Social Work Practice across Disability

Juliet C. Rothman

University of California at Berkeley

Boston   New York   San Francisco
Mexico City   Montreal   Toronto   London   Madrid   Munich   Paris
Hong Kong   Singapore   Tokyo   Cape Town   Sydney

Executive Editor: Karen Hanson
Series Editor: Patricia Quinlin
Series Editorial Assistant: Annemarie Kennedy
Marketing Manager: Taryn Wahlquist
Production Editor: Annette Pagliaro
Editorial Production: Walsh & Associates, Inc.
Composition Buyer: Linda Cox
Manufacturing Buyer: JoAnne Sweeney
Cover Administrator: Kristina Mose-Libon
Text Design and Composition: Publishers' Design and Production Services, Inc.

For related titles and support materials, visit our online catalog at www.ablongman.com.

Between the time Website information is gathered and then published, it is not unusual for some sites to have closed. Also, the transcription of URLs can result in typographical errors. The publisher would appreciate notification where these errors occur so that they may be corrected in subsequent editions.

Library of Congress Cataloging-in-Publication Data

Rothman, Juliet Cassuto, 1942–
    Social work practice across disability / Juliet C. Rothman.
      p.   cm.
    Includes bibliographical references and index.
    ISBN 0-205-37462-X
    1. Social work with people with disabilities.   I. Title.
HV1552.R68 2003
362.4—dc21   2002071171

Printed in the United States of America

10 9 8 7 6 5 4 3 2 1 {printed abbreviation} 08 07 06 05 03 02

Photo credits: pp. 21, 22, 23, Disability Social History Project; pp. 28, 37, 266, 237, HolLynn D'Lil; pp. 46, 165, 225, 229, Howard Petrick; p. 49, 292, ADAPT; pp. 160, 161, Juliet Rothman

For my husband
Leonard

My daughters,
Susan and Deborah

And in memory of my beloved son
Daniel

Contents

Preface

It is the goal of this book to assist social workers and social work students to practice in a caring, sensitive, and effective manner across disability. As we begin, it is important to consider some of the common assumptions our society makes about people with disabilities because, as members of that society, we ourselves can carry some or all of these assumptions within ourselves as well. Their effect is profound, regardless of whether we consider ourselves as persons with disabilities.

By placing the assumptions here, at the very beginning of our work together, it is hoped that they will be present in your thinking as you consciously and carefully work to dismantle them and consider the field of disability in all of its richness as a wonderful opportunity for growth, for both you and your clients.

These assumptions are defined by Michelle Fine and Adrienne Asch in their article "Disability Beyond Stigma: Social Interaction, Discrimination, and Activism" (2000):

> *First assumption:* "It is often assumed that disability is located solely in biology, and thus disability is accepted uncritically as an independent variable."

This assumption locates the disability within the body of the person: The person is both the cause and the effect of the condition. Early theories about disability were grounded in this assumption, as we shall see, and these still influence societal and personal beliefs about disability. More modern theories have begun to consider the impact of the societal milieu on the "location" of disability.

> *Second assumption:* "When a disabled person faces problems, it is assumed that the impairment causes them." (Fine & Asch, 2000, p. 203)

This assumption is critical for each of us to examine as we provide services across disability. People come to us for assistance with problems, and there are an infinite variety of possible problems and causes of problems. Assuming that when someone with a disability walks into your office, the disability is at the center and is the principal causative force in his or her problem both denies your client's reality and diminishes him or her as a person. Of course, it can also lead to inappropriate planning and interventions.

> *Third assumption:* "It is assumed that the disabled person is a 'victim'." (Fine & Asch, 2000, p. 204)

Victimhood is associated both with helplessness and self-blame, neither of which is necessarily a part of the life experience of clients with disabilities. Victimhood diminishes the person; rather, a disability can be both a challenge and an opportunity for growth.

> *Fourth assumption:* "It is assumed that disability is central to the disabled person's self-concept, self-definition, social comparison, and reference groups." (Fine & Asch, 2000, p. 205)

The centrality of the disability to the person varies enormously and is affected by many factors, such as life experiences, character and personality, age at which the person has become disabled, type of impairment, and the social milieu within which the person functions at home, at work, and at play.

> *Fifth assumption:* "It is assumed that having a disability is synonymous with needing help and social support." (Fine & Asch, 2000, p. 205)

While disability historically has been viewed as associated with helplessness and dependence and disabled people were often kept apart from others in a state of social isolation, this is not the current experience of people with disabilities in our society. Thus, this assumption discounts the ability of the person to adapt, develop alternative ways of meeting needs, and use societal resources to maximize independence at every level. All human beings share this amazing capacity to adapt and to develop a positive and meaningful lifestyle. This should not be taken to mean that people with disabilities are *never* in need of help. Help may be needed—but it is important that the individual determine the kind of assistance and the circumstances in which it may be needed.

Three different, but equally vital qualities are need to work effectively across disability: (1) *knowledge* of theoretical constructs, history, and various impairments and conditions, as well as about people, adaptation, and identity; (2) *skills* for effective practice to enable workers to effectively build relationships, communicate, assess, and assist people toward change, as individuals, as communities, and as groups within a wider society; (3) *self-awareness* and a deep insight into one's own personal feelings, experiences, stereotypes, and biases and the possible impact of these on clients. Competent practice involves all three, and it is hoped that this book will assist you to achieve the goal of competent, professional social work practice.

Acknowledgments

The process of preparing this book, talking with people about disability, teaching the material included here, searching for resources, and struggling to define practice methodologies has been one of the most rewarding of my life—a wonderful experience made especially meaningful by the many people who helped me along the way by sharing their stories, offering support and encouragement, and providing special insights and ideas.

I would like to thank, first of all, the people who helped me to understand the lived experience of disability from so many different perspectives: John Mannick, Gary Heaton,

Deedee Remenick, Thad Smith, Connie Lewis, Susan Commoss, and the many, many other people who shared their experiences but preferred to remain anonymous. People in positions from receptionists to executives to clients helped me to understand the function, mission, and services of private sector agencies such as the Multiple Sclerosis Society, Canine Companions for Independence, and the Arthritis Foundation and provided me with literature that helped me to understand each agency's history. Professionals with special training and insights, such as Lester Butt, Sharon Everson, and John Michael helped me to broaden my own knowledge about disabling conditions. Disability rights activists Kitty Cone, Gerald Baptiste, and HolLynn D'Lil shared their experiences with the movement's early days and continuing efforts to address civil rights for people with disabilities.

My colleagues have provided a forum for discussion and have enabled me to pursue my interest through the development of a course on social work practice with people who have disabilities: Paul Terrell, Diane Driver, Kurt Organista, and others have been instrumental in focusing my efforts in this direction. I would also like to thank the reviewers—Martha Sheridan of Gallaudet University, Heather MacDuffie of University of Maine, Mike Meacham of Valdosta State University, and Andrew Bein of California State University, Sacramento—whose comments and suggestions were very helpful throughout the preparation of this book. My students, both past and present, were a source of inspiration, and their unflagging enthusiasm was truly special.

My husband Leonard has given up evenings and weekends to this project, read each chapter (often in the middle of the night), and supported me at moments when the work seemed overwhelming.

Introduction

Who and *what* are we talking about when we talk about disability? The response to the "who" question is easy. We are talking about people, human beings, who, like all human beings, are attempting to live their lives in a meaningful way. Human beings who value family, relationships, freedom and independence, productive employment, recreation and leisure, and the opportunity to achieve the life they desire. We are talking about Plato and Poe, Milton and Homer, Handel, Spinoza and Shelley, Van Gogh and Julius Caesar, and Voltaire. We are talking about FDR. We are talking about Helen Keller. We are talking about Stephen Hawking and about a Vietnam vet named Ron Kovic (names from Kleinfeld, 1979, p. 25).

The "what" question is much more difficult and complex, for the very large and very diverse group of people we are talking about are human beings who are viewed by other human beings—and sometimes by themselves—as somehow different, or special. The "difference," and the "specialness," come from a quality, behavior, or ability that they either have or lack that is somehow not shared by all human beings, though it is by quite a number of them. This special characteristic may make it more difficult for this group of people to achieve the meaningful life that is so essential to each of us personally within our societal structure. As we shall see, different societies have viewed special people in different ways at different times. As we are professionals in the United States in the twenty-first century, we will focus primarily on the way in which our society presently assists or impedes this "special" group of people from reaching their life goals and values.

Our society labels this group, as it labels many other groups within the wider social structure. The label given has variously been *impaired, disabled,* or *handicapped.* We must begin by understanding what we mean when we use each of these terms. The World Health Organization (WHO) definitions may be helpful here:

(1) Impairment: A disturbance in body structure or processes that is present at birth or results from later injury or disease; a loss or abnormality of psychological, physiologic, or anatomical structure or function.

(2) Disability: A limitation in expected functional activity due to an underlying impairment; a restriction or lack of ability to perform an activity within the range considered normal for human beings. This restriction or lack of ability is often socially created.

(3) Handicap: No longer a popular term; originally derived from "hand-in-cap," an image of a person whose difficulty places him or her in a position of dependence and necessitates charity, thus "hand in cap." The WHO definition of a handicap is that of

a social disadvantage experienced by people as a result of impairment or disability that occurs because they do not meet social expectations for performance.

Professional social workers often work with people who have a disability. Disability can affect not only societies and individuals, but also the client-worker relationship. Self-awareness and insight into the ways in which disability is understood by individuals, families, and communities can assist social workers to provide sensitive, caring, and competent services for clients.

The Disabled Person in Society

Although the WHO definition applies to all societies, it is important to note at the outset that definitions of what constitutes a disability vary greatly by culture. In Dahomey, for example, facial scarring that would be considered disfiguring in the United States is valued. Until fairly recently, when it was made illegal, foot-binding in China was considered a mark of rank and beauty (Philips & Rosenburg, 1980, p. 11). Footbinding in early childhood left women able only to hobble and sometimes unable to walk at all. It was prized for the underlying rationale: If you were wealthy, you didn't need to walk because servants would carry you.

There is great variation in the role of disabled people in non-Western societies: Disabled people are rulers, outcasts, warriors, priests—they may be regarded as having a special connection to supernatural powers, as pariahs, as an economic liability; tolerated and used by society; limited in their participation in the social order; or subjected to benign neglect under a laissez-faire policy (Philips & Rosenberg, 1980, p. 11).

Another example of a variation in societal perception by both time and culture relates to the role of crippled children. In some societies, crippled children were to be eliminated: The Greeks and Romans often abandoned such children, unless they came from very wealthy families able and willing to care for them. Social Darwinist ideas of "survival of the fittest" left crippled children to their regrettable but necessary fate. In other societies, crippled children were ostracized, kept separate, hidden in closets, and denied any possibility of a life of self-esteem and relationships. In still others, crippled children were accepted, perhaps as different, but still as part of society. Dwarfs in fairy tales are examples of this kind of societal attitude.

Other possible societal attitudes toward crippled children include *salvage,* where the society believes it can, and desires to, save the child; *prevention,* where the focus is on scientific advance to eliminate the possibility of crippled children; and the *education* of members of the society about crippling conditions and crippled children (Auld, 1927, pp. 138–143).

Societies also vary greatly in their attitudes toward mental disabilities. Mental illnesses are heavily stigmatized in some cultures. In others, a mental illness is viewed as a special gift that connects the person to higher power. In still others, people with mental illnesses or differences are endowed with special status and special abilities, such as foretelling future events, untangling riddles, and resolving difficult and complex societal issues. People with mental illnesses advise on matters of state and are often consulted on family matters. Understanding societal and cultural variations helps us to broaden our thinking about how mental illnesses are defined and how they are manifested in different cultures and ethnic groups.

Disability as an Individual Experience

The way in which disability is understood in the society in which the disabled person lives has a strong impact: Positive, inclusive societal structures enhance self-esteem, empower, and value each individual, regardless of disabling conditions. Exclusive societal structures limit functioning, interaction, and access to the goods of the society to persons with disabilities in many ways that may be environmental, social, institutional, or any combination of these. Exclusion has a profound impact on any person, with or without a disabling condition, regardless of whether the exclusion is deliberate or unintentional.

The lived experience of disability varies greatly among individuals. The kind of disability, the limitations experienced, environmental factors, the family and social milieu, and personality characteristics and identity create a unique experience with disability for each person. While there are often common themes—the experience of difference, oppression, empowerment through activism, disenfranchisement, stigma, and frustration—that may transcend any one specific disability experience, each person "lives" disability different. It is important to understand the themes—but at least equally important to *listen*—and to get in touch with the common humanity that transcends any disabling condition.

Enhancing Our Professional Skills

The professional skills we use in working across disability are no different than the skills we use in every context of practice. One of the most important considerations in working across disability is to develop an understanding that the disabling condition may be, or may not be, the reason the client has come to see the worker. Assuming the centrality of disability in the life of the person is often inaccurate and nonproductive. People with disabilities have marital issues, problems with children, traumas and painful experiences, difficulties with relationships—the same kinds of issues that people without disabilities have. As always, we must take our cues from our clients in regard to their understanding of issues and problems.

There are some areas that may require special attention in working across disability. Where there is difficulty in communication, special skills and sensitivity may be needed. Where there is a need for advocacy or assistance with special needs, special knowledge and skills are essential.

Resources and Networks

There are times, however, that our clients' needs require resources that are specialized and focused on meeting particular needs. The public sector has recognized that people with disabilities often have many needs that cannot be met through family and social networks and community resources. Special programs addressing needs in health care, housing, employment and income maintenance, attendant care, and recreation and leisure have been developed to meet these needs by federal, state, and local governments.

Complementing these is a complex system of private, nonprofit agencies that address specific needs. Some agencies work under contract to provide services mandated by laws. Others provide supplementary services, meeting needs that may be outside of the scope of government. Private organizations advocate, provide direct services, fund research, and also provide social and peer support. They are often a forum for discussion, activism, and empowerment.

The Structure of This Textbook

Recognizing the importance of each of the aforementioned areas, a model for competent and effective social work service has been developed. The model is built around the client-worker relationship, the most basic and essential unit of professional service, for it is within this unit that change and growth occurs. The "client" may be an individual, a family group, a couple, a community—all levels of practice from micro to macro are included as clients. To maximize the opportunity for client change and growth when working across disabilities requires specialized knowledge and special skills. The textbook units and chapters have been structured around this model.

Drawn from the client-worker relationship, four parts are developed, focusing on four primary areas. Two of these, the Individual Framework and the Societal Framework, are closely interwoven. Using the person-in-environment perspective and focusing on first the society and then the individual, these two units help us to learn about and understand the way in which society and people with disabilities affect each other. The part that focuses on society, Part I, presents a series of theoretical models for conceptualizing disability, chronicles the history of disability in the United States, explores the disability rights movement, examines laws and acts that affect people with disabilities, and provides some demographic data that can describe people with disabilities in the United States in terms of functional impairment, age, gender, employment, and other parameters.

Part II focuses on the individual. Recognizing that disability may be integrated into personal identity in many ways, a number of theories about disability and identity are presented. The way people use and understand disability classifications also impacts strongly on individuals. The primary focus of this part is on understanding the lived experience of disability in all of its variety and possibility. Personal narratives offer special insights into both the uniqueness of individual experiences and the commonality of major themes.

The third essential component is the development of professional skills that are specific to disability and supplement the general skills of social work practice. The development of trust, the vital importance of self-awareness and self-monitoring, and special skills for communicating across disability are presented to enhance meaningful interaction.

The resource network for people with disabilities is broad and comprehensive. In Part IV, this network is separated first into public and private sectors, and specific pro-

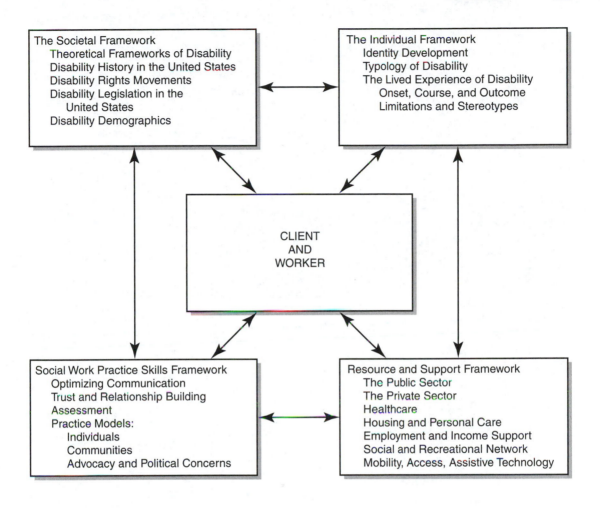

grams, organizations, and services are presented as examples. Part IV then explores public/private intersections in meeting special needs.

While there are many books and print resources for working with people with disabilities and for meeting special needs, the Internet has become a primary source of information. Internet resources are current, and a broad base of information is available to meet every need. Learning about some of the most comprehensive sites is important for both worker and client, and specific sites have been recommended to help you to begin to become familiar with these excellent Internet sources.

Part I

The Societal Framework

In Part I, we will be focusing on the societal framework. We know that the relationship between individuals and the society in which they live is complex and multifaceted. Societies influence the way in which individuals perceive themselves, their worldview, their values and goals, their expectations of themselves and others, social and group affiliations, and almost every other area of life. Individuals influence society also, for society is an aggregate of individuals. Individuals create and sustain society, and society is thought to be the expression of the group values, ideals, aspirations, and worldview of its members.

In an ideal world, the "fit" between individuals and society is perfect, and each is a reflection of the other. In the real world, societal values, goals, expectations, and aspirations rarely if ever completely "match" those of individual members, and vice versa. For all of us, there exist certain areas where our interests and those of society are not the same. The person-in-environment framework that social workers use to describe and understand people considers this reciprocal relationship and attempts to optimize the "fit" between all members of society and the society as a whole.

In general, "society" tends to best represent those people who are members of the dominant and powerful groups within it. Conversely, it least represents those whose voices are rarely heard and still more rarely accepted. Members of groups that are subordinate and undervalued, oppressed, and without power in our society tend to have difficulties with the "fit" between themselves as individuals and as a group and the wider society in which they live.

For centuries, people with disabilities have been silent members of our society; their voices were rarely heard. Hidden in attics and basements, sequestered in large impersonal institutions, deprived of opportunities to participate meaningfully in society, people with disabilities were viewed sometimes with fear, at other times with pity or disdain. Only in the twentieth century, through the disability rights movement and the legislation it has produced, have the voices of the disabled been heard. And what they are saying asks each of us to think about his or her conception of disability and the role society plays in both creating potential difficulties for people with disabilities and in resolving them.

Disability and society have a long mutual history; there were people with disabilities before there were any written records. Archeological exploration has unearthed skeletons and other evidence of people with disabilities, and it is thought that disability was not uncommon in prehistoric times.

Because of the complexity of the interaction between society and a person with a disability, some of the chapter divisions used will seem quite arbitrary. They have been created to provide a structure and a continuity for the reader that enables each chapter to build upon the one that precedes it. Chapter 1 will assist you in exploring some of the theoretical frameworks that, from antiquity to this new millennium, have informed the way in which people think about disability. Because we live in a Western society, much of the theoretical concepts that affect the way in which we think about disability is drawn from a European American perspective. This does not mean that, in other societies and in other times, other views might not have prevailed, but only that in this time and in this society, the views included here appear to have had the strongest influence. The organization of this chapter provides some chronological order, because many of the theoretical constructs followed one upon another, although none have disappeared and each still influences the way in which our society thinks about disability.

Chapter 2 focuses on the history of disability in the United States and attempts to provide an overview upon which the material presented in Chapter 3, which presents the Disability Rights movement, and Chapter 4, which addresses legislation and the ADA, can be superimposed.

Chapter 5 provides information about disability demographics: numbers of people with disabilities, their employment, income, race, gender, age, and other parameters drawn from the U.S. Census and from other studies of disability in the United States. It will be clear from the studies included here that the Census Bureau tends to study disability in terms of functional impairments—that is, the ability to perform the activities of daily living and the instrumental activities of daily living, rather than by the medical categories that, as we shall see later, are often used to determine eligibility for programs. This chapter also presents data gathered by the Centers for Disease Control, which establish a current (2000) baseline for people with disabilities in several areas.

1

Theoretical Frameworks

What creates disabling conditions in people? How can responsibilities for people with disabling conditions be met? Who should be meeting them? To answer these and other foundational questions about disability, it is important to understand the theoretical frameworks we use for thinking about disability. Disability models, or constructs, can assist us by providing a framework, a possible cause-and-effect perspective, and possible parameters for responsibility. In this chapter, we will explore the principal models for thinking about disability that have been used in Western civilization.

Disability models can be divided into two broad categories: individual and societal. The *individual* model conceptualizes disability as a problem of the person who carries the disability. Individual models have as their underlying assumption that disabled people have something wrong with them individually, something that has been caused by forces outside of society. Therefore, causation, blame, and responsibility rest exclusively with the individual. Most of the older models for thinking about disability use this individual context for discussion. Individual models have provided a framework for thought and action throughout most of recorded history. In today's world, in spite of newer models that provide alternative ways of thinking, both disabled and nondisabled people often use the individual models to think about problems, causes, and responsibilities. Whenever someone says, "What did I do to deserve this?" or "Why did this have to happen to me?" he or she is using an individual model to frame the thought process.

The *societal* model, on the other hand, views disability in the context of the surrounding milieu, which is composed of many different kinds of things, including the natural environment, the built environment, societal values, societal institutions, and people, including social groups, public images, and the disability culture. Rather than viewing disability as a problem of the individual, societal models view disabled people as a *group* who are considered and/or treated differently in terms of their value and the consideration given to them as *individuals.* Societal models of disability are primarily twentieth-century phenomena. These models are grounded in the concept that it is not the individual who is disabled; rather, it is the society itself that creates the disability. Variations among people occur naturally with our humanity, societal models say, but they become a problem, a "disability," because of the way society has structured itself.

Our movement from the individual model to the societal is reflected in recent laws and policies, such as the Americans with Disabilities Act. However, the impact of the individual models, so long dominant, persist both within ourselves and in the social milieu. Most of us, whether we consider ourselves "disabled" or not, were raised during the time when individual models prevailed as the commonly understood way of thinking about disability. We have created an uneasy alliance of individual and societal models within ourselves. Because the societal models are more acceptable in today's environment, we often *talk* in terms of these constructs. But we often *think* in terms of the individual models.

Contained within these two broad categories, the *individual* and the *societal,* are the complex and entangled strands of two others: the *spiritual* and the *scientific.* As we explore the frameworks, we may be able to see the way in which this dualistic view of causation and responsibility, value and purpose form a part of each model.

Individual Models

Locating the problems of disability within the individual implies an inherent fault or responsibility somewhere in the individual. In early times, it was thought that sin caused God's displeasure, and punishment came in the form of a disability. Later, a more secular view regarded disabled people as flawed and in need of repair. Disabled people were imperfect in some way, and, for the general societal good, should be changed; if change was not possible, isolation, denial of civil rights, and ultimately extermination were considered as alternatives. It was felt that the presence of disabled people prevented the perfectability of the human race, a perfectability that was inherent in humanness. For, after all, wasn't God perfect, and wasn't man made in God's image?

Separation of Physical and Mental: The Earliest Models

Early Neolithic tribes considered persons with disabilities as shamans. Evidence of osteoarthritis, tubercular spine, and dental malformations have been found in mummies, giving evidence to early deformities and disabilities (Albrecht, 1992, p. 37). During the Classical period, the idea of disability as something evil, or inferior, provided a grounding for a range of behaviors. Perhaps the most severe of these was that practiced in the ancient Greek city-state of Sparta. With its strong cultural emphasis on the body, strength, and physical fitness, Spartans commonly left helpless disabled people, often the newborn or very young and the very old, to die alone of exposure and hunger. Athenians, too, abandoned or isolated disabled people as inferior members of society, not entitled to the privilege of citizenship nor the society of others (Albrecht, p. 37). It is interesting to note that this treatment was aimed primarily at people with physical disabilities. Because Greek religious beliefs incorporated seers and people who were possessed of spirits and given special powers, people with mental disabilities were sometimes considered sacred and used for interpreting signs, foretelling events, and reading omens.

Classical Rome was not as absolute in its abandonment of people with disabilities, but expected that those who required assistance be complacent and accepting of the needs and desires of those who provided it as a form of thanks. Reciprocity demanded that something had to be given by both parties in exchange: care for money, care for acquiescence, care for complacency. The Romans also viewed disability and chronic illness as something in need of treatment, and both exercise and hydrotherapy were used to heal (Albrecht, p. 37). The famous baths, such as those of Caracalla in Rome and in Bath, England, were not for cleanliness alone: The hot baths relieved conditions from arthritis to nerves, and the massages that often accompanied them soothed and relaxed body and mind. This seems to support a more scientific understanding of illness and disability in Roman society.

The Moral Model

Within the context of Western civilization, the moral model is generally drawn from the religions that have influenced moral thought through the ages. There are two dominant strands of thought, existing side by side and simultaneously, that have influenced much of our thinking today: disability as a punishment for wrongdoing or sin and disability as creating an obligation in others to care for people.

Disability as Punishment for Sin or Wrongdoing. Ancient Judaism recognized in God the source of health, but also of all illnesses, including disabilities. Because illness and disabilities came from God as creator, they could be viewed only in terms of a punishment for sins (Castiglioni, 1941, p. 65). Diseases of all kinds came from God not only as a punishment, but also to educate the people about the powers of the Almighty, who was able to cause diseases and also to cure them, such as leprosy (Exodus 4:6) and the malignant ulcers on Job (Job 2:7) (Castiglioni, p. 66). The biblical texts do not discuss the importance of physicians or healers; rather, they support the idea that all disease and disability is caused by God and can be cured only by God (Castiglioni, p. 78). This belief was carried over into Christianity and gave rise to the belief in faith as the ultimate healer and savior of both mind and body (Castiglioni, p. 79).

During the Middle Ages, the birth of a child who was abnormal was viewed as the result of evil and sin on the part of the parents. Similarly, people with mental illnesses were also viewed as being under the control of evil forces (Barnes, Mercer, & Shakespeare, 1999, p. 18).

The Imperative to Care for the Disabled. The other powerful moral strand found in religions is the obligation to care for diseased and sick people in society. Benevolence, kindness, and concern for others are woven through every biblical text, and there is a strong injunction to provide for those in need. People with disabilities were viewed as being in need, and therefore were often given extra consideration. During the Middle Ages, people with impairments were seen as worthy of healing and care, at the same time that they were viewed as being punished for sins (Barnes, Mercer, & Shakespeare, p. 17).

Medicine during the Middle Ages incorporated both lay physicians and ecclesiastical healers. Ecclesiastical healers were viewed as workers of charity, who had been given the power to heal from the divine source. Hospitals were often built near monasteries, and the religious often provided care for sick and disabled people (Castiglioni, p. 293). Medical schools were also often attached to monasteries (Castiglioni, p. 295). Disabled people were viewed as "worthy poor." This inherent worth made it imperative that they be provided with the care and necessities to survive.

A Continuing Dichotomy.   In today's context, it is clear that both strands—disability as punishment, and disability as deserving of assistance—continue to exert a strong influence upon people both disabled and nondisabled. The Christian Council on People with Disabilities (2001) provides an excellent example of these simultaneous, nonexclusive beliefs. Some of the statements in the CCPD perspective will help to illustrate. CCPD's Statement of Faith says, "We believe the Bible to be the inspired, the only infallible, authoritative Word of God." *Principles of Ministry* states CCPD's beliefs "That all people are made in God's image in order to serve him in all the arenas of life," and "That human life has become broken through sin, and one of sin's consequences is suffering." In *Our Confession Has at Least the Following Implications,* CCPD states:

> Christ teaches the sanctity of life, no matter how severe the disabling condition.
> Christ's example and the law of love demand that we compassionately respond to the needs of persons who have disabilities and their families. . . .
> We must make public the gifts of people whom society defines as disabled, so that they may participate mutually in our interdependent family.

As we consider the implications of the moral model, perhaps we need to follow the guidance offered by James Charlton:

> The relationship between religion and disability must be analyzed on two levels. First, what kind of message do various religious doctrines convey about disability? That is, do they contribute to, or help break down the myths and stereotypes about disability? Second, what is the social and political role of religion as an institution? That is, does the church foster or hinder the movement for social justice? (Charlton, 2000, p. 65)

The Deficit Model

The deficit model is an early iteration of today's medical model. It was developed during the Enlightenment and the Industrial Revolution, when major advances in sciences and art led to a new view of human nature and human potential (Albrecht, 1992, pp. 42–46). Rather than viewing people as static, the Enlightenment presented a dynamic view of the human being. People could change, or be changed, through the new advances in science. Those who were imperfect, who lacked function or ability, were missing something very concrete: the ability to see, to hear, to move, to reason. Scientific method would develop new methodology for eliminating these "deficits." Perfection, both in function and in potential, was believed to be achievable for everyone.

Despite good will and much effort, the sciences developed at the time were unable to remedy all the needs and impairments of people who were disabled, and this model was judged to be a failure. The scientific efforts that spawned it, however, continue into the present day and have come to a fuller development and general acceptance as the medical model, which is presented below.

The Social Darwinist Model

While Darwinists might have been horrified to be associated with the Spartans of ancient Greece, in effect there is a core of commonality between the two models. Darwin's famous work, *The Origin of Species,* describes the process of evolution, presenting the concept that the species that become successful and dominant are those best suited to survival in the environment in which they are living. Survival demands, in Darwin's view, not only positive qualities well suited to the environment and the ability to reproduce successfully, but also the ability to change and adapt to the conditions in which the organism is living.

> I should premise that I use the term Struggle for Existence in a large and metaphorical sense, including dependence of one's being on another, and including (which is more important) not only the life of the individual, but success in leaving progeny. (Darwin, 1985, p. 116)

Plants and animals that are unable to adapt and change, cannot reproduce successfully, and/or are unable to function in the environment in which they live do not survive. They do not survive individually, nor do they survive as species. Because of the emphasis on the possibility of change and adaptation that was basic to the deficit model, people with disabilities were at first considered to be in need of such changes. Whether the changes came about through scientific discoveries, through personal effort, or through any other means was not relevant—only the change that would enable the individual to compete with others for survival mattered. Survival in this Darwinist model involves competition for needed resources, such as food, shelter, clothing, and medical care.

Though some people were able to adapt, change, and use the new scientific discoveries, most were unable to do so. People with disabilities were often unable to meet their own needs. In Darwin's world, where everyone was concerned about his or her own survival, people who were unable to survive on their own due to a disability could be left to their fate, thus mirroring the abandonment of imperfect newborns, disabled people, and the elderly in Sparta.

The Eugenics Model

Using the theme of "survival of the fittest," supporters of eugenics took Darwin's position even further. If only the fit should survive, the eugenicists said, then not only should we abandon those who are "unfit," we should also isolate them from the rest of society and above all impede reproduction and thus the continuance of the disability in the next generation. Reproduction in this new view should be limited to the desirable elements of the population only—and people with disabilities were clearly not desirable.

The eugenics movement had a strong influence on both European and American society in the nineteenth and early twentieth centuries, and advocates on both sides of the Atlantic were heard and accepted as the vanguards of a new social order, one composed of what was considered to be the best that humanity could offer. Thus, the achievement of human perfection would be rendered possible through the elimination of all people who were judged to be imperfect. Institutionalization of people with disabilities and restrictions on having children were common.

In the 1930s and 1940s, Nazism and Hitler took their theory to its "final solution." Why wait, the Nazis reasoned, until undesirable people simply died out? Why waste time and resources on them? Why not hasten the process by simply exterminating them? People with mental and physical disabilities, developmental disabilities, and deformities were marked for extinction, and estimates of up to 250,000 were exterminated during the Nazi regime (Disability Social History Project).

In the United States, the eugenics model caused children with disabilities to be objects of shame and disgrace to their parents, who quickly hid them away in institutions, sometimes from birth. Adults with disabilities were discouraged from having children, in order not to perpetuate the imperfection to another generation. Traces of this attitude persist into the present day. Children with developmental disabilities, severe and multiple disabilities, or mental illness continue to be institutionalized, although at a significantly lower rate. It is not uncommon for parents of a developmentally disabled or mentally ill child to request that their child be sterilized upon reaching puberty. While there may be a stronger desire to protect the child from physical and emotional demands the child may be unable to fulfill, the concomitant desire not to perpetuate the child's problem is generally present as well.

The Medical Model

As major advances in science, biology, and medicine began to occur, the rationale for the medical model, a later iteration of the original deficit model, gained new popularity, and a preeminence among models that it still maintains today. The medical model views people with disabilities as lacking some vital element or function: that is, they cannot see or hear, cannot walk, cannot act prudently, and/or cannot perform simple calculations. Disability is viewed as a functional loss, the inability to independently and effectively do the things that other people can do. This way of thinking is *norm based:* The assumption is that there is a standard, or a norm, for what human beings are, how they should look and act, and what they should be able to do. People who deviate form the norm are lacking in some way. When the interventions of medical science cannot resolve the problem and enable the individual to function within the norm, the person is considered to be permanently flawed.

As we shall see in Chapter 6, when we discuss identity development for people with disabilities, the medical profession, with its emphasis on loss of functioning, is also charged with diagnosing and "labeling" people. However, disability labels drawn from the medical model generally have a negative connotation and can have a powerful negative effect. Stereotyping, discrimination, and prejudice often accompany medical labeling. Because society today retains strong traces of the earlier moral model, people who carry a disability label, especially those with mental disabilities more easily perceived as the "fault" of the person (who "could" control them, but "won't"), are still often viewed negatively. Disabled people also internalize the label, complete with all of its negative connotations, and suffer a lack of self-esteem directly related to their label.

People with disabilities have frequent contacts with the medical establishment, where they obtain needed treatments, medications, and assessments. This dependence on the medical establishment continues to support the use of the medical model. Benefits, assistance, and support services are often connected with the medical establishment. Often, a diagnostic label or assessment is required to determine eligibility for benefits and services. Medical model terminology is in our laws, is used by the media, and is the most common method for communicating about disabilities today.

Societal Models

Societal models were developed during the twentieth century in response to a growing recognition of the role of society in the determination and maintenance of disability. The nature-nurture debate, which continue today, acknowledges the possibility that at least some things previously thought to be located within the individual are, in fact, created, exacerbated, promoted, and supported by the environment. Negative self-image, within the individual, is drawn from negative stereotypes and public images of a quality of the individual in society. Viewing people as different and groups of people who share a particular kind of difference as "other" begins the destructive process of stereotyping, isolation, and invisibility. Creating a built environment sensitive only to the norm further isolates and disempowers those of us who don't fit the standard mold and dehumanizes everyone by limiting understanding of the broad range of human qualities and needs. All of the societal models place the cause and responsibility for the problems that affect disabled people squarely on society itself, rather than on the individual, and take the position that the needed changes must occur in the society, not in the individual. Thus, the societal models require a paradigm shift and a new locus; society, rather than the individual.

The Oppression Model

> Disabled people are oppressed and share this experience. Emphasizing differences validates the disabled person but supports separation as "Other." (Wendell, 1996, p. 72)

When able-bodied people define disabled people as "other," disabled people become psychologically, socially, and economically oppressed (Wendell, p. 271). Oppression harms individuals; stifles growth, hope, and ambition; and fosters self-hatred and dependency.

Developed by Franz Fanon (Bulhan, 1985) and others as a framework for understanding race, the oppression model develops the concept that those who are viewed as different and "other" and who are excluded from society are oppressed. Oppression affects groups and individuals. An important aspect of the oppression model is the concept that oppressed people are not only stereotyped and disenfranchised: They actually become *invisible* to the dominant society.

Hegel argues that an individual becomes conscious of his or her self only when his or her existence is acknowledged by another (Bulhan, p. 102). When a person is not "seen" and *recognized as a person* by others in society around him or her, the loss of self-awareness engendered is very destructive. One can easily see how this applies to disability. When people with disabilities are hidden away, isolated, placed in institutions, attics, and basements, when they are deprived of their civil rights, when the environment is not accessible, they do in fact become invisible—in a very concrete, physical way. "Out of sight, out of mind" is an apt description of the conditions of disabled people during much of history. Disabled people are often kept at a "physical and social distance by others, and are viewed with caution and trepidation" (Albrecht, p. 7). Stereotypes, prejudice, and discrimination, which flourish with lack of contact and an acknowledged condition of difference, are an integral part of the disability experience.

Disabled people are affected by discrimination in all aspects of their lives. Lack of employment opportunities lead to unemployment, underemployment, and the poverty that accompanies the inability to secure the necessities of daily living. We shall see how people with disabilities compare with others in employment in Chapter 5. Social isolation leads to loneliness, withdrawal, and depression. Lack of access to education leads to lower levels of educational achievement. People who are doubly or even triply oppressed—by being disabled and a racial or ethnic minority, disabled and elderly, disabled and female, disabled and poor, or multiply disabled—experience oppression even more severely. The public image of difference and, even more, of dependence, provides support for either a negative reaction from others or an overly protective one: Both diminish the individual.

The interaction between the institution of "society" and individual members is a delicate and extremely complex one. The oppression model views the individual as personally integrating the negative images, the oppressive ideas, and the stereotypes that appear all around him or her in society into self. Oppressed people at a deep level often *believe* all the stereotypes, and thus develop a lack of self-esteem or, more deeply, self-hatred. These feelings blunt possibilities for change, desire for improved status, and motivation for risking new experiences.

"The oppressor identifies himself in terms of the sublime and beauty, while depicting the oppressed in terms of absolute evil and ugliness" (Bulhan, p. 141). Fanonian oppression theory suggests that, in order to break this cycle, the members of the oppressed group must rise up and risk everything they have to change their position in the society (Bulhan, pp. 114–151, 121–122). This theoretical framework was a strong influence in the Civil Rights movement of the 1960s, which itself then influenced the development of rights movement for other groups: women, gays and lesbians, and people with disabilities. The Disability Rights movement, which is discussed in Chapter 3, is closely related to this theoretical model.

The Diversity Model

Shifting the primary focus from oppression to diversity changes the perspective on groups and interactions between them. In the diversity model, people with disabilities are seen are a group of people in society that share certain qualities or characteristics. There are groups based on race and ethnicity, groups based on language and nation or origin, groups based on religion, class, gender, age, and also groups based on disability. All groups that are minorities share something of the minority experience with prejudice, stereotyping, and oppression—negative experiences. But all groups also share a common culture, with common language, interests, life experiences, and worldviews.

Thinking about this group context, we can begin by exploring what the "disability group" shares and what unifies all people with disabilities. In general, this group shares decreased access to all of the goods and services in society. It's often harder to go to school, harder to get jobs, to make friends, to get around. They also share in the negative stereotypes associated with disability and dependencies. They share the stigmas, both visible and internal, that are associated with being viewed as flawed or imperfect. They may also share a desire for a sometimes elusive integration in the wider society.

Within this broad group there can be major cultural differences, for each disability forms a cultural subgroup, and develops its own unique way of communicating, relating, and dealing with the broader society. Additionally, within each group, individuals may choose to identify and embrace the culture, or to remain apart from it. Culture involves a choice, and not all disabled people choose to affiliate in a cultural way. In this manner, disability culture may be compared to ethnic group cultures. There is Asian culture, and there is within this group subgroups of Chinese culture, Japanese culture, Indian culture, and Korean culture. Within Latino culture, there may be Mexican culture, Guatemalan culture, Brazilian culture, and so on. People often chose to affiliate with an ethnic culture or to remain apart from it.

The specific disability often defines some of the characteristics of a culture. Deaf culture is perhaps the most widely known, having a distinct and separate language, educational system, social milieu, and network of services from within the culture. Blind culture provides a network of support services including books, schools, and residential arrangements. Developmental disability culture has special ways of communicating and understanding. People who share a culture share a way of thinking, a way of feeling, a way of understanding events and the world around them.

There are some special problems in the diversity model for people with disabilities. Because of a frequent experience of isolation and powerlessness, and because of dependence on others who do not share the disability, it is often much more difficult for people with disabilities to participate in a disability culture. Also, many disabilities affect individuals rather than families; the person who is disabled may not have the commonality of experience and support of those who are closest to him or her. Children are more easily socialized into the cultures of their parents, grandparents, and other family members. But if you are the first person in your family to be blind, you cannot rely upon this socialization-through-family experience.

Research on children with disabilities has indicated the vital importance of early association with other children who share a similar disability (Mackelprang & Salsgiver, 1999, p. 67). Awareness of others who are similar to you is an important resource for identity development, which is grounded in an understanding group as well as individual characteristics. This will be explored further in Chapter 6.

The Social Construct Model

The social construct model grounds disability theory in a manner uniquely suited to disabled people. Rather than building upon established theories, such as the oppression and diversity frameworks have done, social construct theory develops a position that demands a rethinking of the ways in which we consider any person's place in society and any person's rights as members of a society. It demands that we think of society not as an amorphous group of people, but as a group of people, some of whom have *built* the world that they all inhabit. This built world includes physical structures, and also institutions, laws, and programs. *Who* builds this world, *how,* and *for whom* all become essential pieces to consider. According to Oliver (1991, pp. 30–31) the social construct model:

...does not deny the problem of disability but locates it squarely within society. It is not individual limitations, of whatever kind, which are the cause of the problem but society's failure to provide appropriate services and adequately ensure the needs of disabled people are fully taken into account in social organization.

Hence disability, according to the social model, is all the things that impose restrictions on disabled people; ranging from individual prejudice to institutional discrimination, from inaccessible public buildings to unusable transportation systems, from segregated education to excluding work arrangements.

The harms created by these conditions fall disproportionately on people with disabilities as a group (Oliver, p. 31). They occur because societal organization, and the built environment, does not take people with disabilities into account. In the social construct model, it is the environment that creates and perpetuates the disabling condition, not the individual. Drawing some elements from oppression theory, the social construct model views the environment as oppressive to disabled people when its constructs systematically deny access to goods and services to a group.

While this model does not specifically focus on the individual experiences of disability, it does not deny their validity. Oliver states (p. 38) that the intent of the model is not to deny the reality of disability, pain, and chronic illness, but rather to explore on a pragmatic level what can be done to change the environmental barriers and social attitudes that impact so negatively on people.

Both the oppression model and the diversity model acknowledge social barriers and problems. The social construct model, however, takes the position that one of the ways in which these negative social forces play out is in the manner in which our built environment is constructed, a manner that is systematically exclusionary to some people. Sidewalks with curbs, high steps onto buses, narrow airplane aisles, buildings with no ramps, theaters with no spaces for wheelchairs, university classes on floors with no elevator access, restaurants that have steps up to the entrance, round doorknobs, street lights and elevators that require the use of one sense only, office counters at standing rather than sitting height, bathroom doors that don't admit wheelchairs, and a myriad of other objects in the built world preclude the active engagement in that world by all people.

Because these objects are designed and built for human use, addressing this problem necessitates the involvement of architects, urban planners, and designers. The Universal Design movement seeks to create structures that are accessible to all people, and buildings and streets that use the principles of universal design are becoming steadily more commonplace. Universal design means just that: *universal* access, not access solely to one group of people. This design method, its history and origin, and examples that can easily be observed in today's everyday world will be discussed in Chapter 3.

The Development of Norms

From the viewpoint of contemporary society, the idea of a "norm" and "the normal" have always existed. This concept is woven so deeply and intricately into our society that we cannot imagine that there was a time when people didn't think of themselves, and of others, in terms of norms. Our world is built around norms: norms for height and weight, for intelligence, for strength, for ability in an infinite number of areas, for behavior, and for lifespan. It is this concept of "the norm" that first distinguishes, in an organized, concrete, and reliable way, people who are disabled from those who are abled. Disabled people are, by "normal" definition, those who are outside the boundaries of the normal. To really understand the separation that is created when we divide the "normal" from the not-normal, we need to explore the function of norms more closely.

We can say that the "problem" of disability, then, really becomes a "problem" of the way we view the norm (Davis, 1997, p. 9). Before there was any idea of a "norm" for bodies and minds, there was the concept of an "ideal." The ideal, as it was viewed throughout history but most especially in the seventeenth century, was a perfection of form and beauty that was not attainable by human beings. It was a compilation of all of the most beautiful and desirable features. No one body existed that had all of these features. Rather, the ideal body had a certain kind of nose borrowed from one person, and hands from another, and hair from a third, and so forth. No one had all of these features, and no one was the personification of the ideal (Davis, p. 10).

The movement from "ideal" to "norm" is related to the development of the field of statistics. The French statistician Adolphe Querelet (1796–1847) was the first to develop the idea that the "norm" was an imperative, something toward which all should strive. He developed the composite of the "average man." Like the "ideal" person, the "average man" was not a real person; rather, it was an abstract composition, the average of all of the human attributes of people in a particular country or area (Davis, p. 11).

The idea of this average or "middle" man was very well received socially at a time when the middle class was gaining in importance in European society. The middle or average, rather than the ideal, became what people strove to become. The average person, rather than the ideal person, came to embody everything that was good, great, and worthwhile achieving (Davis, p. 12).

Karl Marx used the concept of "average" when he developed his idea of the "average" worker, and the "average" day of labor. Other statisticians, many of whom were sympathetic to the eugenics movement presented earlier in this chapter, developed the idea of "the norm" and "normal distribution," and the bell curve came into existence (Davis, pp. 12–13).

As often happens, what "is" quickly becomes what "should be." With this shift from *state of being* (is) to *imperative* (should be), the "norm" became the "ideal." The average, rather than the perfect, became the preferred state.

In terms of ability and disability, this shift came to represent the societal aspirations of the nineteenth and early twentieth centuries. The emphasis on nationalism and national fitness supported the idea that there were norms in every society that represented the way people "should" look and act. When the statisticians did their work and made their bell curves, some people were left out of the "norm." These people included those with disabilities, as well as criminals, people with a low IQ, and even poor people. Negative connotations were attached to people who were outside the "norm" (Davis, p. 18). As time went on, the concept of norms was accepted for a wide variety of applications from designing advertising to door handles, clothing sizes to typewriter pages. "There is probably no area of contemporary life in which some idea of a norm, mean, or average has not been calculated" (Davis, p. 9).

A Feminist Model of Disability

> Femininity and disability are inextricably entangled in western culture.... Female bodies—*all* female bodies—are deviant from the "norm" of maleness. (Thomson, 1997, p. 286)

Many cultures have practices that emphasize this relationship by actually disabling and disfiguring women. Chinese footbinding, African scarification and clitoridectomy, and Euro-American corseting are all forms of female disablement. While an analysis of the reasons and rationale for these and other practices that disable women is outside of the scope of this book, the association of femaleness and disability is obvious here.

In addition, as we think about norms and the body, we must consider how the ideas of the feminine are intricately connected to maleness; in fact, they developed out of deliberate contrasts to maleness. Where male bodies are strong, female bodies are weak; where males are active, females are passive; where men are hairy, women are hairless, or make themselves so by artificial means; where men are viewed as hard, women are seen as soft. In effect, this makes all women deviant from the norm of maleness (Thomson, p. 287).

More than half of disabled people are women, and disabled women are 10 percent of all women (Wendell, 1996, p. 267). In the preceding section, we discussed the concept of norms, and the effect of norms and the bell curve on disabled people. Women must address an additional issue: the "normal" or "average" person has always been represented as male. From the early moral models of man as made in God's image and women as deviant and sinful, women have been viewed historically as imperfect men. Womanhood has been seen as a condition that is further from God, and therefore dark and evil. Merely being born a woman set a person apart and different from the idealized norm, and less valuable. In some societies, girl babies are aborted, exposed, or given away to orphanages as undesirable. Thus, many of the problems that women must address in relation to the dominant (male) society are very similar to those that must be addressed by disabled people in the dominant "able" society.

One of these problems is a conceptual one; however, the position one chooses to take in relation to it has very real implications in the world. Women are different from men, but also very similar to men in many ways. Should the differences be emphasized or the similarities?

Women, as varying from the norm, have bodies that are imperfect. So do people with disabilities, in the sense that they, too vary from the norm. However, when we oppress women, or people with disabilities, we are, in effect, oppressing everyone. For as the "norm" is an artificially created abstract construct, in effect, no one "fits" the norm in all aspects. We are each of us different from the norm in many ways. If we view these as imperfections, sins, or deficiencies, we must view each person, male and female, able and disabled, as imperfect.

Disabled people, Wendell says, are devalued for their bodies. But they also serve as reminders to people with "normal" bodies that they, too, can become disabled. It is this reminder that motivates much of the avoidance of people with disabilities in our society. We make disabled people into "other" socially, for they are the symbol of what we hate and what we fear (Wendell, 1996, pp. 268–271).

Stigmas and Other Marks

A stigma is a sign or mark upon the body of a person that reveals something bad, unusual, or hidden about the person. In ancient Greece, stigmas were cut or burned into the body to define a person who should be avoided or ostracized. When we use the word today we are talking not only about the body, but also about a state of condition of disgrace or discreditation. It can be used as a quality of a person or of a relationship and does not always refer to specific attributes. What is stigmatized varies between cultures and periods of history (Goffman, 1997, p. 203). As Coleman states, "all human conditions are potentially stigmatizable" (Coleman, 1997, p. 217).

Aside from being avoided and ostracized, people with stigmas were often viewed as less than human. People who are stigmatized have absorbed and internalized the oppression that accompanies a stigmatized state. They are aware that they are not accepted, and are not given self-respect. People with physical disabilities carry a visible sign, a mark as obvious today as the cuts and burns of the ancient Greeks. People whose disabilities are not immediately obvious carry the stigma within themselves: They are aware that, if their stigma could be seen, they too would be avoided or encounter discrimination.

Because a stigma is so closely associated with an individual person, stigmas are viewed as qualities of individuals rather than representations of the society that defined them (Coleman, p. 217). Stigmas that are obscure, easily misunderstood, or rare can evoke fear in others. They are viewed as fearsome because they are unknown, their behavior is unpredictable, and they are not what is expected. There is also a deep fear of contagion by association, even when people know intellectually that the condition is not catching. These fears tend to cause people to avoid those with stigmas, which only serves to reinforce their separation from the society as a whole (Coleman, pp. 225–27).

Chapter Summary

This chapter has focused on exploring various models from which we can draw ways to conceptualize disability, its causes, and the assignment of responsibility for care and for change. When we examine these models in light of our own experiences with disability, however, it is very clear that none of these exist in our society in a pure form, and that each and every one of them exists in some measure. The way we frame disability in the United States is a complex blending of all these models. Although the medical model continues to be dominant and provides the language most people use in talking about disability, there have been major changes in our views and the development of dynamic and exciting new models during the last half of the twentieth century. We have been moving slowly away from the individual model and toward the social model of disability. We are considering our ideas of norms and averages in light of defining humanity, not just one part of it, as "normal," and the experiences of womanhood as related to disability in a very immediate way. It seems reasonable to assume that these changes and paradigm shifts will continue into the new millennium. As Funk states (1987, p. 9):

Disability history in the United States is a history of the humanization of disabled people: Humanization is defined as a recognition that disabled people have human needs and characteristics and that public policy must be designed to reflect and further this human potential.

Questions for Thought and Discussion

1. How do you see the moral model in action today in relation to disability? In what other ways do we use the moral model in thinking about people and what happens in their lives?

2. Eugenics suggests that it is possible to have a society form which all "undesirable" elements are eliminated. Who should determine what these might be? Do you think this would be beneficial to society as a whole? What do you think about recent trends in genetics that may enable parents to select many physical and mental qualities for their children?

3. Which of the models included in this chapter appeal to you most? Do you think that you would be able to use this model in working with people across disability? Why or why not?

4. The medical model is used to classify people and to determine eligibility for many programs and benefits. If we wanted to eliminate it because it is grounded in deficit thinking, what would we substitute to determine eligibility for assistance and special programs?

5. The diversity model develops the concept that disabled people are a group that shares characteristics of a culture and thus are similar in many ways to other cultural groups in our society. What do you think are the defining characteristics of a "disability culture"?

2

A Historical Perspective

Current trends and developments in addressing disability issues cannot be understood without exploring, however briefly, some of the past events that provided the framework and the context of present-day laws, policies, research, and statistics about disability. The next three chapters will provide this framework and enable an understanding some of the major ideas and events in our history that impact disability concepts today.

In Chapter 1, we presented some of the models and theoretical frameworks for understanding disability and noted that each of the models continues to be present in our society today. This chapter will move from the theoretical to the historical and present the chronology of disability in the United States. The treatment of disabled people in the United States was not unaffected by the attitudes and beliefs imported from Western Europe and other areas of the world; they arrived in ships and planes, right along with the people themselves. Where the impact of international events affects the history of disability in the United States, these have been included to provide some insight into the context of American developments. However, because American culture is itself distinct from others, and because some of those distinctions strongly impacted thinking about disability, it is important to understand the evolution of our understanding about disability from a uniquely American perspective.

This American perspective has several strands of interwoven themes. The Puritan influence was and continues to be strongly felt, and hard work was a value strongly connected to both to religion and family in Puritan life. America is a capitalist society, and disability is strongly associated with the ability to work or to return to work. This creates a close identification of disability and employability (Albrecht, 1992, p. 22). America as a society values independence, physical strength, and freedom, all values that disabled people also cherish but may be unable to fulfill in the same way as nondisabled people. Built into our social contract is also the assumption that disabled people are a part of our society and their problems and concerns require a response from society (Albrecht, p. 33). Like other vulnerable populations, such as children and the elderly, society has a special responsibility toward people with disabilities.

We can divide the country's disability history into four periods: the colonial era and early nationhood, the nineteenth century, the early twentieth century, and the late twentieth century, where the strong impact of the Civil Rights movement changed much of society's thinking about people with disabilities.

The Colonial Period and Early Nationhood

> Had clumps of handicapped people settled in the colonies, most disabled people believe, America today would be totally accessible to the handicapped. But that wasn't the way it happened, and the halt and the lame have been mired in obscurity for 200 years. (Kleinfeld, 1979, p. 22)

When the Puritans arrived in the United States, they brought with them their strong religious practices. These framed their thinking about disability, and the framework they used was, not surprisingly, the moral model. All things were either good or evil, right or wrong. Everything that happened to anyone came directly from the hand of God. Disability was evidence of God's displeasure. The Puritans believed that God had withheld His blessings from disabled children and adults.

During colonial times, disabled people, from child to adult, were hidden in attics and basements, kept unseen and often unacknowledged by the society around them, totally dependent upon family members, and with little to occupy minds or hearts. "In the early years of the United States responsibility for assisting disabled people rested with the extended family. If there was no family, the community assumed support" (Funk, 1987, p. 9).

Elizabethan poor laws were adopted intact in the colonies. Within this system, the "hand-in-cap" image prevailed, and disabled people, who were often poor as a result of their disabilities, were seen as objects of charity. Basic needs were provided, but little else, and benign neglect characterized societal attitudes toward disabled people.

The Nineteenth Century

The attitudes toward disability that are so well illustrated by Charles Dickens's Tiny Tim were very prevalent in the United States during much of the nineteenth century (Beyond Affliction: The Disability History Project: Inventing the Poster Child). The moral model still prevailed in public attitudes toward disability, and there was a strong religious belief that disability was related to sin and evil.

By the turn of the century, things were beginning to change in Europe for people with disabilities. Schools for the deaf were opened, first in Germany, then in France, England, and Italy. Proponents of education for all deaf children, such as Arnoldi, a German pastor, believed that their education should begin as young as age four. There were also schools for the blind in all of the major centers of Europe. In 1799, in a Paris hospital, people with mental illness were finally unshackled from the bonds that had held them captive for hundreds of years (Disability Social History Project).

In the United States in 1805, a Chicago physician named Benjamin Rush wrote *Medical Inquiries and Observations,* the first modern attempt to explain mental disorders in a scientific manner (Disability Social History Project).

Deafness and Communication

In 1815, Thomas H. Gallaudet left America for Europe, with the goal of seeking methods for teaching deaf people to communicate and learn. Two years later, in 1817, the Connecticut Asylum for the Education of Deaf and Dumb Persons opened in Hartford. It was the first school for the deaf in the United States, and teaching methodology was based on information gathered by Gallaudet on his trip. The American School for the Deaf, added vocational education to its curriculum in 1822, with the goal of training employable deaf people. *American Annals of the Deaf* began publication in 1846, at the American School for the Deaf in Hartford. Five years later, Thomas Gallaudet died. A monument to him was dedicated in Hartford in 1854. Ten years later, Congress authorized the board of directors of Columbus Institution to grant college degrees. Originally an all-male institution, the National Deaf Mute College finally admitted women in 1887. The name of the school was changed to Gallaudet University in 1894 in honor of the deaf education pioneer and remains a primary educator of deaf people today (Disability Social History Project).

One of the most intense debates over the methods and goals of deaf education and communication occurred in the late 1800s, and traces of it continue to be felt today: the debate between the "auralists" and the "manualists"—between oral and sign communication. The auralists advocated for teaching the deaf to speak, so that they would be fully integrated into society, rather than living in what was, in effect, a separate community. Teaching both speech and lip reading were the educational methods they preferred. The manualists, on the other hand, claimed that sign language was easier and faster to use and therefore better for deaf people. The manualist point of view prevailed, and signing is the predominantly used method of communication for deaf people today. (Beyond Affliction: The Disability History Project: The Overdue Revolution).

Alexander Graham Bell was also interested in deaf education. In 1872, he opened a speech school for teachers of the deaf in Boston. Four years later, he received a patent for his invention of the telephone. Louis Braille invented the raised point alphabet in Paris in 1829. It took thirty-one years for his invention to cross the Atlantic. In 1860, it was used for teaching at the St. Louis School for the Blind (Disability Social History Project).

The Industrial Revolution

Both mines and early industrial enterprises were dangerous places to work. Mining accidents, black lung disease, and cancer caused disability often for hardworking family men, leaving their families dependent upon charity and the benevolence of others. This was the era of the "company towns," where families lived closely together and were dependent on an ever-ready line of credit at the company store. That credit disappeared when the miner was no longer able to work. While some companies continued to care for the miners and their families, others did not feel that such ongoing responsibility was necessary (Disability Social History Project).

Assembly lines and steel production created other kinds of problems, such as deafness, electrocution, exposure to hazardous chemicals, lung conditions from inhalation of fibers, and dismemberment (Albrecht, 1992, p. 43). Upton Sinclair's factories were dark, unsafe, and unsanitary places, where workers often became disabled, and little concern on the part of employers toward these workers was the norm.

While company liability for injuries to workers was not assumed, there was public sentiment expressed for the victims of such accidents. Disabled people, along with the family members whom they could no longer support, were considered a part of the "deserving poor." After all, had they not worked hard, tried to provide for their families, and been upstanding members of their communities before disaster struck?

Freak Shows

A special feature of the American scene from the mid-1800s to mid-1900s was the freak show. Freaks shows traveled from town to town, and audiences came to view people who were considered freaks. P. T. Barnum's Freak Show, at the American Museum in New York, attracted audiences from all over the world (Disability Social History Project).

People who were disfigured, disabled, or had congenital anomalies were used for these shows, which provided a good income to their organizers and to the disabled people themselves. Disabled children who were born into slavery were considered to be of little use to the slaveowners, were often separated from their families, and died. Those among them who had unusual visible disabilities were sold to freak show owners. An example from the Disability Social History Project is illustrative of such situations: The Siamese twins Millie and Christina (see Figure 2.1) were born into slavery in 1852. They were sold by their owner for $30,000. After being kidnapped and victimized, they eventually went to school and trained as singers. After the Civil War, Millie and Christina were freed and were able to command a good income through appearances at sideshows and other venues (Disability Social History Project).

People with disabilities and their owners or promoters often developed a public image in order to earn money and fame. Robert Bogdan, author of *Freak Show*, states: "How we view people who are different has less to do with what *they* are physiologically than with who *we* are culturally. 'Freak' is a way of thinking, of presenting, a set of practices, and institution—*not* a characteristic of an individual" (Bogdan, quoted in Disability Social History Project).

Unusual qualities such as size (dwarfs or giants), conjoining body parts, missing or undeveloped anatomical parts, and other visible characteristics were used to develop these public ideas of anomaly. "Freaks" often participated willingly in the development of these images and enjoyed the fame and fortune produced. Freak shows did not fade from the social scene until the 1940s (Disability Social History Project).

The Civil War

During the years of the Civil War (1861–1865), many soldiers suffered injuries that left them disabled. Among the soldiers of the Union Army alone, there were 30,000 amputations. Caring for amputees and enabling them to lead meaningful and productive lives became a national task (Disability Social History Project). Rather than having an entire cadre of disabled and dependent veterans living unhappily in federal hospitals, government planners encouraged disabled veterans to return home to their families. They were to be

FIGURE 2.1   *Millie and Christina, Siamese twins born in 1852.*
Disability Social History Project

employed as able in positions suitable to their disability and given a pension from the government. Because of the large numbers of Civil War veterans, that pension had become the single largest government expense by 1900 (Beyond Affliction).

The Early Twentieth Century

Babbitt founded the Society for Crippled Children in Elyria, Ohio, in 1910. This society was the forerunner of the Easter Seals, a major organization serving the needs of disabled people today. During the Depression years, Franklin Delano Roosevelt, himself disabled and in a wheelchair, was instrumental in the establishment of the March of Dimes (Figure 2.2), an organization dedicated at first to polio research and today to research on birth defects in children (Disability Social History Project).

While organizations to assist disabled people proliferated during the early twentieth century, the public image of disability was that seen on posters soliciting funds and services on their behalf (Beyond Affliction: The Disability History Project: The Poster Child). The poster child was always a child, appealing and vulnerable, an object of pity and fear, as well as of hope. Poster children gave Americans a distorted image of disability by presenting the helplessness and vulnerability, rather than the strengths, of disabled people.

Braille became the primary method of reading for blind people and, in 1916, British Braille became the English language standard. However, in the United States, New York Point and American Braille were also used. Helen Keller developed the American Founda-

For Crippled Children

Community Chest—I Have Given (1924)

Suppose Nobody Cared?—I Cared

The National Foundation for Infantile Paralysis Inc.—Celebrate Our President's Diamond Jubilee Birthday—Join the March of Dimes

FIGURE 2.2 *Campaign buttons in support of a cure for infantile paralysis, early to mid-1900s.*

Disability Social History Project

Be Thankful You Can See
Sight and Blind Aid

Be Thankful You Can See

Be Grateful You Can See
San Francisco Center for the Blind

FIGURE 2.3   *Campaign in support of the blind, early to mid-1900s.*

Disability Social History Project

tion for the Blind (Figure 2.3), a nonprofit organization charged with advocating for and providing services to blind people (Disability Social History Project).

The Move toward Institutionalization

By the 1920s, most disabled people had been moved from attics and basements to large, impersonal institutions, which we think of as "warehouses" today, where they were expected to remain for life. Many such institutions served a particular disability only: There were institutions for people who were blind, deaf, children, mentally ill, and retarded. The distinction between the "deserving disabled poor" and the "undeserving" continued well into the twentieth century, and traces of it persist today. You were "deserving" if you became disabled as a result of an industrial accident or were a veteran with injuries sustained in the course of service. You were also deserving, of course, if your family could pay for a private institution to care for you. You were "undeserving" if you became disabled though other means and were poor.

While many institutions functioned with limited funding, science and technology spawned new specialties in a new field: the field of rehabilitation. Physical therapists, occupational therapists, nurses, rehabilitation counselors, and disability research flourished as the country attempted to meet the needs of large numbers of disabled veterans (Disability Social History Project).

World War I

The First World War, with its trench warfare, mortars, guns, and rockets that maimed thousands of soldiers and its gasses that poisoned the brain and injured the blood supply, ended in 1918. Veterans returned home without limbs, eyes, or hearing. Surely these were the *very* deserving disabled people—injured during the course of service to their country. As during the aftermath of the Civil War, the government took responsibility for assisting these veterans, some of whom were severely disabled. Vocational rehabilitation programs provided training and services for vets, and assisted them to locate a job that could accommodate their disability (Disability Social History Project).

This large group of disabled veterans returned home to the government system of appropriate employment and government pensions. If a person was disabled but not a veteran, however, not much existed in terms of support in the early years of the twentieth century. By 1920, worker's compensation and vocational rehabilitation programs assisted some people with disabilities. By the 1930s, the federal government had acknowledged its responsibilities to disabled people and wanted to include them in the new Social Security program. However, the outbreak of World War II interrupted this planning (Beyond Affliction: The Disability History Project: What's Work Got to Do With It?).

An Early Protest

One of the earliest protests involving blind people was held in New York in 1935. The League for the Physically Handicapped was originally formed to protest WPA (Works Progress Administration) discrimination against handicapped people. Most of the 300 members of the league had been disabled by polio and cerebral palsy, and all had been turned down for jobs with the WPA. New York's Home Relief bureau, which took the original WPA applications and then forwarded material to the WPA itself, was found to have been stamping the applications with PH, for physically handicapped. Upon receiving applications with this stamp, the WPA immediately turned the applicants down. League members organized a sit-in at the Home Relief Bureau for nine days, followed by a weekend sit-in at the WPA. Their courageous actions eventually generated several thousand jobs for disabled persons through the WPA nationwide (Disability Social History Project).

Eugenics and the Nazi Exterminations

However, that same year, Dr. Alex Carrel, a Nobel Prize winner, published *Man the Unknown,* in which he advocated for euthanasia by gassing for people with disabilities and criminals. Dr. Carrel's position was that espoused by the eugenics movement, presented in Chapter 1 (Disability Social History Project).

The extermination policies of the Nazi regime in Germany actually began with people with disabilities. These policies were grounded in the eugenics movement in the United States, of which Dr. Carrel was a representative. The idea of sterilizing and euthanizing undesirable people was not original with the Nazis. They were, however, the only nation to put these ideas into action (Disability Social History Project). When World War II broke out, the Nazis effected their Aktion T4 program, the "mercy killing" of sick and disabled persons as having a "life unworthy of life." The following year, 908 German patients were transferred from Schoenbrunn, an institution for retarded and the chronically ill people to Eglfing-Haar, where they were gassed. At Hadamar Mental Institution, Dr. Adolf Wahlmann supervised euthanasia with hydrocyanic acid. In 1941, Hitler suspended the Aktion T4 program due to public pressure, after euthanizing almost 100,000 people, but continued the initiative by using drugs and starvation instead of gassing. Estimates show that about 250,000 disabled people were killed during the Nazi regime, and the work of slaughtering people with disabilities continued as late as May 1945 (Disability Social History Project).

Public Health

During past centuries, all over the world, many lives had been lost when infections and communicable diseases spread rapidly among populations. Plague, diphtheria, tuberculosis, typhoid, and other diseases decimated entire populations, including, of course, people with disabilities. Often weaker and less mobile, people with disabilities were even more vulnerable than others to severe illness and death.

Epidemics were often blamed on certain members of the population, who were then punished, ostracized, or exterminated. Often, however, these epidemics were seen as God's punishment for sin. Individuals who were stricken were regarded as sinful, and the epidemic itself could also be seen as God's punishment for the evils in the society. The moral model flourished during epidemics, and prayers for deliverance and forgiveness were often the only remedies available to the people at large. The United States, of course, was not immune to these epidemics, nor to the moral model, which dominated social thinking about disability at such times (Disability Social History Project).

As scientists and physicians gained a clearer understanding of the mechanisms of disease and communicability, however, public health measures were enacted to control them. Vaccines, isolation, and treatment stopped the spread of major epidemics. The last of these was the polio epidemic; people who contacted polio as children are generally among the older members of our population today. Societal understanding moved from the moral model to a more scientific model in understanding illness and disease.

No longer struck in such disproportionate numbers by epidemics, people with disabilities lived longer. Albrecht attributes the lengthening of lifespan for people with disabilities to: (1) preventive measures and advances in pharmaceuticals, (2) medical care management of illness, such as trauma centers intensive care units, and others, and (3) a widespread diffusion of technologies (Albrecht, 1992, p. 49).

World War II

During the years of World War II, enormous numbers of "able-bodied" men were con-scripted or volunteered in the armed services. They left behind them jobs that needed doing, in the factories, the industries, and the offices. While images of Rosie the Riveter appeared on posters all over the country and captured the imagination as women rushed in to fill the now-empty positions in factories and industry and to work in essential wartime industries, a quieter group, not on posters, was also moving into these abandoned posi-tions. Disabled people were hired in record numbers by desperate employers. Ford Motor Company, for example, had 11,000 disabled employees. The new workers were exem-plary: absenteeism declined, positive attitudes flourished, and responsibilities were met (Kleinfeld, 1979, p. 23).

However, when the war ended, disabled workers suffered the same fate as Rosie. Almost all the wartime employees lost their jobs to returning veterans. In a development that paralleled that of all the Rosies, disabled people who had gotten a taste of freedom, accomplishment, and self-respect refused to return to the cellar and the attic. They demanded an education, recognizing that good educations were necessary for good jobs. And they were willing to organize to achieve their goals.

Disability advocacy organizations were born from this recognition. The first to orga-nize as a group were deaf people, followed quickly by blind people and those with cerebral palsy. Many others soon followed.

Mid-Century Changes for Children

Prior to the 1950s, parents with children who had cognitive impairments such as mental retardation and Down syndrome had little control over the treatment and care their children received. Primarily sequestered in large and impersonal institutions, their care and treat-ment was in the hands of staff who were often poorly trained and unable to work with the children to optimize their skills and abilities. With the help of activists and social workers, parents began to resist institutionalization around mid-century and treat these children as full members of the family, keeping them at home and providing the love and care them-selves. The National Association for Retarded Citizens was one of the fruits of these efforts (Beyond Affliction: The Disability History Project: The Overdue Revolution).

The Late Twentieth Century

The story of the second half of the twentieth century is a story of freedom, empowerment, and infinitely greater access to the goods of society for persons with disabilities. The Civil Rights movement of the 1960s was the forerunner of other movements as disempowered and oppressed groups often simultaneously sought civil rights and equality. The women's rights movement, Latino rights and La Raza movements, gay and lesbian pride, and the Disability Rights movement all used the Civil Rights movement as a model for action, from parades to sit-ins to lobbying Congress for a voice. Because of the richness of mate-rial around the Disability Rights movement, the next chapter has been dedicated to that

·exclusively, while the following chapter will present disability laws and regulations passed with the public acknowledgment of disability rights.

By the late 1950s, large, total-care institutions provided most of the care for disabled people. Some of these institutions specialized in training people with specific kinds of disabilities for employment. Board, care, training, and work institutions often provided "sheltered workshops" where people with disabilities could learn a trade and work under close supervision, albeit for very low and noncompetitive wages. Advocacy, advances in science, and a new group of disabled veterans who didn't want to live in institutions created movements toward public entitlements for people with severe disabilities as an alternative to life in the institutions. Rehabilitation became more sophisticated, and the numbers of trained professionals to work with people with disabilities increased. Research efforts, often supported by special interest organizations such as the Heart Association, the Cancer Society, United Cerebral Palsy, and the Muscular Dystrophy Society brought money and attention to disabilities (Disability Social History Project).

Deinstitutionalization

As the moral model slowly gave way to the societal models of disability in the latter half of the century, the lines between "deserving" and "undeserving" blurred and lessened in importance. People came to feel that all people could, and should, be a part of mainstream society. Major legislation closed down the large institutional warehouses and demanded that disabled people, particularly retarded and mentally ill people, be integrated into the community and provided community-based services. As we shall see in Part IV, some of these mandated services were not funded, so that programs to assist disabled people in the community may be excellent or nonexistent depending on location and community interest and support. This has been particularly true of services for people with mental illnesses, possibly demonstrating a trace of the "deserving/nondeserving" dichotomy through which our society still sometimes categorizes people.

The Disability Rights Movement Begins

Just after mid-century, in 1953, a major change in both the rights of disabled persons and the public image of disability began as Ed Roberts arrived on the campus of University of California at Berkeley. He was in an iron lung part of each day and was in a wheelchair. During the time that he was at Berkeley, Ed and his friends, both disabled and abled, became a force that resulted in major changes in the history of disability in the United States. His experiences will be shared in Chapter 3.

By 1973, the National Association of Deaf Americans counted 1.8 million Americans who were deaf—a major political force to be reckoned with (Disability Social History Project). And, indeed, Jimmy Carter took notice of the rights of disabled people during his campaign for office in 1976. He promised to sign regulations that would have a profound effect on the disability community nationwide. During that same year, the FCC authorized reserving Channel 21 on television sets nationwide for closed captions, but it was not until 1981 that Sears Roebuck began selling decoders for closed captioning (Disability Social History Project).

However, when Carter took office, he did not live up to his promises to the disability community, which had supported his election. HEW instead began revising and changing the previously proposed regulations. Much to their disappointment, neither HEW nor Carter sought advice and input from the disabled community (Disability Social History Project).

Protesting Secretary Joseph Califano's refusal to address disability concerns legally though new regulations, a group of people, mostly with disabilities, took over the San Francisco offices of HEW. They remained there for almost a month, the longest sit-in in a federal facility up to that time. For the first time, disabled people advocated strongly and publicly for their rights, and the legal support they were seeking, Section 504, was passed (Disability Social History Project).

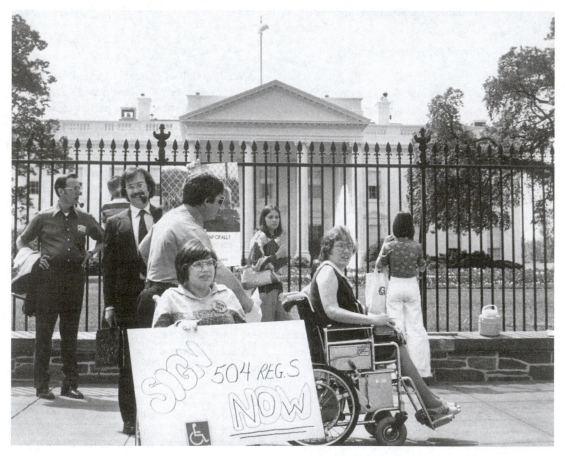

Judy Heumann, who later served in the Clinton Administration as Assistant Secretary for Education, and Kitty Cone of the World Disability Institute in front of the White House, Washington, DC, advocating for the passage of the 504 regulations.

The National Disabled Women's Educational Equity Project was begun in 1980, dedicated to studying disability and gender and to providing training programs for disabled women. The organization conducted the first national study, and later held the first National Disabled Women's Conference (Disability Social History Project).

During this same period, another major movement toward disability rights, American Disabled for Accessible Public Transit, was founded in Denver by Wade Blank. ADAPT's mission was the attainment of accessible public transportation for people with disabilities. In 1989, ADAPT declared its primary mission of making it possible to cross the country by public transportation and took on the cause of the inaccessible, though private, Greyhound Bus system. ADAPT's mission and experiences will be described in Chapter 3 (Disability Social History Project).

Effects of Lifespan Changes

Because of the way we define and measure disability, the limitations that affect individuals due to a disability may vary over the lifespan. Most children with a disability have little or no limitation on daily activities. Exceptions include mental retardation, epilepsy, speech impairments, blindness, and deafness in both ears (Albrecht, 1992, p. 50).

For adults, however, disability is often measured by employability limitations. These problems and limitations increase with age. The most likely causes of work limitations, and therefore perceived disability, include mental retardation, absence of legs, lung cancer, blindness, multiple sclerosis, cerebral palsy, and paralysis (Albrecht, p. 50).

As medical sciences and technology continue to advance, the general lifespan is increasing, and so is the lifespan of people with disabilities. More disabilities are found in the old and oldest old. Heart problems and cancer are frequent disabling conditions for older men, while arthritis and diabetes are more prevalent in older women (Albrecht, p. 52).

Entering the Mainstream

Today, people with disabilities can be found in every part of society. They are employed in all fields, live independently in homes and apartments, take buses to visit friends, and fly across the world for meetings. These achievements are due both to individual strength and courage and to strong advocacy and empowerment that has enabled legislation to support equality and eliminate discrimination.

The Poster Child: Still with Us in the New Millennium

The role of the "poster child" continues today, though the frameworks are somewhat different. Shapiro (1994, p. 12) writes:

> The poster child is a surefire way to our hearts. The children picked to represent charity fund-raising drives are brave, determined, and inspirational, the most innocent victims of the cruelest whims of life and health. Yet, they smile through their "unlucky" fates . . . no

other symbol is more beloved by Americans than the cute and courageous poster child—or more loathed by people with disabilities themselves.

In reaction, Cyndi Jones, publisher of *Mainstream,* a disability magazine, says that the feelings a poster child is meant to arouse in viewers is actually oppressive. "Pity oppresses," she states (Shapiro).

The flip side of the poster-child-to-be-pitied image, Shapiro observes, can quite as damaging. Currently, the media celebrates the inspirational disabled person—the over-achieving "supercrip" hero who overcomes all obstacles and triumphs against all odds. Neither image, Shapiro believes, presents a true picture of people with disabilities. "It's just normal people trying to lead normal lives," he says, "neither objects to be pitied nor heros to be admired" (Shapiro, p. 16).

Chapter Summary

This chapter has presented a brief history of disability in the United States. Several trends can be traced through the 300 years included here. There is a shift from the moral model to the medical model and a new movement toward understanding disability as a social construction. Disabled people were cared for at first in attics and basements by family members and later in large, impersonal institutions. At present, people with disabilities generally live in homes with family or in independent living arrangements. The field of rehabilitation, born out of urgent need for assistance for the veterans of three wars, has become a highly specialized professional endeavor, with its goal to optimize the ability of each person to function in society in a meaningful manner. Research and advances in medical science have extended lifespans, resulting in more people with disabilities living longer, but have also cured chronic illnesses and conditions that were debilitating to previous generations. Advocacy has given a strong voice to people with disabilities, and disability rights and empowerment have become a major political force. No longer invisible, people with disabilities have moved from attics and basements to corporations, businesses, and laboratories.

Although barriers remain and the need for advocacy continues, the last half of the twentieth century has ushered in major changes in the lives of people with disabilities. The changes continue to enable meaningful, pleasant, and productive lives for many people, who are living Shapiro's goal of "normal people living normal lives."

Questions for Thought and Discussion

1. The "poster child" is indeed still with us in the new millennium. Would it be possible to raise the same funds without the poster child images commonly found in fund-raising advertising? If not, do you think the end (of raising needed funds) justifies the means (of using the poster child image)?

2. In Shapiro's view, people with disabilities are "just normal people trying to lead normal

lives." In the context of the previous chapter's discussion of "norms" and "normal," how do you understand this comment?

3. Do you think that it will be possible to eliminate institutional care for people with disabilities completely? Consider that "disability" is a broad term and includes mental illnesses, cognitive losses, developmental disabilities, people who are life-support dependent, and others.

4. In light of what we now consider important to a good quality of life, design an institution that would care for people with severe disabilities in a way that enhances and supports their quality of life. What would you consider to be vital elements?

5. In relation to disabilities and poverty, do you think the terms "deserving poor" and "undeserving poor" still indicate an element of public opinion about disabilities? If so, how would you address this issue?

3

The Disability Rights Movement in the United States

Rights are not established easily; the successful legitimation and institutionalization of rights typically results from political struggle. (Scotch, 2001, p. 42)

The Disability Rights movement became a significant force for change and advocacy during the twentieth century and, like other similar movements for women, Latinos, and gays and lesbians, took its inspiration from the great Civil Rights movement of the 1960s, which fought for equality and freedom for African Americans. Advocacy, nonviolence, sit-ins, protests—these tactics were used by all the movements in their efforts to achieve parity for their constituents. Public actions were particularly difficult for people with disabilities because the built environment, at the time that the Disability Rights movement began, was not accessible to many people with disabilities, and there were few opportunities for meeting as groups for planning and organizing. Despite these difficult barriers, there was great interest in and dedication to the cause of disability rights, and the movement is a major force in U.S. politics today.

Early Efforts

Disabled people in colonial times and during the early years of nationhood were not able to organize effectively to advocate for civil rights. In the context of the "attic or basement" living conditions, the total dependence on families, the lack of contact with other disabled people, and the scarcity of information about what was going on around them that we learned about in Chapter 2, we can easily see the extreme difficulty any individual disabled person would have had in attempting to improve his or her condition in a formal and official sense during this period.

Although the first sheltered workshop was organized for blind workers by Samuel Gridley Howe in 1840, such work opportunities were scarce until the early 1900s, when over half a million people were employed in such workshops. People employed in sheltered workshops had few rights. They were paid less money than other workers and often worked long hours under difficult conditions. There were no opportunities to meet other people. Although organizations that supported workers in sheltered workshops, especially those for the blind, attempted collective bargaining in order to secure wages and conditions comparable to other workers, their efforts were largely unsuccessful. Occasionally, strikes did occur. One documented strike occurred at a sheltered workshop in Pittsburgh in 1937. There was good media coverage of the event, but the focus was not on the discrimination and inequities the strikers were attempting to remedy, but rather on the oddness and unusual occurrence of a strike by people who were disabled (Disability Social History Project).

Although employment was a major issue for people with disabilities, there were other major problems as well: lack of access to buildings impeded voting, applying for programs and services, and recreation and leisure activities as well. Living arrangements often kept people with physical disabilities locked into homes and institutions, limiting social, educational, and employment opportunities and fostering a sense of frustration and helplessness. Public education programs did not address special needs, and access to higher education was often impossible. Vocational rehabilitation was limited and often not accessible. Employers could not be penalized for refusing to hire people with disabilities. Lack of transportation affected employment as well (Disability Social History Project).

The First Advocacy Organization

The League for the Physically Handicapped, originally formed in New York in 1935 as a group of six people, eventually grew to a membership of several hundred. As noted in the preceding chapter, its original mission was to protest the Emergency Relief Bureau's refusal to refer people with disabilities to the Works Progress Administration fairly (Figure 3.1). The media attention gained by this landmark protest increased interest and membership, and the organization continued its mission of fighting unfair employment practices through picket lines and organized demonstrations for years. Members of the league spoke with labor unions and other organizations to educate people about disabilities and the skills disabled workers could develop. The league was accused of leftist "red" membership and influences, as were many other trade union organizations during the 1930s, and eventually dissolved itself at the end of that decade (Disability Social History Project).

Precipitating Influences

There were several other movements that had a strong impact on the formation of the Disability Rights movement. Some of these began prior to disability rights, while others

"DEATH WATCH"

On December 6th, Mr. Ridder announced to the press that within ten days jobs will be given to the unemployed members of THE LEAGUE FOR THE PHYSICALLY HANDICAPPED. There was to be no more discrimination against handicapped workers.

WE ACCEPTED THIS PLEDGE OF THE ADMINISTRATION.
WE WITHDREW OUR PICKET LINES FROM W.P.A. HEADQUARTERS
at 111 - 8th Ave.

BUT THE ADMINISTRATION DELIBERATELY BROKE ITS PROMISE !!

WE ACCUSE !!!
The Administration of

UNJUST DISCRIMINATION AGAINST THE HANDICAPPED.
DISREGARDING THE NEEDS OF THE HANDICAPPED EVEN AFTER OUR
PROBLEM HAD BEEN BROUGHT TO THEIR ATTENTION. ASSUMING A
CALLOUSED AND INHUMAN ATTITUDE TOWARD US. DEPRIVING US OF WHAT
IS RIGHTFULLY OURS -- THE RIGHT TO LIVE.

OUR NEEDS ARE DESPERATE !!!

****
We will honor the dead promises of the administration with a "DEATH WATCH" at 111 - 8th Ave. starting on Friday, Dec. 20th at 4 P.M. and continue through the night.

WE WILL FIGHT UNTIL WE WIN -- WE WANT JOBS !!

****
Since the Administration has ignored our problem, we appeal now to the highest law of the land -- PUBLIC OPINION.
WRITE-WIRE-OR-PHONE YOUR PROTESTS DEMANDING
That Discrimination Be Stopped !!
That the Promised Jobs be Given !!
YOU AND YOUR FRIENDS CAN HELP US.
Phone Watkins 9-3500.

LEAGUE FOR THE PHYSICALLY HANDICAPPED
929 Broadway - New York City
UNEMPLOYED SECTION MEETS EVERY MON. 7:30 P.M.

FIGURE 3.1 *Early disability rights efforts: Flyer for League for the Physically Handicapped, New York, 1935.*

Disability Social History Project

occurred simultaneously with it. All of these movements continue to exert a strong impetus toward change in society today.

Deinstitutionalization

As noted in the preceding chapter, this movement was an attempt to move people out of large institutions, where there was little opportunity for growth and integration into society, and back into their own communities. People who were mentally ill and retarded people (now often called developmentally disabled) were the primary groups affected by deinstitutionalization.

The leaders of this new movement were parents and families as well as care providers, and the theoretical framework was "normalization"—the idea that if people were treated "normally" they would behave normally, as originally framed by Wolf Wolfensberger. Wolfensberger's "social role valorization" theory suggests that, by enabling and supporting positive social role development in the individual with the disability, a positive image will be incorporated into the public image of both the person and the disability, which will, in turn, enable the development of self-esteem and a positive personal identity (Thomas & Wolfensberger, 1982). Until this movement became effective, young people with disabilities often resided in nursing homes for the elderly.

The Civil Rights Movement

People with disabilities and those who cared for them watched the development of the Civil Rights movement with interest. Although the movement itself, and the legislation that was passed as a result, specifically did not include people with disabilities, a major precedent had been set. Civil rights could be advocated for, and won by, an entire class of people.

Leaders of the Disability Rights movement learned advocacy techniques from civil rights: protests, sit-ins, lobbying, gathering consensus, and other techniques that had worked effectively in securing civil rights for African Americans would be used to secure them for disabled Americans as well. As R. K. Scotch observed (2001, p. 164): "Linking accessibility and civil rights meant that altering buildings and redesigning transit systems, at a considerable cost, was equated with providing equal opportunity."

Self-Help and Peer Support

Self-help movements, which began with Alcoholics Anonymous, also provided a useful model for disability rights. The concept that those who could best understand and assist an individual with a disability was another individual with a similar disability grew out of the self-help movement. As one person became empowered, gained independence, and found meaningful work, he or she was able to serve as an inspiration and as a model for others. (McDonald & Oxford, 1999).

Demedicalization

While the medical model was still a major force in conceptualizing disability, the general societal movement toward a holistic understanding of human beings drawn from Asian tra-

Guards at the HEW Building in Washington, DC refused to allow disabled activists into the building. The group was petitioning for the signing of the 504 regulations, the first U.S. law to prohibit discrimination against people with disabilities.

ditions gained popular acceptance. This movement, toward empowerment and responsibility for defining and meeting one's own needs, had a great impact on people with disabilities, whose needs were traditionally defined and met by others. Self-help and peer support provided some of the conceptual framework for advocating choices in living arrangements, caregivers, and medical care, which enabled people to gain self-respect and self-esteem (McDonald & Oxford).

Consumerism

Consumer movements stressed the rights of the consumers to choices about goods and services, and emphasized the responsibilities of the providers of such services directly to the consumers. Although focused originally on products from dishwashers to cars, the thrust of the movement broadened and became more inclusive until it included goods and services traditionally not regulated and chosen by consumers, such as medical care, rehabilitation, and education. Terminology changed to reflect the new paradigm: from patient and client to consumer. Both in the public and in the private sector, consumer movements had a strong effect on disabled people, who internalized the image of empowered consumers rather than of passive patients and clients (McDonald & Oxford, p. 2).

The Independent Living Paradigm

The desire to live independently and to make choices about lifestyles, caregivers, and relationships came to fruition with the development of a new paradigm for living with a disability: the independent living paradigm. Independent living shifted the locus of the "problem" from the individual who is impaired to the society that is disabling and demanded that accommodations be made that maximized the functioning of each person (McDonald & Oxford).

Ed Roberts and the Centers for Independent Living

Ed Roberts wanted to go to college. Childhood polio had left him dependent on an iron lung eighteen hours a day and unable to walk independently or to move his arms. An excellent student, he had sailed through high school, only to be denied graduation by his inability to meet two requirements: that he pass physical education, and that he complete driver education. He was unable to have these waived at the school level and was forced to take his arguments to the California School Board. After strong persistence and advocacy, he was finally granted his high school diploma. Continuing his advocacy, Ed went on to secure rehabilitation funds for himself. He then applied to college and was accepted at University of California at Berkeley (Scalise, 1998).

Arriving on campus in September 1962 with his iron lung and push wheelchair, Ed quickly discovered that he couldn't get into his dormitory room. He tried International House and other campus locations, all without success. Finally, the director of Cowell Hospital, recognizing that Ed was only the first of a group of young people who had survived polio and wanted to continue their educations, gave him a room in the hospital. Ed was able to enroll, the first severely disabled student to attend the University (Scalise, 1998).

Living arrangements weren't Ed's only problem. Classrooms were often located at the top of steep flights of stairs. Quick to make friends on campus willing to help him, Ed was carried up and down flights of stairs and through classroom buildings daily. Another major problem for Ed was toileting. Doors, stalls, and hallways were too narrow to accommodate a wheelchair. He was once threatened with arrest by the Berkeley campus police for not using "proper" toilet facilities.

Over the next eight years, a dozen students followed Ed's path to, and through, the Berkeley campus. With other activists, they formed the first disabled students organization, calling themselves the "Rolling Quads." Like other students at Berkeley, Ed and his friends wanted to be able to go off campus and enjoy the shops along Telegraph Avenue. He was hampered by needing assistance to get on and off the sidewalks and across the streets. The Rolling Quads took on the City of Berkeley, advocating for sidewalk cuts so that they could move independently along Telegraph Avenue. The measure to provide cuts was passed in 1970, and the street was adapted for wheelchairs. There is still a plaque today on Telegraph proclaiming it as the street with the very first sidewalk cuts in the nation (Scalise, 1998).

Mechanically inclined and wanting still greater independence, the Berkeley students designed and built a whole fleet of motorized wheelchairs. Suddenly, Telegraph Avenue and the Berkeley campus were open to them without great effort or the assistance of others! In that same year, Roberts and John Hessler created the Physically Disabled Students Program (Duffy, 1997).

As the students enjoyed their newfound independence, living at Cowell Hospital became less than ideal. Some began to try to move out of the hospital and into independent housing. They adapted the environment to meet their needs, installing ramps and widening doorways. Others left Cowell and came to join them, and the first Center for Independent Living, or CIL as they came to be called, was founded on Haste Street in Berkeley. The year was 1972 (Scalise, 1998).

Students who came to live at CIL not only organized their physical environment, but also took responsibility for hiring caregivers and meeting needs such as cooking, housekeeping, and shopping. CIL became a philosophy, not just a place to live: a philosophy that recognized the importance of choice and empowerment for people with disabilities, as well as their right and ability to organize and manage their own lives. This was a major change from the dependency model that had dominated thinking until that time (Scalise).

Ed himself became the first disabled person to head a government department. He was named director of California's Department of Rehabilitation in 1975. Ed was president of the World Institute on Disability, a position he held until his death in March 1995. Using an iron long at night and a respirator by day and able to move only one finger, he inspired all who knew him in any of his roles: as disability advocate, organizer, intelligent person, father, adventurer, and the "normal guy" who enjoyed having a good time (*World Institute on Disability*, 1995).

The CIL movement spread quickly, first nationwide, and later internationally. Today, there are CILs in many of the world's major cities, serving the needs of disabled people not only in housing but in all aspects of life. As of 1997, the twenty-fifth anniversary of CIL, the 175,000 mark had been passed in terms of numbers of people served, and hundreds of CILs were in operation.

Organizing Demonstrations and the Rehabilitation Act of 1973

In 1972, Congress passed the National Rehabilitation Act (see following chapter for information on provisions). Then-president Richard Nixon vetoed the act. Judy Heumann, a disability rights advocate, organized and staged a protest in New York with about 80 other disability rights advocates. The bill was finally passed in 1973.

Regulations were needed to enforce the act, however. In 1977, HEW Secretary Joseph Califano refused to issue them. Demonstrations by civil rights activists were staged in ten cities across the country. The 150 demonstrators in San Francisco took over the Federal

Building and refused to leave. Califano issued the regulations, which were reviewed by the demonstrators before vacating the federal premises (History of Independent Living).

Wade Blank and ADAPT

In 1974, Wade Blank, living in Denver, Colorado, wanted to help others who wanted to be able to live on their own. He located a house and began with himself as the attendant for nine disabled people in the community who had been forced to live in nursing homes because their needs could not be met in a community setting. His project became the Atlantis Community, a community-based, consumer-controlled organization that provided personal assistants for people in the context of community independent living (McDonald & Oxford, p. 2).

Wade's clients enjoyed their new independence, but found that getting around Denver was impossible for them. The Urban Mass Transit Act had been passed by the federal government in 1970, but cities across the country were ignoring it, and it remained largely unimplemented. Wade realized that access to public transportation was a vital need, and a right for all people. He founded ADAPT, American Disabled for Accessible Public Transit. ADAPT began with a focus on city transit, in order to make city buses and subways accessible to all—in other words, to force compliance with the already passed Urban Mass Transit Act. In 1978, Wade and his fellow ADAPT members held a public bus hostage in Denver, bringing the public's attention to the law and the fact that it was not being enforced. Later, ADAPT broadened its advocacy and took on the Greyhound Bus Company, a major provider of intercity and cross-country public transportation, whose inaccessible buses precluded some people from traveling (McDonald & Oxford, p. 3).

ADAPT grew from a Denver-based grassroots movement to a national one, addressing disability rights and advocating for the enforcement of the 1970s Urban Mass Transit Act. It was not until 1990, however, that the Secretary of Transportation issued regulations mandating lifts on all buses (McDonald & Oxford).

With the passage of the Americans with Disabilities Act in 1990, ADAPT's mission was essentially fulfilled. The organization shifted its focus, while keeping the same name: ADAPT is now American Disabled for Attendant Programs Today, an organization that works toward a national policy of providing community-based attendant services for people with disabilities (McDonald & Oxford, p. 3).

Other Disability Rights Organizations

Throughout the 1970s and 1980s, disability rights organizations were formed, and major issues confronting people with disabilities were addressed. Disabled in Action was formed in May 1970 by some handicapped New Yorkers and became the first *militant* disability rights organization (Kleinfeld, 1979, p. 25–26). In 1974 the American Coalition of Citizens with Disabilities was founded in Washington, DC. Today, the organization represents more than seven million people in the United States (Kleinfeld, p. 35). In 1975, the sit-in protesting government inaction on legislation ensuring disability rights during the Carter administration took place in San Francisco, organized and maintained by the disability community. In 1980, Max Starkloff, Charlie Carr, and Marcia Bristo founded the National Council on Independent Living.

The numbers of members of organizations addressing disability rights grew exponentially during the last decades of the twentieth century. Organizations dedicated to special interests or a specific disability have become powerful political forces, and activism has become a major part of their mission.

The Universal Design Movement

As accessibility became the norm in the designing of structures for the built environment, awareness of the other groups benefitting from these changes grew. Mothers wheeling carriages found sidewalks easier to maneuver. Lowered sinks, light switches, and elevator buttons made children more independent. Handles, rather than knobs, could be operated by someone who was carrying things, someone with no hands, and someone with limited finger dexterity.

The Universal Design movement caught the imagination and inspired the creativity of architects and designers, both students and professionals. Designing dwellings and objects that could be used by everyone in society was a challenge, one that could be met with ingenuity and thought. New materials, gadgets, and styles enabled everyone to use the built environment, removing restrictions not only for disabled people, but also for children, the elderly, and others.

Chapter Summary

The Disability Rights movement is actually a coalition of various organizations and interest groups advocating for equality and civil rights for Americans. These organizations were strongly influenced by the Civil Rights movement, consumerism, deinstitutionalization, self-help, and other movements occurring during this period. Disability rights organizations advocated for community-based housing; access to buildings, transportation, education, and employment; and other rights, demanding that people with disabilities be able to enjoy with all others their rights to goods and services nationwide.

For Further Reading

Additional information about the Disability Rights movement may be found in Pelka (1997). This comprehensive history includes 150 years of disability information and focuses on recent movements and trends. Scalise (1998) details information about 1960s disability activists in a collection of papers and histories compiled at UC Berkeley with funding from the U.S. Department of Education and the National Institute on Disability and Rehabilitation Research. Information is available through the University of California at Berkeley Public Affairs Office.

Questions for Thought and Discussion

1. What are some of the major challenges faced by people with disabilities in addressing their civil rights and basic needs? How have leaders in the movement overcome these challenges?

2. What do the various civil rights movements have in common? Are there any characteristics of the Disability Rights movement that make it unique?

3. Explore the Disability Social History Project website. What do you see as the strengths of the project? What still needs to be accomplished?

4. When the Disability Rights movement talks about "access," what do you view as included in the term? Is it a question of physical accessibility only, or are there broader implications in the use of the term in reference to disability rights?

5. In this age of mass media, what do you think is the appropriate role for the media in relation to disability rights advocacy?

4

Disability Legislation and the ADA

> Disability history in the United States is a history of the humanization of disabled people: humanization is defined as a recognition that disabled people have human needs and characteristics and that public policy must be designed to reflect and further this human potential. (Funk, 1987, p. 8)

Legal protections and recognition for people with disabilities developed in the twentieth century. It began with a national concern for returning veterans who were injured and disabled in World War I and who needed assistance in locating employment and vocational rehabilitation. Clearly, these veterans, who had sacrificed for the well-being of all citizens, were deserving of assistance, consideration, and reintegration into society as expeditiously as possible.

From this military beginning, rights for people with disabilities grew slowly over the course of the century. The first Rehabilitation Act for Veterans was passed in 1916. It took seventy-four years of struggle to reach the Americans with Disabilities Act of 1990, which guaranteed wide access to employment, transportation, and goods and services to all.

This chapter will trace the development of disability rights within the framework of the chronology of major laws that, over the course of the last century, have expanded the rights of people with disabilities. Information on the laws listed below has been obtained from federal government law websites unless otherwise noted.

While a full description of federal laws relating to disability must remain beyond the scope of this book, a brief overview is presented here to help the reader become familiar with major legislation. These laws and policies were developed over the course of the twentieth century. It is important to consider this chronological presentation in the context of major events in United States disability history and world events. It is also interesting to note the way in which legislation reflects the theoretical models presented in the first chapter and the shifting paradigms that moved us from individual to societal models for conceptualizing disability over the course of the century.

Federal Laws

1916: National Defense Act

This law was enacted to meet the needs of World War I vets returning to the United States. Many veterans had become disabled but were returning home as heroes who had sacrificed for their country and were deserving of assistance in returning to the world they had left. Vocational rehabilitation was seen as the avenue for achieving this goal. The cost of the program was to be shared by the states and the federal government.

1920: National Rehabilitation Act

This law expanded the people eligible for vocational rehabilitation through the 1916 act to include all disabled people, not just veterans. The focus of intervention was job training, job counseling, job placement, and work-enabling accommodations such as prosthetic devices and assistive devices. Cost of the program was shared by state and federal governments, with the states also assuming the responsibility for program development and planning.

1935: Social Security Act

The act provides insurance and permanent public assistance to elderly people, blind people, and children with disabilities, but not to other people with disabilities.

1956: Social Security Disability Insurance Act

This entitlement program covers insured workers who are under 65 and are disabled for a year or more, widows, widowers, or divorced wives who have disabilities and are between the ages of 50 and 59, and the disabled sons and daughters of an insured worker. If a worker is covered for SSDI, the spouse and child might be as well. Eligibility is determined by employment and by payment of social security insurance through place of employment—it is not income or resource dependent. However, the person must have contributed insurance payments for a specified number of quarters in order to qualify.

Disability is defined by what a worker cannot do. To be eligible, workers must be unable to engage in gainful activity due to physical or mental impairment. The person must demonstrate inability to perform previous work or any other substantial work. The impairment must be such that continuing to work will result in death or serious injury, must have lasted more than twelve months, or must be expected to last more than twelve months. The burden of proof is on the person who is claiming the disability (Hermann, 1997, p. 343). Disability payments are similar to the payments to which the person would have been entitled at age of retirement.

1963: Community Mental Health Centers Act

This act supported the concept of the deinstitutionalization of people with mental illnesses by providing for the establishment of outpatient treatment centers (Hermann, p. 144). However, resources in these centers have often proved inadequate due to lack of necessary funding.

1964: Civil Rights Act

The Civil Rights Act did not include any provisions for people with disabilities.

1968: Architectural Barriers Act

This act mandates access to federal buildings for people with disabilities. The Architectural Barriers Act was the first national accessibility law and the first to recognize barriers in the built environment.

1970: Urban Mass Transit Act

Wade Blank and the ADAPT disability rights organization he founded were vital to the passage of this act, which requires that all new mass transit vehicles have wheelchair lifts. Although this act was passed in 1970, it was not implemented for twenty years (McDonald & Oxford, p. 3).

1973: National Rehabilitation Act

After Nixon's veto of this act in 1972, Judy Heumann and other civil rights activists advocated for its passage over Nixon's veto, and Congress did override the veto in 1973 (McDonald & Oxford, p. 5). The act prohibits discrimination in the basis of disability in federal programs or programs receiving federal assistance, in federal employment, and in the employment practices of federal contractors. Title V addresses employment specifically. Major provisions include:

Section 501, which requires affirmative action and nondiscrimination by federal agencies of the executive branch to provide "adequate hiring, placement, and advancement opportunities for handicapped individuals."

Section 502, which creates a special board to oversee efforts to make public transportation and public buildings accessible to people with disabilities.

Section 503, which requires affirmative action and nondiscrimination by federal government contractors

Section 504, which states, "No qualified individual with a disability in the United States shall be excluded from, denied the benefits of, or be subjected to discrimination under" any program or activity that receives federal assistance or is conducted by any executive agency or the United States Postal Service.

Thus, the act prohibits all programs receiving federal funding from discriminating against an individual with a disability. Priority in receiving disability-related services is to

Although the Urban Mass Transit Act was passed in 1970, implementation was very slow. Disability rights advocates stage a protest in support of accessible transportation at the Transbay Terminal, San Francisco, 1978.

be given first to those most disabled. Affirmative action imperatives are also incorporated into programs for persons with disabilities.

Two new agencies were also created through provisions in the act: the Architectural and Transportation Barriers Compliance Board and the National Institute of Handicapped Research.

1974: Supplemental Security Income

This insurance provides an income floor for those who have never been employed, are not otherwise entitled to benefits, or have an income less than that set annually by the Social Security Administration. Thus, SSI is a means-tested program: to qualify one must have little or no income and a medically documented mental or physical disability. People who qualify for SSI also automatically qualify for Medicaid or MediCal.

1975: Developmental Disabilities Bill of Rights Act

This provides and establishes protection and advocacy for people with developmental disabilities.

1975: Equal Education for All Handicapped Children Act

Renamed the Individuals with Disabilities Education Act (IDEA), this act states that all children with disabilities between the ages of three and twenty-one are entitled to be educated in the least restrictive environment. Specific "handicaps" include mental retardation, hearing impairment, deafness, speech or language impairment, visual handicap, serious emotional disturbance, orthopedic or other physical impairment, and children with specific learning disabilities. This act does not protect children who have difficulty learning and requires that a diagnostic label in one of the categories listed above be given to the child's problem. Borderline children present a difficulty, falling between the "handicapped" and nonhandicapped levels.

Individual Education Programs (IEPs) are the core method for planning education for each child. Early intervention (by age three) and family involvement throughout the educational process are cornerstones of the program.

Federal funds are available to states developing policies that comply with the act; however, states do not have to comply if they do not receive funds. In cases where states elect not to receive federal funds, children with special needs are protected under the Equal Protection Clause of the Fourteenth Amendment (Hermann, 1997, p. 333).

Part H mandates that early intervention services to children with developmental disabilities be provided between birth and three years of age. As with other parts of IDEA, states are not required to participate, but there are strong federal incentives built into the act to encourage states to develop programs.

1978: Amendments to the Rehabilitation Act of 1973

These amendments provide for consumer-controlled centers for independent living (CILs) for people with disabilities and provide for services for people with disabilities in the community.

1983: Amendments to the Rehabilitation Act of 1973

Further amendments provide a client assistance program and an advocacy program for consumers living in rehabilitation or independent living centers.

1985: Mental Illness Bill of Rights

This bill requires protection and advocacy services for people with mental illnesses, similar to the protection and advocacy services for people with developmental disabilities included in the 1979 Bill of Rights for persons with developmental disabilities.

1988: Civil Rights Restoration Act

This further clarification of the 1973 Rehabilitation Act was necessitated by bad case law to ensure that any program or service that receives federal funding is—in its entirety, not just the affected section—illegal if it discriminates against people with disabilities.

1988: Fair Housing Act

The Fair Housing Act prohibits housing discrimination (both sale and rental, single or multifamily dwellings) on the basis of race, sex, disability, familial status, and national origin. The act applies to both state and federally funded housing and private housing. Landlords must make reasonable exceptions to policies to accommodate people with disabilities. For example, a landlord who rents a "no pets" building must accept a guide dog. Renters with disabilities may make reasonable adaptations to their units; however, the landlord is not required to pay for these. Any new housing of four or more units must be designed to allow access by a disabled person to common areas, kitchens, bathrooms, and the like.

1988: Air Carrier Access Act

This act prohibits discrimination in air travel and provides equal access to air transportation for people with both mental and physical disabilities.

1990: Americans with Disabilities Act

The most comprehensive law addressing the rights of disabled people is the Americans with Disabilities Act. It provides a clear mandate for the elimination of all forms of discrimination through the development of enforceable standards and clarifies the role of the federal government in overseeing enforcement of the provisions of the act.

The ADA defines disability as a physical or mental impairment that substantially limits one or more of the major life activities, having a record of such impairment, and the person being regarded as having such an impairment.

Title I: Employment.   Title I defines job accommodations in the work environment for companies employing more than fifteen people and prohibits discrimination in recruitment, the application process, hiring, or the assignment of benefits, and requires that people with disabilities be reassigned as needed to jobs whose essential functions can be performed. Employers must also make "reasonable accommodations" for employees with disabilities.

Exceptions to note: Religious organizations may preferentially hire members of the religious group if the intent is to provide services to the religious group. Title I also excludes people who are using illegal drugs, compulsive gamblers, pyromaniacs, kleptomaniacs, and people with mental illnesses that result from current use of illegal drugs (Hermann, 1997).

Title II: Transportation and Public Facilities.   Title II supports earlier acts that require access to public facilities and transportation, including all federal, state, and local government offices and services.

Title III: Private Accommodations. This section mandates access to private accommodations, services, and facilities, and also states that service providers such as insurance companies cannot discriminate against people with disabilities. Right of access includes restaurants, hotels, theaters, and other private facilities.

Title IV: Telecommunications. Telephone and television access for people with speech and hearing disabilities is addressed in this section. Common carriers (telephone companies) are required to establish interstate and intrastate telecommunications relay services (TRS) available 24/7. Closed captioning of federally funded public service announcements is also required.

1997: Civil Rights of Institutionalized Persons Act

This act provides authorization to the attorney general to investigate the conditions of confinement in any state or local government institution, such as a prison, a jail, a pretrial detention center, a juvenile correctional facility, a publicly operated nursing home, or an institution for people with developmental or psychiatric disabilities that may have violated the civil rights guaranteed under the Constitution of any person so confined.

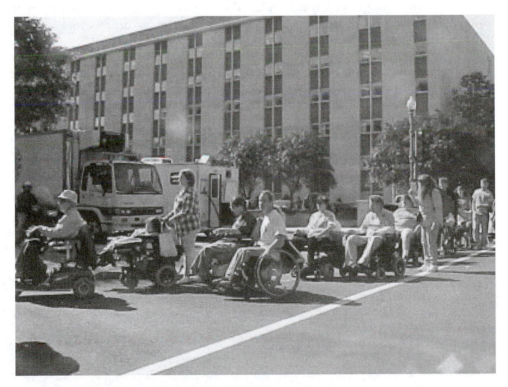

March in support of the passage of the ADA, 1990.

2000: National Family Caregivers' Support Act

The first act to address the needs of caregivers provides support and services to people who are caring for an elderly person, a disabled person, or grandparents over sixty who are caring for a grandchild. This act recognizes the vital role of family caregivers in providing personal care and in assisting disabled people to remain in the community or to retain maximum independence.

Funding for this new program will come from the federal government; however, each state will develop its own plan to administer the program and provide services to caregivers.

2001: Plan for Achieving Self-Sufficiency Act (PASS).

This important piece of legislation enables people with disabilities to keep their medical insurance (Medicare or Medicaid) while they are employed to help offset the heavy cost of medical care for people who are disabled.

State Laws

In addition to the federal laws, each state has a system of state laws that address disability issues. State laws may provide additional rights or programs, but may never provide *fewer* civil rights and protections than the federal system has required. State laws are generally found within the codes of law for the particular state.

It is important to be aware of the disability codes of law for the state in which you are practicing. Some states, such as California, New York, and Texas, have both civil and criminal codes of law available on the Internet. They may be located by going to the official state government site of the state you are researching. You may also obtain information about state laws and statutes from government offices, the attorney general's office, disability rights and advocacy organizations, and state bar associations.

Case Law

Since the passage of the Americans with Disabilities Act, challenges and requests for clarification of laws related to disability have increased geometrically. The EEOC estimates that between 18,000 and 19,000 claims a year are made related to the Americans with Disabilities Act alone (Disability Law Update). Such challenges and requests for clarification may be found on both state and national levels. Cases often involve a dispute or need for clarification of specific wording and/or sections of disability law. You may locate these, and also find the most recent cases, by checking Disability Law Update at *www.disabilitylawupdate .com.*

Some claims and counterclaims reach the Supreme Court, which has taken an active role in defining disability and attempting to clarify what it believes was intended by Congress in the passage of the Americans with Disabilities Act. Cases in 2001 and 2002 have included two women pilots who were turned down for positions with United Airlines because they needed glasses to correct their vision and a woman whose case involved carpal tunnel syndrome accommodations requested from Toyota and supported by the lower courts. The Supreme Court ruled that these limitations did not constitute "disability" as intended by the ADA, thus supporting a more limited definition of "disability." An excellent source for current information on Supreme Court and other case law is DREDF, the Disability Rights Education and Defense Fund (*www.dredf.org*).

Additional Information on Disability Laws

To locate current information about disability laws and implementation, the National Council on Disability has provided *National Disability Policy: A Progress Report,* which is available on the web at *www.ncd.gov/publications/policy* and is updated regularly. This comprehensive report includes information on demographic and research, civil rights, education, health care, long-term services and supports, immigrants and minorities with disabilities, Social Security–related information, employment, welfare to work, housing, transportation, and technology.

You may also locate information on disability laws at the federal and state level by accessing the relevant government websites. The American Bar Association lists helpful information as well. Some additional helpful websites:

> *www.fedlaw.gsa.gov/legal61.htm*
> *www.pueblo.gsa.gov*
> *www.abanet.org/disability*
> *www.usdoj.gov/crt/ada/*
> *www.disabilitylawupdate.com*

Chapter Summary

This chapter has provided a description of the major federal laws that provide and support civil rights for persons with disabilities. Case law, congressional action, and presidential order may modify or negate some of the provisions of the laws included here. It is important to be aware of current changes in working with clients in order to render optimal service.

In the twentieth century, the legal rights of persons with disabilities have been formalized and special circumstances addressed so that people can participate fully in our society. Changes in the built environment and in the social system do not occur overnight, unfortunately, and many of the provisions of disability laws have yet to be implemented on a nationwide and on a local basis.

Disability at some level affects one in five Americans today. The previous chapters have provided the historical and legal grounding for work with people with disabilities. In the next chapter, we will present some data on the prevalence and effect of disabilities in the population of the United States.

Questions for Thought and Discussion

1. To practice using the laws to advocate for client rights, develop a set of five "clients" who are having difficulties with civil rights and in obtaining access to programs. Exchange "clients" with a classmate. Review and explore the laws included in this chapter and determine which would apply to each client's problems.

2. Do you think that all the legal needs of people with disabilities have been addressed? What needs have not been included?

3. For a social worker, familiarity with the laws is important, as is advocacy. However, there are times when legal help is necessary. Using web resources, locate lawyers in your area who specialize in disability rights law. (Hint: The ABA maintains listings by state and location.)

4. Select one of the laws included in this chapter's overview. Research it and present to your classmates the information you found.

5. To meet the federal definition of disability and qualify for federal programs and protection, people with disabilities must have a disability that limits life activities, have a record of such a disability (usually a medical record), and "be regarded as having" such a disability. How do you think that the necessity to "prove" disability in this way affects the right to privacy guaranteed by the Constitution? What happens if the disability is "invisible," and someone is not "regarded" as having a disability?

5

Disability Demographics

In the previous chapters we explored various frameworks for conceptual thinking about disability, disability issues and movements in the United States, and some of the major laws and statutes that have been designed in the twentieth century to ensure the civil rights of all people. In this chapter, we will examine some demographic information: who has been designated as disabled and by what measures disability has been established. We will look at disability and age, race and ethnicity, employment, and other parameters.

Demographic information about disability is essential for social work practice. On the macropractice level, it informs decisions about resource allocation, program planning, and areas of unmet needs. For social workers in direct practice, demographic information helps us to understand our clients' unique circumstances in the broader context of needs and problem areas for people with disabilities as a group. Information that correlates disability by age, sex, race, and Hispanic origin helps in the development of programs that are culturally sensitive and appropriate. As income and employment is a basic issue for everyone, demographic information can assist social workers in planning services that will support employment and help to maintain income.

Part IV addresses resources that are available to assist people with disabilities in areas such as health care, housing, employment and income maintenance, assistive devices and technology, and others. When considering resources and needs in the disability community, it is important to use demographic information to interpret the possible impact of new programs and services, and of the discontinuance of programs and services.

Sources of Demographic Information

The data used in this chapter is drawn primarily from the United States Bureau of the Census. Specific data on disabled persons from the year 2000 census will not be available until 2003. The Census Bureau uses three primary sources for data on disabled people:

1. Survey of Income and Program Participation (SIPP)
2. Census
3. Current Population Survey (CPS)

Data from SIPP have been collected since 1984. Over the years, an extensive panel of questions have been included, and this is perhaps the most comprehensive source of data available. The census has included questions on disability on the long forms for 1970, 1989, 1990, and, of course, 2000. The third data set, the CPS, collects information in March of every year. It identifies people who are unemployed because of a disability, and people who have a health problem that limits employability.

Most of the information in this chapter has been obtained from SIPP. The SIPP questionnaire includes people over fifteen years of age and covers limitations in functional activities (seeing, hearing, speaking, lifting and carrying, using stairs, and walking) in activities of daily living (ADLs: bathing dressing, eating, toileting, getting out of bed or chair, getting around inside the home), and in instrumental activities of daily living (IADLs: going outside the home, keeping track of money, preparing meals, doing light housework, using the telephone). SIPP surveys also include information about use of assistive devices, mental functioning, work disability, and the disability status of children (United States Census Bureau, Survey of Income and Program Participation).

Additional information on people with disabilities included here is drawn from the Centers for Disease Control. The Healthy People 2010 Initiative has gathered baseline information about people with disabilities that will be used to evaluate the initiative over the 2000–2010 decade. The CDC states that at least 54 million people in the United States are currently experiencing some limitation in activities due to a chronic health problem. (The U.S. Census Bureau sets the figure at 53 million.) There is an expectation that this number will rise by 50 percent, to about 108 million people, by the year 2010. The baselines determined current health and well-being of people with disabilities as well as the gaps and disparities between this group and nondisabled people (Centers for Disease Control, 2001a).

In considering the demographic data included here, it is important to note that each set of data includes groupings and categories selected by the researching organizations. Therefore, data for some disabilities and not for others appears in each study.

Americans with Disabilities, 1997

The latest SIPP data was collected in 1997. Because of its centrality in presenting information about disability in the United States, the official report is shown in Figure 5.1.

Prevalence of Disability by Age, Sex, Race, and Hispanic Origin, 1997

In addition to the information included above, two other tables (Tables 5.1 and 5.2) are helpful in understanding the prevalence and severity of disabilities in the United States. Table 5.1 addresses the prevalence of disability by age, sex, race, and Hispanic origin.

AMERICANS WITH DISABILITIES: 1997

Household Economic Studies
Current Population Reports P70-73
Americans With Disabilities: 1997
By Jack McNeil

Introduction

The Americans with Disabilities Act of 1990 (ADA) defines disability as a substantial limitation in a major life activity. The Survey of Income and Program Participation (SIPP) contains questions about the ability to perform a number of activities. If an individual reported having difficulty performing a specific activity, a follow-up question usually determined if the level of difficulty was severe or not. Responses to these and related questions were used to arrive at two overall measures of disability status. The criteria used to classify individuals by disability status are explained in the box on this page.

This report presents information on the number and characteristics of individuals with disabilities and is based on data collected in wave 5 of the 1996 Panel of the SIPP. Wave 5 data were collected from August - November 1997. The SIPP is a household survey, and the estimates in this report exclude the population in institutions. Approximately 32,000 households were interviewed during wave 5 of the 1996 Panel.

Definitions of disability status, functional limitations, activities of daily living (ADLs), and instrumental activities of daily living (IADLs)

Individuals 15 years old and over were identified as having a disability if they met *any* of the following criteria:

1. Used a wheelchair, a cane, crutches, or a walker;
2. Had difficulty performing one or more functional activities (seeing, hearing, speaking, lifting/carrying, using stairs, walking, or grasping small objects);
3. Had difficulty with one or more *activities of daily living* (the ADLs included getting around inside the home, getting in or out of bed or a chair, bathing, dressing, eating, and toileting);
4. Had difficulty with one or more *instrumental activities of daily living* (the IADLs included going outside the home, keeping track of money and bills, preparing meals, doing light housework, taking prescription medicines in the right amount at the right time, and using the telephone);
5. Had one or more specified conditions (a learning disability, mental retardation or another developmental disability, Alzheimer's disease, or some other type of mental or emotional condition);
6. Had any other mental or emotional condition that seriously interfered with everyday activities (frequently depressed or anxious, trouble getting along with others, trouble concentrating, or trouble coping with day-to-day stress);
7. Had a condition that limited the ability to work around the house;

FIGURE 5.1 *Americans with disabilities: 1997.*   *(Continued)*

8. If age 16 to 67, had a condition that made it difficult to work at a job or business; or
9. Received federal benefits based on an inability to work.

Individuals were considered to have a *severe* disability if they met criteria 1, 6, or 9; or had Alzheimer's disease, or mental retardation or another developmental disability; or were unable to perform or needed help to perform one or more of the activities in criteria 2, 3, 4, 7, or 8.

The disability questions that were asked as part of the SIPP wave 5 Topical Module can be found at the following web site: http://www.sipp.census.gov/sipp/top_mod/1996/quests/folder.htm.

Highlights

(Table A presents the confidence intervals for the estimates cited below.)

- In 1997, 52.6 million people (19.7 percent of the population) had some level of disability and 33.0 million (12.3 percent of the population) had a severe disability.
- About 10.1 million individuals (3.8 percent of the population) needed personal assistance with one or more ADLs or IADLs.
- Among the population 15 years old and over, 2.2 million used a wheelchair. Another 6.4 million used some other ambulatory aid such as a cane, crutches, or a walker.
- About 7.7 million individuals 15 years old and over had difficulty seeing the words and letters in ordinary newspaper print; of them, 1.8 million were unable to see.
- The poverty rate among the population 25 to 64 years old with no disability was 8.3 percent; it was 27.9 percent for those with a severe disability.

TABLE A   *Selected Disibility Measures: 1997*

Categories	Number with specified characteristic (in thousands)		Percent with specified characteristic	
	Number	90-percent confidence interval (+/-)	Percent	90-percent confidence interval (+/-)
All ages	267,665	(X)	100.0	(X)
With a disability	52,596	814	19.7	0.3
Severe disability	32,970	673	12.3	0.3
Needed personal assistance with an ADL or IADL	10,076	390	3.8	0.1
Age 15 years and over	208,059	(X)	100.0	(X)
Used a wheelchair	2,155	183	1.0	0.1

FIGURE 5.1   *Continued*

Used a cane, crutches, or walker (not a wheelchair)	6,372	313	3.1	0.2
Had difficulty seeing	7,673	342	3.7	0.2
Unable to see	1,768	166	0.8	0.1
Had difficulty hearing	7,966	348	3.8	0.2
Unable to hear	832	114	0.4	0.1
Age 25 to 64 years:				
With any disability	26,493	612	100.0	(X)
In poverty	5,669	295	21.4	1.0
With a nonsevere disability	9,794	385	100.0	(X)
In poverty	1,018	126	10.4	1.2
With a severe disability	16,700	496	100.0	(X)
In poverty	4,651	268	27.9	1.4
No disability	112,604	1,007	100.0	(X)
In poverty	9,376	377	8.3	0.3

(X) Not applicable.

Prevalence of disability by selected characteristics

Out of a total population of 267.7 million noninstitutional individuals, 52.6 million (or 19.7 percent) had some type of disability. Among those with a disability, 33.0 million (or 12.3 percent of the total population) had a severe disability, and 10.1 million (or 3.8 percent of the total population) needed personal assistance with one or more ADLs or IADLs (see Table 1, printed in this chapter as Table 5.1 on pages 66–70).

The likelihood of having a disability increased with age. Among those 45 to 54 years old, 22.6 percent had some form of disability, 13.9 percent had a severe disability, and 3.6 percent needed personal assistance. For those 65 to 69 years old, the comparable estimates were 44.9 percent, 30.7 percent, and 8.1 percent. For the oldest age group shown in Table 1, 80 years old and over, the estimates were 73.6 percent, 57.6 percent, and 34.9 percent.

Among the population 15 to 24 years old, the prevalence of disability among women (9.8 percent) was lower than the prevalence among men (11.6 percent). The relationship was reversed for older age groups: Among those 45 to 54 years old, the proportion with a disability was 24.2 percent for women, and 20.9 percent for men; and among those 55 to 64 years old, the rates were 37.2 for women and 34.0 for men. Overall, women made up the majority of the individuals with disabilities: 28.3 million women compared with 24.3 million men. Among those with a severe disability, 18.2 million were women and 14.8 million were men, and among those who needed personal assistance, 5.9 million were women and 4.1 million were men.

The likelihood of having a disability varies by race and Hispanic origin[1]. For all ages, the prevalence of severe disability was 8.5 percent for Asians and Pacific Islanders, 9.7 percent for Hispanics (not statistically different from the rate for Asians and Pacific Islanders) , 12.2 percent for non-Hispanic Whites, and 15.7 percent for Blacks.

FIGURE 5.1 *Continued*   *(continued)*

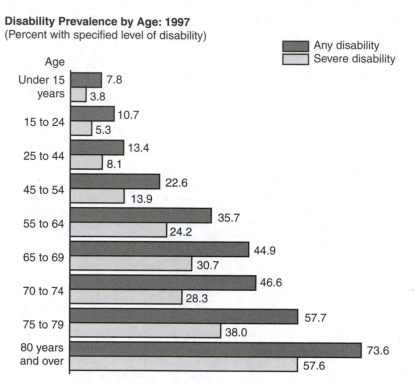

Disability Prevalence by Age: 1997
(Percent with specified level of disability)

■ Any disability
□ Severe disability

Age

Age	Any disability	Severe disability
Under 15 years	7.8	3.8
15 to 24	10.7	5.3
25 to 44	13.4	8.1
45 to 54	22.6	13.9
55 to 64	35.7	24.2
65 to 69	44.9	30.7
70 to 74	46.6	28.3
75 to 79	57.7	38.0
80 years and over	73.6	57.6

Source: U.S. Census Bureau, 1996 Survey of Income and Program Participation: August – November 1997.

Some of the overall differences cited above reflect differences in the age distributions of the populations. For the population 25 to 64 years old, the rates of severe disability were 7.9 percent for Asians and Pacific Islanders, 11.0 percent for non-Hispanic Whites, 11.7 percent for Hispanics (not statistically different from the rate for non-Hispanic Whites), and 19.3 percent for Blacks. For individuals 65 years old and over, non-Hispanic Whites had a considerably lower rate of severe disability than individuals in the other categories: 35.3 percent compared with 49.2 percent for Asians and Pacific Islanders, 47.0 percent for Hispanics and 51.8 percent for Blacks (the rates for Asians and Pacific Islanders, Hispanics, and Blacks are not statistically different).

Prevalence of specific types of disabilities

Table 2 (not included in this chapter) shows the prevalence of specific disabilities for the population 15 years old and over and for three age groups.

The number of individuals with a disability in one or more of the activities of seeing, hearing, or speaking was 14.6 million, or 7.0 percent of the population. A relatively small proportion (2.9 million, or 1.4

FIGURE 5.1   *Continued*

Percent Needing Personal Assistance by Age: 1997

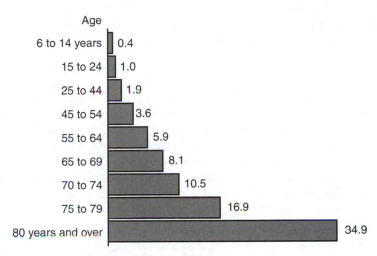

Source: U.S. Census Bureau, 1996 Survey of Income and Program Participation:
August – November 1997.

percent of the population) had a severe disability[2]. For these activities, individuals were considered to have a disability if they *had difficulty* seeing the words and letters in ordinary newspaper print, if they *had difficulty* hearing what was said in a normal conversation with another person (even when wearing a hearing aid), or if they *had difficulty* having their speech understood. They were considered to have a severe disability if they were *unable to* see words and letters in ordinary newspaper print, if they were *unable to* hear what was said in a normal conversation with another person, or if other people were *unable to* understand their speech.

Approximately 25 million individuals 15 years old and over had an ambulatory disability—defined as having difficulty walking a quarter of a mile or up a flight of 10 stairs, or using an ambulatory aid such as a wheelchair, a cane, crutches, or a walker. About 14.7 million people had a severe ambulatory disability, defined as using an ambulatory aid (8.5 million), being unable to walk a quarter of a mile (9.9 million), or being unable to walk up a flight of stairs (5.9 million).[3]

Eighteen million individuals had difficulty lifting and carrying a ten-pound bag of groceries or grasping small objects, and of these almost 8 million had a severe disability performing either or both of these activities.[4]

The survey asked about the ability to perform six activities of daily living, or ADLs, and six instrumental activities of daily living, or IADLs. In 1997, 8.7 million had a limitation in at least one ADL, and of this total, 4.1 million needed personal assistance. Of those who needed personal assistance with one or more ADLs, 1.5 million needed assistance with one, 0.7 million needed assistance with two, and 1.9 million needed assistance with three or more. In the case of IADLs, 12.9 million had difficulty with at least one, and 9.4 million of this total needed personal assistance.

FIGURE 5.1 *Continued*   *(continued)*

When both ADLs and IADLs are considered, 9.9 million individuals needed personal assistance to perform one or more of the 12 activities. Of those who needed personal assistance, 0.4 million were 15 to 24 years old, 4.1 million were 25 to 64, and 5.3 million were 65 or older.

The survey asked a number of questions designed to identify individuals with mental disabilities. Questions were asked about four mental conditions (a learning disability; mental retardation; Alzheimer's, senility, or dementia; or any other mental or emotional condition), and about certain symptoms (frequently depressed or anxious, trouble getting along with others, trouble concentrating, trouble coping with day-to-day stresses). If one or more of the symptoms was reported, a follow-up question asked if the problem seriously interfered with the ability to manage everyday activities. Finally, the IADL question about any difficulty keeping track of money and bills was used as an indicator of mental difficulties. In 1997, 14.3 million had a mental disability; 8.1 million had one or more of the specific conditions; 6.9 million had one or more symptoms that seriously interfered with their ability to manage day-to-day activities; and 4.6 million had difficulty keeping track of money and bills.

In terms of specific mental conditions, 1.4 million individuals had mental retardation, and 1.9 million had Alzheimer's, senility, or dementia. The number with a learning disability was 3.5 million, and about the same number had some other mental or emotional condition.

Among the 6.9 million individuals with one or more specific mental symptoms that seriously interfered with their day-to-day activities, 5.6 million were frequently depressed or anxious, 4.7 million had trouble coping with stress, 3.8 million had trouble concentrating, and 1.8 million had trouble getting along with others.

Questions about whether a physical, mental, or other health condition prevented or limited the work that could be done at a job or business (that is, had a "work disability") were asked in each wave of the 1996 SIPP Panel. In addition to the core questions, the wave 5 disability supplement also asked about the presence of a condition that has made it difficult to remain employed or to find a job. In 1997, 18.5 million individuals 16 to 64 years old were identified as having a work disability by either the core questions or the disability supplement question. The core questions identified 9.7 million individuals as prevented from working and 7.2 million as limited in the kind or amount of work they could do, but not prevented from working. The disability supplement question identified 11.3 million as having a condition that had made it difficult to remain employed or to find a job.

Of the individuals 16 years old and over, 17.6 million were limited in the kind or amount of housework they could do, and of those, 4.4 million were prevented from doing housework.

The final section of shows the number of individuals within three disability domains: communication (seeing, hearing, or speaking), physical (unable to perform a specific physical activity or who had a specific physical condition), and mental as defined above. Individuals may have a disability in more than one domain, and, in some cases, the domain of the disability cannot be identified. The latter situation could occur if an individual has a disability in a general activity such as working at a job and does not report a specific condition as the cause of the disability. In 1997, 28.0 million individuals had a disability in one domain (21.1 million physical, 3.9 million mental, and 2.9 million communication); 13.6 million had a disability in two domains (7.5 million physical and communication, 5.3 million physical and mental, and 0.7 million mental and communication); and 4.3 million had a disability in all three domains. Finally, 2.1 million had a disability whose domain could not be identified.

The survey included a question about the use of a hearing aid, although the use of a hearing aid was not a criterion for determining disability status. The number of individuals who used a hearing aid was 4.0

FIGURE 5.1 *Continued*

million; 1.7 million of these individuals reported difficulty hearing what was said in a normal conversation and 2.3 million did not.

Selected characteristics by disability status

Table 3 (not printed in this chapter) shows the relationships between disability status and a number of other characteristics for two groups: individuals 25 to 64 years old and 65 and older.

Individuals with a severe disability are much less likely than individuals with no disability to be a householder or a spouse of a householder in a married-couple family, and they were much more likely to live as an unrelated individual. In 1997, 46.1 percent of individuals 25 to 64 years old with a severe disability were householders or spouses of householders, and 33.4 percent lived as unrelated individuals. For those in the same age group but with no disability, the comparable figures were 66.3 percent and 20.0 percent.

For individuals 65 years old and over, 42.0 percent of those with a severe disability were householders or spouses compared with 60.1 percent among those with no disability in the same age category. In addition, 44.8 percent of those with a severe disability lived as unrelated individuals, compared with 32.5 percent for those with no disability.

There is a strong relationship between disability status and perceived health status. Among those 25 to 64 years old with a severe disability, 14.5 percent reported very good or excellent health and 58.9

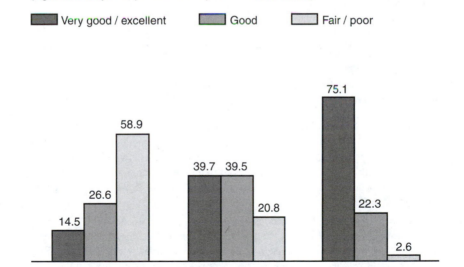

Perceived Health Status by Disability Status: 1997
(Age 25 to 64 years, percent with specified health status)

■ Very good / excellent   ▢ Good   ▢ Fair / poor

Source: U.S. Census Bureau, 1996 Survey of Income and Program Participation: August – November 1997.

FIGURE 5.1 *Continued*   *(continued)*

percent fair or poor, compared with 75.1 percent and 2.6 percent of those in the same age group with no disability. Among those 65 years old and over with a severe disability, 8.8 percent reported very good or excellent health, and 68.0 percent fair or poor. Among those 65 years old and over with no disability, 50.7 percent reported good or excellent health, and 10.5 percent fair or poor.

Individuals with a severe disability are less likely to be covered by private health insurance. Among the population 25 to 64 years old with a severe disability, 47.5 percent were covered by private health insurance compared to 82.3 percent of those with no disability. Among people 65 years old and over with a severe disability, 67.0 percent were covered by private health insurance, compared with 79.7 percent of those with no disability. Among those 25 to 64 years old, 17.2 percent of those with a severe disability and 15.4 percent of those with no disability lacked any form of health insurance.

Disability status is associated with sharp differences in levels of educational attainment. For individuals 25 to 64 years old with a severe disability, 32.6 percent had not finished high school compared with 10.7 percent of those with no disability. In 1997, 9.4 percent of those with a severe disability had graduated from college compared with 28.5 percent of those with no disability. Among those 65 years old and over with a severe disability, 46.2 percent had not finished high school compared to 25.9 percent with no disability .

The presence of a severe disability is associated with an increased likelihood of receiving welfare benefits, of having low levels of income, and being more likely to live in poverty.

Among individuals 25 to 64 years old with a severe disability:

- 20.3 percent received Supplemental Security Income (SSI);
- 5.8 percent received some other form of cash assistance;
- 16.2 percent received food stamps; and
- 9.2 percent lived in public or subsidized housing.

For those in the same age group with no disability:

- 1.2 percent received cash assistance;
- 2.1 percent received food stamps; and
- 1.9 percent lived in public or subsidized housing.[5]

The proportion of individuals 25 to 64 years old with an annual personal income less than $20,000 was 80.2 percent for those with a severe disability compared with 43.7 percent for those with no disability. When the income measure was household income, 41.8 percent of those with a severe disability, and 13.9 percent of those with no disability, lived in a household with an annual income below $20,000. In 1997, 27.9 percent of those with a severe disability and 8.3 percent of those with no disability in this age group lived in poverty.

Income differentials by disability status also existed for individuals 65 years old and over. Among those with a severe disability, the proportion with an annual personal income less than $20,000 was 83.5 percent, the proportion living in a household with an annual income below $20,000 was 52.6 percent, and the proportion in poverty was 16.6 percent. The comparable figures for those in the same age group with no disability were 68.4 percent, 34.1 percent, and 6.9 percent, respectively.

FIGURE 5.1 *Continued*

Employment and earnings by disability status

Table 4 (printed as Table 5.2 on pages 71–75) shows the employment rate and median and average annual earnings for individuals 21 to 64 years old by overall disability status and by specific disability categories. Individuals with a severe disability had an employment rate of 31.4 percent and median earnings of $13,272, compared with 82.0 percent and $20,457 for those with a nonsevere disability, and 84.4 percent and $23,654 for those with no disability.

The first section of Table 4 (Table 5.2) shows selected data on the relationship between disability status and program participation status. One reason for examining this arrangement of the data is to examine whether individuals with a disability who participate in a major program such as Medicare, SSI, or Social Security, or who are identified in the survey as having a condition that prevents them from working, have a reduced availability for employment. Of the 17.4 million individuals aged 21 to 64 with a severe disability, 6.9 million were either covered by Medicare or received SSI payments, and an additional 1.2 million received Social Security benefits. In other words, 8.1 million individuals with a severe disability participated in one or more of these three programs. Of the 9.3 million individuals with a severe disability who did not participate in one or more of the three programs, 3.3 million reported that they were prevented from working and 6.0 million did not.

These three categories of severely disabled individuals (participated in one or more major programs, did not participate but who had a disability that prevented them from working, and did not participate and were not prevented from working) might prove useful when examining their employment situation. If

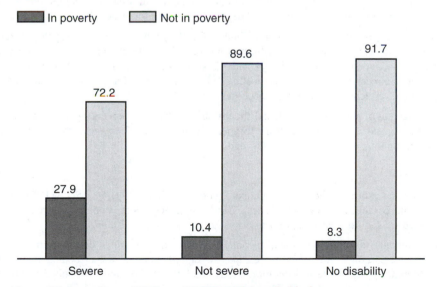

Poverty Status by Disability Status: 1997
(Age 25 to 64 years, percent in and out of poverty)

■ In poverty   ▢ Not in poverty

	Severe	Not severe	No disability
In poverty	27.9	10.4	8.3
Not in poverty	72.2	89.6	91.7

Source: U.S. Census Bureau, 1996 Survey of Income and Program Participation:
August – November 1997.

FIGURE 5.1 *Continued*   *(continued)*

individuals with a severe disability who were not employed are to become employed, the 8.1 million who participated in a major program may need special transition assistance, and the 3.3 million who did not may need to be convinced that changes to the physical and social environment can make employment feasible. Many (73.5 percent) of the 6.0 million individuals in the third category were already employed.

The remainder of Table 4 (Table 5.2) shows data by type of disability. For example, individuals with a limitation in seeing had an employment rate of 41.5 percent and median earnings of $16,791. Those with a mental disability had an employment rate of 37.0 percent and median earnings of $13,534. And those who had experienced difficulty finding a job or remaining employed had an employment rate of 21.1 percent and median earnings of $7,975.

For additional information on employment and earnings, see the materials referenced below in the section on "Related material."

Disability status of children under 15 years old

The survey asked two questions about the disability status of children under 3 years old and two questions about the disability status of children 3 to 5 years old. Two percent of children under 3 had a disability with either a developmental delay or a condition that limited the ability to use arms or legs. In 1997, 3.4 percent of children 3 to 5 had a disability with either a developmental delay or a condition that limited the activities of walking, running, or playing.

A longer set of disability questions were asked for children 6 to 14 years old: 11.2 percent had some disability and 4.8 percent had a severe disability. Children in this age category were considered to have a severe disability if they met any of the following criteria: (1) They had mental retardation or some other developmental disability; (2) they had some other developmental condition for which they had received therapy or diagnostic services; (3) they used an ambulatory aid; (4) they had a severe limitation in the ability to see, hear, or speak; or (5) they needed personal assistance for an activity of daily living.

In terms of specific disabilities, 6.8 percent of children 6 to 14 years old had difficulty doing regular schoolwork, 5.2 percent had a learning disability, 1.5 percent had a developmental disability (including mental retardation, autism, or cerebral palsy), and 3.7 percent had some other developmental condition for which they had received therapy or diagnostic services. The proportion who used an ambulatory aid (wheelchair, cane, crutches, or a walker) was 0.3 percent.

In 1997, 0.7 percent of children 6 to 14 had difficulty seeing, the same percentage as those who had difficulty hearing, and 2.1 percent had difficulty speaking, the same percentage as those who had difficulty walking, running, or taking part in sports and games.

Related material

This report updates estimates shown in "Americans with Disabilities: 1991-92," Series P-70-33, and "Americans with Disabilities: 1994-95," Series P70-61. The latter report can be found on the U. S. Census Bureau's disability web site: *http://www.census.gov/hhes/www/disability.html.*

The Census Bureau's disability web site also contains additional tables about disability in 1997, as well as "Employment, Earnings, and Disability," a paper by John McNeil that was presented at the 75th Annual Conference of the Western Economic Association International, June 29 - July 3, 2000.

FIGURE 5.1 *Continued*

Accuracy of the Estimates

Statistics from surveys are subject to sampling and nonsampling error. All comparisons presented in this report have taken sampling error into account and meet the U.S. Census Bureau's standards for statistical significance. Nonsampling errors in surveys may be attributed to a variety of sources, such as how the survey was designed, how respondents interpret questions, how able and willing respondents are to provide correct answers, and how accurately the answers are coded and classified. The Census Bureau employs quality control procedures throughout the production process—including the overall design of surveys, the wording of questions, review of the work of interviewers and coders, and statistical review of reports.

The Survey of Income and Program Participation employs ratio estimation, whereby sample estimates are adjusted to independent estimates of the national population by age, race, sex, and Hispanic origin. This weighting partially corrects for bias due to undercoverage, but how it affects different variables in the survey is not precisely known. Moreover, biases may also be present when people who are missed in the survey differ from those interviewed in ways other than the categories used in weighting (age, race, sex, and Hispanic origin). All of these considerations affect comparisons across different surveys or data sources.

1/ Hispanics may be of any race.

2/ Totals for individuals with selected disabilities in 1997 were (numbers in parentheses are those with a severe disability in that category): sight — 7.7 million (1.8 million severe); hearing — 8.0 million (0.8 million severe); speech — 2.3 million (0.5 million severe). The number of individuals with a sight disability was not statistically different from the number with a hearing disability.

3/ 19.5 million had difficulty walking a quarter of a mile; 19.8 million had difficulty walking up a flight of stairs (not statistically different from the number that had difficulty walking a quarter of a mile); 2.2 million used a wheelchair; and 6.4 million did not use a wheelchair, but used some other ambulatory aid such as a cane, crutches, or a walker.

4/ 15.2 million had difficulty lifting and carrying a bag of groceries (of those, 7.7 million could not lift and carry a bag of groceries); 6.8 million had difficulty using their hands and fingers to pick up objects such as a glass or pencil (of those, 0.6 million could not use their hands and fingers to pick up a glass or pencil).

5/ For individuals with no disability, the percent living in public or subsidized housing is not statistically different from the percent receiving food stamps.

For further information on statistical standards and the computation and use of standard errors, contact Sam Sae-Ung, Demographic Statistical Methods Division, at 301-457-4221 or on the internet at *Smanchai.Sae.Ung@census.gov.*
Source: U.S. Census Bureau

Contact the Housing and Household Economic Statistics Division's Statistical Information Staff at (301)457-3242 or mail to mailto:*hhes-info@census.gov* for further information on Disability Statistics.

Created: *March 1, 2001*
Last Revised: *March 16, 2001*

FIGURE 5.1 *Continued*

TABLE 5.1 *Prevalence of disability by age, sex, race, and Hispanic origin, 1997 (August–November 1997 data from the Survey of Income and Program Participation. Numbers in thousands.)*

| | Total | With a disability by severity and need for assistance | | | | | |
| | | All severities | | Severe | | Needs assistance | |
		Number	Percent	Number	Percent	Number	Percent
BOTH SEXES, ALL RACES							
All ages	267,665	52,596	19.7	32,970	12.3	10,076	3.8
Under 15 years	59,606	4,661	7.8	2,256	3.8	224	0.4
15 years and over	208,059	47,935	23.0	30,714	14.8	9,851	4.7
15 to 24 years	36,897	3,961	10.7	1,942	5.3	372	1.0
25 to 44 years	83,887	11,200	13.4	6,793	8.1	1,635	1.9
45 to 54 years	33,620	7,585	22.6	4,674	13.9	1,225	3.6
55 to 64 years	21,591	7,708	35.7	5,233	24.2	1,280	5.9
65 years and over	32,064	17,480	54.5	12,073	37.7	5,339	16.7
65 to 69 years	9,555	4,291	44.9	2,930	30.7	777	8.1
70 to 74 years	8,514	3,967	46.6	2,407	28.3	898	10.5
75 to 79 years	6,758	3,897	57.7	2,565	38.0	1,140	16.9
80 years and over	7,237	5,325	73.6	4,170	57.6	2,525	34.9
MALE, ALL RACES							
All ages	130,985	24,331	18.6	14,754	11.3	4,149	3.2
Under 15 years	30,494	3,015	9.9	1,502	4.9	130	0.4
15 years and over	100,491	21,316	21.2	13,252	13.2	4,019	4.0
15 to 24 years	18,663	2,166	11.6	1,007	5.4	216	1.2
25 to 44 years	41,571	5,403	13.0	3,323	8.0	846	2.0
45 to 54 years	16,418	3,427	20.9	2,138	13.0	535	3.3
55 to 64 years	10,342	3,518	34.0	2,364	22.9	584	5.7
65 years and over	13,498	6,801	50.4	4,421	32.8	1,838	13.6
65 to 69 years	4,338	1,813	41.8	1,171	27.0	333	7.7
70 to 74 years	3,722	1,695	45.5	1,022	27.5	392	10.5
75 to 79 years	2,800	1,494	53.4	881	31.5	381	13.6
80 years and over	2,639	1,800	68.2	1,347	51.1	732	27.7

FEMALE, ALL RACES

All ages	136,680	28,265	20.7	18,216	13.3	5,927	4.3
Under 15 years	29,112	1,646	5.7	754	2.6	95	0.3
15 years and over	107,568	26,619	24.7	17,462	16.2	5,832	5.4
15 to 24 years	18,235	1,795	9.8	935	5.1	156	0.9
25 to 44 years	42,316	5,797	13.7	3,470	8.2	789	1.9
45 to 54 years	17,202	4,158	24.2	2,536	14.7	690	4.0
55 to 64 years	11,250	4,190	37.2	2,869	25.5	695	6.2
65 years and over	18,565	10,679	57.5	7,652	41.2	3,502	18.9
65 to 69 years	5,217	2,478	47.5	1,759	33.7	444	8.5
70 to 74 years	4,792	2,272	47.4	1,386	28.9	506	10.5
75 to 79 years	3,958	2,404	60.7	1,684	42.6	759	19.2
80 years and over	4,598	3,525	76.7	2,823	61.4	1,793	39.0

BOTH SEXES, WHITE NOT HISPANIC[1]

All ages	193,234	39,478	20.4	23,627	12.2	7,413	3.8
Under 15 years	38,505	3,173	8.2	1,492	3.9	127	0.3
15 to 24 years	24,307	2,727	11.2	1,206	5.0	286	1.2
25 to 64 years	103,353	19,239	18.6	11,386	11.0	2,823	2.7
65 years and over	27,069	14,338	53.0	9,544	35.3	4,177	15.4

MALE, WHITE NOT HISPANIC[1]

All ages	94,664	18,266	19.3	10,460	11.0	2,988	3.2
Under 15 years	19,642	2,054	10.5	980	5.0	71	0.4
15 to 24 years	12,236	1,502	12.3	611	5.0	157	1.3
25 to 64 years	51,372	9,160	17.8	5,430	10.6	1,354	2.6
65 years and over	11,414	5,550	48.6	3,439	30.1	1,406	12.3

(continued)

TABLE 5.1 *Continued*

| | Total | With a disability by severity and need for assistance | | | | | |
| | | All severities | | Severe | | Needs assistance | |
		Number	Percent	Number	Percent	Number	Percent
***FEMALE, WHITE NOT HISPANIC*[1]**							
All ages	98,570	21,212	21.5	13,167	13.4	4,425	4.5
Under 15 years	18,863	1,119	5.9	512	2.7	56	0.3
15 to 24 years	12,071	1,225	10.2	595	4.9	129	1.1
25 to 64 years	51,982	10,079	19.4	5,956	11.5	1,469	2.8
65 years and over	15,655	8,787	56.1	6,105	39.0	2,771	17.7
BOTH SEXES, BLACK							
All ages	34,369	7,338	21.3	5,382	15.7	1,495	4.3
Under 15 years	9,584	800	8.4	397	4.1	32	0.3
15 to 24 years	5,589	672	12.0	421	7.5	27	0.5
25 to 64 years	16,538	4,136	25.0	3,187	19.3	776	4.7
65 years and over	2,659	1,729	65.0	1,376	51.8	660	24.8
MALE, BLACK							
All ages	16,048	3,380	21.1	2,511	15.6	621	3.9
Under 15 years	4,858	517	10.6	285	5.9	25	0.5
15 to 24 years	2,685	342	12.7	224	8.3	12	0.4
25 to 64 years	7,457	1,879	25.2	1,493	20.0	371	5.0
65 years and over	1,048	643	61.4	509	48.6	214	20.4
FEMALE, BLACK							
All ages	18,322	3,957	21.6	2,871	15.7	873	4.8
Under 15 years	4,726	284	6.0	112	2.4	7	0.1
15 to 24 years	2,904	330	11.4	197	6.8	15	0.5

25 to 64 years	9,081	2,257	24.9	1,695	18.7	405	4.5
65 years and over	1,611	1,086	67.4	867	53.8	446	27.7

BOTH SEXES, ASIAN OR PACIFIC ISLANDER

All ages	9,159	1,192	13.0	776	8.5	223	2.4
Under 15 years	2,089	63	3.0	34	1.6	5	0.3
15 to 24 years	1,454	77	5.3	33	2.3	5	0.4
25 to 64 years	4,971	647	13.0	390	7.9	87	1.7
65 years and over	645	404	62.6	317	49.2	125	19.4

MALE, ASIAN OR PACIFIC

All ages	4,445	537	12.1	337	7.6	87	2.0
Under 15 years	1,117	58	5.2	29	2.6	5	0.5
15 to 24 years	733	52	7.1	18	2.5	5	0.7
25 to 64 years	2,307	257	11.1	158	6.8	26	1.1
65 years and over	288	171	59.4	132	45.7	50	17.3

FEMALE, ASIAN OR PACIFIC ISLANDER

All ages	4,713	655	13.9	439	9.3	136	2.9
Under 15 years	973	6	0.6	6	0.6	-	-
15 to 24 years	720	25	3.5	15	2.1	-	-
25 to 64 years	2,664	391	14.7	232	8.7	60	2.3
65 years and over	357	233	65.3	186	52.0	75	21.1

BOTH SEXES, HISPANIC[1]

All ages	30,086	4,151	13.8	2,906	9.7	820	2.7
Under 15 years	9,133	533	5.8	275	3.0	61	0.7
15 to 24 years	5,398	414	7.7	251	4.7	39	0.7
25 to 64 years	13,966	2,297	16.4	1,632	11.7	391	2.8
65 years and over	1,590	907	57.1	748	47.0	329	20.7

(continued)

TABLE 5.1 Continued

| | Total | With a disability by severity and need for assistance | | | | | |
| | | All severities | | Severe | | Needs assistance | |
		Number	Percent	Number	Percent	Number	Percent
MALE, HISPANIC[1]							
All ages	15,372	1,937	12.6	1,311	8.5	387	2.5
Under 15 years	4,676	329	7.0	174	3.7	32	0.7
15 to 24 years	2,917	230	7.9	138	4.7	29	1.0
25 to 64 years	7,094	1,002	14.1	712	10.0	178	2.5
65 years and over	686	376	54.9	288	42.0	148	21.6
FEMALE, HISPANIC[1]							
All ages	14,714	2,215	15.1	1,594	10.8	433	2.9
Under 15 years	4,457	203	4.6	101	2.3	29	0.6
15 to 24 years	2,481	185	7.4	113	4.6	10	0.4
25 to 64 years	6,872	1,295	18.9	920	13.4	213	3.1
65 years and over	904	531	58.8	460	50.9	181	20.0

—Rounds to zero.
[1]Hispanics may be of any race.

Source: U.S. Census Bureau

TABLE 5.2 *Disability status, employment, and annual rate of earnings: Individuals 21 to 64 years old, 1997 (August–November 1997 data from the Survey of Income and Program Participation. Numbers in thousands.)*

	Total	Employed		Median earnings		Mean earnings	
		Number	Percent	Value	Std. err.	Value	Std. err.
Both sexes	152,886	119,616	78.2	$22,941	$151	$30,155	$358
DISABILITY STATUS							
With a disability	27,802	13,991	50.3	$17,669	$423	$23,373	$731
Severe	17,409	5,464	31.4	$13,272	$651	$18,631	$800
Covered by Medicare, or received SSI	6,920	909	13.1	$4,944	$671	$8,836	$849
Covered by Medicare	4,330	536	12.4	$4,493	$716	$8,215	$1,033
Received SSI	3,627	466	12.9	$4,737	$1,037	$8,808	$1,215
Not covered by Medicare did not receive SSI	10,490	4,555	43.4	$15,541	$676	$20,586	$930
Received Social Security	1,196	135	11.3	$5,939	$1,923	$7,803	$1,614
Prevented from working	865	—	—	—	—	—	—
Not prevented from working	331	135	40.6	$5,939	$1,923	$7,803	$1,614
Did not receive Social Security	9,294	4,420	47.6	$15,989	$669	$20,976	$954
Prevented from working	3,279	—	—	—	—	—	—
Not prevented from working	6,014	4,420	73.5	$15,989	$669	$20,976	$954
Not severe	10,393	8,527	82.0	$20,457	$508	$26,412	$1,078
Received Social Security	492	191	38.8	$6,815	$976	$8,998	$1,515
Did not receive Social Security	9,901	8,337	84.2	$20,795	$515	$26,810	$1,100
No disability	125,084	105,624	84.4	$23,654	$157	$31,053	$394
Received Social Security	2,015	714	35.4	$7,690	$741	$10,972	$1,470
Did not receive Social Security	123,068	104,910	85.2	$23,775	$157	$31,190	$396
FUNCTIONAL LIMITATIONS							
Had difficulty seeing words/letters	3,664	1,519	41.5	$16,791	$974	$21,559	$1,229
Severe	669	200	29.9	$15,781	$1,815	$19,714	$3,782
Not severe	2,995	1,319	44.0	$17,109	$1,271	$21,838	$1,293

(continued)

TABLE 5.2 *Continued*

	Total	Employed		Median earnings		Mean earnings	
	Number	*Number*	*Percent*	*Value*	*Std. err.*	*Value*	*Std. err.*
FUNCTIONAL LIMITATIONS continued							
Had difficulty hearing conversation	3,514	2,176	61.9	$23,483	$971	$29,290	$2,122
Severe	323	150	46.5	$21,750	$4,058	$31,889	$5,903
Not severe	3,192	2,026	63.5	$23,574	$963	$29,098	$2,237
Had difficulty with speech	1,281	476	37.1	$14,836	$1,543	$17,802	$1,680
Severe	252	61	24.1	$3,084	$7,294	$10,712	$3,837
Not severe	1,029	415	40.3	$15,315	$1,566	$18,837	$1,811
Had difficulty walking	9,150	3,108	34.0	$16,445	$806	$20,990	$1,515
Severe	3,915	882	22.5	$14,677	$1,823	$18,222	$1,413
Not severe	5,235	2,226	42.5	$17,205	$1,025	$22,085	$2,037
Had difficulty using stairs	9,436	3,304	35.0	$16,172	$807	$20,860	$1,160
Severe	2,333	450	19.3	$11,529	$2,407	$17,979	$2,200
Not severe	7,103	2,854	40.2	$16,650	$824	$21,315	$1,296
Had difficulty lifting/carrying 10 lbs.	7,247	2,178	30.1	$15,883	$1,173	$20,218	$993
Severe	3,304	666	20.2	$13,556	$1,988	$19,024	$1,694
Not severe	3,943	1,512	38.4	$16,746	$1,216	$20,743	$1,218
Had difficulty grasping objects	3,628	1,403	38.7	$16,268	$1,467	$20,723	$1,226
Severe	265	87	32.8	$17,226	$7,762	$31,985	$10,579
Not severe	3,362	1,317	39.2	$16,189	$1,509	$19,979	$1,088
ACTIVITIES OF DAILY LIVING							
With an ADL limitation	4,016	1,055	26.3	$14,857	$1,966	$21,460	$1,731
Needed personal assistance	1,668	280	16.8	$8,731	$3,340	$16,985	$3,040
Did not need personal assistance	2,348	775	33.0	$17,225	$2,134	$23,078	$2,068
Had difficulty getting around inside	1,459	222	15.2	$10,857	$3,218	$17,437	$3,206
Needed personal assistance	662	62	9.3	$2,474	$1,466	$8,122	$3,066
Did not need personal assistance	796	160	20.1	$13,552	$3,686	$21,022	$4,091
Had difficulty getting in/out of bed/chair	3,028	797	26.3	$14,402	$2,175	$21,279	$2,053
Needed personal assistance	1,078	183	17.0	$9,965	$5,263	$17,892	$3,604
Did not need personal assistance	1,949	614	31.5	$15,425	$2,315	$22,288	$2,431
Had difficulty taking a bath or shower	2,061	407	19.8	$11,386	$3,311	$20,572	$2,640
Needed personal assistance	1,019	136	13.3	$9,991	$7,664	$19,661	$5,135

Did not need personal assistance	1,042	271	26.1	$12,153	$3,829	$21,028	$3,012
Had difficulty dressing	1,608	312	19.4	$13,710	$3,872	$23,293	$3,688
Needed personal assistance	903	145	16.1	$10,062	$4,733	$18,009	$4,107
Did not need personal assistance	706	167	23.7	$17,449	$4,329	$27,877	$5,767
Had difficulty eating	619	130	21.1	$14,934	$8,331	$23,640	$4,750
Needed personal assistance	250	22	8.6	$31,865	$16,794	$28,855	$11,432
Did not need personal assistance	368	109	29.5	$12,286	$7,832	$22,600	$5,190
Had difficulty getting to/using the toilet	868	117	13.5	$11,018	$5,756	$17,725	$4,230
Needed personal assistance	500	46	9.2	$8,218	$13,888	$18,433	$6,967
Did not need personal assistance	368	71	19.2	$11,538	$5,233	$17,263	$5,306

INSTRUMENTAL ACTIVITIES OF DAILY LIVING

With an IADL limitation	5,776	1,427	24.7	$11,767	$1,357	$18,406	$1,355
Needed personal assistance	4,021	825	20.5	$9,423	$1,536	$15,959	$1,815
Did not need personal assistance	1,755	602	34.3	$16,612	$2,119	$21,765	$1,989
Had difficulty going outside alone	3,421	543	15.9	$9,054	$1,778	$15,639	$1,929
Needed personal assistance	2,377	310	13.1	$4,964	$2,433	$13,741	$2,705
Did not need personal assistance	1,044	232	22.2	$14,608	$3,437	$18,176	$2,642
Had difficulty keeping track of money/bills	2,056	424	20.6	$5,519	$1,332	$11,169	$1,735
Needed personal assistance	1,646	342	20.8	$4,492	$903	$9,375	$1,787
Did not need personal assistance	410	82	20.0	$11,999	$4,841	$18,636	$4,497
Had difficulty preparing meals	1,916	286	14.9	$7,744	$3,005	$15,250	$2,739
Needed personal assistance	1,491	194	13.0	$4,189	$2,458	$11,606	$2,620
Did not need personal assistance	425	92	21.6	$15,059	$4,808	$22,962	$6,075
Had difficulty doing light housework	2,804	534	19.1	$12,037	$2,626	$19,470	$2,340
Needed personal assistance	1,943	305	15.7	$12,525	$3,526	$20,401	$3,307
Did not need personal assistance	861	229	26.6	$11,339	$3,513	$18,231	$3,210
Had difficulty taking prescriptions	1,636	355	21.7	$6,989	$1,848	$12,205	$1,972
Needed personal assistance	1,202	237	19.7	$4,979	$2,164	$11,902	$2,647
Did not need personal assistance	434	118	27.2	$10,020	$2,743	$12,814	$2,631
Had difficulty using the telephone	988	352	35.6	$18,547	$2,776	$24,979	$3,421
Unable to use ordinary phone	371	110	29.7	$16,018	$8,951	$23,631	$7,813
Able to use ordinary phone	617	242	39.2	$19,758	$3,242	$25,593	$3,481

(continued)

TABLE 5.2 *Continued*

	Total	Employed		Median earnings		Mean earnings	
		Number	Percent	Value	Std. err.	Value	Std. err.
USE OF AMBULATORY AIDS							
Used a wheelchair	877	194	22.2	$21,240	$6,207	$28,307	$4,559
Used a cane/crutches/walker	2,173	539	24.8	$17,358	$2,477	$21,119	$1,968
MENTAL DISABILITIES							
With a disability	8,987	3,328	37.0	$13,534	$697	$20,353	$1,653
With one or more selected conditions	5,370	2,213	41.2	$13,293	$764	$21,111	$2,393
Had a learning disability	2,468	1,360	55.1	$16,042	$1,368	$25,645	$3,798
Had mental retardation	1,071	337	31.5	$5,423	$1,700	$8,191	$1,113
Had Alzheimers, senility, or dementia	621	141	22.7	$11,610	$3,545	$12,932	$2,341
Had other mental/emotional condition	2,599	764	29.4	$10,578	$1,612	$15,424	$1,299
With one or more selected symptoms that seriously interfered with everyday activities	4,723	1,414	29.9	$12,643	$1,190	$18,081	$1,204
Was frequently depressed or anxious	4,055	1,228	30.3	$12,752	$1,254	$18,688	$1,346
Had trouble getting along with others	1,239	284	22.9	$7,090	$1,793	$13,103	$2,001
Had trouble concentrating	2,459	571	23.2	$8,682	$2,124	$15,130	$1,621
Had trouble coping with stress	3,356	906	27.0	$11,571	$1,672	$16,559	$1,252
Had difficulty keeping track of money/bills	2,056	424	20.6	$5,519	$1,332	$11,169	$1,735
WORKING AT A JOB							
With disability-related employment problems	17,526	6,114	34.9	$13,848	$606	$19,086	$845
Has had difficulty remaining employed or finding a job	10,744	2,271	21.1	$7,975	$761	$13,823	$888
Was limited in kind or amount of work that could be done	16,081	5,487	34.1	$13,889	$599	$19,216	$920
Was prevented from working at a job	9,371	—	—	—	—	—	—
Was not prevented from working at a job	6,710	5,487	81.8	$13,889	$599	$19,216	$920

DISABILITY DOMAINS

With a disability in one domain	16,984	9,830	57.9	$18,608	$501	$24,452	$955
Communication	1,981	1,660	83.8	$24,668	$982	$31,274	$2,678
Physical	12,239	6,508	53.2	$17,708	$591	$22,869	$983
Mental	2,765	1,662	60.1	$14,704	$1,095	$23,838	$3,122
With a disability in two domains	7,389	2,976	40.3	$15,731	$740	$20,622	$876
Communication and physical	3,184	1,678	52.7	$18,480	$1,556	$23,594	$1,215
Communication and mental	497	250	50.2	$9,261	$2,677	$12,986	$1,968
Physical and mental	3,708	1,049	28.3	$12,679	$1,254	$17,685	$1,410
With a disability in three domains	2,017	368	18.2	$13,231	$2,576	$17,209	$2,235
Domain(s) not identified	1,412	818	57.9	$16,281	$1,922	$23,186	$3,636
No disability	125,084	105,624	84.4	$23,654	$157	$31,053	$394

— Rounds to zero.

Source: U.S. Census Bureau

Employment and Income, as Related to Disability Status, 1997

Table 5.2 includes data on employment and annual rate of earnings for people twenty-one to sixty-four years by disability status, functional limitation, ability to perform ADLs, IADLs, and use of assistive devices.

Census Bureau Data, March 2001

The Census Bureau also reports (U.S. Census Bureau press release, March 16, 2001) that one in five Americans—53 million people—said they had some level of disability in the SIPP 1997 survey. Of these, one in eight—33 million—reported a severe disability. The report also states that the survey found that severe disability is often accompanied by a greater frequency of receiving welfare benefits, having a low income, and living in poverty. People with severe disabilities were also much less likely than the general public to have health insurance coverage. Among twenty-five- to sixty-four-year-olds, only 48 percent had coverage compared to 80 percent for those with a mild disability and 84 percent for the general population.

For people fifteen and older, significant findings include:

1. 25 million people have difficulty walking a quarter mile or climbing a flight of stairs, or use a wheelchair, cane, crutches, or a walker.
2. 18 million people have difficulty lifting and carrying a ten-pound bag of groceries.
3. 7.7 million people have difficulty in reading a newspaper, even with glasses.
4. About 14.3 million people have mental disabilities, which include Alzheimer's, senility, dementia, and learning disabilities (3.5 million).
5. The poverty rate for twenty-five- to sixty-four-year-olds was 8 percent for people with no disability, 10 percent for people with a mild disability, and 28 percent for people with a severe disability.
6. 9.7 million people aged sixteen to sixty-four had a disability that prevented them from working, and another 7.2 million were limited in the amount or kind of work that they could do.

The United States Department of Education statistics for students with disabilities include data on 4.7 million students who have been identified as disabled in grades 1–12. Of these, 51.2 percent have learning disabilities, 21.2 percent have speech or language impairments, 11.3 percent have mental retardation, and 8.7 percent have emotional disturbances. (Kennedy, LaPlante, & Kaye, 1997).

Healthy People 2010 Baseline Data

The Healthy People 2010 program promotes health and well-being in the entire population of the United States and includes people with disabilities as a subpopulation within the general population.

Baseline data on health and well-being have found that, at present, people with disabilities have:

- High rates of pressure sores in nursing homes
- High rates of emergency room visits and hospitalizations for the primary disabling condition
- Low rates of formal patient education
- Low rates of treatment for mental illness
- Activity limitations and difficulties with personal care
- Preventable secondary conditions, such as fractures, amputation, or unemployment
- Early deaths from the primary disabling conditions, such as asthma
- Early deaths from co-morbidities, such as kidney failure

The study also notes four significant gaps and disparities between people with disabilities and others:

- Less health insurance coverage and use of the health-care system for preventive measures such as Pap tests, mammography, and oral health exams
- Higher rates of chronic conditions such as diabetes, depression/sadness, elevated blood pressure and blood cholesterol, obesity, and tooth loss
- Lower rates of social participation, emotional support, life satisfaction, employment, children who are in regular education classrooms, and high school completion
- Lower rates of recommended health behaviors, such as smoking cessation and physical activity (Centers for Disease Control, 2001b)

Chapter Summary

As we can see in this chapter, disability affects an enormous number of people in the United States. For every person with a disability, there are also numbers of family members who are impacted by the disability: families in poverty because a parent is unable to work, children who are neglected because a parent is physically or mentally unable to care for them, parents whose lives and incomes are affected by the disability of a child, and children who are caring for parents who are disabled. Disability touches almost everyone in some way. Surely we must rethink some of our ideas about norms and normal presented in Chapter 1. And addressing problems related to disability becomes a necessary and vital service we as professionals can provide to all our clients.

The Healthy People Baseline Data provides a good overall view of problem areas related to people with disabilities. These may be useful to you in working with clients and can help define individual and group goals and objectives that can be addressed through the resources discussed in Part IV.

Questions for Thought and Discussion

1. Do you think that the data collected by the Census Bureau on people with disabilities is sufficient? What additional data might help you in your work with people with disabilities?

2. Review the section on disparities. What do you think causes these disparities? Choose one of the four areas of disparity and design a program to address it.

3. In Table 5.1 it is noted that there is a disparity between men and women of all races in the percentage of people with disabilities. Except for the "under 15" category, there is a higher percentage of disabled women than men. What do you think may account for this disparity?

4. One of the major areas of disparity and difficulty is that of health insurance. What do you believe to be some of the factors that contribute to lower rates of health insurance for people with disabilities? How could these factors be addressed?

5. People with disabilities have a lower rate of employment and a lower income than people without disabilities. Review the ADA provisions relative to employment presented in the previous chapter. What do you think might be the impact of the ADA on employment rates and incomes over the next ten years?

Part I Summary

Part I has provided some of the information needed to understand the "environment" part of the person-in-environment framework. The societal pieces include the theoretical frameworks that are used to define disability, establish causation, and determine responsibility that were presented in the first chapter. We have seen that society has moved from a primarily individual model, which places the focus on the person with the disability and defines the problem in individual terms, toward a more contextual approach where disability is determined and created by society, whether through culture and groupings, oppression and discrimination against difference, or the way in which society has ultimately constructed and organized itself.

As we moved from the theoretical to the historical, we have focused primarily on the United States. In exploring the role and place of the person with disability in society from colonial times to the present day in the second chapter, we have traced the major changes that have transformed the way in which formal and informal social systems understand disability. We have seen in Chapter 3 how early efforts to secure reasonable living conditions and rights for people with disabilities by those most intimately concerned with their well-being, and the Civil Rights movement of the 1960s spawned the "other" movement, the Disability Rights movement, which addressed a number of concerns such as housing, rehabilitation, education, access and mobility, and civil rights issues.

While early disability legislation addressed the needs of disabled veterans who "deserved" the nation's gratefulness and assistance, later legislation became more inclusive and more comprehensive in terms of addressing the rights of disabled members of society. The culmination of efforts to pass legislation guaranteeing rights for disabled people has been the passage of the Americans with Disabilities Act of 1990. The chronology of disability-related legislation was presented in Chapter 4.

In Chapter 5, some of the available statistical data on people with disabilities in the United States provided an insight into numbers: Between 53 and 54 million people have activity limitations that affect their daily lives. We have learned of the major impact that the severity of disability has on employment, and consequently on income, of the person who is disabled. We have seen that disability increases dramatically in the population with age and that older people often have multiple disabilities. In using the information presented, we have learned the kinds of categories and groupings the government has established for learning about disabled people in this country and defining their needs and resources.

Part I Assignment

The legal material presented in Part I has, of necessity, focused primarily on legislation at the federal level. However, it is vitally important that social workers be informed of state laws and regulations that affect people with disabilities in the state in which they are providing services.

Federal laws always supercede state laws: In other words, states cannot make laws that render federal laws void or detract from the provisions of federal laws. Many states, however, provide laws and protections for disabled people above and beyond the federal law. It is important to know about any variations and differences between federal and state laws for the state in which you will be practicing.

Using the state government website for your state, code and statute books, or other resources, search for state laws that address issues related to disability. Prepare a reference guide for yourself listing the information you have found and how to locate it.

Select one area of the state laws: housing, education, access and mobility, rehabilitation, or income supports are a few possible suggestions. Research state codes, laws, and statutes relative to that area. Summarize your findings in a three- to five-page paper.

Part II

The Individual Framework

Life experiences occur within the complex and interwoven relationship between the individual and the world in which he or she lives. Part I explored that world by examining the ways in which society has developed a theoretical framework for understanding disability, presenting an overview of disability history and legislation in the United States and tracing the development of the Disability Rights movement. Statistical information was also presented to assist the reader in understanding some of the demographics of disability in this country in terms of age, ethnicity, gender, employment status, and severity of disability.

Each person with a disability both affects and is affected by events in society that relate to disability. But each individual experiences these events in a unique way that is related to his or her life experiences. People with the same disability do not necessarily react to their condition in the same way. People who become disabled as children vary in their identification with the disability community. And experiences of onset are as unique as the people experiencing them. Part II will focus on understanding the individual: the complex, unique, and special person who, among many other life experiences and characteristics, also has a disability. We will explore some of the theories of disability identity development and examine systems for grouping people with disabilities to understand some of the commonalities of their individual experiences. We will then focus on exploring the unique experience from two different frameworks: first, from an understanding of the possible effect of onset experiences, course of the condition, and expected outcome on the person's relationship to disability, and second, from an understanding of the effect of living with limitations in activity or function. Personal narratives are included to help the reader to develop insight and to empathically share in the experiences of the writers.

It is very important to recognize here that the vignettes and personal narratives included are unique to the experience of the individual. They are personal stories. They may relate to the general experience of disability in some way, but should not be considered as representative of all people with the specific disabling condition they are describing. Experiences, reactions, and ideas that are quite different from those included here are also encompassed within the "disability experience."

6

Disability and Identity Development

In Chapter 1, we explored the conceptual frameworks for thinking about disability. The individual frameworks, such as the moral model and the medical model, placed the disability and its meaning squarely within the individual or the individual's parents. The societal frameworks conceptualized disability as something created and framed by the society in which the individual is living, and thus external to the person.

When we review the history of disability in the United States in Chapter 2, it is clear that traces of both the individual and the societal models are evident in the way in which disability is framed today. Additionally, culture greatly influences perceptions of disability. What is viewed as a disability in one culture may be seen as a desirable attribute in another. Certain forms of mental illness, for example, are viewed as a disability in one culture and as a sign of special status in another.

How does this translate when we think about a disabled individual, living in contemporary U.S. society? What meaning does the person ascribe to the disability? What are some considerations for thinking about people with disabilities who also are experiencing racial, religious, ethnic, cultural, gender, and/or sexual orientation differences in our society?

Facets of Our Identity

If someone were to ask each of us "Who are you?" and "How do you see yourself?" we each would understand the question as related to the context in which it was asked and respond within that context. We also would answer in a closely interwoven mix of our own understanding of ourselves and the characteristics commonly ascribed to us by others. Our identities are complex and multifaceted and are composed of a wide variety of qualities.

If the context in which the question is asked is school, we are students and teachers;

at work we are social workers, supervisors, directors, and owners; at home we are sons and daughters, mothers, fathers, and siblings. We all carry multiple *roles,* and each of the roles we carry has specific role functions attached to it. In a different kind of context, we might answer the same questions a bit differently. Instead of viewing ourselves through roles, we might explore personal *attributes*. We might answer with our age, our race, our religion, our ethnicity, our gender, our place of residence, and our nationality. We might also answer with descriptive information, such as height, eye color, or hair color.

We can also define ourselves according to the way in which we view our *personality characteristics*. We may see ourselves as shy or outgoing, disorganized or thorough, creative, peaceful, or confrontational. We could answer this question by defining ourselves according to our *abilities*. We might see ourselves as good at math, a poor speller, an athlete, a reader, a questioner, or a computer whiz. Especially within U.S. culture, we are defined by what we *do*. Often, what we do tends to relate to what we perceive to be our abilities.

Last, we can view ourselves in terms of our *values* and our *ideals*. In a very real way, our ideals and values define the essence of who we are. We might value freedom, equality, friendship, justice, truth, life, honesty, loyalty—the list is practically endless. We value these things as ideals, as our preferred conception of the kind of people we want to be. Although we are not always all of these, knowledge of our ideals helps us to live a life as close to them as possible.

How does disability fit in to these definitions? For a person with a disability, one of the facets that make up "who I am" addresses the disability and the person's relation to it. The size and quality of this facet varies according to a variety of factors, such as kind and severity of disability, the social and cultural context, and the person's understanding of the disability. The disability "facet" can become so overwhelming that other facets appear insignificant and relatively meaningless. Or the individual may minimize, hide, or deny the disability, shrinking the outward-facing part of the disability facet almost completely.

Disability identity is a global term that contains a number of other facets, or possibilities. It is possible to identify generally as disabled or to identify with a specific disability. It is also possible to identify with a particular community of disabled people. Particularly with disabilities that have a strong cultural community, such as Deaf culture, it is possible to identify culturally, individually, or generally in terms of being a person with a disability. Identifying with a community is often validating and empowering for the individual who makes that choice. However, it may also isolate the person from the broader society, which often includes relatives and friends who do not share the disability.

Adaptation

One of the special and distinctive qualities of human beings is their ability to adapt to a variety of environments and circumstances in an intelligent and meaningful way. Adaptation can assist and even ensure our survival in difficult circumstances. Everyone adapts to both the environment and his or her own qualities and functioning. We adapt to new jobs and new schedules, to parenthood, to marriage and divorce, to new homes and new neighborhoods. Each time we go through the adaptation process we gain a greater understanding of our personal capacity to adapt to changes in our life situation.

When we become disabled and have some limitations in functioning, whether we believe they are within us or in the world around us, we must make some changes in ourselves and in our environment. We learn new communication skills, new mobility skills, and often we redefine our relationship to the world around us to include our new condition. While the idea of "adapting" to a disability tends to have a negative connotation, this does not have to be so. Adaptation can be seen as a strength, as the ability to consider new situations and manipulate our world such that we can prosper within it in our changed circumstances. With adaptation to disability can come awareness of a whole other set of strengths and abilities: We can discover, and create, whole new facets of ourselves.

Mackelprang and Salsgiver's Life Stage Development Concept

Mackelprang and Salsgiver note that there is little in the literature that addresses identity formation and life stage development for person with disabilities (Mackelprang & Salsgiver, p. 63). Neither Freud, nor Piaget, Erikson, Maas, or others included disability in their theories of life stage development (p. 74). Utilizing the stage method found to be descriptive and functional in other theories, Mackelprang and Salsgiver developed a theory that addresses the integration of disability within the identity of the person from a social and cultural perspective.

Birth to Three Years

Children who are disabled from birth or who acquire a disability during their early years learn to view the world from a disability perspective: That is, they have become disabled before the development of cognitive skills that would make them aware of the difference. All of their life experiences are within the framework of their disability, and their first experiences with others occur accompanied by disability and the reactions of those around them to the disability (pp. 63–64).

Parents of a disabled infant or toddler are themselves going through processes that will affect the child. Parents may grieve, for a brief or extended period, for the "perfect" baby they envisioned and desired. They may be overwhelmed as they try to grasp the child's needs and what will be required to meet those needs over the course of a lifetime. Some parents may reject their children, however briefly, and resist making the commitment to love and care for their child.

Parents also have the tendency to overprotect and shelter the child with disabilities, keeping the child close to them and preferring not to let babysitters, neighbors, or other family members assist them with the care of the child. Children cared for in this way develop a strong sense of trust in their environment. However, overprotective parents often don't encourage children to learn developmental tasks appropriate to their level, and children do not have those first opportunities to learn to struggle, to fail, and to keep trying until they have mastered the task. Low parental expectations can hamper the development and learning of children with disabilities. In some cases the parent-child bond is also affected by some of the uncomfortable and painful procedures parents must perform to assist their disabled child (pp. 64–65).

Three to Six Years

Words and language increasingly become vital tools of communication for children aged three to six years. Children with disabilities may acquire verbal skills later than other children, and it is important to provide the alternatives that enable the child to communicate effectively. When the focus of effort becomes communication, rather than verbal speech, children are able to learn and develop alternative ways of communicating that are effective (p. 66).

Children in this stage need to experience some control over their environment and themselves, a task that may be rendered more difficult by possible physical dependence upon parents or other caregivers. Children should be offered choices and encouraged appropriately to "take charge" of themselves so that they can gain a sense of separateness from their parents and other caregivers (p. 66).

It is also important for children to be with other children, both children with the same disability and with others. The reactions of others may give children their first experience in "being different," and support and coping strategies can assist them to mitigate the effects of feeling different. Active play should be encouraged and playground interaction is important (pp. 66–67).

Six to Twelve Years

Children grow enormously during these years: physically, intellectually, and emotionally. Educating children in classrooms with other children with and without disabilities is now mandated by the Equal Education for All Handicapped Children Act. Supportive school environments assist children to develop a positive self-image.

By this age, children with disabilities have internalized the view of physical beauty and body image that is so prevalent in the culture around them. Often the personal images they develop about their own bodies are not consonant with reality, and they deny their own disability. They may be surprised to view themselves in a mirror and learn that their body does not fit their imagined picture of themselves. Body dissonance is not an uncommon phenomenon at this stage of life (p. 68).

As in earlier stages, frequent and regular interaction with peers both able and disabled is very important to the child's development. Contact with other children and with environments where their disability is "the norm" is often critical to positive identity development (p. 68).

Children who become disabled during these years can often have a difficult time. Their bodies have changed, and they must often change their habits and activities to incorporate the new changes. Both parents and children can experience grief and mourning for the nondisabled child they loved. However, these children have not experienced disability from birth or early life; they have not had the experiences of rejection and discrimination, and if they have developed a healthy sense of self-esteem and respect, they will be able to keep it. Skills and mastery over many subjects and activities may be maintained, although perhaps in a different way (pp. 68–69).

Twelve to Eighteen Years

The primary tasks of this stage of development involve developing and affirming a personal identity, increasing independence from parents, and developing of a sexual identity. For teens with disabilities, each of these can be formidable tasks.

The task of seeking personal identity, coupled with increasing separation from parents, can be especially troublesome to teenagers who remain dependent upon parents for physical assistance, mobility, or other activities of daily living. Needing assistance but wanting independence, teens often feel frustrated and ambivalent in their relationship with parents. Outside attendants can sometimes help but can also create additional problems in upsetting the traditional family roles. Technological aides can be very helpful at this time (pp. 69).

Identity seeking, along with many other activities of the teen years, requires a great expenditure of energy—energy that disabled teens often do not have. It takes disabled teens extra time and extra effort to prepare for their day and extra time and effort during the day to address educational needs. There may be little energy left for engaging in relationships, participating in activities, or just having fun (p. 69).

Developing a sexual identity may also be problematic. In a society that values external beauty rather than internal qualities, teens who believe they do not match that (impossible) standard of physical beauty may need assistance from others to develop a positive sexual identity. It is important for families, friends, and people working with the teen to assume that he or she will grow up, fall in love, get married, and have children. It is also important to be aware of the potential for sexual abuse and exploitation of teens with disabilities (p. 70).

Teens who become disabled face a challenging task in shifting roles and identity to include disability. By their teen years, they have absorbed the ableist images and ideas about disability prevalent in society and have difficulty in accepting themselves as disabled. Sometimes friendships are lost, activities and interests must be refocused, and exposure to others with the same disability becomes extremely important in order to allow normalization of their condition (pp. 70–71).

The development of a positive disability identity during this time is fostered by family, school, and community supports and close relationships with disabled and nondisabled peers. Teens can be helped to understand that disability is a construct of the environment, and not a personal failure in themselves. They can become advocates for justice and equality for all people.

Young Adulthood

Reaching maturity and independence in young adulthood often means assuming responsibility for organizing and hiring and arranging for personal care and a comfortable environment apart from parents. It is important that the young adult be aware of resources and supports in the community to assist him or her to plan. The existence and accessibility of jobs, educational resources, and transportation and services becomes very important (p. 71).

Young people often seek role models or other people with the same disability with whom they can identify. They are often eager to immerse themselves in disability culture and develop pride and self-esteem from activity in the Disability Rights movement. Well-known media stars who have a disability, such as Christopher Reeve, can become essential role models.

People who become disabled during these young adult years often face major life adjustments. They have developed self-images and identities prior to becoming disabled. Newly developed relationships are particularly fragile and often do not survive the onset of the disability, creating a sense of loss and change even beyond the disability itself. Young adults, especially young men, often become disabled as a result of accidents incurred through athletic, recreational, or driving activities. With support, newly disabled young adults can successfully develop strong identities that include disability and strong affiliations with the disability culture (p. 72).

Middle Adulthood

People this age begin to focus outward from home and family and become deeply immersed in community. Expanding interests and options often enable people to explore alternative lifestyles and affiliations. It is people in this age group who have been the prime movers of the disability movement, leaders of disability culture, and passionate advocates for the legal changes that have occurred in recent years. They serve as role models and mentors for younger people with disabilities and work to change the image of disability in the general culture (p. 72).

Many people acquire disabilities during these years. Newly disabled middle adults have a strong identity and have developed close relationships, both outside of the disability culture. They tend to keep their nondisabled sense of identity and do not make the shift to disability identity. They are the same people they always were, in their eyes, with an additional problem that does not change their basic identity, interests, or avocations (p. 73).

Although they tend not to affiliate with disability movements in a strong way, newly disabled middle adults do often attempt to use the experience of disability as an opportunity for personal growth and a developing insight about the nature of the world (p. 73).

Older Adulthood

As we have seen, aging greatly increases the likelihood of acquiring a disability. Many older people have multiple disabilities, some major, some less incapacitating. Visual, hearing, and physical disabilities are the most common late-onset disabilities. Most people who become disabled in older adulthood do not identify with disability culture or with others who share the same disability. Because of this, and because of the social isolation that often accompanies both disability and old age, offering social supports and resources to people who become disabled in older adulthood can be particularly helpful (p. 73).

People who age with a disability are often more knowledgeable about needed resources and better able to navigate "the system." However, having a long-term disability may create problems that newly disabled older adults do not experience, because they are a side effect, or aftereffect, of the disability itself (p. 73).

For disabled elderly as well as for all elderly, maintaining maximal independence is very important, as is maintaining social relationships and meaningful activities.

Disability Identity as a Learned Social Role

We can also understand disability and identity through social role theory. The basic premise is that the person *learns* the behavior that is socially acceptable for a person with a particular kind of disability. Using blindness as an example, Stone says:

> The disability of blindness is a learned social role. The various attitudes and patterns of behavior that characterize people who are blind are not inherent in their condition but rather are acquired through ordinary processes of social learning. Thus, there is nothing inherent in the condition of blindness that requires a person to be dependent, melancholy, or help-less; nor is there anything about it that should lead him to become independent or assertive. Blind men are made by the same processes of socialization that have made us all. (Stone, 1977, p. 14)

Much of the conceptual framework for disability as a learned social role comes from the seminal work of Talcott Parsons. Parsons developed the theory that the adoption of a "sick role" provides a sanctioned form of social deviance for people with chronic illness and disability. There are three conditions that must be met by the individual: (1) He or she must consult with a physician and receive confirmation of the "sickness" from the medical establishment; (2) he or she must view the condition as undesirable; and (3) he or she must then be relieved of all the normal social role expectations (Barnes, Mercer, & Shakespeare, p. 40).

We learn the roles that are expected of us. We are rewarded with praise, attention, and approval. Hopefully, we learn positive roles, roles that enhance self-esteem and support independence. However, some people learn disability roles that have a negative effect, such as helplessness or passivity. When society reinforces these negative roles, we learn these in the same way that we learn the positive ones and for the same reasons: to gain approval, attention, and praise. It is thus quite obvious that social role theory places much of the responsibility for developing a disability identity on the society, rather than primarily on the inner processes of the individual's character.

All people learn the social roles expected of disabled people. When a disability is acquired, these expected social roles of which the person has been aware become a part of his or her identity. They are internalized—the disabled person believes in their validity, no matter how dysfunctional the roles may actually be in assisting the individual toward life goals.

Piastro (1999) writes about the transitions in identity that can come with disability. Internalized negative images had induced within her feelings of shame and low self-worth.

She believes now that these negative images are often developed in the context of the medical model of disability, which, as we know, continues to be the prevalent conceptual framework for understanding disability today. She was able to change these internalized images through affiliation with the independent living movement and with disabled professionals to develop an identity that incorporated personal empowerment and pride.

Empowering and Normalizing Disability Identity

The disability movement, positive role models, and the availability of resources and supports assist people to develop and create a positive, empowered disability identity. In order to foster such an identity, it is important to live in a milieu that includes both disabled and nondisabled people. Relationships with other people with similar disabilities can help people to normalize their lives—in such groups, the disability experience is the norm, and people who do not share that disability are the ones who are viewed as different. This sense of belonging is important to the development of a positive identity related to disability.

Understanding and relating to disability history, to major events in that history, and to the people who were involved in them is also important. Learning about the lives of the leaders of the movement, like learning about civil rights, women's rights, gay and lesbian rights, and other twentieth-century movements, reinforces pride and develops a strong affiliation.

People with a disability also develop pride and self-esteem as they learn a sense of mastery over their condition and recognize the growth potential inherent in both the integration of disability into one's self image and in the strengths and values that enable them to achieve lives of meaning within the context of the disability.

The development of a positive, self-respecting disability identity can be achieved through affiliation and identification with movements, individuals, and historic events. However, another important avenue toward a positive and empowered disability identity comes from the experience of socializing with nondisabled people, with being *normalized,* that is, being, and being seen as being, "just like everybody else." When people can relegate disability identity to a facet only, instead of the primary characteristic of their identity, they are able to enjoy the brilliance of each facet and to "grow" those that are most meaningful to them.

Sascha Bittner's experience is an excellent illustration of the empowerment/positive self-identity process.

I've had cerebral palsy since birth. As a child, I knew I was different, but I just didn't really understand what it meant. My mother was wonderful—she loved me and did everything she could to help me. When we would go out, people would look at me. I thought they were looking at me because I was pretty. I didn't think it had anything to do with my being in a wheelchair. But I learned differently, eventually.

I wanted to go to school with nondisabled kids, and I finally was able to do that in sixth grade. Later, with DREDF (Disability Rights Education and Defense Fund), I sued the school district for access and accommodation at extracurricular activities, and my school district changed its policies as a result.

My mother and I both became really involved with the disability rights movement, and it gave us both a strong feeling of identity. We became very active, and I even got to know two of my heros, Ed Roberts and Judy Heumann. I joined ADAPT and protested with them in San Francisco and in Washington, DC and was arrested with them as a juvenile. I was put on probation, but the juvenile hall probation offices were not accessible, and I had to meet with my probation officer in a parking lot!

I also went to Washington to speak before the National Press Club about barriers to work for people with disabilities. My mom and I present disability awareness programs in the public school system through K.I.D.S. (Keys to Introducing Disability in Society), and I have spoken with thousands of children over the years. It's a project we share, and we do it every year. I want to bring the importance of disability rights to the forefront, to make everyone aware of the issues. I also work with young people with disabilities, to give them a sense of pride about their community and culture. I conduct leadership training workshops for disabled youth, enabling them to co-teach workshops on disability issues, and facilitate peer support groups for students with disabilities.

I'm a student at UC Berkeley now, and I'm Vice President of the Disabled Students' Union. I often must deal with the misconception that people who are disabled aren't very bright, especially if they have a speech disability, as I do. Sometimes I use interpreters, including my mom. However, most of the time when I'm out in the community or talking in class I can make myself understood, though it's hard sometimes.

(Sascha Bittner, Personal Statement, 4/30/02)

Taub and Greer explore this process in their study of school-aged children with physical disabilities (Taub & Greer, 2000). Children with disabilities often experience indifference and lowered interaction from peers in school. They may be excluded from physical activities, and thus from the social and recreational opportunities these provide. When this occurs, the researchers note, children feel diminished, and their disability becomes the most important quality about them. During sports activities, they may be spectators rather than players, and social interactions with able-bodied children in those situations are often quite limited.

Children who participated in the study were provided with opportunities for direct involvement in sports and physical education and then were interviewed about their reactions to their experiences. All the children reported positive experiences and enjoyed engaging in both the activity and the socialization that it enabled. Children gained feelings of competence, they made and interacted with new friends, and they developed a feeling of normalcy. In spite of some of the negative experiences that occurred (not being among the first selected for a team, being made fun of by peers), overall the children gained from the experience and wanted to continue an active role in sports programs. Children were also aware of the beneficial physical effects of exercise and felt that their sports achievements changed some of the negative stereotypes held by other children. They experienced a sense of mastery as they achieved in their sports endeavors, of pride, and of achievement (Taub & Greer, 2000).

Both the development of a strong identification with disability culture and immersion and normalization into nondisabled society can provide the individual with the sense of empowerment, mastery, and self-esteem needed for an optimal life experience.

Rolland's Three Categories of Disability Identity

Rolland posits that the way in which people relate to a disability and integrate the disability into personal identity is strongly related to the kind of disability they have. He develops three broad groupings (Rolland, 1988).

Progressive Disabilities

These are characterized by an ever-increasing degree of severity and impairment, such as Alzheimer's, diabetes, ALS (Lou Gehrig's disease), and certain forms of arthritis. When a person is given a diagnosis of a progressive disability, the task of integrating the disability into personal identity must include not only the present condition of the person, but also the awareness of a greater degree of impairment as time goes on. While at first it may even be possible to deny any impairment or association with a future condition, this may become more difficult as the disability progresses. However, there is often a wide divergence in reactions to progressive disabilities, even to the same disability.

Constant Disabilities

Whether occurring at birth or later in life, constant disabilities remain the same throughout the lifespan. Certain kinds of constant disabilities, such as spinal cord injury or loss of a limb, occur as the result of trauma, and the person often has a memory of life and identity prior to the disability. The change is sudden and permanent. Crisis intervention may be the methodology of choice for assisting clients with sudden-onset, chronic disabilities. Sudden-onset disabilities may also create a real crisis in identity as the person struggles with the impact of a changed life expectation.

Other constant disabilities, such as blindness or deafness, may occur from birth or occur later. When they occur at birth, the disability is integrated into the child's developing personality and identity. Conditions such as certain forms of blindness and deafness occurring later in life may create the same needs for intervention and integration as those of the person with spinal cord injury.

Relapsing or Episodic Disabilities

Relapsing or episodic disabilities create a different set of circumstances and problems for the individual in terms of identity. The disability is not always present; therefore, concerns like telling others about the disability, adapting lifestyles and goals, and integrating a disability identity are often complex issues. A relapsing or episodic disability that is not severe is easily forgotten or denied when it is not present. Disabilities that require work or school accommodations when they are present, and not at other times, may prove challenging. Relapsing or episodic disabilities can also create an ongoing sense of anxiety—

after all, you never know when the disability will make its presence known. Multiple sclerosis, lupus, and epilepsy are examples of these kinds of disabilities. These three categories will be presented in depth in Chapter 8, as we explore the disability experience.

Avoidance of Disability Identity

Many people with a disability do not identify themselves as disabled. This is especially true of people who become disabled as adults or later in life. Disability is often closely associated with the inability to work. Since people who are older and retired do not work, they do not have the experience of losing a job, needing vocational retraining, needing to change jobs, or needing special accommodation—situations that may force the individual to accept a disabled status.

Some people who are disabled do not require assistance through public agencies and services for people with disabilities. Need for personal assistance, transportation, and technological aids are often viewed as accompanying disability. If the individual's needs are met within the family, among friends, through purchasing equipment through private sources, or through hiring private caregivers, the disabling condition can more easily be deemphasized or ignored.

People who have invisible disabilities and those with relapsing or episodic disabilities can also often avoid identifying as a disabled person. Reasoning that there are periods of relative nondisability enables people with relapsing or episodic disabilities to identify with those periods as truly representative of self, rather than the periods of greater disability. If the disability is not obvious, the person may choose the "public," abled identity others presume they have rather than integrating disability into identity.

The word *disability* tends to have a negative connotation that many people prefer to avoid. Disability implies inability, incompetence, and dependence. Disabled people constantly hear these negative stereotypes reinforced all around them—is it any wonder that, in many cases, they might prefer *not* to identify as a disabled person?

In their article "The Reluctant Identity," Iezzoni and Israel explore perceptions of disability among people with disabilities. While many of their respondents did view themselves as disabled, a significant number of others answered the question with more than a simple yes or no. They mentioned others who were more disabled and needed more help. They talked about trying to stay independent, doing for themselves, not being a burden to others, and assuming responsibility for their own lives (Iezzoni & Israel, 2000, p. 1160).

People with disabilities who view themselves as able may think about disability in terms of severity, as noted above, and be able to identify others whose disability is more limiting of daily activities. They may also believe that they help others as others help them—a give and take that, in a sense, eliminates disability and dependence from the equation. Others feel that the technological devices they use enable them to live in the world in much the same way as everyone else (Iezzoni & Israel, p. 1162).

The problem, Iezzoni and Israel state, is that people often *need* to be identified by a disability label in order to have access to the supports and resources that they need to keep their nondisabled identity. Each person who is identified as disabled has allowed another person, usually a physician, to "pronounce" them disabled and to give them this identification (Iezzoni & Israel, p. 1163). The medical model continues to be the primary route of access to services, and it is often nearly impossible to avoid a disability label if resources are needed.

Avoidance may be related to other factors as well. Because people with disabilities are oppressed and stigmatized in our society, people may try to avoid the label and the accompanying stigma. Because of the enormous variation among disabilities and severity and functional impairments experienced, it may be difficult at times to locate a generic idea of "disability" with which to identify.

Disability and the Minority Experience

While the focus of the present textbook is on disability, it is vital to recognize the special experiences of people who are disabled and are also members of racial, ethnic, cultural, religious, gender, or gay and lesbian groups. People may be doubly, or even triply, oppressed and stigmatized within the broader society. In addition, understanding of disability is very much related to culture and worldview, as has been noted in Part I. Differences in cultural attitudes can hamper or facilitate social relationships and interactions for people with disabilities.

Because disability crosses all racial, religious, cultural, ethnic, gender, and sexual orientation boundaries, people with disabilities are members of many other groups as well and are often a cultural subgroup of the larger group. When the personal choice is made to identify with both groups, people with disabilities can find an active role in more than one movement.

Gender also plays an important role in the development of disability identity. Parallels between female gender and disability and the application of feminist theory to disability were presented in the first chapter. It is important to be aware of the special vulnerability that disability often creates for women, a group already vulnerable in society from both a personal and an institutional viewpoint.

Racial, cultural, and ethnic issues may impact on a disabled person as well. The oppression of racial and ethnic minorities combined with disability may create additional difficulties. On the other hand, the inclusiveness of extended families, the heightened sense of family responsibility, and a different view of disability itself may provide additional support and nurturance for people who are disabled in many ethnic groups

Chapter Summary

The development of a disability identity is a complex issue, influenced by age, experiences, cultural norms, type and severity of disability, and personal choice. A strong identity can be a source of strength and empowerment. Conversely, the refusal to identify as disabled and to normalize one's life such that one sees oneself as a part of the broader society can also be a source of strength. Either will support the individual, and provide a firm grounding for an understanding of self in society. Disability identity becomes a negative only when people attach a negative connotation to disability and the disability experience and feel diminished and helpless to control their personal lives. This may occur when people internalize some of the negative stereotypes that disabilities carry in our ableist society.

Questions for Thought and Discussion

1. If you are disabled, how do you feel about disability and personal identity? Do you think that the effect of disability on identity is something each person needs to explore? How much, and in what way, does your own disability impact on your ideas about disability and identity?

2. Do you think it may be good for some people to refuse or reject a personal identity that includes disability? If so, under what circumstances might it be good?

3. Assuming the "sick role" seems to occur more frequently in older people. Are there other developmental or life-cycle issues that impact on older adults that might lead them to choose this kind of identification?

4. When children are disabled at birth or at a very young age, their parents' feelings about disability may influence their own identity development. Do you think that parental influences on identity are greater for children with disabilities or about the same for all children?

5. People with disabilities can "normalize" their experience by socializing with other people with the same or a similar disability. If a client chooses to associate *only* with people who share her disability, would you feel that this might be symptomatic of problems and thus a useful area to explore with the client?

7

Systems for Grouping Disabilities

One of the most important methods people use to try to understand the world and our place in it is that of sorting or categorizing things. In ancient Greece, Aristotle recognized our ability to sort and categorize things in nature. His foundational work, *The Categories*, develops a way of sorting out everything in the world we live in. Many hundred of years later, German philosopher Immanuel Kant echoed Aristotle, but with a major difference. In his *Critique of Pure Reason*, Kant posited that the categories are not "out there" in nature; they do not exist external to us. Rather, he said, it is part of our internal structure as humans to group things together by various traits of similarity and difference. We bring the structure of our mind, Kant believed, and the way that we organize things, to the objects and construct groupings or categories. This enables us to understand the world we live in.

Modern philosophers talk about the uses of language and logic and about the theories of sets, or classes, or things. Using modern terminology, disability is a class. Within this class are other classes, such as vision impairments or cognitive impairments. We construct the classes and keep the broad term *disability* to represent a class that includes all other classes. In this chapter, we will explore several ways in which the broad class "disability" has been subdivided.

As we know, "disability" covers a vast area of problems, symptoms, and conditions. In Chapter 6, we began our exploration of disability in relation to its meaning for the person with the disability and for others in terms of identity development and group affiliation—or nonaffiliation. Understanding the sets, classes, or categories we use when we talk about disability will give us further insight into how an individual might perceive himself or herself in the context of society.

The way that a person's disability is defined helps both the person and others in the person's environment relate to the disability. Some kinds of disabilities may carry negative connotations, or engender fear, such as AIDS. Others may be viewed as catastrophic, such as severe brain injury. Still others contain an element of responsibility that our society places on the person who has the disability, such as mental illness. Some disabilities are associated with young people, such as learning disabilities. Others are often associated with old age, such as arthritis or poor vision.

People absorb their idea of how their disability is viewed in society, and therefore how they "fit" into society, from the kinds of categories that have been developed for thinking about their disability. If someone chooses to identify with a group or movement, this choice will often be determined by the way she or he perceives her or his disability in the context of other disabilities.

Disability categories are used by governments to chart demographic changes and maintain data on people. As we saw in Chapter 5, the U.S. Census Bureau and other government agencies have a number of ways in which disabilities are categorized, such as severity of impairment, amount of assistance needed, ability to work, and earnings. Government categories also are used to determine eligibility for programs that require a disability determination.

Specialized disability organizations also use categories, often diagnostic categories, to define whether an individual is eligible for services and assistance through the organization, since generally only one or several related disabilities are served by these special organizations. For example, the Lighthouse serves people who are either blind or visually impaired. It does not serve people with developmental disabilities, people who are paraplegic, or people with a mental illness, unless such conditions accompany visual impairments.

Knowing about disability categories can also assist us in understanding a particular client's problems. Using categories, we can begin to understand something of the course of the disability, the physical effects, and related problems and conditions. Knowledge about a client's specific disability, like knowledge about race, ethnicity, gender, and sexual orientation, provides another kind of framework for thinking about the person.

Most of the categories included here are grounded in the medical model of disability—a further testimony of the strength of this model in influencing the way that our society thinks about disability.

National Health Interview Survey: Grouping by Activity Limitation

One possible way to group disabilities is to use the system developed by the National Health Interview Survey. Disability "refers to a state of being limited, due to a chronic mental or physical health condition, in the type or amount of activities that a person is expected to perform" (LaPlante, 1996). In order to determine this, the survey defines disability in terms of normative activities related to the age of the person. For children under five, these are defined as the ability to partake in "ordinary play"; for children five to seventeen years, they are defined as attendance at school; for adults eighteen to sixty-nine, as working or keeping house. In addition, there must be a capacity for self-care such as ability to bathe, dress, feed, toilet, get around the house, care for the house, shop, and conduct personal business in an age-appropriate manner (National Institute on Disability and Rehabilitation Research, 1992, p. 3).

Work limitations are defined as limitations in the amount or kind of work one is able to perform or whether one can work at all. Personal care (ADL) limitations include those mentioned above and also getting in and out of bed or chair, getting outside, continence, and walking. Instrumental activities of daily living (IADL) limitations include preparing meals, shopping for personal items, managing money, using the phone, doing laundry and heavy housework, doing light housework, taking medications, getting around outside, and walking in the neighborhood. This system is generally used by the government in grouping disabilities. It is the system used to study trends in disability rates, such as the study by Kaye, LaPlante, and colleagues (Kaye, LaPlante, Carlson, & Wenger, 1996).

It must be noted here that there is no necessary association between these categories and a medically related diagnostic label. A person who is a quadriplegic, one who is severely developmentally disabled, one who has had a serious stroke, and a fourth who is psychotic can have similar limitations and thus share a grouping when this system is used.

The Disability Statistics Center: Grouping by Causative Condition

Another possible system for grouping uses two broad categories with subgroupings within these. The Disability Statistics Center's research groups disabilities by:

I. **Impairments**
   Orthopedic impairments
   Learning disability and mental retardation
   Visual impairments
   Hearing impairments
   Paralysis
   Deformities
   Absence or loss of limb or other body part
   Speech impairments
   Other

II. **Diseases and Disorders (Causes)**
   Diseases of the musculoskeletal system
   Diseases of the circulatory system
   Diseases of the respiratory system
   Diseases of the nervous system and sense organs
   Endocrine, nutritional, and metabolic diseases and immunity disorders
   Conditions from the perinatal period and symptoms, signs, and ill-defined conditions
   Mental disorders, excluding mental retardation
   Diseases of the digestive system
   Neoplasms
   Injury and poisoning, not involving impairment
   Infectious and parasytic diseases
   Diseases of the skin and subcutaneous tissue
   Congenital abnormalities
   Diseases of the blood and blood-forming organs

This system differentiates between "impairments," which limit function, and "diseases or conditions," which also limit function but are caused by an underlying condition.

Access Unlimited: Grouping by Impairment in Learning and Working

Access Unlimited is a disability organization that monitors access and accommodation and advocates for accessibility for people with disabilities. The agency has developed a very specific system for categorizing disabilities (Access Unlimited, 1999):

1. *Physical impairments* include musculoskeletal and connective tissue disorders that might require adaptation of the environment, such as cerebral palsy, absence of body member, clubfoot, nerve damage to hand and arm, CVA, head injury and spinal cord injury, arthritis and rheumatism, intracranial hemorrhage, embolism, thrombosis (stroke), polio, MS, Parkinson's disease, muscular dystrophy, and other congenital malformations and muscular disorders.

2. *Hearing impairments* include hearing losses of 30 decibels or more, with a pure tone average of 500, 100, 2000 Hz ANSI, unaided, in the better ear, and include conductive hearing impairment, sensorineural hearing impairment, high- or low -tone hearing loss, acoustic trauma hearing loss, and deafness related to any of these losses.

3. *Vision impairments* are disorders in the structure and function of the eye causing visual acuity of 20/70 or less in the better eye with corrective lenses, a peripheral field so constricted that it affects functioning, or a progressive loss of vision.

4. *Learning disabilities* limit listening, speaking, writing, reading, reasoning, mathematical abilities, or social skills, such as dyslexia, dysgraphia, dysphasia, dyscalculia, and others.

5. *Speech impairments* include disorders of language articulation, fluency, or voice that interfere with communication, learning, or social adjustment and include stammering, stuttering, laryngectomy, and the aphasias.

6. *Attention deficit hyperactivity disorder* in and of itself, is, according to the agency, insufficient to qualify for accommodation.

7. *Cardiovascular or circulatory conditions* include congenital heart disease, rheumatic fever, arteriosclerotic and degenerative heart disease, and other heart or hypertensive diseases.

8. *Mental, psychoneurotic, and personality disorders* include psychotic disorders, alcoholism, drug dependence, and other character and personality disorders.

9. *Traumatic brain injury* includes neurobiologic disorders resulting from accident or injury that create cognitive and behavioral disabilities such as memory loss and difficulty concentrating, decreased self-awareness and insight, and impairment in reasoning, and physical disabilities including impairments in speech, vision, hearing, motor skills, and balance.

10. *Respiratory disorders* include asthma, TB, emphysema, pneumoniosis, chronic bronchitis, and others.

11. *Diabetes, epilepsy, and other conditions.*

Disability Classifications "Commonly Used" by Schools

This set of categories is frequently used in educational settings to communicate about students and their needs (AOL, iVillage Better Health Network, 1998). Examples provide insight into the broad groups of disabilities that fall into each category. Use of this system may be somewhat limited for our purposes but is included here because many clients continue to be a part of the educational system or the vocational education system for many years as adults.

1. *Physical disabilities:* This category of disabilities includes those that are apparent at birth or soon after, such as cerebral palsy, spina bifida, cystic fibrosis, and Down syndrome (which may be a physical as well as mental disability).
2. *Acquired disabilities:* These disabilities can occur at any time in any person without regard to other factors. They include Acquired Immune Deficiency Syndrome (AIDS), spinal cord injury, multiple sclerosis, and Alzheimer's disease.
3. *Developmental disabilities:* These include any congenital anomalies that disrupt growth, development, or maturation. Learning disabilities may be often linked to developmental disabilities but are not always seen together. Developmental disabilities include attention deficit disorder, dyslexia, Down syndrome or mental retardation, learning disorder, and learning disability.

U.S. Department of Education: Grouping by Frequency of Occurrence

In the 1997 study of Department of Education Statistics released by NIDDR, the categories cited are related to extent of occurrence in the population studied. Because there are relatively few students with physical disabilities, that category is not given the primacy that it is often given in other systems of categories. The primary categories for schoolchildren in order of frequency, as we saw in Chapter 5, are learning disabilities, speech and language impairments, mental retardation, and emotional disturbance.

Disabilities Classifications for Sports Participation in Special Events

Sports organizations such as the International Paralympic Committee have specific categories developed for competition between people of similar disabilities. Two examples are included here to demonstrate how exact and specific it is possible to be in the development of categories and subcategories:

1. "Lawn Bowls Classification," International Paralympics
   Categories here include wheelchair bound, needs special bowls, wheelchair bound combination of upper and lower limb disability, lower limb disability, upper limb disability, totally blind, partially sighted

2. "Functional Classification for Table Tennis," Table Tennis Association
   - Sitting mode includes five classes of players in wheelchairs by level of impairment, such as quadriplegics (tetraplegics), paraplegics, and amputees (International Paralympic Committee, 2001).
   - Standing mode also includes five classes of players, such as amputees, players with lower limb impairments, or players with upper limb impairments (Tabletennis.org, 2001).

Rolland's Disability Categories: A Typology of Disability

Rolland has been a major contributor to our understanding of disability and chronic illness, both in individuals and in the context of the family life cycle. In the previous chapter, Rolland's understanding of the effect of the type of disability on the development of a disability identity was presented. The three identity-impacting categories Rolland identified were (1) progressive disability, which requires a possible change, or alteration, in identity over time; (2) constant disability, which offers the possibility of a continuous and stable relationship to the disability; and (3) relapsing or episodic disability, where predictable or unpredictable fluctuations in severity impact on the development of a stable self-concept. All three of these relate to his category of "course" of the disability, as we shall see below.

Rolland also identifies four broad distinctions applicable to the development of disability categories (Rolland, 1989). Each disabling and/or chronic condition can be grouped according to these four parameters: onset, course, lifespan, and incapacitation.

1. Parameter One: Onset

Onset of a disability may be either *acute* or *gradual.* Acute-onset disabilities often create a crisis for people and families, as they struggle to address the impact of major, permanent changes in roles and identities. Stroke is an example of an acute-onset disability, as are any disabilities caused by accident or trauma, such as spinal cord injuries, brain injuries, or trauma-related deafness or blindness. Gradual-onset disabilities, such as Alzheimer's, allow time for adjustment and integration. The way in which individuals and people around them adjust to these two kinds of onsets will be at least in part dependent upon their personality and values.

2. Parameter Two: Course

This is the categorization presented in Chapter 6 as relevant to identity, but it is also an important way in which to categorize disabilities. *Progressive* disabilities follow an ever more disabling course as the condition becomes more severe. AIDS, the progressive form of multiple sclerosis, and cancer are examples of this type of disability *Constant* disabilities, such as deafness, blindness, and paralysis, remain at the same level throughout the lifespan. If one is a paraplegic, for example, there is no expectation that the impairment will "progress" to quadriplegia. If one is blind but able to distinguish light from shadow, this ability will be expected to remain. If someone has a developmental disability, he or she may learn new life skills, but basic level of functioning remains the same. *Relapsing or episodic* disabilities, on the other hand, offer little predictability. There are periods of remission, where a person can resume usual activities, and periods of exacerbation, when activities may be curtailed or strongly affected by the disability. Lupus, the episodic form of multiple sclerosis, fibromyalgia, and some forms of mental illness may follow this pattern.

3. Parameter Three: Outcome

Outcome relates the disability to *lifespan* issues: Will the disability also shorten the lifespan? Where it is expected to do so, people must also address issues around death and dying, along with disability identity. AIDS, many forms of cancer, and ALS (amyotropic lateral sclerosis) generally shorten the lifespan, although there are many, many variations among people. Painful quality/quantity of life issues may need to be addressed over time, and previously set life goals must be adjusted to integrate changes in projected lifespan.

4. Parameter Four: Incapacitation

Disabilities also occur with varying degrees of severity or intensity, therefore causing differences in the degree of *incapacitation* among people with the same condition. To use examples from Rolland (1989):

- Impairment in Cognition: A condition such as Alzheimer's can cause a wide spectrum of impairment from very minimal to severe.
- Impairments in Sensation: Visual impairments may be very minimal and resolved with glasses or cataract surgery, or severe, such as macular degeneration.
- Impairments in Energy Production: Cardiovascular and pulmonary diseases create a broad range of impairments, from ability to sustain heavy activity to ability to sit up in a chair. The disease label alone does not of itself address the degree of impairment a person might experience.
- Disfigurement: Leprosy and severe burns may cause a wide range of disfigurement. An element to consider also is the location of the disfigurement—whether it is noticeable immediately or hidden.
- Social Disability: This may be due to a contagious disease, such as AIDS, or to a mental illness or developmental disability also has a wide variation in severity and impact upon functioning.

Disability Categories and the Medical Model

The medical model does not group disabilities by any of the categories explored thus far. In fact, this model does not address disability as an entity separate from the disease or condition that is the cause. Rather, the medical model groups "diseases" by "system": the part of the body or the groups of tissues and organs that are together affected by the condition. This is very important to consider in working with clients, because clients with disabilities are very much influenced by the medical labels and categories, and these affect the way the client perceives himself or herself in relation to the disabling condition.

Examples of "systems" classifications and disabling conditions found in the *Merck Manual* (Berkow, 1992) include:

System	*Examples*
Infectious and parasitic diseases	Leprosy, sarcoidosis
Cardiovascular disorders	Arteriosclerosis, congestive heart failure, coronary artery disease
Pulmonary disorders	Asthma, chronic obstructive pulmonary disease, occupational lung diseases
Gastrointestinal disorders	Tumors, cancers
Hepatic and biliary disorders	Hepatic neoplasms, fibrosis, cirrhosis
Endocrine disorders	Goiter, cancer, diabetes
Hematologic disorders	Anemia, hemophilia, leukemia, Hodgkin's disease
Musculoskeletal and connective tissue disorders	Arthritis, collagen diseases, fibromyalgia
Neurologic disorders	Dementias, head injury, spinal cord injury, neoplasms, Parkinson's disease, Huntington's chorea, myasthenia gravis, muscular dystrophy
Psychiatric disorders	Drug dependence, personality disorder, psychoses, schizophrenia
Renal and urologic disorders	Neoplasms, renal failure/dialysis
Otorhinolaryngology	Deafness, hearing loss, carcinoma, vocal cord paralysis
Ophthamologic disorders	Macular degeneration, glaucoma, conditions causing blindness

Chapter Summary

Because of the enormous number of impairments, conditions, and diseases that are included in our general understanding of "disability," it is helpful to be able to organize or group them in a form that is useful and accessible for both social workers and clients. In this chapter, we have presented a number of different systems for classifying disabilities: (1) by limitation in activity, ADLs, and IADLs; (2) by conditions causing the disability; (3) by limitations in learning and working; (4) by prevalence in the school setting; (5) by level of ability to participate in a sport; (6) by medical model classifications; and (7) by Rolland's typology of onset, course, outcome, and incapacitation. We can see that each system is related to the purpose for which the classifications are to be used and to the frame of references of the designers.

Rolland's categories appear to best illuminate the kinds of stresses and problems social workers must address in working with clients with disabilities, and they provide an overarching framework within which the other classification systems can be encompassed as well. Therefore, in the next two chapters, this typology will be used to explore the individual framework in greater depth. Chapter 8 will address issues around onset, course, and outcome, while Chapter 9 will focus on limitations by exploring some specific limitations, such as mobility, sensory limitations, communication, reasoning ability and mental functioning, and differences that are either visible or invisible.

Questions for Thought and Discussion

1. When people are disabled as children, their relationship to disability may be affected strongly by life experiences, which include school. Do you think that the school-based categories for disability can impact identity in adulthood? If so, in what ways?

2. When people incorporate disability into self-identity, they incorporate a very personal and individual view of the disabling condition. How do we balance our understanding of the individual with the general knowledge we can draw from understanding disability groupings?

3. When a person interacts with society, society's groupings greatly impact personal identity. Which of the groupings presented in this chapter do you believe to have the greatest influence on people in terms of identity in our society?

4. One of Rolland's parameters for disability groupings is "outcome," which addresses possible changes in lifespan that result from disabling conditions. How much of an impact might changes in expected lifespan have on personal identity?

5. Create your own list of "essential" activities of daily living (bathing, toileting, transferring, eating, and so on) and instrumental activities of daily living (shopping, housecleaning, driving, using the phone, and the like) that are important for your sense of self and independence. Rank each group by prioritizing the activity in terms of its importance to you. Do you think this ranking applies to people generally, or is it specific to you only? If you think it is specific to you only, in what ways might other people differ from you?

8

Understanding the Disability Experience: Onset, Course, and Outcome

In the next two chapters, we will attempt to develop some insight into the *process* of living with one or more disabilities. We will explore the experience of disability from birth or early childhood, the experience of getting a disability diagnosis, of working with the medical establishment, of dealing with friends and family members and others in the social world, and of having a mobility limitation, a hearing limitation, a vision limitation, and several other kinds of limitations. We will learn about the special problems people face with exacerbation/remission cycle disabilities and how this uncertainty affects daily life. We will also explore the experience of having an invisible disability, an experience that goes beyond the diagnosis and into self-perception and issues of disclosure, and the experience of having a disfiguring condition that immediately calls attention to itself. Personal narratives will help us to relate to experiences that may be quite different from, or only outwardly similar to, our own.

In gathering personal stories, it is noted that although people with disabilities were willing to share personal information and experiences readily, and even welcomed the opportunity to share their experience with social work students and professionals, they were in large measure not willing that their identities be made public. For this reason, both this chapter and the next have a large number of "anonymous" contributors.

This chapter will explore three of Rolland's four categories for understanding the context of disability: onset, course, and outcome.

Onset and Beyond

Getting Diagnosed

The way in which a person becomes disabled has a major effect on self-perception and on the person's understanding of his or her disability. We may have had the disability from birth or early childhood and have no knowledge of self without the disability. We may acquire the disability suddenly and traumatically, through an automobile accident, ski injury, or fall. We may also have experienced a very gradual onset of disability, a period when no one understood what was happening—neither doctors, nor family, nor even ourselves.

Experiencing Disability in the Early Years.   As we have seen in the chapter on identity development, for children who are born with a disability or acquire one in early childhood, the disability is immediately a part of who they are. Depending on the kind of disability they have, there may be a greater or lesser early awareness of difference in their immediate experience. Awareness, however, often comes from the realization of being treated differently from other children: perhaps overprotected by mom and dad, shunned by other children, feared by other parents, or expected by teachers to perform poorly.

Adults in the child's world may at first be uncomfortable talking with the child about her or his difference and may be dealing with their own very private guilt and fear, drawn from the moral model, that the child is somehow carrying the mark of their own failures. They may be angry with the child for having disappointed them—they were expecting a picture-perfect baby and were instead presented with a child who was less than perfect in some way. This may be their first contact with disability and they may have had no preparation: They may not know what to expect, how to assist their child, what the course of the disability is likely to be, or how or what to tell family members, friends, and neighbors.

Children are expected to be dependent on others at first, but for some children, dependence upon others is a way of life. Because of this dependence, it's easy for the adults in the child's life to assume complete control, to regulate not only daily routines, but also friendships, relationships, and, with adolescence, sexuality.

Many parents and family members may also deny a child's disability. Sally French, in *Can You See the Rainbow?* (2000, p. 195), describes some of her early childhood problems with lack of vision:

> The adults would also get very perturbed if ever I looked "abnormal." Being told to open my eyes and straighten my face, when all I was doing was trying to see, made me feel ugly and separate. Having adults pretend that I could see more than I could, and having to acquiesce in the pretense, was a theme throughout my childhood.
>
> . . . As a child, explaining my situation without appearing disagreeable, sullen, and rude was so problematic that I usually denied my disability and suffered in silence. All this taught me from a very early age that, while adults were working themselves up about whether or not I could see rainbows, my own anxieties must never be shared.

She summarizes her feelings about disability that were built upon this denial in earliest childhood (French, p. 200), stating her reasons for denying the reality of her disability:

1. To avoid other people's anxiety and distress
2. To avoid other people's disappointment and frustration
3. To avoid other people's disbelief
4. To avoid other people's disapproval
5. To live up to other people's ideas of "normality"
6. To avoid spoiling other people's fun
7. To collude with other people's pretenses

We receive information about sexuality and our future roles as adults from our parents and from teachers, peers, and other adults in our lives. A child with a disability is often discounted as a sexual being. Peers don't include him or her in secret conversations about sex as children, and adults relate as though the child had no sexual identity. Developing a sexual identity under such circumstances is often difficult or even impossible, yet is very much an essential part of development.

In *Making Choices* (1996, p. 25), Mary Duffy gives us a moving insight into her experience:

> *somebody's daughter*
> *CHILD*
> *i am your daughter.*
> *i was born in your double bed.*
> *you thought that i was half bird*
> *that i had wings*
> *afterward you thought*
> *god had chosen you specially for me*
> *and you were going to love me so much*
> *it wouldn't make any difference*
>
> *they blamed it on sputnik and the russians and gave me*
> *artificial arms*
> *when i was eight months old*
> *they came out of the airing cupboard every morning*
> *to help me develop a body image that included arms*
> *while we all waited for technology to catch up.*

Looking back at her childhood experiences with lupus, one woman writes:

> My autoimmune disease deeply impacted my self-image and my worldview. While coming to grips with this disorder as a child, I defined myself by it. I saw myself as a person with ill health, and subsequently doubted my ability to participate in normal activities. I later saw I could still accomplish many things while having a disease. I realized that my disease was simply a part of who I was rather than what I was. I redefined myself. (Anonymous, personal statement, 10/1/01)

Experiencing a Sudden-Onset Disability.   Unless you have had a disability since birth or early childhood, receiving a diagnosis of a condition that will create major life changes is often fraught with terror, anxiety, and moments of panic. However, there are some situations where receiving a diagnosis can actually be a kind of relief. These first experiences with becoming a person who is disabled remain an important part of the "story" of the person, a story that is told and retold, to oneself and to others, throughout a lifetime.

The way sudden-onset disability happens to people with disabilities is usually related to the cause of the disability. If you have an automobile accident that causes spinal cord injury, the diagnosis follows closely behind the trauma and there is little time to adjust to either. Strokes, trauma-related head injuries, and amputations create an instantaneous permanent change. The physical shock mirrors the emotional and intellectual one. Often, pain accompanies the initial trauma. Medication, surgeries, intensive-care stays, complex and uncomfortable diagnostic tests all add to the disorientation that is a part of the first hours, days, and sometimes weeks of disability.

There's only so much the mind can take in at once. Trying to stay alive, to understand what is said, to deal with pain and immediate needs is often as far as a person can go at first in these circumstances. There will be time, hours or days later, to address and absorb the permanency of the changes that have occurred, to become physically aware of them as only the person affected can do.

Family members may have a slightly different reaction and timetable. They may be readier than the newly diagnosed person, or less ready. They don't have the body signals that indicate change, but neither do they have the medications that can dull sensation and confuse thought. Their reactions and behavior to the change the newly disabled person is experiencing will have a major impact on adjustment and planning for the future. After a period of time, which varies with the condition and with the people involved, the person and the family members will be ready to ask questions and to begin to try to understand the changes that have occurred.

Here are the recollections of a newly injured teenaged quadriplegic:

First day post injury: Wow! This is weird. What a joke! I can't move. I can't feel anything below my head. I'm lying here in this bed and people keep coming in and adjusting things, moving things on my body but I can't feel them. I can see them, but I can't *feel* them. I wonder how long this will last. Am I going to miss the first day of summer school? I bet my mom and dad are really mad at me.

Five days post injury: I can't really ask anyone anything. I can't talk because there's this tube stuck down my throat. I have to learn to breathe again. Every day this guy comes to work with me, but I can't do it. I like when my friends come at night. They tell jokes and I show them how I can move my head a little bit with my neck muscles and we all laugh.

Twelve days post injury: This isn't funny any more. I still can't feel anything. I can't move. No one tells me anything but this is taking too long to go away. Everyone is worried about me, I can tell. Do they think I'm going to die?

I work on moving all day long. I try really hard. I move a muscle and my head moves. Then it goes right back to where it was. Maybe I'm not doing this right? Got to keep trying. Everyone's working, or going to school. They come every night, but it's not fun when they come. I told the nurse I don't want any visitors.

Twenty days post injury: I am *so* uncomfortable. I can't make myself be comfortable. I'm sick of all this, and I think it's not going to go away. I wish I was dead. I wish I could kill myself. I get so mad I bite my tongue till it bleeds and my mom gets really upset. (Anonymous, diary, 1992)

A woman who was involved in a drunk-driving accident as a teenager recalls her experience:

> I woke up in the hospital. I couldn't move anything. I couldn't talk. I thought I was going to go crazy but my best friend came to see me every day and held my hand. I couldn't do anything for myself. I was like a newborn baby. They had to teach me how to crawl, and then how to walk. They taught me how to talk, but I know I don't talk right. I can't talk fast like I used to. I never got to go to college. I never talk about my problems with people. My friends want me to join a bookclub, but they don't know I can't read very well. I don't think about it too much, but I know there are lots of things I can't do—that I never got to try to do. (Anonymous, personal interview, June 1996)

Experiencing the Gradual Onset of a Disabling Condition. While sudden trauma is often the more familiar scenario for thinking about diagnosis, it is only the most immediately dramatic. Many people experience diagnosis quite differently. For months, there may have been a vague awareness that something was wrong. Visits to the doctor, blood tests, X-rays—all may have been inconclusive. "You just need to rest," "Anyone would feel like that in your situation," "You should feel pleased that all the tests are negative," or, worst of all, "There's nothing wrong. If there was, we would have found it. It must be all in your head."

"All in my head?" And yet it doesn't go away. Often people try psychotherapy, change jobs, change life routines and lifestyles, rethink relationships—all in the process of believing, "It's all in my head" and adding to that "I must be losing my mind." Family members and friends, concerned but reassured by the physician, often discount the symptoms also, adding to the person's distress.

Frustration mounts as visits to the doctor continue. In these kinds of situations, receiving a diagnosis is often not a shock, rather, it is experienced as a relief. "I'm *not* losing my mind after all. There really is something wrong." And that something has a name and includes all the symptoms the person has been experiencing! This kind of diagnostic experience can occur with multiple sclerosis, some forms of mental illness such as depression, rheumatoid arthritis, chronic fatigue syndrome, and lupus.

John, who has primary progressive MS, explains what it was like to get diagnosed:

> I first noticed that I couldn't keep the beat of some music with my left foot. I've always been musical and left-handed and that seemed really strange to me. The diagnosis process was awful. I went from doctor to doctor for eleven months. Each doctor just shrugged his shoulder, and that was really frustrating. I asked them if it was in my head. I thought it was. But it wasn't. I had a myelogram and lots and lots of tests. But everyone shrugged their shoulders. I remember one doctor who said he had good news. I thought he had found out my problem, but instead he told me I didn't have a brain tumor. That wasn't good news to *me*. Finally one doctor said I didn't have anything else, so I must have MS. I didn't even know what MS was, then. (John Mannick, personal interview, 9/7/01)

Diagnosed with rheumatoid arthritis in her early thirties, a woman shares her experience:

> Some conditions begin in a way that is similar to many other illnesses that a person commonly experiences. Mine is such a condition. I had symptoms that were typical of a cold in

the beginning: fever, nausea, sneezing, and a headache. Before these began, I was recovering from mononucleosis. Unlike mono, this new illness took hold in just a few days. I saw my doctor several times. Finally she asked me to drop my head down and asked me if it hurt. I said yes and she sent me to the emergency room to test for meningitis. That was what I had, and I spent five days out of it, in the hospital.

When I got back home, I woke up one morning with pain in one finger. Within a few days, I had pain and stiffness in all my fingers, and in my feet. My doctor said it was a residual response to the meningitis. A week went by and it got worse and worse. I couldn't do everyday tasks, and every movement was painful. The doctor kept saying it was the residual response.

One day she said maybe it was arthritis but she didn't think so. She took a test but said she was sure it would be negative. I didn't know what arthritis was. I didn't ask and she didn't tell me. The test came back negative. But I just kept getting worse and worse.

Finally, she sent me to a rheumatologist. He did another test, and it came back positive. It took weeks before I could start any treatments because they had to observe and test me to be sure. During those weeks I was in terrible pain. Finally, I got my diagnosis and started medications. I take a lots of medications every day now. (Anonymous, letter, 8/26/01)

After this initial feeling of validation and relief, however, people begin to learn about their condition and how it will affect their lives, not only in the here-and-now of still vague and often fairly minor symptoms, but later, when the progression of the disabling conditions impacts functioning much more severely. Depending on the personality characteristics and values of the person, her or his family and friends, employer and colleagues, and various other considerations, the disability can be denied, accepted, integrated in a positive way, or in a negative one.

Becoming a Long-Term "Patient"

The point at which a person is diagnosed with a disability is also the very beginning point of a lifelong, sometimes ambivalent, and often quite complex, relationship with the medical world. Disability means treatments, medications, tests, prostheses and assistive devices, sometimes pain, frequent checkups, the ever-present possibility of hospitalization, and a profound awareness of a new kind of dependency—on the medical world.

What does it take to keep a disabled person functioning at an optimum level? Depending on the disability, of course, the answer to this question will vary. However, the one constant for nearly all people is the larger-than-life role that medicine and physicians will play in their lives. Even if one chooses alternative medical treatments and attention, the medical world that is such a strong presence in our society will never be far away.

Specialists are available to meet needs—provided, of course, that you have medical insurance, for one of the absolutes of disability is that your medical costs will increase exponentially. If you do not have "good" coverage (and that word takes on a whole new meaning in this new context), just obtaining medical care becomes a major quest. Medical assistance provides coverage for low-income people. Medicare, which can provide medical coverage for people with disabilities, has a waiting period. What happens in the meantime? Working to address medical needs in such circumstances can become an all-consuming task.

When funding needs have been addressed, other major questions remain. Do I choose a doctor who is accessible or one who is well-known for his or her skill in working with my disability? Do I follow doctor's orders all the time, or do I do what I think my body needs? Do I choose someone I like or someone whose office is near home or work? Doctors are often rushed, and people with disabilities often speak or move more slowly than other people. Do I hurry through and not tell the doctor all my problems, or do I risk impatience and annoyance and share every concern?

Dependence creates other worries as well. A very expensive medicine may be needed on a daily basis. Ongoing physical therapy becomes a necessity to keep muscles functioning. Oxygen may be required on a continued basis in order to maintain life. Awareness of what *might* happen, should access to medical care, medicines, and treatments stop, can create anxiety and stress. The awareness that medical care stands between a person and certain death can create both insecurity and an ever-greater recognition of dependence.

Leaving the area you live in, for any reason, involves additional stress. Vacations become involved affairs, and it's hard to do any last-minute kinds of things. What if I lose my medicines? What if I have an attack? A seizure? Moving to another location does not involve only the usual problems of housing, schools, and jobs, but also locating and beginning a relationship with a new medical establishment.

Entering the world of medical dependence and expensive medications: The young woman with arthritis continues her story:

> When I was finally diagnosed with rheumatoid arthritis, I didn't know what that meant at first. I wasn't in the hospital, and I was working full time. Every night, I'd go on the Internet to try to learn more about arthritis. What I learned was very depressing.
>
> My joints were all swollen and I hurt so much I couldn't sleep. The doctor put me on a lot of medicines. I kept having to go in for more tests and X-rays, and to have my medicines adjusted. Nothing seemed to really work well.
>
> I didn't want to complain. I tried not to call the doctor too often because I didn't want to bother him. Sometimes I just kept the pain rather than call him. Then I got so depressed, I really needed help. Finally I called and got anti-depressants and my medications were adjusted again.
>
> I have to go to the doctor every six months and have a lot of tests to see if my arthritis is arrested or not. That means taking time off from work, and making appointments. It's hard because I don't want people at work to know I have arthritis. I haven't told anyone.
>
> Sometimes when I have a problem it takes the doctor a day or two to call back. But I'm off anti-depressants now, and my arthritis is stable as long as I take all my medicines. Even if I feel OK, though, I still have to go in every six months. And I still have to go to other doctors for other things, too. It just seems like there's a lot of doctors and medical offices and labs in my life that weren't there before.
>
> I'm really lucky because I have very good medical insurance. My medications cost more than $1,000 a month. I don't know what I'd do if I didn't have insurance. It's so scary because what if I can't work and lose my medical coverage? How will I get my medicines? If I don't take them all the time, I'll be completely crippled. (Anonymous, letter, 8/26/01)

Yet facing a permanent disability is also an opportunity for growth, for reordering priorities, for setting new goals. A nurse shares her story:

I knew right away after they told me. I had worked with people that had this, and I knew how it affected them. I was really frightened. Even though I knew about my disability, I started to gather everything I could find about it—books, articles in medical and nursing journals, leaflets, stuff from the web—anything. I joined chat rooms and I went to support groups. But that stage only lasted for a little while.

Then I tried alternative therapies. I tried megavitamins and special food and all that did was cost a bundle and not help at all. I knew it wouldn't hurt me, so I tried everything anyway. I never stopped the medicines my doctors gave me though. I was afraid to go against their advice. And I felt that doing what they said would minimize my disability best.

Anyhow, then I got really afraid about my mind. I decided I could deal with the rest of it, but not with not being able to use my mind. I knew I'd have cognitive difficulties at some point, and I needed my mind. I needed it to do the work I did. This made me really nervous.

Then some more time passed and I started thinking that getting this was really a wake-up call. A wake-up call to reorder my life, and to decide what was really important. I decided what was really important to me was my family—not my job, or power, or prestige—just having the time to be with my family. So I quit my job and took another one that was just part-time. I can keep this job for a long time, I think. And it gives me so much more time for family and to do the things I really care about. I'm living each day like a gift . . .

So that's what I'm doing now. I go regularly for check-ups and stay on medications and my symptoms haven't been too severe. (Anonymous, telephone interview, 9/2/01)

Facing the World

Although it is the individual who carries the disability and whose life is most affected, interactions with others are also affected by disability. Reactions and attitudes of family members, friends, and co-workers can provide a supportive network. However, at times, these are also sources of difficulty and stress.

Family Members and Caregivers

Family members are often a person's closest relationships and are also those most affected by the disability. Parents of children with disabilities often have as many needs, and as many problems, as do the children with the disability. Overprotective parents often try to shield children from difficult or painful experiences and keep the child in a state of dependency beyond the necessary one created by the disability. They may worry about what will happen to their child when he or she is grown, and the parents are old and no longer able to care for the child, or die.

Used to providing all the physical care their child needs, they may actively or passively resist their child's efforts to grow independent and make their own arrangements for housing and personal care. Parents of children with developmental disabilities and mental illness worry about strangers, sexual exploitation, accidents, or disappearances. All parents worry about the reactions of others to their child and how such reactions will affect both them and the child.

Families often include other children without disabilities. How do parents balance time and attention between them such that the disabled child's needs are met, but the able children are not set aside? How to help siblings to understand? How much should they rely on a sibling to provide care and supervision? And preventing abuse and exploitation can also be a concern in families.

Often, it is not the child in the family who is disabled, but an adult. Multiple sclerosis, lupus, rheumatoid arthritis, traumatic injuries—all of these affect adults, often adults with children. It's difficult not to be able to parent your child as fully as you would like, to be dependent upon someone else to fulfill household roles you saw as your own, and to ask your own child for help with eating, toileting, or transportation. Families can use such experiences to grow as a family and become a strong, positive entity that meets the needs of all members.

Older adults in our society are by far those members who carry the greatest frequency, and the greatest number, of disabilities. We have seen in Chapter 5, "Disability Demographics," that the likelihood of becoming disabled increases with age. Older disabled adults are often cared for by family members and do not identify as disabled people. Family relationships tend to remain stable with disability. Because there are so many more older adults who are disabled, it's much easier for older people to retain their former roles, friendships, and family relationships. It is not uncommon for an older person to use a cane, walk slowly, wear thick glasses, or use a hearing aid. The realm of disability is probably the only one on earth where older is often better!

Family members are not the only people providing care for people with disabilities. Caregivers can be friends or more distant relatives as well. Caregivers may experience some of the same kinds of reactions as immediate family members: They can experience fear and anxiety; they can be overprotective, trying to shield the disabled person from both physical and emotional harm; and they can struggle with new roles and chores. They also must reflect on the changes that have occurred in the relationship and perhaps restructure it to incorporate disability.

Peers.   People with disabilities spend most of their time in an ableist world. Their schoolmates and workmates are not disabled (or so they think). Children have a difficult time avoiding staring and asking questions, questions that a disabled child might find distressing. Children, especially in the elementary grades, may avoid, mimic, tease, and harrass a disabled child. Alert and responsive teachers and other adults are necessary to observe interaction and to intervene when necessary. Playgrounds are especially fraught with problems: Children who cannot play a sport, participate in a game, or understand a peer's directions may have an especially difficult time, and these early experiences have a strong effect upon the development of identity and self-worth.

A older man who had very poor vision shares his early school experiences:

> I always had to sit up in the front of the room so I could see the board. I didn't know there was anything wrong with me, and I thought everyone could only see the board from the front row. I didn't understand how some kids could pick to sit in the back. Luckily my last name started with a C and teachers often sat us in alphabetical order so I was always in the front.
>
>   Still, when the board was freshly washed and the chalk the teacher used was new, I couldn't see even from the front row. Then I had to try to get up and walk right up to the board to look. But even if the teacher let me do it, I was really embarrassed to have to stand up in front of everybody.

I got away with it until third grade. That year, the teacher said it wasn't fair that people were always seated alphabetically with the first letters of the alphabet in the front row. She decided to do it backwards—to put the last letters in front and the first letters at the back of the room to give everyone a chance to be in a different spot. My seat was in the back row. I couldn't see anything. It felt as though I couldn't hear, either, even though I knew I could. I asked the teacher if I could sit in the front. I ended up crying. I think she called my parents because after that I was taken to the eye doctor.

At recess, I had problems too. I never got picked to play baseball. When I did get picked, I never once hit the ball. I couldn't see it coming until it was too close to swing the bat. I'd swing and the ball would be way past me. The same with basketball. I couldn't see the basket clearly so I never got a basket. (Anonymous, personal interview, 9/21/01)

It's important for disabled children and adults to have contact with people with their same disability, we have learned, in order to normalize the experience. And often people with disabilities find close friendships among others with whom they can truly be open and sharing about this most difficult aspect of their lives. It's also important to have friends who are not disabled. When a person becomes disabled as an adult, many close friendships have already been formed. Disability is a litmus test of relationships: Some will fall by the wayside, others will be strengthened in the process of learning and understanding and sharing. Newly disabled people often grieve not only for the life they lived, the future they envisioned, but also for the friends and relationships who have moved on, often leaving a dead space in their place.

As we learned in Chapter 6, the most vulnerable of these kinds of relationships is a newly formed romantic attachment followed by the onset of a disability in one partner. Very often these relationships don't survive the disability diagnosis, and this can be very painful. Not only is there the loss itself, but the awareness that this person, who was loved and trusted, did not love enough to transcend the disability.

A young lady writes:

I was married for two years before I became disabled. I felt that my husband cared about me, and that he would help me when I became disabled. He did at first—he brushed my hair and helped me to get dressed. He put my shoes on. But he wouldn't help with any of the housework, or cooking. We both worked full-time, and for very long hours, but I had always been the one to take care of everything around the house. When I couldn't do it, and he refused, we had to hire someone to clean. He made me take it out of my salary.

After a while, he got tired to taking care of me. He started screaming at me all the time. It got worse and worse. He wouldn't go to counseling and he wouldn't stop screaming so one day I locked him out of the house and started divorce proceedings.

This isn't the way I thought life was going to be. I thought we'd be together forever. And now I have to cope with two things—my disability and my divorce! (Anonymous, telephone interview, 3/14/98)

Out in Public.   What about meeting strangers? Going out in public, on the street, in the subway, at the movies? People may stare, but they may also often avert their eyes and avoid making any eye contact. In a society where eye contact is an important part of relationship, people with disabilities are often excluded. And then the disabled person must always be left to wonder, "Am I so awful, is my existence so upsetting to people that they cannot even look at me?" "Is my condition so bad that people are afraid to look at me?"

Sometimes people don't avert their eyes. And they don't stare either. Instead, they treat the disabled person as an object of charity, someone to be infinitely pitied. In a desire to overcompensate for the eye averters and the starers, some people become oversolicitous and kindly, treating the disabled person as inferior, all the while offering to help. Often, this kind of help is worse than no help at all.

Fortunately, as our built environment becomes more accessible, more and more people are able to be out in public spaces. With a greater and more obvious presence, people with disabilities are becoming an everyday part of public life. Self-propelled wheelchairs, chirping traffic lights, accessible buildings, special seating in theaters—these and many other changes in our world, the products of legislation and policy changes, have made the world friendlier, and differences less remarkable, than they were even ten or twenty years ago. Starers and averters are gradually giving way to people who note, or ignore, the person with disabilities in the same way they would note or ignore anyone else they encountered.

John, who uses a wheelchair, describes his experiences out in public:

> One of the hardest things [is that] I might be remembered just because I'm in a chair. It makes me sad because I'd like to be remembered because of my personality or something about me being enjoyable or friendly. Now it's real sad that even though I have the same personality, that's what would be remembered. Someone says, "Do you remember John Mannick, the person in the wheelchair?" I think of myself the same way I used to. I see myself walking down the beach, going surfing. I started surfing when I was eight. I don't expect anyone to see me as any different. But they do. I know I can't even bathe myself— my wife has to bathe me. (John Mannick, personal interview, 9/5/01)

This excerpt from "Being Sam's Mum" can help us to understand some of the feelings of disabled adults with young children:

> If you saw me and Ann and Sam together, what would you decide about us? What story would you tell yourself to make sense of the picture we make? Of course, one of us must be his mum, that's obvious. Who would you choose? Perhaps you'd wait and see who picked him up and perched him on her hip, who buckled him into his buggy and strode off to the shops with him. Or perhaps you'd wait for that biggest of all giveaways, who changed his nappy.
>
> She who swoops and grabs, she who totes, she who is in physical possession, is the mother. This is the public image of motherhood, so much part of our culture that it's never spoken of, never challenged.
>
> If these are the signs you'd be looking for to help you decide who the real mother is, you wouldn't choose me. I'm disabled. I don't go to the shops with Sam on my own, we've always needed a third party; my swooping and grabbing has been strictly limited and I haven't changed his nappy since he decided that it was good fun to be chased around the room by somebody waving a fresh nappy at him and shouting, "Come back, come back."
>
> When Sam was a baby sometimes we'd walk around a shopping center precinct or down the high street with him sitting on my lap whilst Ann pushed me in my wheelchair. For the odd half-hour, I would occupy that public space, be that public image, woman in possession of baby. . . . Not so . . . we were two women and a baby. To the public eye, I

looked an unlikely candidate for motherhood. The wheelchair disqualified me. (Polio, pp. 77–78)

Course

A second vital element in the way a person experiences disability is related to the expected course of the disability. The tasks of adjustment and identity integration differ with three possible courses of disability described by Rolland and discussed in Chapter 5. In some cases, it may take quite a while before the course of the disability becomes apparent. For example, there are two forms of multiple sclerosis, with two different kinds of courses. One is progressive, where losses in functioning ability increase steadily with time, sometimes very slowly, over years, and sometimes quite rapidly, over weeks or months. The second course is one of exacerbations and remissions—an acute period where functioning is quite impaired, followed by a period of wellness and relative stability. Obviously, the tasks of understanding and integrating the disability into life are quite different in these two circumstances.

Rolland identifies three possible courses: progressive, constant, and relapsing or episodic. These present three very different types of experiences.

Progressive Disabilities

Some disabilities follow a steady or uneven course toward an ever-greater level of impairment. Many of these also shorten a person's individual lifespan. Living with a progressive disability often means addressing not only the changes that have occurred in the present, but making preparation for the changes that will occur in the future. It is often difficult to predict any timetable with accuracy, however, and progressive disabilities may become more disabling over many years, even decades. Receiving a diagnosis of a progressive disability can be especially difficult and frustrating. Progressive conditions can be physical, such as ALS (amyotrophic lateral sclerosis), the progressive form of MS, progeria, scleroderma, cancers, and many others; or they can be mental, such as Alzheimer's and forms of senile dementias.

The experience of a progressive disability can be one of anger, frustration, and fear, but it can enable enormous spiritual growth and a reassessment of life priorities and values. Always, there is a much greater sense of the here and now and, of the importance of the moment, whether because it is fleeting or because it is valuable, or both.

The reactions of family members and loved ones play a major role in the person's struggle to accept both the disability and its progressive nature. Support and understanding from family members is essential in assisting the person to accept future dependence and a narrowing of physical or mental horizons. In some ways, progressive disability echoes the life path of all of us, for we each look forward to a lessening of capacities and functioning in old age. The timetable may be different, but the process of acceptance can be much the same.

As happens frequently with old age, people with progressive disabilities may worry over the future and anticipate functional losses, grieving for them as we grieve for all losses. But there are at least two other courses open to them: They can learn about the future, understand it, and accept it, enjoying each moment to the fullest; or they can address some of the issues and lay the rest aside, feeling that there will be time to adjust to losses when they occur.

A woman with metastatic cancer in rural New Hampshire shares her philosophy:

> I don't know why this happened to me. I don't like it. I don't like being weak and tired and just feeling terrible. But I'm going to do everything I can to slow things down, to gain days and weeks. I can't work full time, but I can work two days a week, and I want to do that for as long as I can. I'll think about what to do when I can't work at all.
>
> Meantime, there's the vegetables to bring in. And I have to plan on wood for the winter. I can't split the logs myself this year. I'm going to have to find someone to do it. I'm going to have him split enough for the whole winter. I'll have him stack it right next to the house, so I can get to it even when I'm tired.
>
> Sometimes I can't get out of bed. Sometimes I am shivering with fever. Sometimes I just sleep and sleep and sleep. I expect those times will get more frequent, and maybe will last longer. But, I'm going to keep right on going.

After the September 11 terrorist attacks on the World Trade Center and the Pentagon, she expressed these thoughts:

> It really changed the way I think. All those people—they didn't have cancer. They just got up on an ordinary morning and went off to work. And they never came back. They didn't get to think about "why me?" They didn't get to have all the days that I have.
>
> I don't understand any of it. But I know that I think differently about getting sicker and about death now—I still have days left! (Susan Commoss, personal interview, 9/20/01)

John has had primary progressive multiple sclerosis since 1980, and shares more of his experiences:

> Now, I'm in a wheelchair 100 percent of the time. I'm on lots of meds. Meds for MS, meds for fatigue, meds for my bladder. I don't drive any more because of the meds. I had to give it up eighteen months ago. Now my sister drives me around, or my wife, or I take paratransit.
>
> I used to be a radiator repairman before I got MS. Then I took computer training through vocational rehabilitation and became a computer programmer. Now I had to stop work and go on disability. I can still type, with one finger. I can move my right arm and my right leg. My left arm and left leg are pretty much weights.
>
> I'm home most of the time, but I never get bored.
>
> (John Mannick, telephone interview, 9/8/01)

Chronic Disabilities

People with chronic disabilities do not face the special tasks of those with progressive disabilities. Rather, if they have become disabled past early childhood, their focus can be on accepting, adapting, and adjusting their world to incorporate the disability within it, knowing that the changes they make will then lead them to the same reasonably stable patterns of life they experienced before becoming disabled.

Those with chronic disabilities from birth or early childhood have never known themselves to be different. Thus the task is not so much adaptation as learning to optimize their ability to achieve the things that are important to them. Guidance, educational opportunities, and positive social experiences can be very helpful.

Spouses, children, parents, family, friends, and employers must also learn to adapt and assist the person to live a meaningful and rewarding life. Because disability often means some dependency, family and friends will need to work through some of their feelings about this. However, once the initial changes have been integrated into relationships, they may remain stable for all concerned.

Walking, parenting, going to school, and running her household can all be done effectively on crutches, says a woman who feels that her condition is stable. She is comfortable with her identity. She is strongly affiliated with the disability movement, and is involved in advocacy. She observes:

> Someone once had the nerve to ask me if I got tired of using crutches all the time. They wanted to know wasn't it tiring. I got so mad. "Do you get tired breathing?" I asked her. Using crutches to me is as natural as breathing. No, I don't get tired! (Anonymous, discussion on disability, 10/9/01)

Relapsing or Reoccurring Disabilities

Learning to understand oneself in the context of relapsing or recurring disabilities is a difficult task, for the unpredictability may make it difficult to find any constants around which to build expectations, goals, or plans. Multiple sclerosis, rheumatoid arthritis, and lupus are three examples of these kinds of disabilities. There is a strong correlation between these relapsing or reoccurring disabilities and gradual onset. While the exact mechanism of the disabling condition is not known, it is thought that these disabilities may have been caused by an earlier exposure to some bacteria or virus that, combined with a possible predisposition, may have caused the disability. Symptoms tend to appear gradually, and people with this kind of disability often have a frustrating and difficult time with diagnosis. Problems, pain, and activity limitations seem to come and go, with no apparent pattern. Generally, it takes a few cycles for both individuals and the medical establishment to determine what is happening. And, once determined, there is still little that either doctors or people with the disability can do to control the cycles.

The differences between an exacerbation, as the most disabling periods are called, and a remission vary among people and among conditions. Some people have very disabling exacerbations, others have much more limited problems. The timing varies not only among people, but even from one event to the other, so that there is no ability to predict when one will feel well or poorly, or for how long.

Exacerbation-remission cycles create a very special set of problems. One of the primary difficulties involves the ability to plan, to work, or to take on responsibilities. Something as simple as being a den mother becomes a major challenge in periods of exacerbation, while during remissions, many people can take on responsibilities like these with ease.

Work becomes difficult to plan for because employers need to rely on any particular employee to fulfill certain functions. The functions don't stop during exacerbations. It may become necessary to make decisions, based on degree of incapacity or pain, about whether to leave employment, make the incredibly enormous effort of going to work anyway, or to attempt to explain and to make arrangements. We Americans have a great deal of our identity wrapped up in the kind of work we do—our work tends to define us. Leaving a job means not only a loss in pay and in productivity but also a very real loss of identity.

During remissions, people with these types of disabilities are very functional and are able to do all the things they have always enjoyed. In new social situations, however, there is always the underlying question: "Should I tell?" "Better now, or later?" Telling often means dealing with the reaction of others, being vulnerable, in a sense, when vulnerability isn't absolutely necessary. Especially among peers, or during dating, the natural trust that develops seems to imply that sharing this information is good and is expected. And, generally, people do react in a supportive and understanding manner.

Exacerbation-remission-cycle disabilities often begin in young adulthood, a time when obligations and responsibilities are greatest in terms of physical demands. It may be difficult to go on trips, do housework, or coach a baseball game. Even if one needs and can afford help during exacerbations, it is difficult to find help willing to work an unpredictable cyclical schedule. Often, spouses, partners, and children must pitch in and complete tasks and projects.

It's frustrating to think you have to lie on the couch all day, when last week you could go for long walks in the sunshine. Frustration can at times become anger and/or depression. A frustrated woman with chronic fatigue syndrome explains her problem:

> I signed up for a really great yoga class. I love it, and I love the teacher. Everything has been fine, but now my I can't lift my arms or legs. Should I push myself? Should I miss classes I've paid for, and enjoy? I told my teacher about this, but what can he do? He can't change the class for just me!

And, about her work she had this to say:

> I had to tell the girl that handles the insurance, because she would see it anyway. I made her promise not to say anything because I don't want people to feel sorry for me. And there are lots of other people they could hire if they think I can't do my work like I'm supposed to. Sometimes I think I'll die just getting there, and it seems like the day will never end. And then the next week I'm fine and loving every minute. I don't know what's real any more. Neither one feels real. (Anonymous, personal interview, 7/16/01)

A middle-aged man with MS observes:

> I really like going to support group. I love the people. It helps a lot when I'm feeling bad. But when I feel good, I don't want to be around them. It depresses me. I don't want to remember that I get like that too. I want to forget and just be like I am now. And then I feel guilty for not going, because I know we all need each other. (Anonymous, personal interview, 5/14/85)

A woman with lupus who is in a supervisory position in a hospital says:

Everyone knows I have lupus. I had to tell them because if I don't come in, someone has to take over and do my job. It worked out OK. I just can't figure out what to do about those in-between days. The ones where I don't have to be in bed, but I'm really tired. Sometimes I go in and just say I'm here but I don't have any energy, so I have to do everything from sitting in my office. People are really nice, and everyone helps me. I'm really lucky I can keep my job, because I really need the money. I have kids to send to college, you know. (Anonymous, personal interview, 3/15/75)

Outcome

The third parameter of understanding disability has to do with expected lifespan changes. Some disabilities may not shorten life, while others shorten it a little. Some disabilities reduce life expectancy drastically. These are often the progressive disabilities discussed earlier.

Preparing for death is not an easy task We tend to avoid thinking about it. Research has shown that although most people today know about advance directives, very few people actually complete them. Few people talk with family members about end-of-life issues. As a society that worships youth, we keep death at arm's length.

When we receive a diagnosis that implies an early death, we come face to face with all of our hidden fears. And it's often hard to find someone who will help us to think about death. People have a tendency to avoid the subject and to think they must be reassuring to the person whose disability is worsening steadily and whose condition is irreversible.

A sixty-year-old woman says:

What I hate most is when I see people and they say, "You look great. You look like there's nothing wrong with you. It's nice you're out walking around," or on the phone, "Your voice sounds so strong. You must be feeling wonderful." And I damn well don't feel wonderful and I'm scared out of my mind and I know they see it and hear it and they make me so mad. There's no one to talk to about how really scary this is. (Anonymous, personal interview, 6/27/01)

People with disabilities that will shorten their lifespan need to be able to talk about it. They need to do life reviews, to plan for themselves, to do the things that they need to do before the disability limits every possibility. Fortunately, there are friends and family members and support groups that can assist them in this endeavor. But sometimes it is not those closest to the person but people much farther removed who will be the ones who are open to helping.

One important task is to ensure comfort when one can no longer be one's own advocate. Planning for the difficult days ahead is painful, but it can also provide enormous relief. Some people are able to do this very successfully, while others struggle on, locked into the knowledge of death and without the ability or desire to integrate this difficult fact and find an inner peace.

Some people also accept what they see as inevitable and reach deep within themselves to find a serenity and a quiet space. Still others think it is better for them to "fight the good fight." A cancer patient states this philosophy clearly and succinctly:

> I'm not just going to get into bed, curl up my toes, and die. I'm going to fight this thing and if I lose, then I'll know I've done the best I can. No planning for death for me! I want to plan for *life!* (Susan Commoss, personal interview, 8/31/01)

And another has a different view:

> I'm so tired. I'm just tired. I did everything I could in life, and I'm ready to go. I just want to be out of pain, and I want to rest. Eternal sleep sounds pretty good to me right now! (Anonymous, personal interview, 4/15/87)

Everyone who receives the knowledge that his or her lifespan will be shortened receives it differently. For it is received in the context of the person's whole life experience, and each of us has a unique life experience. It is impossible to generalize here without taking away some of that uniqueness.

Chapter Summary

We have begun our work of understanding the lived experience of disability by exploring three of Rolland's parameters. *Onset,* the experience of being or becoming disabled, has been explored through three different possibilities: being born disabled or acquiring a disability very early in life; becoming disabled instantly, as through an accident; and becoming disabled through a gradual process without clear benchmarks and often accompanied by difficult experiences with diagnosis. Onset experiences include interaction with the medical establishment, which now plays a much more major role in life, and with going out into the world as a person with a disability. *Course,* the second parameter, addresses some of the experiences and issues faced by people whose disability course differs. People with progressive disabilities face steadily deteriorating conditions, which will leave them in a substantially more disabled state than the one they currently are experiencing. Those with constant-course disabilities have conditions that do not change, and the process of adaptation and adjustment to change can lead to a long period of stability that enables a return or remaining in "normalcy" for that person, in a sense. People with relapsing or recurring cycle disabilities face uncertainty every day, issues of disclosure or nondisclosure, and the difficult task of creating a meaningful life with little permanency.

The third parameter, *outcome,* addresses expected lifespan changes related to the disability. Progressive disabilities often lead to a more limited lifespan and necessitate addressing issues of mortality and spirituality, as well as the need to plan for times when a person's limited capacity may hamper genuine self-determination.

Each person approaches a disabling condition differently. While conditions may carry the same name or the same general symptoms and causative agents, each of us is different, and each of us will approach disability from our own unique viewpoint. It is important to recognize that there are an infinite number of possible ways a person can react to a change in functioning ability, and that, although some appear more functional and productive for the person than others, each person is doing some of the work that he or she needs so do in the way that is most suitable to them.

Questions for Thought and Discussion

1. Over and over again, people's stories seem to indicate a lack of general public knowledge about disability and disabling conditions. How can we address this problem and provide meaningful public education about specific disabilities?

2. Most people encounter a disabling condition as a part of the aging process: vision and hearing decrease, fingers lose dexterity, and muscles can lose their strength. Do you think that this much greater frequency of disability in older people affects the way in which the disability is perceived, by the older adult and by others in society?

3. How would you feel if you had a disability that would substantially shorten your lifespan? How do you think that your own feelings might impact your work with others?

4. In small groups, share an experience with disability, either your own or of someone you know. What are the commonalities? What are the differences?

5. Many people have difficulty in accepting themselves as "disabled" even though their condition may limit activities, sometimes severely. Are such clients in denial? Under what circumstances do you think this may be a problem for clients?

9

Understanding the Experience of Disability: Living with Limitations and Stereotypes

With onset, course, and outcome, Rolland's fourth parameter addresses the specific limitations experienced by people with disabilities. As we have already seen, "disability" is a very broad term encompassing a wide variety of conditions. It is well beyond the scope of this book to attempt to address or even to mention all of them. However, because understanding the lived experience of people with disabilities is important to our work, this chapter will explore a number of conditions and personal experiences to help readers to understand both the wide differences in experiences and disabilities, and the common themes that seem to transcend any one particular person. Understanding these lived experiences and themes will help us to prepare for the work of Part III, which will address skills for working across disability.

Accordingly, we have grouped disabilities into four *very* broad categories: limitations in mobility and energy, sensory limitations, limitations in communication, and limitations in reasoning ability and mental functioning. A fifth grouping, invisible and social disabilities, addresses conditions that are not immediately obvious to others and conditions that are very obvious and provoke strong reactions, such as burns, amputations, and deformities.

As we saw in Chapter 8, some conditions can cause limitations in more than one area. Strokes can cause limitations in energy, mobility, communication, and mental functioning. Developmental disabilities can cause limitations in communication, reasoning ability, and mobility. Mental illness can cause limitations in mental functioning, energy, communication, and sensory capacity. Additionally, mental illness may or may not be invisible.

Many disabilities are impairments only because of the limitations of the social context and the built environment. They are, in effect, *defined* as disabilities by the social environment. An example that personifies these conceptual differences is dwarfism. In terms of ability to function, a dwarf is not disabled because of being a dwarf. In the dominant medical model, dwarfism is included as a disabling condition. However, it is very clear that the disability is not in the person, but in the way in which the environment has been built around him or her. If the environment were built to accommodate people in a wide range of heights, a dwarf would not be disabled in any way. This is what is meant by the conceptual framework that posits that disability is a social construct, rather than something inherent in the individual. In the first chapter, we discussed models for conceptualizing disability. It is a good idea to reread that chapter now, in preparation for the work of this chapter, and to consider disability from more than one perspective.

Mobility Limitations

When we think of "disability," mobility limitations come immediately to mind. Mobility limitations personify disability in our society. The ubiquitous sign that indicates "handicap" or disability is a white wheelchair pattern against a blue back ground. This sign "represents" you whether your disability involves sight, hearing, communication, energy, or mental functioning. It is the symbol of generic disability.

Using the social construct model, mobility limitations occur because the built world does not readily accommodate people using alternative means of transportation.

Independent Wheelchair Mobility

People in wheelchairs were among the first to organize themselves into a politically active force and to advocate for change. Advocacy rights pioneers like Ed Roberts used a wheelchair for mobility, and people in wheelchairs were prominent forces in early disability rights sit-ins and protests. Sidewalk cuts were mandated primarily to enable people using wheelchairs to use the public streets. Today, wheelchairs and scooters, both manual and electric powered, are common sights on city streets. We have become accustomed to all these alternative forms of mobility and no longer regard them as an interesting rarity.

People use wheelchairs for many different reasons. Some users are paralyzed from an accident or injury causing paraplegia or quadriplegia. Some have degenerative diseases that make ambulation difficult and painful. Some users' physical weaknesses or energy levels make use of wheelchairs necessary. The condition that causes a person to use a wheelchair for mobility is not generally obvious; we see only the effect—the need to use an alternative means of mobility.

Although wheelchair mobility in public areas and within homes is assumed throughout much of the country today, people who use wheelchairs for mobility still do have to address some unique circumstances. It is generally necessary to look *up* to make eye contact with people who are standing, a position that is not always the most comfortable to maintain, especially with certain kinds of disabilities that make holding such a position tiring and painful. It's harder to get attention, harder to use appliances, and harder to use many public facilities. While newer pay phones are at waist level, the older ones may still be uncomfortably out of reach. Counters are often chest high—at the cleaner's, at restaurant cashiers, and at reception desks in busy offices. It's hard to get attention sometimes as people often look right through you to the person standing next to you.

Public transit is accessible—to a point, for not every bus along the route is equipped with a wheelchair lift, and the waits are often long and uncomfortable. Restrooms have a stall that accommodates wheelchairs, but it's often at the farthest end of the room and difficult to reach during theater intermissions. And at the theater, at the movies, at a concert, you can't choose where to sit but must use the allotted wheelchair spaces. Grocery store aisles are wider now and you can steer through them, and wonderful electric devices with baskets attached are often provided. But to do a really "heavy" shopping, you will need someone with you, for only a small amount of groceries fits into the little baskets. And once you have checked out, you may need to arrange for help to get your groceries home.

People who use wheelchairs, even for brief periods of time, are quick to notice the obstacles that are often invisible to walkers. Small cracks or uneven spots on the sidewalk become difficult problems. The texture of floor coverings is important—smooth textures work best. Tightly woven carpeting is sometimes all right. Deep piles make floor surfaces exhausting to traverse. And handicapped entrances aren't always where you think they will be: Sometimes they are at the farthest reaches of a building. One museum-loving tourist in Washington, DC, notes:

> I rolled myself along the Mall to the Museum of Natural History next to my husband, looking for a handicapped entrance near the main steps. There was none. The only handicapped entrance was on the opposite side of this massive building. Although I hate being pushed, it was farther than I could roll. (Anonymous, personal interview, 5/18/97)

In addition to the frustrations of maneuvering through the built environment, people in wheelchairs need to pay special attention their own bodies. Our bodies were not designed for sitting unmoving for long periods of time. We become stiff and sore after only a few hours. While time and adaptation helps to mitigate some of the discomfort, many people experience discomfort after a long time in a seat. Wheelchair padding helps a lot, as does a well-fitting wheelchair. But it's important also to change position, to move around during the day. This may be difficult if you are working in an office and sitting at a desk all day long. Sometimes, depending upon your condition, you may be unable to move yourself but must depend on others to assist you.

Your wheelchair becomes an extension of your body. It is a part of you in a very real sense. Wheelchairs require care and servicing. Battery-operated chairs require charging. Seats fray, and wheels become worn. Choosing a wheelchair and caring for it is an important task, and to the greatest extent possible, people in wheelchairs need to know all they can about how wheelchairs function.

People using wheelchairs become instantly aware of other people in wheelchairs around them. After all, it's easy to make eye contact with them! And there is often an immediate bond and an immediate understanding.

Dependent Wheelchair Mobility

Certain disabilities limit the use of arms, hands, legs, and feet. People who have strokes, for example, often lose the ability to move one or both sides of the body. In addition to being in a wheelchair, there's often a greater level of dependence in personal care, such as eating, bathing, toileting, and transfers. Electric wheelchairs can keep people independent, but are often bulky and heavy and may require a wheelchair van to move them from place to place in the community. When electric wheelchairs are not an option, it may be necessary for people to depend on other people to assist them with mobility needs.

Thad has multiple sclerosis and uses a wheelchair for mobility. He shares some of his experiences:

Personal Narrative

Some people are disabled from fatigue and there aren't any obvious signs. You can't make any assumptions about how people's problems will manifest themselves. People with MS can have cognitive issues that are hidden also—there are often memory losses and problems in processing information. People can get overwhelmed by too many stimuli. The stimuli mean we must encode things and then store them. Well, the encoding doesn't work as well. When we try to remember things, many times it's the pre-MS things that we remember easiest.

I was diagnosed in 1986. I had a really difficult time because I didn't have any medical insurance. That made me realize how important medical treatment was—because I had no insurance I couldn't get an MRI and so I couldn't get a definitive diagnosis. When I entered remission after my first exacerbation, I made sure to find a job that had good health insurance. The second time I had an exacerbation, I finally could get a definitive diagnosis.

When I first got MS, it was the exacerbation-remission cycle kind. Now it has become secondary progressive, and two years ago I had to stop working altogether. At first I refused to have a disabled parking permit, but later, I did get one.

My company was very good about job accommodations for me. The first thing I asked them was to change from a job that involved driving to one that was mostly desk work, and they did that. Later, I had to ask to come in later in the morning, and they adjusted my schedule. Then I moved from a position where I had to drive at times to one where I stayed in the office. That gave five more years of working full time.

I think you have to be flexible about work. You have to educate people about your disability. And you have to do the work of finding the accommodations that will work for you. The higher up you are in a company, the more likely you'll get support if you're disabled because the jobs are more flexible. At first, I was a service rep—you have to be there—so they might put you in another job entirely so you can have the flexibility you need. Employers don't like to do that.

Anything that's out of the ordinary—people don't like change. If you can think of another job, or a way to adapt your job, you'll have a better chance than if you expect them to do it. I think disability affects promotions. People look at you differently if you're disabled—but also they tend to work with you, especially if they see you are making an effort.

When I first got my diagnosis of MS, I went into denial. I went through all the stages of grieving and I made a very gradual change. Now I'm a peer counselor, and also I have many friends with MS. And one thing I found—*disability frees you from having to compare yourself with others*. That's a big thing.

Becoming disabled was a real transition I had to make. I came from a family that's very independent. I ran marathons. Now that I'm disabled, I recognize I need help from the community—from my wife, from my neighbors, from the Unitarian Church, from the MS Society.

For a long time, I was very frightened. But I learned that I have no control over this disease. Twenty years ago, I couldn't imagine not running. But you adapt.

I do have some observations about the disability community. There's this dichotomy between people in wheelchairs and people who aren't. There's fear. There's people who are working and people who are not working. I don't work but I go to the Jimmy Heuga Center and I go to a physical fitness program. You can be in the program whether you're in a wheelchair or not.

Jimmy Heuga was an Olympic skier who developed MS in his twenties at a time when the general consensus was that physical activity was bad for MS. This was very frustrating to him as an athlete. He developed a five-day educational program focused on proactive ways people with MS could help themselves live with the disease. The program is now given at different times in different areas for people with MS and their significant others to learn more about MS and develop a physical training program that works with their current condition. I really enjoyed the program because it was very positive and made me realize for the first time that just because people are in a wheelchair doesn't mean they couldn't walk a little bit and that they didn't have to be totally sedentary.

To work with people with disabilities, *listening* is important. And sometimes I think people say what's "expected" of them, but the feelings aren't there. You need to catch up— you need to *catch your feelings up to your words.* People are pretty decent. They want to help you. It can be an act of kindness on your part to let people help you—you can be giving as much as you are receiving.

People always look at me and smile. It can be annoying. I recognize that I used to do that too, before I became disabled. I think disability is more likely to expose you to decent people in the world. People who aren't decent just ignore you.

Community and relationships are what makes things rich in my life.

(Thad Smith, personal interview, 10/9/01)

Limitations Due to Energy Levels

Many limitations in mobility are caused not by trauma or directly by an illness or condition, but by the loss of energy that occurs as a side effect of the condition. Sometimes, simply *having* a condition or disability, or being treated for it, can use up enormous amounts of energy and leave the person feeling tired and weak. Medications can cause weakness, as can chemotherapy and radiation. It is not uncommon for people to sleep most of the day away after receiving debilitating treatments. Sometimes just getting out of bed is an effort beyond imagining.

Certain kinds of disabilities are particularly associated with losses in energy and exhaustion. Chronic fatigue syndrome leaves people feeling unable to perform the necessary daily tasks. Because this is one of those gradual-onset, hard-to-diagnose relapsing conditions, people with chronic fatigue syndrome often carry anxiety and stress along with the severe drop in energy level that is the principal feature of the condition. People with fibromyalgia have disrupted sleep patterns. Lack of proper sleep causes exhaustion and pain and a sharp drop in energy levels as well.

Another group of conditions that cause difficulties with energy are related to oxygen use and lung capacity. People with chronic obstructive pulmonary disease, asthma, emphysema, or adult respiratory distress syndrome also experience drops in energy levels that affect daily functioning. Connie is a psychologist who uses continuous oxygen. She describes her experience:

Personal Narrative

About twelve years ago, I started to be really affected by emphysema and asthma. I saw my X-rays, and I stopped smoking. My sister had it. My father died of it. But still I thought *this won't happen to me*. But it did. Now I am on continuous oxygen day and night. I'm in a wheelchair. I am tired a lot. I can't drive.

I really feel the loss of power that comes from the loss of independence. I am lucky to have a wonderful husband, who takes complete care of me. If I didn't have him, I'd have to go to an institution. He pushes me to try to do things, to try to do some things still.

He took me on a trip recently. We drove across the country. It was exhausting. We have this machine that makes oxygen from the air. But it broke at 10,000 feet, up in the mountains. Every stop, he had to find oxygen for me. I'm very much afraid of being without air. It's terrifying. My heart pounds.

I used to be very vain. I really cared about how I looked. Now I'm in a wheelchair and am connected to this machine all the time. I don't like how that makes me look, but there's nothing I can do about it. When I was living in the city, I was drinking too much. And I was feeling really suicidal. Now that I live out in the country, I stopped drinking and I don't feel suicidal any more.

I had lots of friends in San Francisco, but we had to move, so that I would have better air. Now we're out in the country and the air is much better, but I still can't do things. And if you can't do things, it's really hard to make friends. I go to a writing group once a week, and to water aerobics even if I can only do half of the class.

I think that people relate to me differently than they used to because of the oxygen. Just the outward appearance of the oxygen does that, and being in a chair. People look over my head all the time. They talk to my husband about me and ask him about me as though I wasn't there. It makes me laugh sometimes, but I don't confront them. I just let them talk over my head.

I have a friend who needs oxygen too, even more than I do. But I see that he never uses it when he goes to parties or meetings, because of the way people will react to him if he does. It makes you feel like a lesser person.

I have a love-hate relationship with my oxygen.

(Connie Lewis, personal interview, 9/7/01)

Physical illnesses are not the only cause of losses in energy levels. Mental illness, especially depression, can create similar conditions. There is an enormous amount of energy expended in addressing or simply living with mental illness. And sleepiness and energy loss is a common side effect of medication.

Sensory Limitations

Vision and hearing are the two primary sources of sensory limitations. Limitations can be a complete absence of the sense, as in blindness or deafness, or a partial absence, where vision or hearing is absent in certain aspects, at certain levels, or under certain conditions.

Education has been one of the earliest issues addressed for and by people who are deaf and/or blind. Schools for the blind and the development of Braille have made it possible for blind people to develop knowledge and skills for almost 150 years. Today, blind students generally attend regular classes, taking notes and doing assignments with the help of new technology. Schools for the deaf developed very early as well, and today classes in signing are offered on college campuses, in high schools, and through vocational education centers. New technologies have brought hearing to many deaf people, but to become a hearing person is a choice, a choice that is the subject of heated debate within the deaf community.

Blindness and Visual Impairments

Blindness and visual impairment is usually measured by tests of visual acuity, based on a medical model. We are all familiar with the expression "20/20 vision." Having 20/20 vision means that one can see, at a distance of twenty feet, what a "normal" eye can see. As visual acuity decreases, the standard 20 that represent "twenty feet" remains the same, but the second number changes. The higher the second number, the greater the visual impairment. To be legally blind, a person's vision must be 20/200, meaning that he or she can see at twenty feet what the "normal" eye can see at 200 feet. A measure of 20/80 in the best eye, with corrections, indicates a visual impairment. Using this model, there are about 500,000 people in the United States who are legally blind (Mackelprang & Salsgiver, 1999, p. 125) and a much larger number who are visually impaired.

Blindness. Most people today view blindness as one of the worst possible conditions that can befall a person, and there is reason to believe that this has been so for a long time. Aristotle notes that vision is our favored sense, the one we believe is the most important. To be without this sense is often considered a major tragedy, and a "normal" life is seen as an impossibility. Because of the general perception of blindness as a tragedy, and as something of which one is a "victim," blind people often epitomize those disabled people who "deserve" the help of others, both financial and otherwise. The image of the blind person is still today one of a poor person standing on the streetcorner, tin cup in hand, with life merely a sad echo of a "normal" life experience. But is it, really? What *is* a "normal" life, anyway? If it is a life with meaning and purpose, beauty, love, and friendship—these are all unrelated to sight.

Blindness, like wheelchair mobility, is also a social construct, and assistive technology has made the world a much friendlier place. Elevators ring once if they are going up, and twice if they are coming down, so they can be used with ease. Traffic lights chirp to indicate walk/don't walk. Railings in many places make walking more secure.

N. Kleege, blind since childhood, writes of her experience in writing her life story (Kleege, 1999, pp. 3–4):

Beyond my taste for the visual, I know what it means to be sighted, because I live in a sighted world. The language I speak, the literature I read, the art I value, the history I learned in school, the architecture I inhabit, the appliances and conveyances I employ were all created by and for sighted people. I find it easy to imagine what it's like to be sighted. I had to write this book to learn what it is to be blind.

The most valuable insight I can offer is this: Blindness is normal to me. As a general rule, I do not spend my days lamenting a lost sight; most days I don't even think about it. Although I can imagine what it's like to be sighted, I have trouble imagining myself as sighted, just as I have trouble imagining myself as Swiss. To analyze the impact of blindness on my life would require me to imagine myself living in a parallel universe of light, I would have to compare events in the life I have actually led to events in a life I can only imagine. Whether that imagined life would be better, richer, or more fulfilling, I can only speculate.

Gary's experience is similar, but also quite different:

Personal Narrative

I started to lose my sight when I was 28, in 1965. Before that, I had 20/20 vision. I was married. For the first six months, the doctors thought it would get better. They tried this and that—medicines, procedures. They said I had cataracts, then glaucoma, then panuveitis. They aren't really sure what I have even now—they still don't know much about it. It took a long time for me to become totally blind.

My wife left me pretty early on. She was divorced and had a kid. She needed financial support and stability and I couldn't give it to her. She became an alcoholic. She died from it later, too.

When my vision got bad, I lost my job. I was a licensed airplane mechanic. I worked one more year, then I went back to school through Cal Rehab and got a BA in general education. I did computers till my junior year, but then I changed because I decided I didn't like computers. I never got a job after I graduated. I just never found one.

One thing that really hurt me—I met a sighted girl while I was in college. She wanted to socialize, and I really liked her. I didn't know she was just pitying me. Finally, I asked her out on a date and she said no, she wouldn't go out with me because I was blind. That really hurt.

I opened my own business in 1970. I opened a cabinet shop and became a cabinet-maker. I always did love to build things. I loved to build since I was a kid. It seemed like a natural thing to do. I really built the business up and did very well. I had six employees. I lost my sight completely in 1982, but I kept my business going anyway. Then in 1991, the complex the business was in burned down completely. I decided to retire—I was 54 by then.

I went through depression at every stage of my loss of vision. I had to cope at each stage. I got really depressed when I lost my eyesight. As long as I had some vision, I functioned as though I was completely sighted. I missed some details in things, and maybe I was slower, but I thought of myself as sighted. After I lost my vision I had moments of despair, but I also felt very positive about a lots of things. I had a really high opinion of myself. Being blind didn't change that at all.

I don't identify with any disability movements or with blind political or grassroots organizations. I think people in those organizations are full of self-pity. And they have their hands out, too.

I think sighted people have a really hard time relating to blind people. They approach you, but they don't really know how to. They really are approaching the stereotype. The person is ignored. I go to restaurants with sighted people and the waitresses talk with them and ignore me. Recently I took some sighted people out for lunch. I got the bill and payed it. But then when the waiter came back, he gave my change to the sighted people.

Sighted people have such stereotypical views of us. Like that we wear dirty clothes or that we eat like slobs. They see us as defenseless and useless. But they don't help us—they don't tell us when our clothes are spotted, they just see us as not neat. And they infantilize us.

I dated a woman for thirteen years. She was blind too. She was walking down the street with her little boy and he said to her, "Look mommy, there's a man with a cane just like yours." We had a good relationship till just a few months ago. I guess most of my friends are blind too. But not because they are blind—it's because sighted people have such a hard time making friends with us. They don't really see us. They just see the cane.

I'm any male with a cane. They mix me up with people who look completely different from me, just because of the cane. When I lost my business in the fire, I went to my competitor to ask for a job. We had bid against each other three or four times a month for twenty years. But he wouldn't give me a job. He said it was because of the insurance.

Another problem, I walk down the street and get to a crosswalk. I start across but then I move out of the crosswalk. People start yelling at me, "Go straight, go straight!" but don't they know I have no idea which way "straight" is? And that that's why I went out of the crosswalk?

When I meet people, they say to me, "I know so-and-so, who is blind too," or "I have a friend who is blind." They try to use that to build rapport with me. In the beginning, when you first become blind, you believe them. But then you realize that they are making it up a lot of the time. They don't really know anyone who is blind.

I have a good life. I love to read talking books. I listen to talk shows on radio and TV. I do miss driving—I loved that freedom. Now I'm dependent on the bus. I use the computer for e-mail. I do have to work hard on my memory—you have to use your memory a lot to keep it. You have to remember where you put things all the time. I tape record everything—addresses, phone numbers, events. I use a scanner to read my mail. And they just adapted a new bar code scanner to read codes on cans. So you can take a can of soup and scan it and know what kind it is. You can shop on your own too, because you can just scan items to learn what they are. But it's not ready to use yet—there are millions of items in a grocery store, and the same thing comes in different brands and different sizes—it's a lot to put into a computer!

I've adapted to being blind. It doesn't bother me. It was harder to lose my business in the fire than to lose my sight. I've been blind now for thirty years.

If I can say one thing to the people who will read this book: Accept an individual for what he *is,* not for what he *represents.* Don't write him off—see him as a human being. You don't have to socialize with me, just accept me as a human being.

(Gary Heaton, personal interview, 10/24/01)

Visual Impairment.   To learn about the experience of vision limitations, the Lighthouse has designed a set of eight pairs of glasses. Each one allows the sight that would be available with a certain condition. For example, the pair of glasses for blurred vision presents a hazy, fuzzy view of the world. The pair for macular degeneration, a progressive condition often found in older adults, has spots of varying sizes randomly placed on the lens. The one for peripheral vision has a darkened center and admits light only from the sides. Using these glasses, as we shall see in Chapter 10, can help us to understand the experience of vision impairment.

While visual impairment allows for easier navigation than blindness does, the effort of trying to focus around and through the limitation is often tiring. People with visual impairments must rest their eyes frequently. Some people actually find it easier to wear dark glasses and give up the broken, distorted sight that they have.

Kleege says she "became blind" and began to use a cane and learn Braille, during the process of writing her book. Her condition, macular degeneration, enables her to have only a very limited peripheral vision. This is her description of what she sees:

> At the 1992 Matisse exhibition in New York's Museum of Modern Art, a man said to me, "You're standing too close to that painting. You have to stand back to really see it."
>
> He was right. I was standing a foot away from a canvas large enough for most people to view comfortably from a distance of several yards. When I look at a painting from a sighted person's distance, macular degeneration, my form of blindness, obscures or distorts the center of the canvas. My peripheral vision is unaffected, so the edges of the canvas are more or less visible. To get a general sense of the overall composition, I scan the painting systematically moving my oversized blind spot around it, allowing different regions to emerge into my peripheral vision. My brain slowly identifies the forms and assembles the picture bit by bit, In effect, my mind sketches an outline, or a map. "To the left, there's a table with a basket of fruit. To the right, there's a window with a view of the sea." (Kleege, pp. 93–94)

Jean lives in a life-care facility for seniors. She describes her experience:

> I never could see really well. I've been wearing glasses since I was 12. I have macular degeneration now. I've had it for five years. I don't know what will happen in the future. I don't want to know my prognosis. I really would rather not know.
>
> When I watch TV, I have to sit really close to the television. And when I go out walking—when I go to San Francisco—I take my cane with me. It makes me feel more secure to take it with me. So if I bump into people, they'll know why and they won't get annoyed.
>
> I do all the things I used to do. I'm lucky to be here in St. Paul's Towers [a life-care community]. They do all the cooking and cleaning and laundry. I wouldn't be able to do any of that. But here, everything is done for me. And I'm here with my husband. He can't hear very well, but he has a hearing aid and he does just fine. We both do.
>
> I don't think of myself as a disabled person. I think of myself the same way I always did. Nothing has changed.
> (Jean Levit, personal interview, 10/15/01)

Deafness and Hearing Limitations

Deafness.   While we think of deafness, like blindness, in terms of the medical model, it is important to understand that there is a strong social component here as well. Rather than focusing on entering mainstream society, a distinct separate deaf culture has developed. As a culture, there are power issues and interaction issues here; however, Deaf culture as a separate entity has proven itself viable and functional in meeting the needs of its members in every sphere.

More than any other group of disabilities, deaf people have developed a distinct and separate culture within the wider U.S. culture mosaic. Deaf culture has all of the distinguishing marks of a culture: a language, terminology and expressions, criteria for participation and membership, and an established way of interacting, as a culture, with other cultures. The growth of Deaf culture was dramatically enabled when the manualists won the communications war and created American Sign Language.

In the last century, there were two schools of thought about deaf communication: The auralists held that deaf people needed to function in the wider society, and that therefore they needed to learn to speak and to read lips. The manualists held that it was faster, easier, and more efficient for deaf people to communicate manually, using sign language. For many years, the arguments raged bitterly through the deaf community and education centers for deaf children. Today, almost all deaf people communicate using ASL.

Deaf culture is a very tight-knit community. In a world where boundaries between groups are permeable and intermarriage is steadily increasing, 90 percent of deaf people marry deaf people (Pray, 1997, in Mackelprang & Salsgiver, 1999, p. 107). In these times of prenatal testing, deaf parents must address the possibility of knowing ahead of time that they will have a hearing child, one who will not be an integral part of deaf culture as they are. There is often a strong ambivalence, if not outright disappointment, when parents learn they will have a hearing child.

Because the community is so strong, it is also able to meet almost all the needs of members within its boundaries. Schools and universities, sports teams, religious groups, employment training, and recreational opportunities are all available within the community. Where members of the community go "outside," to school or to work, they generally choose to socialize and associate with other community members within the larger entities.

This exclusivity often makes it more difficult for a hearing person to understand how the Deaf community operates. It is necessary at the very least to learn ASL, and to demonstrate a willingness to understand and value the institutions of Deaf culture. Without knowledge of ALS, people must communicate through the use of interpreter, often a cumbersome and expensive process.

It is important to remember that using a diversity/cultural model for thinking about deafness, though helpful in many ways in understanding and valuing deaf society, ideals, and cultural richness, also justifies and supports the separation between deaf people and hearing people. If we think, instead, in terms of deafness as a social construct, we can consider that it is quite possible for each person to learn many ways of communicating. We see this clearly in multilingual classrooms, where children are routinely taught not only the language of their culture but several others as well. The same values that underlie this approach—that we live in a world where we need to be able to interact with many different people—could support the teaching of ASL as routine in U.S. classrooms. This would dissolve the social construct that keeps deaf people separated from hearing people in society. However, it would be important to consider both the preferences of the deaf community and the value of continuing deaf culture as a culture in the future.

Hearing Impairments.   Of the 21 million deaf and hard-of-hearing people in the United States, more than 20 million are hard of hearing. Limitations in hearing increase in frequency with age but can affect people of any age. The technology of assistive devices has grown enormously in the past decade, and smaller and more accurate devices have been able to minimize the effects of hearing limitations for many people.

People who are hard of hearing rarely identify with Deaf culture and generally do not learn sign language. Because such high numbers are elderly, they tend to identify as hearing people with a problem. When hearing aids and louder voices no longer help, people who are hard of hearing often learn lip reading and can become quite efficient at this technique. They also may prefer written communication—a message board or pad and pencil, kept close at hand, assists with communication.

Deedee shares her experience of gradually losing her hearing:

Personal Narrative

I noticed I had a problem while I was in college. I could hear better in one ear than in the other. I couldn't hear people on the phone if I held the phone to my right ear. I lost my hearing over a period of over thirty years.

It gets tedious not to hear well. I always had to ask people to repeat things. It was tedious for people to have to do that. A lot of times, you answer a question totally inappropriately. You don't even realize it. So you learn to use facial clues—you watch people's expressions to see if what you answered had nothing to do with the question. Then you say, "I'm sorry, I misunderstood." I couldn't hear people saying my name either. So then I would get a reputation as a snob for not acknowledging people.

I work in the school system as a speech therapist. Funny, isn't it? A speech therapist with a hearing problem. But it never affected my work in any way.

When I got to the point that I wanted hearing aids, I had a real fight about it. They told me I wasn't deaf enough. Now the technology is better, but then the problem was that if your hearing wasn't really bad, they couldn't screen out all the background noise with an aid. I got them anyway—got hearing aids that fit in my ear, for both ears. The only problem I have now happens when things are *really* loud around me. My aids are digitally set to my audiogram: If it gets really loud I have to take them out. If you don't have hearing aids, I think your brain adjusts to really loud noises and screens some of the noise out. My hearing aids don't do that, though. I went to New York to see a Broadway show with a friend who didn't use hearing aids. We were in the front and it was really loud. I just took my hearing aids out, but she really suffered.

When I got my hearing aids, people asked me if I was going to change my hairstyle. I wear my hair back over my ears. If I wore it down, no one would know I had hearing aids because they are the in-the-ear kind. But I like my hairstyle, and I didn't change it.

I walk with girlfriends a few times a week around Baltimore. The first time I walked with them after I got my aids, nobody said anything. When we finally stopped for coffee, I asked them why they didn't say anything about my hearing aids. They said they hadn't even noticed.

I think appearance is a factor though. People accept people with glasses really easily, and they are an aid too. But they don't accept people with hearing aids as much. They better start, though, because we're going to have a lot more people with hearing aids in the country soon—all those rock and rollers lose hearing when they listen to all that loud music. And people that play in orchestras lose hearing too. They often wear little ear plugs in their ears because of how loud the instruments can be.

If you're working with someone with a hearing impairment, face them. Don't talk louder. If they have a hearing impairment, it doesn't help for you to talk louder.

(Deedee Remenick, personal interview, 10/16/01)

Limitations in Communication

In the previous section, we discussed one form of limitation in communication: the limitation that occurs because deaf people cannot speak, and hearing people cannot sign. This communication limitation has a major impact on our society because of the large number of deaf and hard-of-hearing people in our country.

There are other limitations in communication, however, and these do not provide the richness of experience and communication alternatives available through Deaf culture. Often, people with aphasia and other communication limitations live locked in a private world of silence, unable to interact or to communicate needs, hopes, dreams, and feelings, and/or unable to understand and process the things that are said to them.

Human beings are social beings. We live in a social world, and much of what gives life meaning occurs in the context of social interactions. We reach out to other people, and we receive what other people give to us. As human beings, the most basic way in which this interaction occurs is through the spoken word.

When the ability to communicate verbally is lost, gesture, expressions, body position—all the nonverbal cues that are hardly noticed but are processed by our brains and integrated into our understanding—become essential. When nonverbal communication is also lost, we talk about being "locked in," one of the most difficult and painful circumstances a human being can experience.

Expressive Aphasia and Other Limitations in Speech

Expressive aphasia, whether complete or partial, often accompanies cerebral accidents and head trauma. With expressive aphasia, people are unable to use the proper words, or to form words at all in order to communicate. People with expressive aphasia often have other limitations that are confining in physical ways. Aphasia is confining in mental and emotional ways.

As with deafness, people with aphasia can use alternative forms of communication. Writing, using a communications board, gesturing, and forming words that others can lip read are some of the ways people use to communicate. However, because of the effort involved in communicating, it is often only the most basic needs that are communicated, and not inner reflections, emotions, or complex material and ideas.

A short essay (Aspen, 1996, p. 181) will help us to understand some of the feelings and experiences of people who have difficulty in communicating:

What did you Soy?

Do you get your nongue in tots? Is your life full of herbal goofs? Do you "Tune off the televasion," or say "Hello Knickers" to Nicky? Do you try to buy "fruit guns" or "jeans with electrocuted waists?" Do you eat a "bowl of sellotape" for breakfast and ask your partner to "sass the mugar?" I do. It's enough to make me suck.

It affects my smelling—I mean "spelling." "Anybordy" is my favorite, but "paynut" and "hoing gome" comes close. I can't get my gear into brain.

I recently warned a friend she was "Making a rod for her own bath." I told another to "Avoid it like a bargepole." "You want your face and eat it," I admonished. It just goes to show how long you can be. Romance is not spared . . . watching a sunset with my partner, I murmur "You don't get evenings like *this* on a plate. "I lug you" is so passionate, don't you think?

That suns it up wall. Mostly I loff but sometimes I get fed enough.

PS If you knees an explanation write to me personably. If you want a replay, send a stomped envelope.

Receptive Aphasia

People with receptive aphasia and other limitations such as some kinds of learning disabilities have difficulty in processing verbal and/or written communication. What reaches the brain is not comprehensible. Unlike people with other forms of aphasia, whose difficulties are readily apparent, people with receptor limitations often struggle in silence to understand and react in an appropriate manner to things that do not make sense to them.

A client with learning difficulties and an inability to read and process language shares this "menu" (Anonymous, 4/15/87). What would you order from this restaurant?

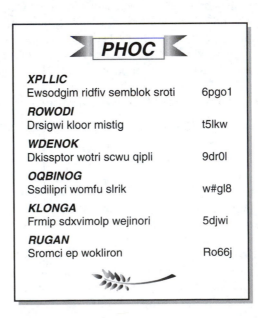

PHOC

XPLLIC
Ewsodgim ridfiv semblok sroti   6pgo1

ROWODI
Drsigwi kloor mistig   t5lkw

WDENOK
Dkissptor wotri scwu qipli   9dr0l

OQBINOG
Ssdilipri womfu slrik   w#gl8

KLONGA
Frmip sdxvimolp wejinori   5djwi

RUGAN
Sromci ep wokliron   Ro66j

Limitations in Reasoning Ability and Mental Functioning

This very broad group of disabilities includes developmental disabilities (also known as mental retardation), mental illness, Alzheimer's disease and the senile dementias, and brain injury. Our ability to reason and to function mentally is basic to our integration into society. When this ability is absent or lost, we are often separated from society, sometimes in very physical ways. This is at least partially due to the differences in the ways in which physical and mental disabilities are viewed in our society.

Many times we think about people with physical disabilities in the context of victim-hood. Bypassing the vestiges of the moral model, we view people as unfortunates who are suffering through no fault of their own. As such, they "deserve" our sympathy, assistance, and consideration. It is illustrative of this concept that early programs for disabled people focused on those who were blind and deaf, and then on "victims" of war, the returning soldiers of the Civil War and World War I. People with physical disabilities still today often live with their families, perhaps with assistance from various programs designed to help people with physical needs. When someone with a profound disabling condition or intractable physical pain wants to end life, we argue about the relative merits and individual rights of "euthanasia," a "good death."

When people with profound mental illness, mental dysfunction, or mental pain want to end life, we call that suicide. Unlike euthanasia, suicide is not a "good death." It was, in fact, a felony in many states until the mid-twentieth century. "American law retains an extremely strong precedent against the legal permission of suicide" (Battin, 1982, p. 17). Where is the difference, and how does that apply to people with reasoning and mental dysfunctions?

Despite medical evidence that links limitations in mental functioning to genetics, predisposition, life circumstances, chemical imbalances, and other causes that are out of the person's individual control, we often continue to regard limitations in mental functioning, particularly mental illness and substance abuse, as "caused" by the person's inability or refusal to "take control" of his or her life and behave in a socially acceptable manner. These constructions of what is and what is not are what help to make limitations in mental functioning and reasoning ability a social construct rather than a physical "fact" like paralysis or blindness.

It is difficult to gain a good experiential grasp of these kinds of limitations, for people who experience them generally do not write about them. However, it is important to understand some of their unique kinds of experiences.

Cognitive Limitations: Developmental Disability

Though developmental disability may not be a "culture" in the way of Deaf culture, there is clearly a "world" of developmental disability. This world is composed of people who have developmental disability and those who love them, care for them, teach them, and hire them. There are behavior rules and independence rules, a structure within which people with developmental disability have optimal independence to run their own lives and make their own decisions. The film *I Am Sam* provides viewers with an excellent insight into the "culture" of developmental disabilities, as well as an understanding of one of the challenging issues—parenting—that faces people with such disabilities.

Because of the constant state of dependency and care in which developmentally disabled people live, the world of developmental disability is a "yes" world. Compliance is a learned social behavior. This assists caregivers and enables people to work, live, and learn. But the sad fact is that over 80 percent of people with developmental disability experience abuse, either physical, sexual, or emotional, at some time during their lives (Everson, 2001). Abuse comes from caregivers and from family members. The learned compliance allows the abuse and enables it to be kept secret in many instances.

Improper physical contact occurs easily because many developmentally disabled people are used to other people touching them in very private areas. They are often assisted with bathing and toileting. How can it be that touching the genitals for toileting is OK, but for other things is not OK? It can be hard to understand this! This example of both learned compliance and a blurring of lines between proper and improper physical contact was offered at a developmental disability workshop for adult protective service workers (Everson):

> "Do you want to go to school?"
> "Yes."
> "Do you want a sandwich?"
> "Yes."
> "Do you like tuna fish sandwiches?"
> "Yes."
> "Do you like me?"
> "Yes."
> "Can I touch your breasts?"
> *You* guess the answer.

People with developmental disabilities are often very vulnerable when they go out alone into the community. Reassurance is offered by traveling and working in groups, which often serve as a protective device. But groups do not protect people from the stares, the rudeness, the avoidance, and the abuse of others.

With education and training, people with developmental disabilities can live pleasantly and productively in the world. The young man speaking here, who has Down syndrome, exudes pride and confidence in his achievements:

> After finishing high school, I worked as a teller at a bank, and now I am working at the Peekskill Chamber of Commerce. I take public transportation to work. I am being trained on the computer and I use the fax machine, the copier, and do filing. I have prepared mailings and special projects, and I answer the phone and provide information. I also help walk-in customers with directions or events in our community. . . . When I am with my family, I like water skiing, downhill skiing, tennis, and ping pong. I enjoy traveling, eating pizza, watching baseball, and wrestling. Every day, I read the newspaper so I know what is happening in the world.
>
> My message to all of you is to keep your minds open to the idea that we should be able to make our own choices. If young people with Down syndrome are given the opportunity to have many experiences in life, we will be better prepared to make decisions for ourselves. My advice to you is to encourage children and young adults with Down syn-

drome to have dreams and goals and to believe that success comes from belief in ourselves. (Nadel & Rosenthal, p. 247–48)

People with developmental disabilities also frequently are not informed about sexual issues, and sexuality and sexual relationships are discouraged. Issues of how to define "consenting" or even "adult" present special difficulties. It is important to recognize that people with developmental disabilities are sexual beings and to provide needed information and discussions when maturity is reached.

As people with developmental disabilities age, other disabilities that are often age-related compound the difficulties they face. Someone with developmental disability experiences the Alzheimer's, or the hearing limitation, or the stroke, in a unique manner, and caregivers often find it especially difficult to care for older people with developmental disabilities and multiple other limitations.

Limitations in Cognitive Functioning: Alzheimer's and Senile Dementia

Limitations in cognitive functioning due to Alzheimer's and the senile dementias differ from developmental disabilities in that they occur later in life, generally after a person has developed relationships with family members, friends, employers, and others based on a different level of functioning. Stressful for both the individuals and families, people with Alzheimer's and dementias experience personality and behavior changes, changes in reasoning ability and perception, and related changes as well.

There is a wide variation in the experiences of people with Alzheimer's and dementias. Some people become anxious, agitated, aggressive, and confrontational with others, while others are peaceful, happy, and pleasant, and every possible permutation between these also occurs. The changes seem to bear almost no relationship to the personality and behavior of the person prior to the onset of the condition. Alzheimer's and dementia are usually gradual in onset, which can enable individuals and family members to try to prepare for the changes ahead.

In the early stages, memory is affected, as well as the ability to use words. Sleep is disrupted and people often fall asleep at odd hours of the day. Episodes of aggressiveness and inability to think in other than black-and-white terms begin to affect relationships at home and work. Later, driving may be compromised, and families often must face the agonizing decision to report the person as an unsafe driver in order to prevent accidents.

Later, more extreme variations in behavior may occur, and medication may become necessary, as well as one-on-one care. Family members are often severely affected: The person they know and loved is gone, and the person who lives in that body is unfamiliar and often unpleasant. Strong support networks are important for both families and individuals.

Because of the nature of this group of disabilities, not much has been written by people with Alzheimer's and dementia. The narrative below is drawn from several separate interviews.

Personal Narrative

My daughter got me a hat I loved. It said, "Of all the things I lost, I miss my mind the most'. I live in a life-care building, and I used to wear my hat in the elevator all the time. Everyone laughed and really enjoyed it. But I don't know what happened to it. One day it was just gone.

I've always been a person who valued work. I've worked all my life, and I still work now, even though I'm ninety-three years old. But I am having a tough time. One of the things I was doing was entering things on a computer at a museum where I volunteer. I was making a list of everything in the collection. I did it for years, and my goal was to finish the project before I die. But I didn't. I started to push the wrong buttons on the computer and things would happen that I didn't understand. Sometimes I worked all day and then it all got lost. I made a lot of mistakes. Now they got a new computer and they are telling me that no one knows how to work it. No one can teach me.

I even forget to go sometimes, because I don't ever know what day it is. It's getting worse and worse. I can't remember anything. Sometimes I make arrangements to do two and once three things at the same time because I don't remember the other things. The other day, I didn't meet people I was supposed to play bridge with. I forgot. It was awful. They tell me I call the nurse all the time but I don't think I do. I don't remember. They say when the nurse comes I don't know why she is here.

But no one tells me what pills to take. I get pills from the doctor and I don't know when I'm supposed to take them. I have a box with the days of the week and the times but I don't know what day it is so it doesn't help me. And then I get new pills and I don't know what I'm supposed to do with them.

I lose things all the time. I lose my cane and my wallet and my pocketbook. I lose sweaters. Sometimes I lose things I really care about. I look for things for hours and hours at a time and it's hard to do that because it makes me very tired. Some things I find, but some things I care about are gone forever. I was taking a little silver dish to my grand-daughter once, in Los Angeles. I didn't want to leave it in the car when we stopped for lunch, so I took it into the restaurant. And then I just left it there. No one ever found it. It was my own grandmother's. That was really hard.

The other day, I had to ask my daughter when my husband's birthday was because I wanted to remember. Then I realized I couldn't remember hers either, or my son's. I wrote them all down, but now I can't find the piece of paper anywhere. That happens all the time. I write things down and then I lose the piece of paper.

I'm so agitated all the time, so anxious. It makes my heart palpitate and that makes it even worse. I don't know why I'm so anxious, except that I worry about things all the time. I worry if I'm supposed to do something. If I have nothing to do and I'm in my apartment, I get even more anxious. Then I call the nurse—and that's when she comes and I don't remember what I was supposed to ask her. I have to be with people all the time. When I'm with other people I'm less nervous.

My mind was the thing I valued the most. I used my mind all my life. I worked as head of the Indexing Department for Americana Encyclopedia for twenty-five years. I did freelance work for the State Department. Now I'm so confused I can't remember anything. And it's getting worse every day. They made me hire someone to come in the morning and help me get dressed. I was afraid she would take my watch and my bedside clock and my picture frame with my mother and my cousin in it and so I hid them. I think she must have

found them because I looked everywhere and I can't find them anywhere. I don't want to accuse her of taking them. What should I do?
(Nelda Cassuto, personal interview, 5/14/98)

Mental Illness

In his book *The Manufacture of Madness,* Thomas Szaz takes the position that mental illness is a myth created by society to explain conduct that is outside of the norm for that society. "We call people mentally ill," Szaz writes, "when their personal conduct violates certain ethical, political, and social codes" (Szaz, 1970, p. 23).

In this sense, we can clearly see that mental illness itself is a social construct. Behavior that is valued and praised in one society may be unacceptable in another. Violation of the social norms, which are social constructs, places a person morally in the wrong, and the moral model is perhaps the most dominant conceptual framework today, providing the lens through which we view "mental illness" in our society. Substances accepted for consumption in one society may be against the law in others. Both the acceptance and the denial are social constructs. The moral model, as we know, places blame directly on the individual for his or her behavior, and this is exactly what occurs in regard to mental illness and substance abuse in our society.

Mental illness affects millions of people in the United States at some period of their lives, or all of their lives, and it affects their families and their communities. Mental illness, along with substance abuse, is perhaps the most negatively judged limitation in our society. It is assumed, as stated earlier, that people with mental illness and substance abusers *could* control their condition if they *wanted* to. They *don't* want to because they are weak, powerless, and/or evil.

The course of mental illness varies greatly among individuals, and also among conditions. Schizophrenia is said to "burn out" in midlife, and people affected by this can often resume, or begin, lives in society at that point. Medications manage people with manic depression, and with depressive illnesses, as well as psychoses.

Mental illness, as well as substance abuse history, are disabilities that are included in the ADA, and accommodations are expected to be made by employers for applicants and employees who become disabled during the course of employment (Mancuso, 1994). However, employees and employers have difficulty with accommodations, particularly with employees with manic-depressive disorder, whose cyclical nature often resembles that of relapsing or recurring kinds of physical disabilities. In addition to the needs of people with mental illness themselves, family members often face stress and anxiety. Community networks that address both needs provide support and a place of refuge for individuals and families.

When Congress enacted legislation that eventually closed the large hospitals where people with mental illnesses were housed, often for a lifetime, and mandated that there be community resources for assisting people to return to their communities, many people with mental illnesses were released. They gravitated to the cities. However, the needed funding and programs were not available, and large numbers became homeless, wandering city streets often without medication, medical care, or any way of meeting basic needs. While mental illness is often an isolating disability, communities of homeless people with mental illnesses have slowly formed. These provide a sense of safety and security, a vehicle for socialization, and a group of people knowledgeable about the resources needed to meet any need.

A client who has depression and anxiety disorder, and a brother with schizophrenia, shares her experiences:

Personal Narrative

My brother is two years older than me. I loved him so much, and still do, and when I was a kid, I really looked up to him all the time. He went into the army after high school (and to Vietnam). When he came home, he was a schizophrenic. My father had to work really hard to get his disability through the veteran's, but finally they gave him 80 percent. He wanted to be on his own, so he got apartments to rent with his disability check. He tore every one of them up. My parents had to keep paying to fix them, and moving him somewhere else. Finally they got him a home of his own. He tore that up too, but at least it was his. It's because he never wanted to take any medications and we couldn't make him do it.

My parents died ten years ago, and I have to look after my brother now. He used to walk over to neighbors' houses and rip off their screen doors, tear up yards and gardens, and mess up cars. The police got called because his neighbors are scared to death of him. He's a pretty big guy, and I can understand that. He's conserved now, and on medications and he's much better. People get conserved when the courts find them incompetent to take care of themselves. The judge appoints what is, in effect, a guardian to make decisions on behalf of the person. People with mental illnesses can get conserved if they injury or damage themselves or others.

I know people with schizophrenia are supposed to "burn out." But it's been thirty years, and he hasn't burned out at all. I don't think he ever will! I started to get really depressed and anxious when my parents died. I was just overwhelmed with the idea of trying to take care of my brother. I had to go into treatment, which was good, because I had a lot of issues about my mother. I still do. I feel as though I never got a real chance to grieve about her, because of my brother. I worry that I can't take care of him. I know I don't have to, any more, now that he's conserved, but I still can't sleep because I just think about it all the time. I can't even work any more. I take medications myself. They help a lot.

Everything makes me so nervous. I worry all the time about everything. I can't stop worrying. I tell people all the things that worry me, but nothing helps. I just know something is going to go wrong, and it's going to be my fault.

(Anonymous, personal communication, 12/6/01)

Visibility: A Special Challenge

When disabled people interact with others in society, the disability itself becomes one of the factors in the interaction, often determining quality and quantity of relationships. A special problem often faced by people is that of visibility: Some disabilities, both physical and mental, may not be instantly visible and recognizable to others; others are instantly apparent. Of these, some are related to a limitation in functioning such as we have been discussing, but others are disabilities *only* in the sense that they create social situations similar to those created by an actual mental or physical limitation. These may be called *societally determined* disabilities.

Invisible Disabilities

Many disabilities are not immediately obvious. Others may be obvious only when they are in a relapsing or reoccurring state. Invisible disabilities pose a special challenge, because sharing is voluntary, not obligatory, much of the time. There are circumstances where invisible disabilities are often shared by necessity: when special arrangements are needed for testing or learning in an academic setting, for example, or when work schedules will be affected. But there are many other situations where relationships can form, and develop, without information of the disability being shared. When do you share this information? With people you date, right away or after three dates, or six? With friends and co-workers, right away, later, or maybe never? With casual acquaintances? With people you meet at an affair or event? If something related to disability comes up, should you share then?

Sharing makes the invisible visible. It identifies you with disability—as different from others. And if you don't have to be different, when and why would you choose to be?

A woman with a learning disability shares her experiences:

Personal Narrative

I'm in college now, and this problem is just always there. It's with me every semester. I did go to register myself as a disabled student, but to get the time I need to do my work, I have to take a letter to every instructor and ask for special accommodations. I know the instructor will keep this confidential, but I really hate to do it anyway. I want to be a student just like everyone else.

When we start the semester, everyone is the same. We have class discussions, we listen to our instructors, and I forget in class sometimes that I have a disability. Each semester I think, can I get away with it? Can I get through the semester without anyone knowing? Everything is fine til midsemester. And then the first assignment comes due. Or a test is being given the next week. And every time, I go through this internal battle. Should I get the accommodation request, or not? In one course, I did the paper assignment and handed it in on time without saying anything. But then the test came up.

I felt that I wanted to try to take the test with everyone else. I think sometimes that people in my class notice that I'm not there, and they guess why. So I decided to try. And then I have to ask myself, what's more important, the instructor and maybe even some classmates knowing, or failing the test? The test wins every time.

When I hand the instructor the accommodation request, I feel as though things are changed. Sometimes instructors become kind of patronizing, or oversolicitous. Or that's how it feels to me, anyhow. And then I'll wish I hadn't made my disability known.

Maybe I'll try without the accommodation next semester.

(Anonymous, class presentation, 4/14/90)

Visible Nondisabilities: Disfigurement

At the other end of the spectrum are people who have visible differences, such as a bone deformity, severe facial scarring or birthmarks, or anatomical differences that can be either congenital, accidental, or necessitated by other circumstances, such as major surgery of cancer for the face, which removes a part of the jaw.

The visible difference stands between the person and other people in society. The difference, in and of itself, is often not disabling. What causes disability, then, is the reaction of others—the horror, the fascination, the fear, the pity, all reactions that erode self-esteem and can easily cause the avoidance of public spaces and public events. Visible difference is, clearly, a *social* disability. Research findings have noted that the difficulties experienced by people are similar, regardless of the kind of difference, and regardless of the severity. Sometimes a relatively minor disfigurement has powerful effects on the life of the person (Robinson, 1997, p. 103).

People who have visible differences feel avoided and rejected by others, and evidence suggests that this is reality and not paranoia on the part of the person. This continuous avoidance and rejection creates social anxiety, a poor self-image, depression, and low self-esteem and self-confidence (Robinson, p. 103) Children who are born with a congenital disfigurement have a greater than average risk of having insecure attachments, and the reaction and sensitivity of the mother or nurturing figure is vital, for it has a major effect on future well-being. The whole family is affected by society's reaction to the disfigured member (Walters, 1997, pp. 113–14, 119). Social support, social skills, and optimism are strong determinants of the ability of the person to cope with being visibly different.

The excerpts included here are from the experience of Maureen, a primary-school teacher in Yorkshire, England, born with a large port wine stain on one side of her face (Williams, 1997, pp. 15–16).

> When I was in fifth form, aged 15 to 16 years old, the specialist at the hospital arranged for me to make a promised visit to Max Factor in London to learn to apply makeup. . . . I learned the basics of applying foundation, powder, and eye makeup. . . . I came home a different person; I thought I looked like a million dollars . . .
>
> Since that day, I have always worn makeup for work and my social life. With the family and on holiday, especially abroad, I don't wear makeup. I feel I am two different people: my made-up self and my natural self. . . .
>
> From school I went on to college and I really took off. I was away from home. I felt attractive and for the first time I had boyfriends. People who met me made up didn't ask questions and so I never told them about my face. . . . I met Richard, my husband, while I was at college and he was at university. After going out with him for some time, I became more anxious that he should know the truth, the terrible truth as I saw it at the time. I was very frightened to tell him in case it changed our relationship. . . .
>
> He said he had guessed my makeup covered some skin disfigurement but he thought from my serious tone that the something important was life-threatening, like cancer. . . .
>
> Isn't that how it is to the people who really know us and care for us? Our disfigurement is not an issue [to them]. We ourselves can make it into a barrier. We ourselves can make it come between us and our dealings with others.

. . . From the little girl who prayed that when she woke up in the morning she might look in the mirror and see a face without an ugly red mark, I have become a woman of 50 years old who still hopes for a miracle but in reality knows that I am as I am.

The feeling is always there, though, that you are different (apart from others). I think you will always feel different because you are different. You are different because you look different. You look different because of that disfigurement, which you can't change. Because of that, you have a whole area of experience that only others who are disfigured as you are can share; but that does not stop you having the same feelings as others, the same emotions, likes and dislikes, responsibilities and enjoyments. You have the same entitlements in life and that life might bring more trials but lots of joys too; perhaps it will make you stronger.

Chapter Summary

In this chapter, we have been given a special window into the minds and hearts of people with disabilities. Each experience has been different, and yet also the same. For each has felt the common prejudice, discrimination, and avoidance that people with disabilities experience every day in the "real world." Yet it is easy to see into each person also, and to see the special qualities that have made it possible for each of them to share such personal events with readers.

It is important to take a moment to think about why each of these contributors have written and shared as they have. Perhaps, in part, writing helps us to "own" our experiences, to make them real, and to validate them. Perhaps there is a sense that, in sharing, we promote understanding and a healthy empathy, rather than a destructive pity and sympathy. For social workers, there is an additional purpose for the writing and the reading. As professionals, we must move beyond stereotypes and generalizations to a genuine and authentic relationship and use our professional skills to assist all people with disabilities to find their "voice," and their special place, in a society that welcomes us all.

Questions for Thought and Discussion

1. What do you see as some of the common themes in the experiences you read about in this chapter? How do you think these themes impact on the life experience of people with disabilities?

2. How do you see differences between physical and mental disabilities? Do you think the societally understood differences are valid?

3. Though visually impaired and hearing-impaired people clearly have a disability that limits their functioning, some of these impairments can be corrected by assistive technology. Should people whose conditions can be corrected with technology be considered "disabled"? Think about this in the context of disability models. What would the medical model say? What would the social construct model say?

4. The ADA definition of disability includes "having a record of such an impairment" and "being seen as having an impairment." How would this work with visually and hearing-impaired people?

5. The ADA definition seems to focus on a definition of disability from the point of view of others: "having a record of," "being seen as," leaves the person with the disability out of the disability determination function. Do you think this is appropriate? Should the views of the person in viewing himself or herself as disabled have a role?

Part II Summary

Part II has presented an individual perspective: We have explored the experiences of people with disabilities from their personal viewpoints through narratives and poems, and we have considered the effects of identity development, onset, course, and outcome of the disabling conditions and the effect of activity limitations on life experiences. We have also explored systems from grouping disabilities that in some instances may negatively affect individuals but also provide us with a broader contextual framework for understanding.

Chapter 6 presented ways of thinking about how people adapt to disability as a facet of themselves. Mackelprang and Salsgiver's identity development theory suggests that the age at which the disability is acquired has a major impact on identity development and that there are major differences in disability identity between people who are born with a disability and those who acquire a disability in later life. One can also think about disability from the perspective of social role theory, where disability is a learned social role—a role that is understood both by people with the disability and by others. Through identification with the disability movement, a person can also develop a disability identity grounded in pride, self-esteem, and self-respect. The development of a disability identity has at least certain elements of choice, however, and many people, especially those who become disabled later in life, choose not to identify as a disabled person at all.

In order to understand the commonalities as well as singularities, Chapter 7 explored ways in which disabilities are grouped by organizations and the government. Disability is defined differently, we saw, according to the purposes and goals of the organization developing the groupings. Some disabilities carry social disapproval, and this has a strong effect upon the individual. Others are associated with age, carelessness, or other kinds of personal behavior. An individual's relationship to his or her disabling condition may also be affected by how that condition is viewed in society, and its relative position among other disabilities. Disability groupings assist us in understanding something about the disabling condition, its expected course and outcome, and the ways in which it affects the individual.

No disability text would be complete without personal narratives that provide evocative insights into the experience of disability. Two chapters have been devoted to understanding the disability experience, both intellectually and intuitively. Chapter 8 presented disability through an understanding of the way in which onset was experienced, the expected course of the disability and its effect on the individual, and the expected outcome in terms of functioning and life expectancy. Chapter 9 explored the disability experience through an understanding of how disability is lived by people, and the way in which the stereotypes associated with disability have impacted upon them.

Parts I and II have presented disability from the perspective of the individual and of society, and explored the complex and delicate interaction between these two. Frameworks and models have assisted us in developing an understanding of the lived experience of people with a disability in our society. Grounded with this understanding, Part III will move us toward the acquisition of practice skills that will enable us to work competently with people with disabilities, whether or not the disability is perceived as central to the problem for which the client is seeking help.

Part II Assignment

Part II has explored the lived experience of disability from various perspectives. Personal narratives have enriched our understanding and provided insights into some very special people who have shared their stories and experiences with us.

Talking with people about their life experiences with disability provides us with many personal insights. For your assignment in this part, interview someone with a disability. Talk with the person about his or her life, what has changed and what has remained constant, how the person thinks about himself or herself, and how the person perceives other people's thinking about him or her. Your interview should last about an hour. While interviewing, be especially sensitive to cultural issues and worldview that might be affected by race, religion, ethnicity, gender, and sexual orientation.

After you have completed your interview, write a paper in two sections about your experience. In the first section, present the personal narrative experience of the person you interviewed. In the second, share your experience in terms of what you gained, how you felt during various parts of the interview, and how you viewed yourself in relation to the person you were interviewing.

Part III

Skills for Social Work Practice

We have explored two parameters of our framework for social work practice in the preceding units. In Part III we will develop the third parameter, the acquisition of specific skills for working with clients across disability.

Clients may come to us for many reasons; disability may or may not be the primary focus of their perceived needs. It is important for us as professionals to consider clients holistically and *not* to give primacy to the disability itself as the salient issue for which the client is seeking our help unless the client so perceives it. As always, it is vital to "start where the client is"—to listen, to understand, and to accept the client's perception of problem and need as the only valid place to begin working.

However, as professionals, we must give attention to the client's disabling condition as it affects the potential client-worker relationship. We must provide services to clients *across* the disability, and that involves learning to communicate, assess, use practice models, and develop programs that take the disability into account while not necessarily giving it precedence over other issues.

One of the essential components for competent social work practice across disability is knowledge of the disability and of some of the major themes or issues that affect people with the disability. If you are working with clients with spina bifida, for example, it is essential to have a good working knowledge of the condition—its onset, course, potential effects on the individual, and models of adaptation and adjustment. If you are working with aphasia, it is important to understand the causes, possible issues in identity development, the course, and the prognosis. Part II defined some of the major components to be considered in working with a client with disability. However, because of the wide range of disabilities, the cultural components, and a variations within each, it must be the individual responsibility of each worker to become knowledgeable about the disabilities that affect his or her clients.

Part III will focus on skills for working across disability whether or not the disability itself is the central issue. It is recognized that many other skills are necessary for effective and competent social work practice; however, it will be the assumption here that readers are familiar with these and have had some experience in using the social work processes on both a micro and a macro level. In addition to these general skills, working across disability requires competence in some disability-specific areas.

Because effective communication is the necessary grounding for any engagement with a client, Chapter 10 will explore communication and some of the ways a client's disability may serve as a barrier to effective communication. Some specific strategies will be offered to assist workers to communicate across the barriers presented by difficulties with communication. Once the possibility of communication exists, making it effective is the next task to be addressed. Chapter 11 discusses the development of trust and relationship across disability and includes a section on the importance of exercising care in avoiding making assumptions about disabled clients based on their disability.

When the problem has been communicated and a relationship has been developed within which change can occur, an assessment is essential in developing an understanding of both the stressors and the strengths of clients and the environmental issues that impact upon them. Chapter 12 will explore several approaches to the assessment process where disability is one of the parameters that must be considered.

Chapter 13 presents several practice models for working with individuals. Models were selected for applicability to many of the special problems that affect clients with disabilities, but they are accepted practice models for work with all clients. Crisis intervention is appropriate when a person is newly disabled, when there is a change in condition, or when any other condition in the client's life creates a crisis. Because clients with disabilities often feel helpless and have a low sense of self-esteem, the empowerment model seeks to assist the client to affirm his or her ability to act and to control his or her life. The advocacy model is appropriate for working with severely disabled clients, where the worker must take a firm proactive stance in addressing client needs. The case management model is often helpful to clients whose disability is of long standing, and where assistance and service coordination are necessary for the highest possible level of functioning.

Social work in the community setting with clients who have disabilities may involve assisting and advising self-help groups, empowering groups of people, and assisting them to work for changes in communities to better meet their needs. These models are presented in Chapter 14, while Chapter 15 explores social work intervention at the broadest level— through the building of coalitions, political action, and the development of social movements.

10

Using Client Strengths and Worker Skills to Optimize Communication

A person is not handicapped.
A person is not disabled.
A person has a disability.

A handicap has been defined as an obstacle which society imposes on a
person with a disability: i.e. inaccessible transportation or buildings, no
signage, etc. Handicapped is not a term to describe human beings. A
disability has been defined as a body function that operates differently. It's
that simple! Just a body function that operates differently. People First
Language seeks to put the person first and the disability second. People with
disabilities are people, first and foremost. (Snow)

Because all social work, whether individual or community based, is grounded in relationship, communication is essential to effective social work practice. It is also essential to our
understanding of humanity.

There are often barriers to effective communication that hinder relationship building
and effective interpersonal interactions. Barriers may be related to client life experiences
or experiences with social agencies, to the precipitating circumstances, to client resistance,
to transference or countertransference, to reporting procedures, and to many other causes.
In addition to these, disabling conditions that potentially limit communication in either
worker or client or both may also be barriers. It is important to understand and address
these so that their effect on practice is minimized. A brief review of several approaches to
enhancing communication will help to prepare the reader for learning about the kinds of

communication problems and possible approaches to them that will be helpful in working with clients.

A particularly useful system for understanding communication and barriers to effective communication involves understanding the various processes that are used in communicating. These include *encoding,* the process of putting the message to be sent into a symbolic form in preparation for sending; *transmitting,* the process of actually sending the encoded message; and *receiving,* the process of interpreting the message that was transmitted. The receiver must then *decode* the message, and *check out* with the sender the accuracy of the message as it has been received and decoded. Additionally, *noise* may affect the communication process by providing extraneous influences that can distort messages (Compton & Galway, 1994, p. 307).

A conversation between two people, then, involves one person encoding and transmitting a message, the message's passing through extraneous noise, being received and decoded by the receiver. The receiver then responds by encoding and transmitting another message, and the process is repeated. Difficulties in communication can occur at any phase of the process, and many factors affect each step. Language use, dialects, thought disorders, inability to verbalize, difficulty in forming words, cultural differences between sender and receiver, inability to hear verbal messages, and potential distortions from noise can affect the accuracy of the communication

"Total communication," Compton and Galway state (p. 309), "in that one can completely understand what another is saying, thinking, and feeling, is impossible." Understanding the validity of this statement can help us to understand that, even with no disabling conditions and in the best of all possible circumstances, it is still impossible to fully understand what another person is trying to communicate. Many factors affect communication. Disability is only one of these, and, with effort and dedication, much can be done to surmount this barrier and to communicate effectively with clients using the client's strengths and abilities as well as worker skills.

Some simple general guidelines are useful in examining the way in which we communicate with others. These are essential for all communication, including communication across disability. Sheafor, Horejsi, and Horejsi's suggestions can assist us in the *planning, sending,* and *receiving* stages of communicating with others. During the *planning* stage, we must think about timing, essential points to be made, and how to organize the message to minimize confusion and misunderstanding. During the *sending* stage, it is essential to use simple and clear language and to break up complex messages into simple and distinct parts, as well as to ask for feedback to ensure the receiver has understood. It is also important to be aware of nonverbal communication, such as body language, so that verbal and nonverbal communications are congruent. During the *receiving* stage, it is important to give cues that demonstrate interest in the communication, to be patient, not to interrupt, and to ask relevant and appropriate questions to clarify the intent of message (Sheafor, Horejsi, & Horejsi, 2000, p. 136–37).

Hepworth, Rooney, and Larsen (1997, pp. 180–81) focus on barriers to communication primarily by asking workers to self-observe and self-examine for problems with communication patterns. They stress the value of physical attending, such as making eye contact (except when culturally dissonant) body position, and awareness of cultural differences and patterns in nonverbal communication. They also focus on verbal communications barriers, such as moralizing, prematurely advising or giving solutions, lecturing, threatening, judging, criticizing, analyzing, or providing too much sympathy, consolation, or excuses for behavior (pp. 183–190).

Any client may experience difficulties in communication. Some kinds of disabilities, however, directly affect communication and pose an especial challenge to both client and worker. These include sensory impairments to hearing and vision, deafness, blindness, mental illness, developmental disabilities, and cognitive impairments. In this chapter, some specific techniques and strategies will be offered to assist the worker in establishing communication across these disabilities that is meaningful and effective for social work interaction. Personal experiences and/or knowledge of specific conditions may provide the reader with additional techniques; the ones included here are meant to serve as general guidelines and are not an exhaustive listing.

It is important to recognize the strengths of each client in developing a relationship. Your client has learned a variety of skills that have enabled him or her to cope with problems and difficulties encountered thus far. Some of these may be very functional in assisting the client toward his or her goals; some may be dysfunctional in terms of goals but functional in other ways. Withdrawal and isolation, for example, may not help your client to achieve goals, but may keep him or her from situations that may be embarrassing, confrontational, or potentially dangerous. Learning about your client's strengths may take a little time, but communicating effectively should provide mutual insights.

Communicating across Sensory Impairment

Many people experience difficulty in communication due to sensory impairments. These include hearing impairments, deafness, blindness, and vision impairments. Using Sheafor, Horejsi, and Horejsi's description of the process of communication noted above, the barrier to communication that is created by sensory loss generally involves the *receiving* process, the step in communication where the person receives that which is communicated by another person. If there is deafness or a hearing impairment, the receiver is unable to receive verbal communication and must use alternative sources to the ear in order to receive communication, while the other communication processes—*encoding, sending,* and *decoding*—are all functional. If there is blindness or a visual impairment, language input is received, but vital nonverbal communications that qualify, describe, amplify, and explain the verbal communications are not received. This limitation in the *receiving* process may then impact on the *decoding* process and limit accurate understanding of the communication. Competent social work practice skills can compensate for sensory losses and ensure accurate communication between client and worker.

Clients with Hearing Impairments

Learning about the Impairment.   Hearing impairments vary broadly in degree, quality, and circumstances. Thus, when working with a hearing-impaired client, it is necessary first of all to attempt to understand the kind of limitation the client is experiencing, so that you can compensate for it in the most effective way. While it may be necessary to ask direct questions about hearing fairly early in the contact, the worker can attempt to gather this information from the client's chart, other professionals, or previous workers. This will enable the client to begin with focusing on the problem that has brought him or her to seek services.

If this is not possible, it is preferable to give the client an opportunity to initiate discussion. Introduce yourself and exchange social amenities, taking a position where you are facing the client directly and speaking in a firm, clear voice. This will assist the client who uses lip reading as a full or partial method of understanding verbal communication. If possible, use a midrange tone, since many hearing impairments affect the high or low pitches more severely. Make sure that you have minimized all extraneous noise by closing the door and turning off radios and televisions. (If this is a home visit, be sure to ask the client's permission first!)

If your client appears comfortable and understands what you are saying, there is no need to focus on the hearing impairment unless he or she initiates the discussion. You client may or may not perceive the impairment as important or relevant to the problem that prompted seeking your assistance. The issue may be raised at some later time or may not ever be discussed.

If the hearing impairment is the worker's, a brief explanation and simple directions for minimizing communication difficulties can be provided initially. It is important not to make the worker's hearing impairment the central focus and, rather, to direct attention to the client's problems.

Enhancing Communication.   Some clients may have difficulty in understanding your spoken communication but may be unwilling to raise the issue with you. You may become aware of this through observation of your client's nonverbal communication. Do the body and facial expression reveal tension? Does the client appear to be concentrating overly closely on your words? Does the client respond inappropriately to your questions or statements? These and other behaviors may serve as clues to you that your client is experiencing difficulty. Your approach may depend upon your degree of relationship and your sense about whether the client would be comfortable with your initiating the subject.

Because clients with hearing impairments often have better audition in one ear than in the other, you may want to try to position yourself differently, seeking the most effective position for communication. You may also ask your client if he of she is clear about everything you are saying, and, if not, whether there is anything that you could do to help him or her. Many clients will then explain what works best for them—lip reading, position, or other method.

Many clients will take the initiative themselves and explain this impairment to you and make the necessary accommodations and adjustments.

Ensuring Privacy.   A frequent problem that occurs with both workers and clients who are trying to work around a hearing limitation is that voices are raised in an attempt to compensate for hearing loss. Your client may speak loudly, either because of inability to hear his or her own voice clearly or because he or she believes it will enable you to understand the message. You may speak loudly in order to try to communicate above the hearing impairment.

Often, clients are unaware that such loud speech impinges on privacy, and it is important for the worker to address this issue. Closing the door or taking the client to a place where he or she cannot be overheard may be helpful in assisting your client to maintain privacy. If necessary, you may need to raise this issue directly with your client, express your concern, and attempt to engage the client with you in addressing the problem. This may motivate the client to explore the possibility of a hearing aid, to modulate his or her own voice (you may have to help remind him or her periodically), or to explore alternative means of communication.

You can also suggest that the client write any private communications rather than speaking them. If a client chooses this option, be sure to destroy the notes in the client's presence so that there is a mutual recognition that the privacy of the contents is being respected.

Hearing Aids.   Many clients with hearing impairments use hearing aids to assist them in communicating effectively. Hearing aids are functional and come in a variety of sizes, price ranges, and degrees of effectiveness. All clients who are hard of hearing are *entitled* to a hearing aid; however, some may elect not to use one for a variety of reasons. Clients who are elderly or confused may often "forget" to turn on their hearing aid. They either remove or turn off the aid at night and simply do not turn it on again until reminded. Always make sure that your client's aid is turned on before you begin working if you find that this occurs.

It is also not uncommon for clients with hearing impairments to refuse to use the hearing aid either at all times or selectively. Especially if your client is in an institutional setting, or in a setting where he or she is unhappy, you may find that the hearing aid is purposely turned off to "turn off the world." This is a strength, in that the client is controlling his or her environment, "admitting" some sounds and excluding others. Building on this strength may lead worker and client to set goals for other means of empowerment or control.

In such cases, the worker's first task is to build a relationship such that the client is willing to use the hearing aid in order to interact with the worker. When the client has a hearing aid and consistently refuses to use it, or "forgets" to wear it that day, the worker needs to clarify whether this behavior is usual for this client or whether there is something in the client-worker relationship that is causing the client's desire to avoid or withdraw from meaningful interaction. It may be necessary for the worker to be explicit in seeking an understanding from the client.

Clients Who Are Deaf

Unless you are working with a client who has recently lost hearing, in which case you are in the "crisis intervention" practice mode, your client will have made some arrangements to compensate for deafness such that communication can be maintained. The client may have learned ASL or other signing method, may lip read proficiently, or may use a qualified interpreter. Each of these requires some different social work skills in communication. It is important for the worker to be comfortable with the communication method the client is using. Clients quickly pick up on worker discomfort, and this may negatively affect interactions.

Learning about Deafness.   To prepare for working with a deaf client, the worker should learn about deafness, its etiology, and its effects, as well as about the common methods of communication used by deaf people. Deaf culture in the United States is a well-developed and very effective subculture in our society. If you are a deaf worker, working within Deaf culture may be a comfortable matter. If you are a hearing worker, you may experience frustration, rejection, and low credibility in your work with clients who identify strongly with Deaf culture. Learning ASL can be an enormous asset to hearing workers who work with deaf clients.

However, many deaf clients do not identify with Deaf culture, especially those who have become deaf in later life. They may also be unable to use ASL. Developing effective communication can be quite a challenge with these clients. Many clients who lose their hearing gradually later in life become proficient lip readers, acquiring the skill as their hearing loss increases.

Communication with Lip-Reading Clients.   As noted above, many clients who lose their hearing later in life have become proficient lip readers in the process. Others may use a combination of ASL and lip reading, depending on the setting and needs.

To enhance your client's ability to lip read, it is important to sit directly facing the client, so that he or she can clearly see your mouth movements. Focus the light in the room such that your face is clearly in light rather than in shadow. Clients who are deaf and lip reading cannot hear you even if you raise your voice, so there is no need to do that. Rather, take especial care to enunciate clearly and carefully. In order to ensure that your client has understood what you have said, ask for confirmation and/or paraphrase your statement to allow another opportunity. If you are presenting vital information or asking the client to make a major decision and want to be sure your client has understood what you have said, you may supplement your verbal discussion with a written statement.

Lip reading is a difficult skill. Clients who have mastered this and are effective lip readers have worked consistently to learn, often over a long period of time. It requires good vision, good intuitive skills, persistence, and a good knowledge of language, all important strengths your client beings with him or her to the social work encounter.

Communication with Clients Who Use ASL.   If you are a hearing worker planning to work with deaf clients, learning to use ASL is an important preparation for competent practice. Communicating with ASL indicates to your client a clear commitment and interest in working with him or her. Courses in ASL are offered in community colleges, high schools, universities, and other settings, such as organizations for the deaf.

Often, however, your client may be more adept at using ASL than you are. While your client may value and appreciate your investment in learning to communicate, it is important to watch for signs of frustration and impatience. ASL is another complete language: You can understand your client's feelings by thinking about some feelings you may have experienced when talking with a person who was not fluent in English, made many mistakes, and spoke slowly. Practice your ASL skills outside of the client-worker relationship until you reach optimum proficiency before using ASL independently with clients!

If you want to use ASL but are not proficient, it is important to exercise special care, for there are important ethical issues involved here. Your client has come to you for professional services and has a right to effective communication. If your own knowledge of ASL is limited, you may be unable to grasp the full content or meaning of what your client is trying to communicate with you. Focusing on your own communication denies the centrality of the client and the client's problem to the interview and deflects attention from client to worker. If your ability to sign is not "effective," it may be preferable to use a qualified interpreter until you have gained mastery.

Communicating with Clients Who Use a Qualified Sign Language Interpreter. Deaf clients may prefer to use a qualified interpreter when meeting with you. Qualified interpreters meet national testing standards and are certified as professional sign language interpreters. Qualified sign language interpreters belong to the National Registry of Interpreters of the Deaf (NRID) and the National Association of the Deaf (NAD). They have a professional code of ethics that includes an obligation to confidentiality.

Qualified interpreters listen to what you say and interpret your statements into ASL for clients. Communicating in this manner is often fast and effective, but introducing another person into the client-worker relationship poses a different set of challenges in establishing good communication.

Although the interpreter is bound to confidentiality, the presence of a third person may affect client-worker interactions. There may also be occasions when the interpreter is not a qualified, certified interpreter but rather a friend or family member. Clients may not feel as free to express themselves, and workers may not feel as free to react to them. Especially if you are a new worker, you may feel that the interpreter is listening to you and judging your competence. You may wonder whether he or she is communicating exactly what you want to communicate and if any comments or reactions are being added in the translation. If the interpreter is someone who is known to the client, such as a friend or family member, you may be concerned about that person's impact on the interaction.

Consonant with the core social work value of self-determination, it is important to ask your client about preferences for communication. The ADA also requires that workers respect the client's wishes in regard to effective communication. Some clients may prefer privacy, while others will elect to use an interpreter. The essential ingredient is that communication be effective from the perspective of the client.

It is helpful to lay clear ground rules from the outset that define the role of the interpreter: the expectation of confidentiality and the importance of accurate communication. The relationship between the worker and the interpreter must remain professional at all times. Both the client and the interpreter should understand that the client, and not the interpreter, is in the central position. This is communicated very strongly through your interaction with the interpreter.

In order to minimize the effect of the interpreter on the client-worker relationship, the interpreter should be positioned slightly behind and to the left or right of you (Phelan & Parkman, 1995). This enables the client to see the interpreter but decreases the possibility of any direct interaction between worker and the interpreter. Always sit facing the client directly, and speak to the client, not to the interpreter. Nonverbal communication is important, and body language, facial expression, and head movements should be directed toward the client. It is also helpful if the worker ensures that there is adequate lighting, and that the interpreter is not placed in front of a bright window (Phelan & Parkman).

While the client must clearly remain the focus of your attention during the interview, it is important to let the interpreter know you appreciate his or her efforts, and value him or

Social work students at University of California-Berkeley practice communication skills with "clients" using a sign language interpreter.

her as a person. This is best done at the end of an interview rather than during the interview process.

When Deafness Affects Speech.   Clients who are deaf often have difficulty with speech because of their inability to hear what they are saying. This may create a difficult challenge for the worker, who does not want to create another potential communications barrier. It is not uncommon for workers to respond with a general "uh-huh" or to nod following a statement from a deaf client that they have been unable to understand.

While the desire to demonstrate acceptance and the reluctance to share his or her own inability to understand the client are both very understandable concerns, it is important for the worker to consider the information that may be lost, the interventions that may be missed, and the statements that may be misinterpreted. If the worker is missing an occasional sentence, he or she may decide to continue with the client without addressing this issue. However, if large and frequent communications from the client are lost, the worker may wish to explore some of the alternative forms of communication discussed below in the section "Communicating across Speech Impairment."

Clients with Visual Impairments

Learning about Visual Impairments.   As with any disabling condition, the first step in working with visually impaired clients involves learning about the impairment. There are several major categories of vision limitations, including tunnel vision, macular degeneration, loss of vision in certain parts of the eye, such as peripheral vision or central vision, blurring of vision, and fading. It is important to understand which kind of vision loss affects the client so that appropriate measures can be taken to compensate for the losses.

Nonverbal Communication.   Our clients hear our words, listen to our intonation, and integrate the accompanying body language to create an overall understanding of what we

Social work students at the University of California-Berkeley practice working with visually impaired "clients" using specialized glasses from the Lighthouse to simulate vision impairment.

are trying to communicate. Clients with vision impairments often miss nonverbal communication, and thus lose a part of our message.

If the client's vision impairment involves partial loss of vision, the worker should position her or himself within the client's area of vision. In the case of clients with peripheral vision only, this may mean sitting directly to the side of the client, rather than facing him or her. While the worker may know about the client's vision loss through records or other workers, to position properly, it is useful to ask for the client's help. A simple "Can you see me clearly from here?" or "Is this a good place for me to sit?" can help the client to feel comfortable in asking the worker to sit in a particular spot.

When the optimal place for the worker has been determined, position the light source so that you are clearly visible to the client. The worker will not need to make exaggerated body movements or positions: If the client can see the area where the worker is positioned, the worker's nonverbal communication will be evident to the client.

There will be instances, however, when the vision impairment is such that positioning alone will not resolve the nonverbal communications problems. In these cases, it is possible for the worker to partially compensate for the loss of nonverbal communication by using more expressive language in communicating verbally and by checking in with the client frequently to ensure that meaning is accurately interpreted.

Clients Who Are Blind

Learning about Blindness.   While blindness, like vision impairment, does not directly impact verbal communication, people who are unable to see miss all nonverbal communication, which often qualifies, assigns meaning to, and amplifies the verbal content.

There is an enormous amount of material available about blindness and about communicating with people who are blind. It is important for the worker to familiarize himself or herself with common problems and issues in order to provide competent services.

Meeting Blind Clients.   Clients who are unable to see you will need some cues from you regarding expectations and behaviors. In an office setting, shaking hands when meeting provides an immediate contact. Explain to your client the location of your office and offer to assist him or her by offering your arm. When you are guiding blind clients, be sure to remain constantly aware of position: You will need a wider area free around you for walking, and you should describe any obstacles such as steps and doorways to clients before you approach them. Your client will feel at ease if you share the same casual conversation with him or her as you would with a sighted client, adding guiding comments as needed and without undue emphasis. When you arrive at the place where the interview will be conducted, position your client so that the back of the legs gently touch the seat and ask the client to sit down. Withdraw your arm at this point as the client is able to be seated independently.

When visiting a blind client in his or her home, remember that drawn blinds and low lighting do not mean the same things as they might with a sighted client but are simply due to the fact that the amount of light makes no difference to the client. If you find that you need more light, politely ask your client for permission to turn on lights or open blinds.

Your client will probably be able to move around his or her own home unaided by you, using cues from furniture and other objects. You may ask your client where he or she prefers that you sit so that client is aware of your location in the room. You may also make one or two positive comments about your client's home, as you would with a sighted client.

As was discussed earlier, blindness may or may not be central to your client's reason for meeting with you. Let the client take the lead and describe the problem, concern, or situation, then you can determine whether blindness forms a part of it.

Guide Dogs.   Guide dogs are extremely helpful in maintaining the independence of a person who is blind. Guide dogs are specially trained to lead clients safely in streets, buildings, parks, and any other public and private areas. There are a number of breeds that are especially gifted in learning and performing their tasks, and guide dogs are a vital part of the lives of many people.

When working with a client who has a guide dog, some simple guidelines will help you.

- Guide dogs are not pets. They are working dogs. Do not pet them, give them treats, or display interest and affection unless your client has asked you to do so.
- Guide dogs are trained to work with their owner. Don't try to lead a guide dog away, or separate the dog from the owner unless your client has involved you in the dog's care.
- Guide dogs remain with their owners at all times. Locations that do not permit dogs will permit guide dogs.

- The guide dog wears a special harness in addition to the leash. When the harness is held, the dog functions as a guide. When held by the leash, the dog knows that he or she is free to sit, stand, or change position. Your client will use the harness while moving about and hold the leash when sitting in your office.
- If large dogs make you uncomfortable or afraid, it is important to acknowledge this to yourself and, if you will be working with blind clients, to attempt to address your fears. Dogs, even well-trained ones, can sense fear in people and may behave erratically. You may also want to share your concern with your client: He or she has heard of this problem before and will keep the dog under close control while in your presence.

Communicating across Speech Impairment

Speech is our basic tool for communicating with other human beings. Where speech is impaired, whether partially or wholly, it is necessary to develop alternative forms of communication to enable clients to express themselves. People with speech impairments often are able to *receive* and *decode* verbal communication. Generally, the problem occurs during the *sending* process. Some clients also have difficulty during the *encoding* process.

A client's speech may be garbled, slurred, or otherwise difficult to understand. Some clients, such as those who have had strokes or those with quadriplegia, may be unable to communicate verbally at all. Some clients may be able to move their lips to form words, though no sound emerges. Other clients may be unable to write or to move, as well as unable to speak.

Because the content of social work–client interactions is often complex and laden with emotion, it is important to receive your client's messages accurately. This may necessitate the use of alternative means of communication. Interpreters may be very helpful in working with clients with some speech impairments, and the guidelines presented in the section on sign language interpreters may be applied to speech interpreters as well.

Depression and apathy often accompany initial difficulties in verbal communication for clients who lose speech. The possibility of these reactions supports efforts to communicate by alternative means. Often, the worker is able to obtain alternative communications systems for clients. Speech therapists and speech pathologists are excellent sources of information about communications systems.

Lip Reading

If your client is able to form words with his or her mouth, you may be able to distinguish them by lip reading. To enhance your ability to lip read, try to have your client's face in the light and sit fairly close to him or her. Ask your client to indicate how "yes" and "no" are communicated (by a nod, a blink, a shake of the head, a lifted finger, or the like).

When you have lip read something that your client has said, repeat the sentence out loud and ask your client to indicate whether this is correct. When you repeat the sentence, use a neutral tone of voice, unless your client's affect and body language have communicated specific feelings. Using a neutral tone decreases any "noise" or distortion you might give, and encourages the client to continue to elaborate if desired for clarity and specificity. Avoid using a monotone in repeating your client's sentence, however, for this will sound artificial and might communicate lack of interest.

If you do not understand what your client is communicating, ask him or her to repeat what has been said. If you need to do this repeatedly, you might want to acknowledge this by saying that you've a really poor lip reader and please to excuse this, or by saying that you know it is hard for him or her to repeat things so often, but you want to be sure you have what he or she is saying just right. If your client sees that you are making a genuine effort, he or she will work hard to communicate with you.

Some people are just naturally poor lip readers. No matter how much they practice or how hard they try, they are unable to extract meaning from the client's lip movements. If you are one of those people, you may want to explain this to your client and suggest trying alternative methods of communication rather than risk creating frustrations on both sides of the encounter.

Communication Boards

Communication boards are useful tools for working with people who are able to move an arm or a hand. Boards may be made up with any combination of words of letters. The simplest board has the letters of the alphabet and a few common terms, such as yes and no. The terms can be adjusted according to the client's circumstances and needs. The client simply points to a letter, a word, or a phrase that says what he or she wants to say. Several alternative systems have been developed to speed communication by grouping letters on boards by frequency of occurrence, position in the alphabet, or other methods.

Communication boards are available commercially, or workers with clients who are unable to communicate may choose to construct a personal board for the client. Any hard surface can be used. Letters and words may be drawn in or purchased at an office supply store and glued on. Words on the board in addition to the letters can be personalized to reflect the needs of the client, such as "toilet," "hot," "tired," "sleep," and so on. Words expressing emotion can be added as well, such as "angry," "happy," or "sad." Engaging the client in the process of selecting words or designing the board creates a mutual relationship that can carry over into other areas of practice and empowers the client in taking responsibility for his or her communication. The more the client has directed the board-making process, the more he or she "owns" the method of communication!

Because communication boards are rather slow and cumbersome as a means of communication, clients tend to use these for immediate needs and to communicate briefly about concrete subjects. It may be a daunting task to use communications board to communicate sensitive or emotional-laden content. Care and patience should be used if the worker is seeking to develop communication on a feeling level.

Finger-Operated Communicating Systems

Commercially available systems in which clients use one or more methods to operate a machine that spells out words are also helpful to clients. Systems may be operated from both sitting and prone positions and enable more efficient communication.

Disability rights activist communicates with police using a head stick and communication board, San Francisco, 1978.

Eye-Movement Communicating Systems

For clients who are "locked in" and unable to speak or move in any way, eye movement systems can enable communication. There systems require a high level of technology and are quite costly. Clients using these systems use their eyes to focus on a letter or a word on a screen placed before them. The eye movement is registered and a letter or word appears. If an error has been made, the client is able to change a letter or a word.

If an eye-movement communicating system is not available for a client, it is still possible to develop a system for communicating using blinks. The number of blinks can signify yes, no, or any other word.

Communicating across Mental Illness

While a thorough presentation of methods for communicating with clients who have a mental illness is beyond the scope of this book, the suggestions offered here may serve as a useful starting point for social workers establishing communication with mentally ill clients. It is important to note that not *all* clients with a mental illness necessarily have difficulties in communication. Many are able to communicate quite effectively. However, it is not uncommon for clients with mental illnesses to be confused, agitated, fearful, or withdrawn. Establishing a positive and effective method of communication can be a challenge.

Clients with a mental illness may have difficulties with any part of the communication process; however, problems with *encoding* and *decoding* tend to occur with greater frequency because of the inner processes the client is experiencing along with the external process of communication.

Mental illnesses vary greatly both in quality and in degree. They vary within diagnostic categories in the way in which they are manifested from individual to individual. They also vary within the individual from one moment, hour, day, or month to the next. These variations are a part of the condition, inherent within it. However, they may create special difficulties for a social worker in developing a communication system with a client that will enable the client to be engaged. The suggestions below should assist the worker in communicating effectively with mentally ill clients. As with any functional limitation, it is important to learn about a client's problem and condition prior to initiating a relationship.

The most important technique for communicating with a person who has a mental illness is to keep your communication clear and simple, brief, and to the point (Woolis, 1992, p. 73). Always try to avoid using professional jargon, complex sentences, or ambiguous terms. Because people with mental illnesses often take every word you say literally, be careful using jokes and indirect terms.

Although you may not have a choice about timing when working with a mentally ill client, it is important to remember that your client may react quite differently to you at different times, depending on what is going on inside of him or her at that moment. This means there may be little carryover from one interview to the next. It is important to be aware of the client's emotional state and to adapt your communication accordingly (Woolis, p. 74). It is very helpful to be aware of your own gestures and facial expressions because your mentally ill client will use them as cues about your feelings toward him or her. These should reflect care, concern, and warmth.

Because people with mental illnesses often have difficulty in communicating feelings, it is important to be aware of your client's nonverbal communication (Woolis, p. 74). A client who tells you that everything is fine but whose body is tense and poised for action is sending you two different messages. It is often the body language message that is the clearest reflection of what the client is actually thinking and feeling. He or she may believe that you want to hear that everything is fine, may want to please you, or may want to believe that everything truly is fine. When the body language tells you differently, you may want to explore this *very* cautiously.

The following chart may be helpful to you in developing a positive communication with a client who has a mental illness. It was developed to assist families in communicating with a mentally ill member but is also very applicable to the social work encounter (Woolis, p. 72).

Communicating with a Person with a Mental Illness

People who have mental illnesses have symptoms and characteristics that require adaptations in the way you communicate to increase your chances of being understood. The following table shows symptoms of mental illness and corresponding adaptations.

Symptom or Characteristic	Adaptation
Confusion about what is real	Be simple and straightforward
Difficulty in concentrating	Be brief, repeat
Overstimulation	Limit input; don't force discussion
Poor judgment	Don't expect rational discussion
Preoccupied with internal world	Get attention first
Agitation	Recognize agitation and allow the person an exit
Fluctuating emotions	Don't take words or actions personally
Fluctuating plans	Stick to one plan
Little empathy for others	Recognize as a symptom
Withdrawal	Initiate conversation
Belief in delusions	Don't argue
Fear	Stay calm
Insecurity	Be loving and accepting
Low self-esteem	Stay positive and respectful

Communicating across Developmental Disability

About 3 percent of the total population in the United States have abnormalities in development related to intellectual ability. Of these, only 1 to 1.5 percent are actually identified (Berkow, 1992, p. 2108). People with developmental disabilities often have an ongoing need for comprehensive social work or case management services, and developing good communication is important in helping clients to function at optimal levels in society.

Communicating with clients who have developmental disabilities involves using a variety of techniques and skills, but always requires using a simple, basic vocabulary that is descriptive but very clear. Very plain language works best—don't use euphemistic terms or allusions when trying to communicate in order to be understood. Because many people with developmental disabilities have a limited vocabulary, it is important to use terms whose meaning cannot be misinterpreted.

Some people with developmental disabilities are quite verbal and communicate well. Some are difficult to understand, while others are nonverbal. Many people have a physical abnormality of the tongue that affects communication and may make it difficult for you to understand speech. The tongue is long and fat and therefore protrudes from the mouth. Because of this, it is difficult for the person to form words and difficult for others to understand what is being communicated (Everson, 2001).

To understand some of the challenges faced by people with abnormalities of the tongue, try placing a large jaw-breaker candy in your mouth and watch what happens when you try to talk. You may find yourself drooling a bit and have great difficulty in forming words. There's no *room* in your mouth for you to place the tongue in a way that creates clear enunciation. You become easily frustrated; you know what you want to say, but others don't seem to understand. This is similar to the experience of people with developmental disabilities when they try to communicate verbally.

People who have difficulty with communication or who are nonverbal often carry a personal communications book to assist them in communicating with others. You may find this helpful as a tool as well (Everson). It is also important to be aware of the nonverbal communication. Observing your client's position, body movement, and affect can provide much valuable information and suggest avenues for exploration with words, pictures, or other means.

Several problems specific to communicating with people with developmental disabilities must be addressed in order to facilitate communication. People with developmental disabilities have great difficulty with timelines; concepts such as tomorrow, last year, or last week are often meaningless, and the social worker must create other systems to help clients communicate about time frames. One way to do this is to use cards with pictures of the seasons. Then it is possible to ask if something happened in summer, winter, or fall, for example. Another useful aid is a series of pictures of a person at different ages—as a baby, a young child, a teenager, an adult, and an older person. Using these cards, it is possible to ask whether an event happened when the person was little or older (Everson).

Another problem in communication of which workers must be aware involves the use of the word *yes.* "In the world of dd," Ms. Everson states, "you are taught to say 'yes.' You *have* to say 'yes.' If you don't say 'yes' you lose your token—soda, coffee, and outing. You comply because you lose if you don't comply" (Everson).

Working with clients who tend to say yes to every question asked poses a challenge to workers seeking information about events or feelings. You may need to rephrase the question several times. An effective technique is to ask a question, and then ask it again on another day, or at another time. Another is to avoid simple yes-or-no questions. Rather, ask questions that require a sentence in response.

Learned compliance may also affect your perception of the client-worker relationship. Clients with developmental disabilities will rarely refuse to see you or refuse to respond to a question. They will quickly agree with any plan you develop. In this sense, developmentally disabled clients are "easy." Because of this, a worker may miss some of the nonverbal objections or negative feelings that a client may be experiencing and miss truly engaging the client in planning for his or her own life appropriately. It is important to empower your client and to encourage a sense of mastery and control over his or her own life. This is often much more difficult, and more time-consuming, than accepting your client's compliance as a genuine expression of his or her will.

In order to facilitate communication, it is also important to understand your client's knowledge base. Your client may be using words inaccurately or may not understand some of the words he or she is using. Ask your client to explain meanings of words you are uncertain the client understands. You can say you want to be sure about what he or she is talking about and ask the client to tell you in other words.

Establishing good lines of communication with clients with developmental disabilities is essential in order to protect clients from abuse. Everson states that 70 to 85 percent of people with developmental disabilities will be abused by the time they reach 18 years of age. One out of every seven men will be abused and one out of every four women. Ninety-nine percent of the abusers are people known to the client. As noted above, because developmentally disabled clients have learned compliance, have learned to say yes to everything, they are at high risk for abuse. Awareness of the abuse potential is important to competent practice with developmentally disabled clients, and workers can use the techniques described above, supplemented with pictures, dolls, puppets, and art to assist clients to communicate accurately about what is happening to them.

Communicating across Cognitive Disability

Cognitive disabilities affect clients' orientation and memory (Morrow, 1993, p. 126). Confusion, disorientation, dementia, disorganized thought processes, poor memory, and insensitivity to others may indicate an impairment in cognitive functioning. In order to ascertain cognitive disability, tests such as the Mental Status Questionnaire (MSQ) and the Mini-Mental State Exam provide confirmation of disability in an easy-to-use format (Morrow, p. 127). Clients often exhibit disorientation more severely for time, less for place, and almost never for self (Berkow, p. 1403).

People with dementias constitute a large portion of people with cognitive disabilities. Many people become demented with age; however, dementia may occur at any age. Dementias affect more than one million people in the United States (Berkow, p. 1403). Dementia may be static or progressive and includes Alzheimer's dementia, multi-infarct dementias, AIDS dementias, and dementias caused by head injury (Berkow). In addition, people with adult attention-deficit disorder, who may exhibit disorganization in thought process, memory loss, and confusion, may also benefit from specialized techniques to enhance communication (Sudderth & Kandel, 1997, p. 112, 125).

Using "Windows of Opportunity" for Empowerment and Decision Making

In support of the principles upheld by the Patient Self-Determination Act, courts have encouraged social workers and other professionals to use "windows of opportunity" in working with clients with dementia. Many dementing conditions vary in degree from day to day, and sometimes from hour to hour. A client may have a period of clarity during which he or she may be able to think reflectively, to understand implications of courses of action, to communicate wishes and desires—social workers can use these "windows" to assist clients toward self-determination.

It is important to recognize such moments and to act promptly. While a social worker can make the judgment himself or herself that a client is lucid at a particular period of time, it is helpful to seek confirmation of the "window" from other health professionals, from family members, or from other interested parties and/or to have discussions witnessed by another person with the client's consent. This additional confirmation will lend credibility to your account of the client's statements.

Optimizing Memory

Clients with cognitive impairments often have difficulty with memory. People with dementia tend to lose recent memory first and distant past memory last. Because of this, clients may have difficulty remembering who you are or may associate you with someone else. To help them connect with you, reintroduce yourself at the beginning of each visit. You can do this casually, just saying, "Hi, do you remember me? I'm ———," should help your client to remember. You may also want to develop a little ritual or a special phrase that will help your client to recognize you. Sometimes wearing a special pin or tie each time you see the client will help him or her to remember you.

Clients with cognitive impairments forget more than who their social workers are; appointments, events, medication regimens, mealtimes, house or room numbers—all may easily be forgotten. To assist clients with some memory loss, suggest writing things down and carrying pencil and paper with them to help them to remember (Sudderth, p. 139). They might try pocket calendars, day planners, or beepers that go off to remind them of appointments with you or others (Sudderth, pp. 139–42). Tape or voice recorders are often very effective for adults with memory loss resulting from ADD, as are cell phones and personal computers (Sudderth, pp. 142–44, 151).

Social workers can ask clients to keep a list of questions or concerns that come up between appointments and to bring that list to the interview for discussion. This will help the client to maintain a sense of continuity from one contact to the next. Helping your client to make a plan for the days between your contacts, and writing the plan down, may also be helpful.

Using Nonverbal Forms of Communication

Clients who are confused and do not speak clearly or at all can respond well to other forms of communication. Creative arts have been used successfully with clients with cognitive impairments; painting, drawing, clay, or other creative activity can provide insight into the client's moods and state of mind and enable you to respond to these both verbally and nonverbally.

An important resource for communicating with a client with cognitive impairments is body language. Clients who are frightened, anxious, or in pain will hold their bodies rigidly and tensely. Clients who feel more comfortable may smile at you, even if they don't know who you are, and their smiles can tell you something about their state of mind at that point in time. Clients can be hostile and aggressive, revealing an inner disquiet, frustration, or anger. Learning to read you client's body language to look for changes and consistencies can be very helpful in establishing a good communication with him or her.

An Important Word of Caution

It is very important to avoid infantilizing the client who is confused, forgetful, and disorganized. Treating the client as a child is humiliating and destroys self-respect. Always treat your cognitively impaired client as an adult. Avoid using first names (without the client's permission), childish terms, and childish activities. Artwork is helpful for developing communication, but avoid children's coloring books!

Communicating across Physical Immobility

As we have noted earlier, only a part of communication is verbal. Nonverbal communication amplifies, supports, or disproves verbal statements and also offers excellent cues to clients' emotional states. In order to understand clients, social workers observe, use, and respond to both verbal and nonverbal communication.

Just as people who are blind miss the worker's nonverbal communication, so workers miss some of the nonverbal communication of immobilized clients. What is missed is dependent, of course, on what part, and to what degree, the client is limited in mobility. Clients who are able to use facial expression or move an arm are able to communicate nonverbally much more clearly than clients who are able to move only their eyes and mouth. Clients who have some paralysis but can move their upper body are able to communicate nonverbally with almost no limitation.

Where nonverbal communication is limited, the social worker can gently try to encourage the client to verbalize feelings, attitudes, and beliefs, as well as emotional states. He or she can also observe carefully for evidence of nonverbal communication and respond carefully to nonverbal cues. Often, a great deal can be learned from observing your client's eyes and facial expressions: They are well able to communicate joy, sadness, anger, frustration, fear, and many other emotions that can provide helpful insights to workers. Recognizing and responding to your client's nonverbal communication at whatever level of expression it occurs encourages your client to continue to express him or herself and also validates the client's feelings.

Social workers whose clients have limited mobility can also pay increased attention to tones of speech and choice of words, using the client's verbal communication to provide some of the cues that may be otherwise missed.

Chapter Summary

Communication is basic to social work practice. It is the tool that we use to build relationships, define problems, and develop and implement plans for change. This chapter has attempted to provide some guidelines and suggestions for communicating with clients whose communication is affected by sight, hearing, and speech losses; by mental illness, developmental disabilities, and cognitive disability. We have noted that the reason that the client seeks help may or may not be a loss in communication. However, these kinds of losses may constrain the client's ability to change his or her circumstances as desired. Because social work practice is grounded in relationship, communication is vital to effective practice. Alternative means of communication and methods that enhance the possibility of effective communication that are appropriate to the client and culturally congruent should be selected.

Communication always involves at least two people. Workers bring social work skills to the encounter with a client and special techniques for alternative forms of communication. Clients bring their years of experience in communicating with and through any impairment and the personal strengths that have assisted them toward optimal functioning. Together, clients and workers can develop helping relationships that assist clients to address problems and develop and effect the changes they desire in their lives.

Questions for Thought and Discussion

1. Each of us has had experiences in communicating across disability. Because communication is such a basic part of our understanding of others, these experiences can have a profound effect on our beliefs about and attitudes toward people with disabilities, creating stereotypes, both positive and negative, in our minds. Think about your personal experiences and assess how they have affected your understanding about people with disabilities.

2. If you are able to do so, look around you at the room in which you are sitting as you read this chapter. If you were communicating with a client who had a hearing impairment, was deaf, had a vision impairment, or was blind, where would you place the client and yourself in the room? Why would you choose those particular places?

3. The infantilizing of older people with cognitive disabilities is a common problem in our society. What are some of the possible negative effects of such infantilization for the client? For you as the worker?

4. Because of the frequency of abuse and sexual abuse that occurs with clients with developmental disabilities, it is important for workers to be able to communicate with clients about sexual activities and behavior in very simple, graphic ways. How would you do this? What are some of the words you would use? Share your words with a classmate. Do they understand your meaning clearly?

5. What do you think about "reorienting" clients who are "disoriented" by mental illness or cognitive impairment? Do you think that being oriented is always preferable? What if your client's "reality" toward which reorientation is directed is painful, difficult, or distressing?

11

Trust and Relationship Building

In the previous chapter, we presented some suggestions for working with clients who may have difficulty using some of the conventional forms of communication and for whom alternative means may offer increased opportunities for understanding and expression, and thus for self-determination and empowerment. Not all clients with disabilities, of course, will need or benefit from these alternative means; most clients are able to communicate using speech and body language.

Having developed and established the conditions that offer the greatest potential for communication between client and worker, the social worker is ready to begin working with his or her client. Perhaps the most important task of the beginning stage of the client-worker relationship is the development of trust and of relationship.

As noted in Sheafor, Horesji, and Horesji (2000, p. 36), the social worker's role in developing a relationship with a client is an art: It requires artistic and intuitive abilities, compassion and courage, capacity and creativity in relationship building under many different circumstances, the infusion of hope and energy, sound judgment, and personal and professional values. It is also a science, in that it requires knowledge of theory and of the client's problems, culture, environment and history, and also the application of specific social work practice skills.

The social worker brings to the encounter all of her or his art and science, expertise, energy, and good will. The client also brings essential ingredients to the encounter, without which the relationship cannot develop. Clients bring knowledge of themselves and their problem, of their culture and their world, of what has been tried before to address the problem, what has worked and what hasn't. Without the client's expertise, energy, and good will, change is not likely to occur.

There is a balance here that is important to acknowledge. The worker brings theoretical knowledge and expertise, a general framework within which the work can occur. The client brings practical and personal knowledge and expertise, a particular framework that is equally necessary. Acknowledgment of the value of the client's contribution—that the client is the expert on himself or herself—enables the client to increase awareness of strengths and to have a sense of mastery that is essential to effective social work interventions.

Acknowledging the value of client knowledge, values, and expertise about himself or herself is basic to all social work practice, but is especially important in working across disability. Keep the focus client-centered, rather than assuming that you or the doctors or the self-help organization know more about the client's condition than the client does—this diminishes the client and discourages a proactive stance. While it may be true and valid that other sources may be more *intellectually* knowledgeable about the client's disability, the client is the most knowledgeable about how that disability is lived *experientially,* and it is on this level that relationship between client and worker must begin.

Social work relationships can be used to "enable clients to explain their situations; to support self-determination; to empower them, when possible, to assume responsibility for their own lives; and to help them contemplate alternative actions" (Meyer & Mattaini, 1995c, p. 115).

Trust Building and Belief Bonding

The development of trust and respect that must underlie the partnership necessary to effective social work practice is a *process*. Processes occur over a span of time, and time is a necessary component of effective relationship-building. What needs to occur during this initial period of time?

Bisman (1994, pp. 79–81) presents this process as one of "belief bonding" and describes three components that are essential to both worker and client: (1) a belief in the competence of the worker to address the client's problem, (2) a belief in the client's capacity to incorporate change, and (3) a belief in the client's worthiness of the efforts of both worker and client.

Belief in the Worker's Competence

One of the major factors in the establishment of a belief in the worker's competence on the part of a disabled client is related to the client's disability. Clients who have had experiences that, in their understanding, are different from those of most other people, often have difficulty in trusting others who have not had similar experiences, especially when the subject under discussion is the experience or is related to the experience in some way. This is one of the reasons why peer support groups and peer counseling are so effective in working with some kinds of problems, from substance addiction to divorce, bereavement to immigration, imprisonment to terminal illness.

Many agencies and resources that provide services to people with disabilities, recognizing this as a major factor in offering assistance, search for and actively recruit people with the same disabling condition as their client population. If they are unable to locate people with the same disability, they may seek others with a different disability, assuming, as we do here, that there is a commonality in the disability experience that fosters increased trust and the development of a helpful professional relationship.

While the worker must be aware that there are also dangers and risks inherent in having a disability similar to that of the client (see below, "Avoiding the Assumptions Trap"), the more obvious problems occur when there are differences between the client's experiences and what the *client believes* to be the worker's experiences. Of course, as we all know, you don't have to have a broken arm to understand what that could feel like; however, if you have, there is an instant understanding and empathy that occurs that is obvious to both parties.

There are steps a social worker can take to assist the client to develop trust in the worker's competence to understand and to work within the client's disabling condition. It is important to become knowledgeable about the condition. Books are an excellent resource for this—not just books about, for instance, the *condition* we call cerebral palsy, but books by and about *people* with cerebral palsy. Other resources are the support and service organizations in your area whose area of special interest and expertise includes your client's condition, such as the Lighthouse, the Muscular Dystrophy Association, or the Cerebral Palsy Association. These resources can provide information, a knowledgeable person to answer questions, and possibly some peer groups the worker can attend. Gallaudet University Press in Washington, DC, offers books and material about deafness, including books by social workers and other mental health professionals. MSW students at Gallaudet organized DHHHSW (Deaf, Hearing, and Hard of Hearing Social Workers' Network) and maintain a website at *http//:academic, gallaudet.edu/dhhhsw*, which offers resources and feedback for social workers.

Still another resource is the selection of films and videos about people with your client's disability, such as *One Flew Over the Cuckoo's Nest, Rainman,* or *The Piano*. A word of caution: Films may present stereotypical images of disability that may be misleading and detrimental to your work with clients. The American Association of People with Disabilities in Washington, DC, and specific disability-related organizations are good sources of films that present more realistic portrayals.

Perhaps even more vital than these activities, the social worker can, as appropriate to the client's problem and unique situation, explore the experience of disability with the client directly. As with other differences between client and worker, such as race, religion, ethnicity, language, and customs, the client himself or herself is often the best resource for information. If the client's disability impacts upon the client's problem, and therefore is important to its resolution, it is appropriate for the worker to tactfully and carefully suggest that it might help him or her to know a little about what it feels like to be a blind person, or a person in a wheelchair, or a person with Lou Gehrig's disease. This approach not only develops the possibility of a common pool of knowledge and understanding about the disability between client and worker, but also places the client in the position of "expert"—a very important and empowering part of the relationship-building process.

In addition to questions about the worker's competence in terms of the client's disability, of course, the client may have other questions or issues: the worker's experience in the field in general, the worker's knowledge of and experience with the problem for which the client is seeking help, or other differences between worker and client. It is important not to approach clients with a strong authoritative stance, but rather by communicating a sense of self-esteem and competence that inspires trust (Bisman, p. 80).

Worker's and Client's Belief in the Client's Capacity to Change

It is important to note that this part of the belief-bonding process involves *both* worker and client. When working with a client across a disability, both client and worker must engage in reflection, introspection, and a mutual sharing of trust.

While many clients with a disability approach problems of any kind with optimism and a strong belief in their own ability to address them, for some the disability itself, or other experiences and personality traits, may diminish their confidence that change can occur. Clients, Bisman notes (p. 80), sometimes are not clear about the nature of their problems, or about what needs to be changed, and a part of the worker's task is to help clients to develop the confidence that things can change and improve.

Clients with disabilities may blame their disability for many seemingly related and unrelated problems. If the disability is permanent, there may be a sense of hopelessness that anything can change and that their situation can improve. For example, a client whose disability is such that he or she has been unable to maintain previous employment may feel depressed and hopeless about future employment and concerned and anxious about financial issues. Belief in the capacity to change means a belief that one is capable of finding a different kind of employment, of vocational training, or of performing another type of work as well and with as much interest and enthusiasm as the previous position engendered.

A client whose child is in trouble may blame the problem on his or her disability, believing that this caused or significantly contributed to the child's school problem, the crime, or the mental illness. In addition to blaming himself or herself, the client may also believe that there is nothing he or she can do to address the problem. While it is possible that the client's disability may have played a part in the child's problem, assuming total responsibility for the actions of another person is generally not realistic and can lead to despair and hopelessness. Helping the client to understand the various components of the situation, and to see that he or she can effect some change creates a vital link in the belief-bonding process.

Clients may also need assistance from the worker in believing that change can be effected when the reasons for the despair and hopelessness are related to conditions other than the disability. All clients, whether disabled or not, may feel a sense of hopelessness that impedes the belief-bonding process. The worker's energy, enthusiasm, and faith in the client are essential in assisting the client to believe that change is possible and within the client's power to achieve.

The worker also needs to believe that the client has the inherent capacity to change and to improve his or her situation. This may be a special challenge for workers whose clients are disabled. Workers may believe that a client's disability is a major impediment in effecting change, or that a client's disability necessarily negatively impacts every aspect of the client's life.

In order to achieve belief in the client's ability to improve his or her circumstances, the worker must self-examine, self-monitor, and self-observe. If the worker feels that the disability in and of itself makes a positive resolution to the problem almost impossible, or that it precludes change, he or she will not be able to bring the necessary energy and belief to the client-worker process. Workers must be sensitive not only to the client's perceptions of the place of the disability in the overall problem, but of their own as well.

Although social workers generally do have a strong belief in human being's capacity to change and adapt to different kinds of circumstances, sometimes a particular disability, or a degree of disability, may engender a sense of hopelessness in the worker. Jonsen, Siegler, and Winslade (1998) believe that helpers' perceptions about life with an illness or disability are grounded in their own position as people without the illness and disability and that not enough credit or understanding is given to the capacity of all human beings to adapt to a variety of circumstances. How many of us have had the experience of thinking we absolutely could not live with some condition or circumstance, only to find that, when the condition or circumstance occurs, we are able to adjust, adapt, and continue to live meaningful and fulfilling lives? The section on empathy and sympathy on page 178 may be helpful in thinking through some of these difficult issues.

It is vital that workers believe that change can occur and that the client's problem can be ameliorated with effort from both client and worker.

Belief in the Client's Worthiness

Clients with problems often have a sense of worthlessness and low self-esteem. They may believe that they have caused their problem or are directly or indirectly responsible for it. They may believe that they don't deserve to be helped, that they themselves are helpless, or that life as they are living it is not worthwhile. One of the first tasks of the social worker is often to assist clients toward an acceptance of their own value, of their worth as human beings, and as people who deserve and need to be helped.

Other clients approach the social work encounter firmly grounded in a strong sense of self-worth. With such clients, workers may quickly form the alliance necessary for the belief bonding to occur, for workers generally approach clients from a clear position of the value and the inherent worth and dignity, of every person.

Workers communicate this sense of client worth by treating clients with dignity and respect, by their manner of address, by consideration for the client's comfort and well-being during the interview process, by the manner in which questions are asked and information is received, and by other cues, both verbal and nonverbal. Clients, especially clients who are in the relationship-building stage of the social work process, are very sensitive to the smallest indications of worth (or lack of worth) the worker provides. Careful self-monitoring can be helpful, especially when a worker is unsure how she or he feels about the client.

Worker feelings about client worthiness to receive services is a major issue in certain kinds of settings, such as prisons or jails, substance-abuse treatment centers, and domestic violence counseling settings. In such settings, issues around worth are openly discussed and addressed in supervision, through in-service education, and special programs and seminars.

Worth, however, may also become an important consideration in working with disabled clients, especially those who are severely disabled. Unlike the discussions of client worthiness that occur in the settings described above, worth in a disability setting is often not openly discussed. In the former instance, lack of worth was ascribed to the client due to behavior and personality. In the case of severe disability, lack of worth may be attached to issues of quality of life or independence. It is thus not the *client* who is worthy or unworthy, but rather the client's *life,* with the disability, that is so considered.

Workers' reluctance to reflect upon these issues may be grounded in an unwillingness to address quality-of-life issues in general and to fully consider the import of their own subjectivity on their beliefs about the client's life and its worth. The code of ethics asks that social workers respect the inherent worth of each person; ability or physical or mental condition is not a qualifier to this directive. To think about one's personal feelings about quality of life in the context of this directive can be a painful experience in self-awareness, but an important one!

Beliefs about the lack of inherent worth of a client's life can occur in mental hospitals, long-term care facilities, Alzheimer's treatment centers, institutions for profoundly retarded people, and other chronic-care institutional settings. Problems with issues of quality of life, like the people who care for these clients, are multidisciplinary. However, it is the ethical responsibility of the social worker to address the issue in her or his setting, and in himself or herself, as well as in the context of work with a particular client.

There is a difference, it is acknowledged, between the person as an individual and the person's life, in terms of worth. However, to the client, this difference may be one of semantics, rather than one of essential meaning. It is important, then, to ask oneself, what is there in this client, and in this client's life, that is worthy of the effort that the client and I together will make to address the client's problem or condition? Our profession's ethical foundations will assist you in searching for, and finding, an answer that will be meaningful to both you and your client.

Empathy and Sympathy

Interwoven through, around, and between the three major components of the belief-bonding process is the concept of empathy and the way in which this is used to build relationship and trust in the professional encounter. It is important to distinguish between empathy and sympathy—or empathy and pity—in working with clients generally, but most especially when working across a disability.

Avoiding Sympathy and Pity

When confronted by a person who is experiencing difficulty, pain, anxiety, or other problems, many people find themselves expressing sympathy. Sympathy says, "How very awful! I know just how you feel." When we offer sympathy, we try to place ourselves in the shoes of another person and think of how *we* would feel if we had the problem ourselves. We then share with the other person the way that we think we would feel and believe that we are being supportive, understanding, and helpful.

It's rare that we are! Most of the time, the person to whom we are offering our sympathy responds politely and appreciatively to our expressions. If we look closely at the nonverbal communication, however, we see quite a different picture: We see frustration, anger, defeat, hopelessness, confusion, and a sense of being violated. The problem or condition may cause these feelings, but, in offering our sympathy, we are adding another, quite distinct layer of difficulty. Sympathy diminishes personhood, uniqueness, and the sense of self. The receiver of sympathy, in a sense, loses ownership of the problem creating the need for sympathy to the person who is expressing it, and who, by saying "I know just how you feel" claims that his or her reactions are the same as, and just as valid as, those of the person who is the object of the sympathy.

Even when the person expressing the sympathy has had an experience or has a problem similar to the receiver of the sympathy, no two lives, experiences, feelings, or reactions can really be the same. No two people whose child has temper tantrums feel the same way about the tantrums. No two people who didn't get into the school of their choice react the same way. Similarly, no two people who become deaf feel the same way about losing their hearing, and no two amputees experience the loss of a leg in the same way. In all of these cases, expressing your knowledge of how the person feels is inaccurate and destroys self-respect and dignity. Professional social workers understand the negative effects of offering sympathy and self-monitor to avoid this reaction to a client's problem.

Even more difficult for the client than sympathy is pity. While the sympathizer places himself or herself in the shoes of the client and expresses feelings and reactions he or she believes are the same as the client is feeling, the pitier does not attempt to identify with the client's feelings. Remaining external, intact, separate from the problem, and very much aware of the separation, the pitier "feels sorry" for the client. People who are expressing pity might say things like "It must be just awful to have cancer and know you're going to die," "This has to be the hardest thing to live with. I know I never could live with it," or "If I had to live like you are living, I know I'd just want to be dead."

While sympathy takes away the client's sense of uniqueness and of self, pity completely destroys the client. Expressions of pity basically communicate that the person does not believe that the client's life can have any qualities of meaning and goodness; the reason for the pity has become the whole person. The message of the pitier is "You *are* your problem or condition. You are defined by it and not by anything else you may be."

Both of these reactions to the client's problem, and/or to the client's disability, are very destructive. In order to avoid expressing sympathy or pity regarding the client's circumstances, before beginning your relationship it is important to reflect on your possible reactions, on the client's strengths, and on the things in the client's life that give, or have the potential to give, his or her life meaning, beauty, and depth.

Enhancing Empathy and Empathetic Communication

Different from either sympathy or pity, empathy is one of the foundational relationship-building tools used by social workers. The empathic worker must be able to "perceive accurately and sensitively the inner feelings of the client and to communicate this understanding to the client" (Hepworth, Rooney, & Larsen, p. 99). There are two steps involved in empathic communication: empathic recognition, and accurate reflection of the recognition.

To be aware empathically of what the client is saying, the worker must tune in to the client on many levels. Language, expression, tonality, body posture, facial expression—together these and other dimensions can help you to become aware of your client's feelings, both openly expressed and concealed. It is important to reach into the client's experiences, but also to understand the meaning that the client attaches to those experiences.

Once the worker understands the client's experiences and their meaning to the client, he or she is then able to communicate this understanding to the client. Empathy is not the same as sharing in the experience: Rather, it is sharing a recognition of the *meaning* of the experience to the client. Empathy conveys "I understand" through tone, gesture, and words.

Social workers use empathy in working with all clients. It is especially important in working across disability, and even more important when the client perceives the worker as having experience with the client's disability. Not "I know just how you feel. I would feel the same way," but rather, "I can understand your feeling as you do, in your situation." A subtle separation is maintained between the worker's experiences and the client's that enables the client to "own" his or her experiences in a way that is not possible when the worker attempts to lose the distinction between her or himself and the client in sympathy.

Empathy will encourage your client to share further details and feelings, while identifying with the client will shut the client down, and create an inner feeling of anger and frustration.

Avoiding the Assumptions Trap

Competent social work practice asks that we become knowledgeable in various areas: practice theory and methods, policy, diversity, human development, and research. It also demands that we become as knowledgeable as possible about the problems and conditions, cultures, and family and social networks of the people with whom we will be working. When we are practicing across disability, this includes becoming knowledgeable about disability in general and about the specific disabilities that affect the clients in our caseload. While this textbook will help you to gain the general information you will need, this should be supplemented by learning as much as possible about the specific conditions and problems of your own clients.

Although the knowledge we acquire is often quite concrete and specific, it is essential to recognize that this is still general, in the sense that any one particular client may not have the conditions, emotional reactions, or experiences that often are found when the group as a whole is explored. "Most" or "average" may not describe your client at all!

It is important, therefore, to approach clients with knowledge, but also with an openness to the specific conditions and details and perceptions of life experience that are unique to him or her. If we assume that clients feel a certain way, or will react a certain way to events, we make at least two very important errors. We make errors in assessment and in the development of a plan for change and therefore in the possibility of successful change. We also undermine the reality of clients' experiences, and undermine ego strengths, self-esteem, and self-determination.

Another assumption social workers often make in working with disabled clients is that the disability itself is, or should be, the focus of the work. Clients come for services for many different reasons, such as problems with a child, marital discord, social isolation, loss of a loved one, or fear of taking exams. When a client with a disability asks for help with a problem, that problem should be the focus of the work. If, in the course of exploring and addressing the problem, the social worker finds that the disabling condition is a part of the difficulty, it can be included in the discourse. Writing about clients with visual impairment, Adrienne Asch (1995) notes:

In the past, social workers tended to adopt the mindset that people with visual or other disabilities needed services from specialists in blindness or disability in general, but such ideas were often wrong then and are now indicative of subtle prejudice and discrimination by social workers or their agencies. It is essential for a social worker whose blind client and spouse come for marital therapy, for example, to concentrate on the couple's dynamics. However, if blindness comes up repeatedly as a source of friction, the worker may properly examine whether the client and his or her spouse know the means of optimal functioning as a blind person.

Workers who share a client's disabling condition themselves must be especially careful about avoiding the assumptions trap. While the shared disability may create and impression of an instant bond, in actuality the experiences of worker and client—both in terms of the disability and in terms of life experiences—will be quite different. Workers must be careful not to assume that clients have the same issues about their disability as the worker. Especially if a client has come for help about something not immediately related to the disability, it is important for the worker to self-monitor and stay where the client is rather than grounding the relationship-building process in the shared disability. Just as workers can make assumptions about client experiences and feelings based on sharing a disability, so can clients. Clients can readily assume that workers "understand" because they share a similar condition. It is important for the worker to recognize this and to focus on the special uniqueness of the client's own experiences, rather than on the presumption of commonalities, while acknowledging the obvious similarities as well.

Developing Patience and Understanding

Communicating with clients and developing a trusting relationship with mutual belief bonding may present some special opportunities for professional growth. Genuine trust may take a longer time to develop, or, with some clients—especially those with some kinds of mental illness or cognitive impairment—may never develop fully. Trust in some instances may have to be developed repeatedly, with the worker and client focusing on belief bonding during a part of every contact.

While many clients will communicate easily and comfortably with the worker, communicating with clients across some disabilities that may require nontraditional methods of communication may be awkward and will always be much more time consuming. Working with clients using communication boards, spelling out each letter of each word, requires an ample supply of both patience and time. Waiting and watching for "windows of opportunity" to support self-determination when decisions need to be made quickly may be frustrating. Repeating instructions several times to ensure comprehension requires persistence and dedication.

However, communicating with clients will enable the worker to develop a great deal of personal insight. In order to maximize these special opportunities for professional growth and develop competence, it is important for the worker to set aside some time for self-reflection. With a sincere respect for clients and a commitment to utilizing client strengths for empowerment and self-determination, workers will be able to develop a professional stance that incorporates patience and understanding and encourages clients to communicate and act in their own behalf.

Reducing Fear and Discomfort

It is not uncommon to experience some fear and discomfort in working with clients with disabilities, especially in the early stages of the relationship. Fear and discomfort occur most frequently when workers are new to the client population and do not have a similar disabling condition. As we know, when people perceive others as different from themselves, they often feel as sense of discomfort, or even of fear. Social workers are not immune to these feelings! It is important that we recognize within ourselves the fears we have about working with certain clients and address them, so that we minimize the effects of our own emotions on our clients and on the client-worker relationship.

Some disabilities, such as AIDS, severe deformities, or psychosis, may engender more fears than others. Fears may be grounded in many things, some realistic, some less so. No matter how remote the possibility, we may be afraid of "catching" our client's disabling condition. We may be afraid of how a client looks or acts or of the potential for violent or erratic behavior. We may be afraid of revealing, in own words and actions, our own fears or even our horror at the client's condition. When clients are near death, fears about our own mortality may intrude upon our consciousness. Fears about "saying the wrong thing" to a client who is disabled and already perceived as vulnerable—and thus adding to the client's problem—may leave us tongue-tied. Fear can make our hearts race, our voices shake, and our hands tremble. Fear can also paralyze and leave us unable to function as the competent professionals clients need. How can we address our fears?

There are several things we can do to help ourselves. Knowledge is our best resource. If we are concerned about "catching" our client's disability, knowledge about transmission and etiology will help to dispel those fears, as will taking adequate and appropriate steps to reduce any potential. If we are afraid of violent or erratic behavior, developing a safety plan with a supervisor or care team will assist us to feel more secure in terms of personal safety. If we are afraid of how our client may look or act, we can prepare ourselves by becoming familiar with these changes in appearance or actions and their meaning and in learning to look beyond them at our client's essential humanity. If we fear death and our own mortality, self-reflection and thought will help us to address this issue that is important not only to our work with clients, but also to our own lives and well-being.

Fear and discomfort generally decrease with time. As we get to know clients, as we develop relationships, our fears will fade. As we learn more about our clients' disabling conditions, we will become more comfortable in accepting them as a part, but *only* as a part, of who our clients are.

Chapter Summary

Whether the context of practice is individuals, groups, or communities, the first social work process—that of establishing trust and a working relationship with a client—is essential to any further work. In this chapter, we have presented several concepts to foster the development of trust, to develop a belief bonding, and to enhance relationship-building skills.

Helping relationships require a belief in the competence of the worker, a belief in the essential worth of the client as a person who deserves dignity and respect, and a belief that, together, worker and client can create a change and an improvement in the client's problem. The client may be seeking help for problems or issues arising from his or her disability, or for other, possibly unrelated, problems. Because the disability is a part of the client's life experience and often affects the relationship-building process for both the worker and the client, it is in some measure a part of that process.

A cornerstone of the relationship-building process is the competent and professional use of empathy. Empathic communication differs from sympathy or pity in that it demonstrates understanding of both the problem and the meaning that the problem holds for the client, and communicates that understanding in a caring and sensitive manner. It is important to try to avoid making any assumptions about the client's experiences, feelings, or relationships. While general knowledge of the client's problem, disability, and life situation is often helpful, workers must be careful to avoid generalizations and consider each client as a unique individual.

Working with clients who have difficulties in communication is an opportunity for professional growth, and workers should make every effort to allow time for self-reflection and for the development of a professional stance that includes patience and understanding, as well as respect for the client. An essential part of this is addressing personal fears and discomfort that may interfere with the development of an optimal client-worker relationship.

Questions for Thought and Discussion

1. Addressing quality-of-life issues when working with severely disabled clients in an essential part of self-awareness and self-monitoring. The first step is to gain an understanding of one's own feelings about the essentials of good life quality. What are the special qualities of your life that make it good? What would make your life poor in quality?

2. Do you think there are certain life qualities that are essential for *everyone?* How would you describe and define these? Do you think these are valid across cultures? Across time frames? Across age and gender?

3. If you and your client share a common quality—a disability, an ethnicity, gender, size, or any other observable quality—how would you respond to that commonality when beginning a relationship with a client? Would you allude to it or ignore it? Would you respond differently based on what the quality was, on what you know about the client population, or on the rarity or commonality of the quality?

4. How would you react if you become aware that your client was making certain assumptions about you and/or your experience and was building a relationship grounded in these assumptions? Do you think it's best to ignore these assumptions, in the interest of creating a strong belief bonding, in order to help your client?

5. For the next week, listen carefully to people around you. Notice how empathy, sympathy, and pity are expressed and watch the reactions of those who are its objects. Do you notice any differences?

12

Assessing Individuals and Communities

> The assessment process (that) begins at the first visit and continues
> throughout the contact. This process includes the definition of the unit of
> attention, or the drawing of boundaries around the relevant areas for inquiry.
> It also includes the gathering of information relevant to the situation and the
> thinking process through which the worker and client attempt to make sense
> out of the information gathered. (Hartman, 1994, p. 27)

The problems, resources, needs, and circumstances of each client or client group are unique. At first, each may be presented and/or perceived as distinct and separate issues, such as social isolation, unemployment, and inadequate housing. The assessment process provides a structure that assists client and worker to view not only each separate part, but also the ways in which each relates to every other; in other words, it connects each experience or perception to the client's life as a whole.

Assessment is potentially an unlimited process; there is always something new to be understood about a client, client group, or community and/or situation, and the assessment process is ongoing throughout the interaction between the client(s) and the worker. However, assessment as the primary function of the social worker–client contact must be structured to enable the process to continue toward intervention and resolution. Thus, during the assessment period, parameters must be drawn that provide information helpful to understanding the client within the context of a specific agency's services and resources, time frame, and client problem (Meyer, 1995b, p. 267).

Meyer (1995b, p. 268) notes that there are five steps to the assessment process: (1) the collection of data and its organization into an understandable system; (2) inference, the process through which the worker uses knowledge and judgment in understanding the material collected during step 1; (3) an evaluation of client functioning; (4) an agreement between client and worker regarding what will be addressed; (5) the development of a plan for intervention.

The assessment process enables the social worker and the client to gain an understanding of the client's world and of the needs and problems that must be addressed. As in all social work practice, assessment is a *mutual* process: Both the social worker and the clients have a vital role in sharing information, experiences, ideas, and approaches.

The importance of mutuality of process in enhancing the client's feelings of empowerment and self-determination make full client involvement in the assessment process essential. Because clients with disabilities often feel disempowered, or believe that their choices are limited by the disabling condition, mutuality becomes even more essential in working with these clients. The preceding two chapters have presented some of the work that is a necessary precondition to effective assessment: the development of communication and the establishment of a relationship that is built on trust.

The social worker brings to the assessment process a wide-angle lens, a lens that can include knowledge of theoretical frameworks for understanding people and life experiences; knowledge of human development; an understanding of the role of culture, ethnicity, belief systems, and experiences of oppression; an understanding of the impact of all life experiences and events on biopsychosocial development; and knowledge of community resources and support networks that can assist an individual to address, resolve, stabilize, or ameliorate his or her problem. The worker also brings skills in relationship-building and in interviewing that can help client and worker together to understand, focus, and address the issues that are troubling the client.

The client brings a telephoto lens, a lens that is focused on the uniqueness of his or her own life experience, an understanding of the world and of events that have impacted on him or her through personal beliefs and cultural experiences, knowledge of what has been attempted previously to address problems, what has worked and what hasn't and why. The client also brings two essential elements without which the social work process cannot be effective: a motivation for change and a willingness to engage in the process. If the client lacks these two essential pieces, the first tasks of the worker are to explore and understand the reasons, to attempt to engage the client in the process, and to help the client to understand that a change in the client's condition is a possibility.

> Through the process of assessment, worker and client seek an understanding of objective facts. . . . Much more exists, however, than objective reality. An understanding of the subjective reality must also be reached. People's views of their inner and outer worlds influence their adaptive and coping responses. Their personal reactions, the meanings attributed to events and processes, and feelings about them, are facts, too. (Germain & Gitterman, 1980, p. 18)

Because disability can complicate and confound the relationship between an individual and his or her environment, it is essential to be especially careful in developing and framing assessment tools. Appleby, Colon, and Hamilton (2001, p. 181) note that people with disabilities must address the same life issues as people without disabilities, with the superimposed additional layers of difficulty that are engendered by the disabling condition.

Practitioners working across disabilities may encounter anger, frustration, hopelessness, and a distinct unwillingness to engage in the process of change. These may be in part the client's reaction to the disabling condition itself; however, it is important to recognize that the barriers that society and environment have placed may so limit the ability to actualize and achieve a meaningful life that the client in effect "gives up."

It is also important to recognize that an "objective reality," as Germain and Gitterman state, such as the loss of use of limbs, the inability to see, or the onset or multiple sclerosis, may carry very different meanings for worker and client; the "subjective reality" may differ according to worldviews, experiences, and coping abilities. It is also important to recognize that, whether worker and client share a disabling condition or not, the disability that must be understood is the *client's* experience and not the worker's. Workers must be careful to understand the "subjective reality" of the client and be aware of the potential difference between that and their own assumptions of what such a reality would entail. Disabilities that may seem relatively minor to a worker may appear to be major obstacles to a client. Empathy, as discussed in the preceding chapter, is the tool that the worker can use to assist in understanding the client's subjective experience.

Social work assessment is understood through the person-in-environment framework, an ecological approach that involves understanding and assessing the goodness-of-fit between an individual and his or her environment (Meyer, 1995b, p. 263). In addition, the strengths perspective provides a focus on the positive strengths of the individual and the environment upon which worker and client can build in order to develop a plan for change. The strengths perspective is especially helpful in working across disability because it assists both client and worker to explore and affirm strengths rather than placing the primary focus on the problems and/or needs that are often related to the disabling condition.

While use of these two frameworks is basic, exploring the client's problem through other perspectives provides additional information and resources that can be helpful. Several other frameworks often used during the assessment process are presented here: the biopsychosocial, disability-specific, and quality-of-life perspectives all contribute meaningfully to assessment. Focusing on quality-of-life issues is an approach often used in working with clients who are ill and/or disabled, but it should not be the only approach used for assessment. Quality of life may be strongly impacted by environmental factors and others. Additionally, as noted in the preceding chapter, assessing quality of life is always a subjective process, and there is a potential for the worker's subjective experiences and understanding to unduly affect such an assessment.

Both the ecological and the strengths-based frameworks may be used to assess communities and groups as well as individuals. The community needs assessment provides an additional method for assessing communities. Groups of clients or communities may encompass a wide range of views, experiences, and perspectives. It is important to understand that the assessment process and the approaches used may vary significantly according to the size of the client system and the theoretical framework being used (Hartman, 1994, p. 28).

When working with a client, a group of clients, or a community, the worker can utilize any or all of the tools presented in this chapter in assessment. Choices may be determined by worker preference, client preference, agency policy, cultural appropriateness, or applicability to the problem or need.

The Ecological Framework

The ecosystems perspective was originally developed in the natural sciences, and in social work it has given rise to both the systems and the ecological methods. This perspective shifts the focus of the problem from the individual to the community and to the place of the individual within the community (Meyer, 1995b, p. 262–63). The individual and the community are viewed as each simultaneously affecting and being affected by the other and are thus understood to affect each other reciprocally (Germain & Gitterman, p. 28). An important implication of this reciprocal nature of the relationship between an individual and his or her environment is that both are "always actually or potentially adaptive to each other and that interventions can be carried out in either sphere of the case and can be expected to affect other spheres" (Meyer, 1995a, p. 19).

When the reciprocal balance between the individual and the environment is upset by an event, experience, or condition, stress is generated "by discrepancies between needs and capacities, on the one hand, and environmental qualities, on the other" (Germain & Gitterman, p. 28). Disability often creates such discrepancies: Needs and dependencies may increase, while the capacity to meet them may decrease. The environment may be unable to meet the increased needs, and the "fit" between person and environment deteriorates, creating stress.

Germain and Gitterman note that stress may occur in three areas: (1) during life transitions and crises; (2) under environmental pressures, such as unresponsive organizations and social structures; and (3) through maladaptive interpersonal processes. In this sense, there is a difference between people with disabilities from birth or early life and those who acquire a disability later in life. Those with disabilities of long standing have generally surmounted any crisis and developed a functional relationship with both societal structures and institutions and with social interactions. However, the occurrence of a disability or a sudden worsening or change in condition may initiate a crisis and a transition that engenders a great deal of stress. Individual coping abilities may be compromised by an unresponsive or inadequate social system and by the reactions of others in their lives to the changes. Professional intervention to restore balance, encourage and/or teach new coping skills, and develop networks and resources to meet new or emerging needs and interventions with family members and others in the client's interpersonal system can assist in the restoration of balance and the resolution of stress.

Allen-Meares and Law (1993, pp. 8–10) have developed a three-dimensional comprehensive ecological assessment system that encompasses six assessment principles:

1. Assessment should include data collected from multiple ecosystems with which the client interacts, such as home, school, place of employment, and so on.
2. Information sources should include the client, significant others in the client system, and worker observation.
3. All variables that describe the client and situation should be assessed, both those within the person (personality, behavior, physical conditions) and in the environment.
4. Information should be as comprehensive as possible.
5. Data should be organized in an intelligible manner.

6. The assessment should be linked to a variety of interventions, both individual and environmental.

The ecological framework also utilizes visual tools to clarify the relationships between the client and various environmental entities. The basic diagrammatic tool of the ecosystems perspective is the *eco-map*. Working with the client, a picture of the client's world is developed that considers each element in the client's environment in relation to him or her. Many variations of the eco-map have been developed (Edwards, 1995, p. 264). The three presented below may be especially helpful in working with clients across disability.

Eco-maps have generally used a person or people as the central focus of study. However, they can be used successfully to explore feelings, social relationships, or any other aspect of the clients' world.

The Classic Eco-Map

The eco-map contains a central circle, within which is placed central focus of the map. This is generally the name of the individual, but can also be the names of all the family members and their relationship to one another, the community, or people with a specific condition or impairment. Around this central circle project other circles, each illustrative of a relationship between the central circle and the others. Variations in importance and in relationship may be indicated in at least three ways: by the size of the circles, by their position, and by the quality and appearance of the lines that extend from the central circle.

While an eco-map form can be adapted to this purpose, it often limits possibilities or encourages emphasis on a particular element because it predetermines sizes and distances from the central circle. Rather, the worker and client can easily create a very personal and unique-to-the-client eco-map simply on a sheet of paper. Colors, shapes, designs, and the like can help to personalize the eco-map and engage the client more fully in the process.

Developing an eco-map is a very empowering process, one that can be accomplished, with worker assistance, by clients with almost any kind of disabling condition. When working with blind clients, eco-maps can be drawn using a variety of other communication methods; the shapes can be three dimensional (a system of rings or circles such as colorforms gives a tactile presentation yet enables the ecomap to be easily integrated in the client's chart) and the words can be written in braille. As always in using eco-maps, include an explanatory key that provides meanings given to lines, shapes, or colors.

The eco-map in Figure 12.1 represents the primary relationships of Stephanie, a sixteen-year-old high school student who attends a high school for the deaf. She works part time doing data entry at National Data Systems. She doesn't like her job because no one at work knows ASL, and she feels isolated and as though people ignore her. She is the only deaf person in her family. John and Sylvia, Stephanie's parents, are close to her, as is her brother Ted. Her older brother, Mark, has difficulties relating to her. He feels his parents have ignored him while taking care of her needs. He has refused to learn ASL, so their communication is superficial. Her best friend, Mandy, and her boyfriend, Connor, both attend school with her. Lately, she's been feeling unsure about her relationship with Con-

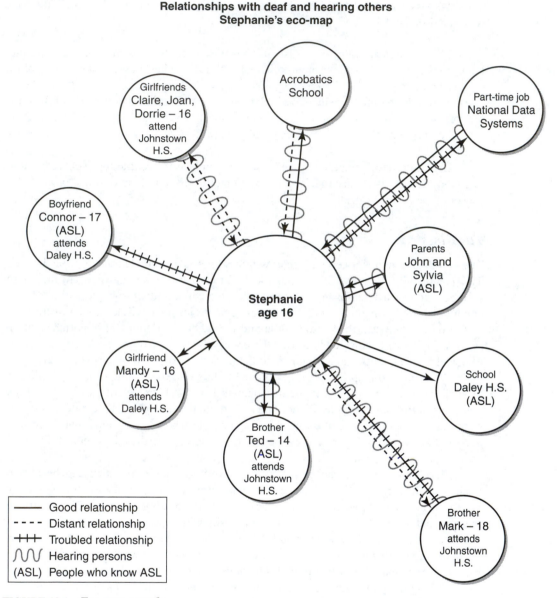

**Relationships with deaf and hearing others
Stephanie's eco-map**

FIGURE 12.1 *Eco-map sample.*

nor, and says she's thinking about breaking up with him. Claire, Joan, and Dorrie live in Stephanie's apartment building. They all played together as children, but lately Stephanie feels their relationship has become more distant, since each is more involved with school friends. The thing Stephanie enjoys the most is acrobatics. She attends afterschool classes three afternoons a week and works hard even though the teacher can't communicate with

ASL and has to use gestures and hand signals. If she has a question, or when events or competitions are planned, her parents have to assist her in communicating.

The PIE Map

The PIE map is an alternative form of eco-map that uses one large circle as the primary element. At the center of the circle is a smaller circle, within which is the name of the client, group, or community.

While the PIE map also uses the person-in-environment framework, the relationship among the various components is shown differently. The client and worker develop a list of all of the essential people, conditions, events, and other elements in the client's life. Generally, the disabling condition will be one of these elements. The client then creates "slices" of the PIE, giving each item on the list importance in relation to the others by varying the size of the slices. It is important to enable the client to engage fully in this process and to avoid providing input in order to arrive at an accurate portrayal of the importance the client gives to each part of his or her life.

The PIE system can be especially useful in assessing the client's view of the role of the disability in his or her life. Clients who do not feel that their condition has a major role will give a relatively minor place to their impairment. Clients who feel overwhelmed and controlled by their disability or who feel that their disability affects every other aspect of their life will, of course, give this a very prominent place in the diagram. It is important not to make assumptions about the meaning of the size of the disability slice: Rather, use this as an opportunity to explore the role of the disability in the client's life.

The example of a PIE in Figure 12.2 (p. 192) eco-map included here does not utilize variations in the slices; however, it provides a view of the system that can be adapted to meet individual, group, or community needs.

The "Environment" Map

Each of the eco-map systems highlights one aspect in the development of a mutual understanding of the client's world. The "environment" map (see Figure 12.3, p. 193) places the client in the central of three concentric circles. Immediately surrounding the client in the closest position is the circle of his or her "nurturing network." Outward of this is the widest circle, that of the "sustaining network."

The "nurturing network" circle is composed of all of the people and structures that provide nurturing to the client, such as family members, friends, and any others the client identifies. Because of the prominence of medical and caregiving people in the client's life, these may be a part of the client's "nurturing network." Support groups and disability organizations may also serve in a nurturing role and be included in this circle.

The more distant "sustaining network" generally includes community resources and institutions, such as clinics and hospitals, vocational rehabilitation, employment, income support systems, community recreation facilities that are accessible to the client, and others.

Relatively few elements placed in either of the network circles may indicate an area of problem that may benefit from social work intervention, and these should be explored

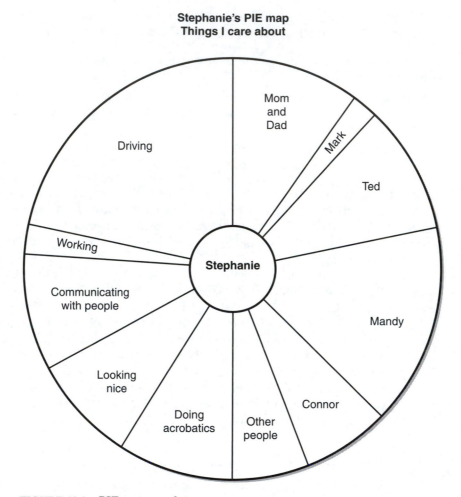

FIGURE 12.2 *PIE map sample.*

further with the client. If there are relatively few friends, or no friends, in the nurturing network circle, this may indicate social isolation and a genuine need for relationships. However, it may also indicate a person who prefers to lead a solitary life. It is important to explore whether the situation has developed as a result of, or after, the disability, or is completely unrelated to it.

If there are no, or few, community resources listed in the sustaining network section, the worker may want to explore why this is so. It may be that the client is unaware of services and resources and would welcome contact; it may be that there are no resources available to meet the clients' needs, and that these need to be developed; and, of course, it may be that the client's preference is not to be involved with outside resources.

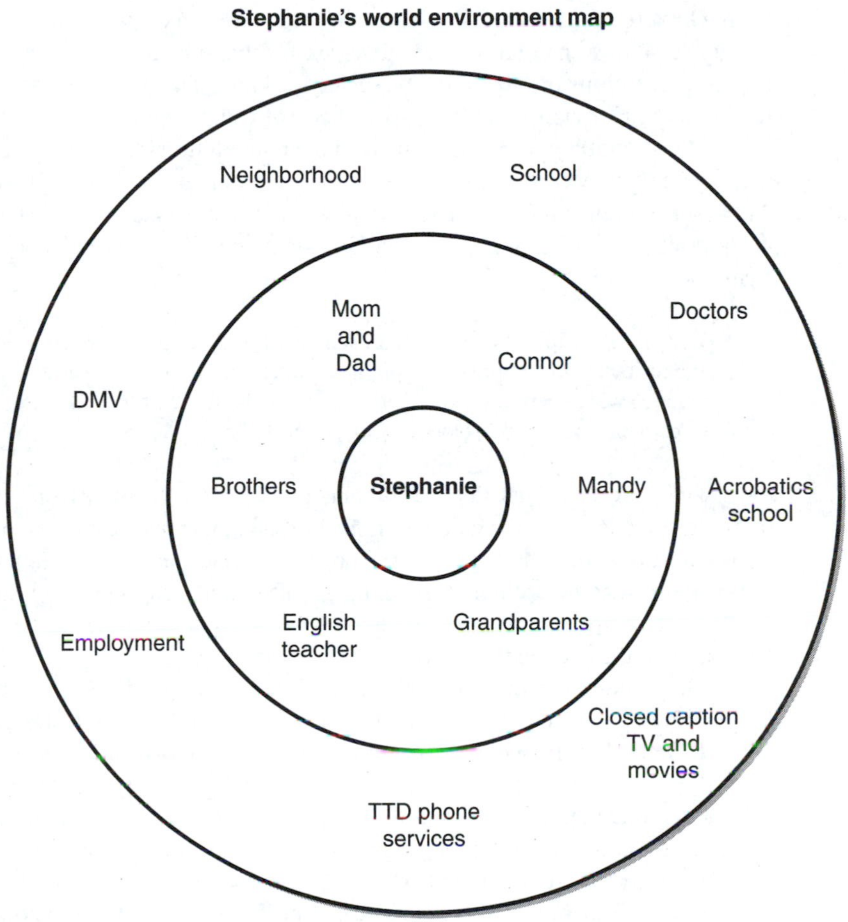

Stephanie's world environment map

FIGURE 12.3   *Environment map sample.*

The Strengths Perspective

While all assessment frameworks, theoretical perspectives, and practice models in social works include client strengths as an important dimension, Cowger develops an assessment tool that gives a preeminent place to an evaluation and understanding of client strengths. Social work practice from a strengths perspective utilizes client strengths in every phase of the social work process. The strengths perspective is empowering; it encourages client self-determination and supports the dignity of and respect for clients that are foundational professional values.

Many clients with disabilities are perceived by others as having few strengths: They may be dependent on personal care, require special accommodations in employment, or be unable to verbalize feelings, participate in sports, drive a car, dress themselves, hear a concert, or see a flower. Often we see ourselves as others see us, and disabled clients internalize the perceptions of others and of society at large. This may lead to low self-esteem, a feeling of helplessness and hopelessness, and of a lack of control over one's own life.

The strengths approach begins with the client telling his or her story, with assistance and encouragement from the worker (Cowger, 1991, p. 141). The process of explaining and describing the problem, of selecting which circumstances are relevant to it, is in itself an empowering one. It recognizes that the client "owns" the narrative and controls what is shared and how it is shared.

> With a little help from a worker, a client can clarify, or perhaps discover, some new insight, and articulate the nature of the problem situation. These questions are based on a model of practice whereby social workers believe their clients, trust their clients' judgment, and reinforce their clients' competency. (Cowger, p. 142)

The "problem," as defined in this perspective, "assumes only a disequilibrium between the client's needs and environmental demands and resources" (Cowger, p. 142). There are no value judgments made here that impact negatively on disabled clients, no implications that the problem rests in the client rather than in the environment. Client and worker can then move forward to explore the possible strengths in the client and in the environment that can be mobilized to address the problem.

The strengths perspective utilizes a simple framework as an assessment tool (see Figure 12.4). Two axes intersect, creating four quadrants. One axis describes personal and environmental factors, while the second describes strengths and needs or deficits (Cowger, p. 142).

Each quadrant represents the two factors noted at the ends of the axes: (1) environmental strengths, (2) personal strengths, (3) environmental deficits, and (4) personal deficits. Worker and client together enter data in each of the quadrants.

While all four quadrants are needed in order to develop a comprehensive assessment, the quadrant that focuses on client strengths may be the most important, for developing an awareness of strengths empowers the client and also can assist the social worker in affirming the client's ability to address and resolve problem situations. Strengths to be included include cognitive strengths, emotional strengths, motivational strengths, coping strengths, and interpersonal strengths (Cowger, pp. 144–46). These kinds of strengths are available to each person, whether or not disability limits some portion of physical or mental functioning.

The strengths perspective makes a number of assumptions: (1) that all people and environments have the capacity to improve the quality of clients' lives; (2) that focusing on strengths increases client motivation to address and resolve problems; (3) that the discovery of client strengths involves a mutual process between client and worker; (4) that focusing on client strengths decreases the possibility of "victim blaming" and increases interest in understanding client survival skills; and (5) that all environments contain resources that can be mobilized to resolve the client's problem (De Jong, & Miller, 1995, p. 729).

Focusing on client strengths helps both worker and disabled client to recognize that, in spite of the severity of the client's problem, the environmental deficits that limit resources and possibilities, and the constraints created by the client's disabling condition,

Stephanie's strengths

Her problem: Should she be a part of Deaf culture only, or should she also go out into the hearing world? If she decides to also interface with hearing world, what would she have to do?

Strengths

Good health	Supportive parents
Self-awareness	Brother Ted
Willingness to think about problems	Mandy
Ability to develop close relationships	Supportive school environment
Willingness to do some things she	Availability of services for deaf
doesn't like if it's for a reason	Acrobatics school has students
Ability to drive	her age
Good grades in school	Old hearing friends in her
	apartment building

Personal ———————————————————————— **Environmental**

Inability to communicate well with	No hearing friends at present
non-ASL speakers	No place for deaf and hearing
Fears of hearing world away from	to meet and interact
parents and Ted	Brother Mark
Doesn't like to take risks	Few hearing adults other than
	family members

Deficits / Needs

FIGURE 12.4 *Strengths perspective assessment.*

the clients *has,* in fact, survived and can call forth the internal strengths that have kept him or her functional until this point. As noted by Appleby, Colon, and Hamilton (2001, pp. 180–81), one of the most valued strengths for persons with disabilities is that of personal resilience, which can help in adapting, coping, and relating to the disabling conditions. Most people with disabilities experience ridicule and abuse by peers at some point in their life cycle; oppression, discrimination, rejection, and invisibility in some measure often accompany disability as well. Recognition of the individual's inner resources and his or her ability to marshal these when needed is an important part of strengths assessment for people with disabilities.

The strengths perspective, with its positive focus, appears to work particularly well in consonance with the social construct theory when the problem for which the client is seeking assistance is directly related to the client's disability. When the problems created by the disabling condition are located in society and in the environment's limitations, rather than in client limitations, and when utilization of the client's strengths rather than concentration on functional deficits are the focus of planning, motivation for change increases, as does client empowerment control over his or her life choices.

One of the key concepts of the strengths perspective is that of regeneration and healing from within. The very words "regeneration" and "healing," as De Jong and Miller note

(p. 734), point toward wellness rather than toward disease. The wellness and regeneration focus does not deny the reality of physical disease or disabling condition. Rather, it emphasizes the client's ability to "heal" in a profound and internal sense. "Regeneration" does not mean that one must re-create oneself without the disabling condition; rather, it implies the possibility of a wholeness that incorporates the disability into self, enabling the disability to become a part of the strengths of the individual, rather than defining his or her weaknesses. This is the true meaning of "wellness" within the disability context.

The Biopsychosocial Perspective

The biopsychosocial assessment addresses the biological, psychological, and social aspects of the client of client system in understanding problems and needs. Lum notes that, in working with multicultural clients especially, it is important to address cultural and spiritual aspects as well (Lum, 1999, p. 39). Cultural and spiritual assessment is vital for all clients, but especially for clients with disabilities. Assessing these dimensions can often provide essential information about the individual's or group's views about disability in terms of causation, effect, and relation to belief system and culture. The very nature of the definition of a disability is culturally dependent and a social construct developed by the culture: a disability in one culture may be a normal part of life in another, and a valued quality in yet a third.

Thus, the parameters of assessment in this framework include:

- Biological: physical functioning
- Psychological: internal, mental, emotional
- Social: external, relational, environmental
- Cultural: external, ethnic, racial, sectional
- Spiritual: transcendent, religious, belief system

The biopsychosocial framework is particularly useful in working with clients across disability because it provides a clear place for assessment of biological functioning and an opportunity to discuss and assess physical functioning or developmental delay with clients who may have avoided a discussion of a condition that limits functioning in the client's environment. The inclusion of psychological assessment also enables the introduction of mental health issues and history of mental illness or cognitive impairments.

Psychosocial assessments focus on client coping skills and stressors. Thus they encompass both the client's social and environmental situation and the client's psychological reactions to it (Lum, p. 39). Clients who are able to cope manage the stressors they experience competently. A sudden-onset disability can overwhelm a client's coping skills and cause a high degree of stress. The crisis intervention model presented in the following chapter can assist the worker to help the client to develop new coping skills or transitional coping skills, or to adapt older skills to encompass a new condition. Workers can assist clients to view their reactions to a sudden-onset disability in the context of a new, often serious stressor and to accept the temporary inability to cope as a disruption in the previous balance between stressors and coping skills that can be restored with time and appropriate interventions, rather than as a personal failure of unsurmountable proportions.

Psychosocial assessment explores not only the problem, but what is accessible to change that will stabilize, ameliorate, or resolve the client's problem (Woods & Robinson, 1996, p. 571). In working with disability, the disability itself—its existence in the client's life and some of its impact (with some notable exceptions, such as some kinds of mental illnesses)—is generally not accessible to change. All the motivation, resources, and efforts possible will not heal a severed spinal cord, enable vision to a person who is blind, restore cognition to someone with advanced Alzheimer's, or eliminate the effects of developmental delays. The change that is possible is in the client's relationship to the disability, in the attitudes of others in the client's environment, or in the responsiveness of societal and organizational institutions to the client's needs—parameters other than the biological and sometimes the psychological.

A Disability-Specific Framework for Assessment

Disabling conditions often demand the development of special adaptation and coping mechanisms. Because each person's life circumstances are unique, and each person's experience with disability is unique, there are infinite variations in the kinds and degrees of adaptations possible. To understand the person in relation to his or her disability, Appleby, Colon, and Hamilton (2001, p. 183) have developed a set of variables for use in assessing a person with a physical disability. These can generally be adapted for use with persons with other kinds of disabilities as well. They are:

1. The specific nature of the disabling condition
2. The person's age at onset
3. The person's character and personality
4. The person's family characteristics
5. The characteristics of the person's environment
6. Socioeconomic status
7. Ethnic group
8. Cultural and societal interactions

All these variables interact with one another, shaping and being shaped by the disability itself and the perceptions of the disability in both the person and in those around him or her. Because of the degree of discrimination, oppression, and stigmatization experienced by people with disabilities, almost all people have some degree of internalization of negative self-concepts.

In order to clarify some of the most important and basic distinctions in the way that people relate to disability, Appleby and colleagues suggest exploring two parameters with clients as a part of the assessment process: functional disability versus socially imposed disability and early age of onset versus later age of onset.

Disability

Functional disability: This term describes the kind of disability and its extent, as well as the effect of the disability on the client. It can be translated into a real inability to perform certain functions; it can be seen and recognized, and it is acknowledged by the health professions and by the general culture (Appleby et al., p. 184).

Socially imposed disability: Functional disability, however, is affected by the person's own perceptions of his or her disability, which in turn are affected by the perceptions of those in the person's environment about the disability. To assess socially imposed disability, worker and client must consider the client's feelings, as well as his or her experiences with oppression and stigmatization, isolation and discrimination. Because the environment itself is disabling, both through the experiences noted above and through its structures and institutions, disabled people often experience feelings of worthlessness, self-pity, and hopelessness (Appleby et al., pp. 184–85).

Age of Onset

Early age of onset: When a child is born disabled or becomes disabled at an early age, much of his or her ability to adapt and cope with the disability is dependent upon the reactions of parents, siblings, and other family members to the disabling condition. Family reactions are affected in turn by ethnic and cultural factors, religious and spiritual beliefs, and socioeconomic issues. The experiences of the disabled child with rejection and ridicule with peers and at school becomes the family's issue as well. Appleby and colleagues (p. 186) note that when parents and family members experience the child's disability as a challenge, they and the child can become empowered to change the oppressive and discriminatory elements in the child's environment. When they experience the child's disability as a loss or as a threat, self-esteem of both family members and child is negatively affected.

Because a disabled child is a part of a family system, assessment must include an understanding of the family, including the strengths of each individual; the level of functional disability in the child; the limitations the child's disability imposes on the family's functioning; the subjective interpretation of the disabling condition by individual and family; the differences between perceptions of functional, social, and subjective disability; and the resources available to the family (Appleby et al., p. 187).

When the individual being assessed is an adult whose disability was of early onset, consideration of the person's childhood experiences using the assessment process described here can provide valuable insights and a greater depth of understanding to both client and worker.

Later age of onset: People who become disabled later in life have experienced living without functional limitations. For them, becoming disabled precipitates a crisis of major proportions. A major factor to be assessed is the effect of the disability on the individual's identity. Often identity must be redeveloped to include the new disabling condition and the resultant loss of function. The degree of readjustment in self-concept may be linked to the kind and severity of the disabling condition but is also affected by age of onset and by social and environmental factors. A person with AIDS may experience disability quite differently than someone with rheumatoid arthritis. Someone with deformities of limbs and spine may have very different experiences from someone who has an invisible disability such as chronic fatigue syndrome. Social and environmental issues affect each of these quite differently. The ability of a person to adapt and cope with a later-onset disability is also very much a function of the person's personality and character (Appleby et al., p. 189).

Addressing Quality-of-Life Issues

In the introduction to his book *Quality of Life for Persons with Disabilities,* David Goode (1994a, p. vi) notes the variation in the perception of the essential components of good quality-of-life in diverse countries and cultures:

> . . . The most basic things, such as the conceptual basis of quality of life, or how it should be studied, are points of contention. Diametrically opposed perspectives will be found on almost any proposition. . . .
>
> This is not to say that there are not trends and consistencies . . . but that . . . there is diversity of opinion on most of these matters.

He goes on to note that, except for the position that challenges the quality-of-life concept altogether, all the authors agree that the way in which individuals construct their quality of life is essentially subjective and that quality-of-life issues are best understood from the perspective of the individual client whose life is being addressed from such a standpoint.

In order to address quality-of-life issues in a meaningful way, it is important to recognize that the more a person has in his or her life of the things the person wants and needs, the better will be that person's quality of life. There are three preconditions to the attainment of a good quality of life using this definition: The person must be *able* to want things, to recognize and *know* what those things are, and to *communicate* those wants to others (Rosenberg, 1994, p. 176).

In 1987–88, a National Quality of Life for Persons with Disabilities project was undertaken in the United States as a result of changes that had occurred in regard to disability in the previous decade: the move toward deinstitutionalization, normalization, advocacy and self-advocacy, and the inclusion of persons with disabilities in the mainstream. Concern for the quality of services and supports led to an exploration of "quality" and how this is understood. In the development of quality-of-life concepts, the project turned to disabled people themselves for guidance. The resulting process for exploring quality of life dimensions is applicable to all people and is not limited to persons with disabilities (Goode, 1994b, pp. 139–40). The model was used by people with disabilities, family members, and professionals to understand and discuss quality-of-life issues in a meaningful manner (Goode, p. 143).

The framework stresses social interactions and relationships, and focuses strongly on subjective understanding by the client of quality-of-life issues. From the complex model first developed by the project, a simpler discussion model was drawn that could be used in a variety of contexts and situations. The central circle in the model defines the desired behavior outcomes, or the quality-of-life indicators that the client has defined.

To use the model (Figure 12.5, p. 200), begin with number 1, a description of the needs of the client: those things that are important factors in a good quality of life. When these have been defined, the client proceeds to number 2, social goals expectations: In order to meet these needs, the client must recognize the kinds of expectations these needs set up in others. For example, if you want to participate in a book discussion group followed by a coffee social on Monday nights from 5 to 7 P.M., because that will contribute to your life quality (number 1), then the expectation (number 2) is that you will read the book,

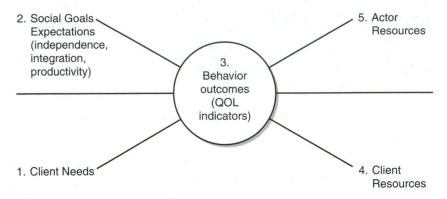

FIGURE 12.5 *Quality-of-life discussion model.*

Goode, D. (1994). The National Quality of Life for Persons with Disabilities Project: A Quality of Life
Agenda for the United States. In D. Goode, *Quality of Life for Persons with Disabilities,* p. 142. Cambridge,
MA: Brookline Books.

think about it in the context of the expected discussion, be available, be prepared to attend
the activity, and be willing to engage with others.

Developing ways to meet these expectations requires the use of resources in the
client (number 4). In our example, the client must read the book; if this requires special
assistance or equipment, such as talking books, large print, or a page-turning system, the
client must arrange these. He or she must be dressed and ready to go and must be willing
to engage with others.

There must also be a recognition that others and the environment can either assist or
hinder the client in meeting his or her need (number 5). To attend the book discussion may
require transportation, either private or through a public service. Being prepared to go may
involve assistance with dressing from a caregiver or a family member or setting aside the
time to dress oneself. Members of the group can contribute to the client's experience or
compromise it by being friendly and accepting or indifferent or rejecting.

Through the discussions engendered by the discussion model, a needs/goals matrix
was developed for assessment (see Figure 12.6). The matrix encompasses the first, second
and third elements in the discussion framework (Goode, pp. 143–44). It is possible to use
these two assessment guides for developing a greater understanding of salient quality of
life issues for the client.

It is important to recognize that these assessment tools focus on the whole individual
and do not emphasize disability. Rather, these methods recognize strength and ability, as
well as the essential similarity of all people in their needs, goals, and expectations (Goode,
p. 147). They enable a very subjective assessment that encourages individual thought and
goal definition. However, one must also recognize that cultural differences in societal goals
related to quality of life and access to services impact on the quality of life of people from
racial and ethnic minority groups. A good "quality of life" as defined by European Americans may not be attainable or desirable to all. Programs and services designed to enhance
the life quality of "all" (read "majority") do not necessarily meet the needs of all ethnic
groups (Laucht & McClain, 1994, p. 189).

Age group: Settings: Other primary actors:

Need (1)	Need Salience	Social Goals and Expectations (2)		
		Independence (Decision Making)	Integration (Participation)	Participation (Responsibility)
Love	H_M_L	*		
Acceptance	H_M_L			
Sexuality	H_M_L			
Friendship	H_M_L			
Personal growth	H_M_L			
Health	H_M_L			
Possessions	H_M_L			
Financial security	H_M_L			
Stable environment	H_M_L			
Recreation/leisure	H_M_L			
Culture/faith	H_M_L			

*Boxes when filled in refer to element 3 of the QOL discussion framework desired behavior outcomes.

FIGURE 12.6 *Needs/goals matrix sample.*

Goode, D. (1994). "The National Quality of Life for Persons with Disabilities Project: A Quality of Life Agenda for the United States." In D. Goode, *Quality of Life for Persons with Disabilities,* p. 144. Cambridge, MA: Brookline Books.

The Community Needs Assessment

The "triple community approach" explored by John Tropman (1995, p. 563) presents three definitions of "community" that may be useful in understanding and assessing community needs in terms of services and accommodations for persons with disabilities. The three definitions used for "community" include a geographical (*locational*) community, such as Des Moines or Arizona; a common activity (work) community (*vocational*), such as farm workers, engineers, or teachers; and a common belief and commitment community (*identificational*), such as Christian Scientists, Jews, Mormons, Latinos, or African Americans.

Who defines the "needs" in a community is often a political matter. Often those who determine needs and develop plans to resolve them are not those affected by the needs. A helpful example of this described by Tropman (p. 384) suggests that those who define "poverty" and develop plans to address this need are generally not those who will be affected by either the definition nor the plan. A problem associated with this is that people, although they may be able to perceive their own needs, often do not perceive the needs of others in their community and therefore are not willing to provide resources to address these.

Ideally, community assessment does involve people who are disabled. Ethical standards of fairness presume that the people who are most affected by the need be involved in assessing it and in the development of a resolution (Tropman, p. 564). People with disabilities often have difficulty making their needs known. Limitations imposed by the disabling condition, unwillingness to call attention to themselves and their problems, and low self-esteem often serve to keep the needs of the disabled people on the fringes of needs assessment and resource allocation. Chapter 15 explores advocacy as a social work practice model that addresses this issue.

Quantitative Assessment Tools

Quantitative measures of assessment involve exploring problems by considering their prevalence in the community. This can be determined using census data, surveys, telephone and personal interviews, mailed questionnaires, consumer surveys, and other methods that assess the need for services (Tropman, p. 565). A specific subset of the community can be assessed as well. It is possible using these methods to focus a needs assessment on people with disabilities living in a particular area, people with disabilities working in banks, or people with disabilities who are members of a faith community or ethnic group. It is important to involve people in the situation being assessed in the development of the assessment tool as well.

Qualitative Assessment Tools

Qualitative assessment provides more in-depth information and uses tools such as focus groups, discussion groups, observation, or representative groups to gather the information needed for assessment. Qualitative assessments includes the variety and richness of experiences and also are able to incorporate varying perspectives with much greater detail (Tropman, pp. 565–66).

Tropman notes (p. 567) that there are differences in the structure of the various kinds of groups that can be used to obtain information. The goals of the assessor and the predetermined parameters defined by the political process may also impact the qualitative assessment process. Three kinds of groups serve different functions in qualitative assessment:

1. Public meetings: These meetings are open to the public in a community and have a preset agenda. While a wide variety of views and perspectives are presented by participants, these public meetings are often attended predominantly by those who have a particular interest or stake in what is being discussed.

2. Focus groups: The focus group is generally a group of people gathered together by the assessor who react to and interact with the subjects raised by the assessor. Access to the group is by invitation, and focus groups are not open to the public.

3. Representative groups: Members of representative groups are often chosen to present the views of a specific group of people in the population of which they are members. In assessing the needs of people with disabilities in a community, for example, a representative group might include people who are blind, people in wheelchairs, people with exacerbation-remission cycle conditions, people who are homebound, and others. Though they share a disability status, the needs of each of these groups in the community are quite different. Representative groups enable each member to share his or her diverse needs and to listen to the needs of others in order to develop a comprehensive understanding of the needs of the disabled in a community.

Because the line between *needs* and *wants* is often unclear in a community, and because the assessor largely determines who will be involved in the assessment and what methods will be used, it is important for the assessor to understand that personal value judgments may affect the decisions about what is assessed and how (Tropman, p. 568). Self-awareness and a mechanism for community oversight can help to minimize these potential difficulties.

Chapter Summary

This chapter has presented several approaches to assessment that are particularly suitable for working with people across disability. The ecological perspective considers the person-in-environment "fit" and suggests that change and adaptation in any part of the system will affect every other part. The onset of a disabling condition, therefore, can affect every area of functioning and interaction in a negative manner. Conversely, an adaptation, the development of a coping skill, or a positive change of attitude will also affect every area. Three diagrammatic systems were presented for assessment, and adaptations of these to incorporate issues specific to people with disabilities were discussed.

The strengths perspective is particularly helpful in assessing people with disabilities and is in and of itself an empowering and affirming tool. Assisting the client to "tell his or her story" immediately places the client in a position of mastery and control. The assessment model, with its four quadrants, should be used in a manner that particularly emphasizes individual strengths. Focusing on strengths rather than on deficits, disabilities, and losses, which have often been the central locus of attention in the client's interactions with health and community systems, enables the client to view himself or herself as positive, resourceful, and able to survive.

Biopsychosocial frameworks, expanded to include the vital elements of cultural and spiritual assessment, can provide helpful insights to client and worker. The focus on "bio" as one of the essential elements of assessment enables the disabling condition to be introduced into the assessment process as a "normative" and not a "special" aspect. The "psycho" portion of the assessment clearly encompasses mental illness and other mental and emotional conditions in a similar "normal" manner. The inclusion of the cultural and spiritual dimensions in the assessment enables the discussion of disability in the context of the client's belief system and culture.

Appleby and colleagues' disability-specific framework focuses on the way in which the person and others in the environment, social institutions, and physical structures relate to the person with disability. It develops a distinction in disability assessment between "functional" and "social" disability, which is essential to both client and worker understanding of the client's relationship to his or her condition. This framework also explores the differences that age of onset have upon the way in which a person adapts and copes with a disabling condition.

No consideration of disability assessment would be complete without an exploration of quality-of-life issues, which play so prominent a role in literature about disability. It is noted that there is a general agreement that determinants of good life quality are both individual and subjective. A diagrammatic model for discussion of quality-of-life needs and goal attainment provides a mechanism for assessment of the client's subjective values regarding life quality. As a result of the Quality of Life for Persons with Disabilities Project, a tool has been developed that addresses elements of life quality that are shared by all people, both with and without disabilities. There is a strong emphasis on commonalities within subjectivity: Most people want many of the same kinds of things to ensure a good quality of life.

While several of the assessment methods presented, such as the ecological framework and the strengths perspective, are readily adaptable as tools for assessing groups and communities, a model for community needs assessment is also included here. Application of this model views the person, or persons, with a disability as members of a group within the community with needs and concerns that can be understood and assessed using community assessment methodology.

Assessment tools are generally used within the framework of a particular practice model. Some work better with certain models, but all of them can be used effectively with the practice models included in the following chapters. Chapter 13 will present models for social work practice with individuals across disability, while Chapter Fourteen 14 discusses models for working with the disability community.

Questions for Thought and Discussion

1. The eco-map and the PIE map can both easily be adapted to reflect feelings instead of relationships. From what you know about the client Stephanie, design a possible eco-map and PIE map that focus on feelings rather than on relationships.

2. Stephanie has come to you with a serious issue, one that may impact her entire life: whether to be a part of the Deaf community only, or whether to be involved in both the Deaf and the hearing communities. Do you think it is possible to be immersed in both? How might you help Stephanie to explore the hearing community?

3. You and your client are assessing his problem, and he does not relate it to his disability in any way. Do you think that knowing about a client's disability is an important part of assessment, whether or not the client views his or her problem as related to the disability?

4. If you think knowing about disability is important and the client has not mentioned it, would you introduce the subject? If not, can you be certain that your client's disability is not impacting the problem in some essential manner?

5. Some people who have disabilities have strong identifications with a specific "disability culture." Deaf culture is the prime example of this kind of group identification, and our client Stephanie is a part of that culture. Do you think that all disability groupings have a "culture"? How would you define "culture"?

13

Practice Models: Working with Individuals

Chapter 12 has presented a number of frameworks for assessment that enable worker and client to incorporate issues around disability into the assessment process. Assessment is an essential element in social work practice, and using a number of assessment methods can increase understanding and facilitate the goal setting and intervention process that generally follows. In that chapter, a generic model of social work practice was assumed. To function professionally in any setting, social workers should be able to intervene with individuals, families, groups, and communities and move across different systems and boundaries (Hartman, 1994). This supports a generalist model that provides for such flexibility. However, the assumptions of a generalist, generic model regarding necessary elements in practice are also applicable to specific social work practice models with individuals (Adapted from Brieland, 1995, p. 2250):

1. Knowledge of the accepted standards of social life and the typical deviations from these standards
2. Use of norms of human life and human relationships
3. Understanding the importance of social history in understanding the needs of a particular individual
4. Using established methods of study and intervention

Practice models provide an overall orientation to the client and to social work and incorporate all the social work processes. Workers are trained to use a variety of models, and the model ultimately selected for work with a particular client may be chosen for a number of reasons. Worker and/or client preference is a strong determinant: Some workers and clients prefer the psychodynamic orientation, others a cognitive-behavioral model, and still others a feminist model of practice. Agencies have often a preferred model that is used with all the agency's clients. Practice models may be dictated by setting or by population, such as crisis intervention for hospital settings, case management for working with the elderly, and psychodynamic models in for clients in mental hospitals. Program and funding sources also influence the choice of models; programs that will provide funding for a maximum of twelve visits per client require short-term models, while others may fund group-work models exclusively.

Because all practice models have a generalist core and are developed around an understanding of the ways in which human beings think, react, live, and feel, grow, and change, any model is potentially appropriate and applicable to working with clients across disability. The models that have been selected for inclusion in this chapter are simply those that tend to be used in working with clients because they address a particular need or problem that occurs regularly in the lives of people with disabilities. They are excellent choices for many other populations and problems as well and are commonly utilized in many settings.

The crisis intervention model is generally the practice model used in hospitals and other emergency settings. It is especially helpful in working with clients who have been newly diagnosed with a disability or those whose condition or life situation has changed or with disabled clients who, like nondisabled clients, are experiencing a crisis in their lives. The goal of this model, as we shall see, is to stabilize the client in a manner that enables optimal functioning within the parameters of the changes experienced.

Because many disabled clients feel isolated, stigmatized, and oppressed, they experience a great loss of self-esteem. The empowerment model addresses the internalized sense of hopelessness and powerlessness and assists clients to assume an active role in shaping and managing their own lives and their care. Using strategies to develop confidence and a sense of mastery over one's own life and life choices, the empowerment model seeks to maximize client independence.

In the empowerment model, the client is the primary source of action and change. However, not all clients with disabilities are able to become empowered sufficiently to attain their goals and meet their needs independently. The advocacy model addresses the special needs of these clients. In this model, the social worker personally takes a much more active role. Doing her or his best to ascertain the client's needs, desires, and wishes, the social worker as advocate works on the client's behalf strives to fulfill these through linking the client with resources and services, advocating for the client in institutional settings, and supporting the family in meeting the client's social and relationship needs.

Because conditions that create disabilities tend to persist, clients with disabilities often require services long term. Often, a number of agencies, programs, and systems are involved in providing support and services to the client. Case management social workers provide the necessary link that enables communication and coordination between service providers. The case manager carries ultimate responsibility for the client's care. Case management is often a less intensive model, but case managers may work with the same client for many years.

Many case managers are often also skilled in the crisis intervention model. When a crisis or change occurs in a long-term client, immediate, intensive intervention and action is needed. Case management often follows a pattern of low-intensity coordination services, interspersed irregularly and unpredictably with high-intensity interventions to meet crisis needs. When crisis intervention is not a part of the case manager's functions, he or she refers the client for these services.

We have come a long way from Chapter 1, where we explored models for thinking about disability. One of the models presented was the social construct model, where the "problem" is located not within the client but in the environmental limitations that limit client functioning. It is important to understand how this model can be used in social work practice with individuals and how shifting from individual deficit to societal deficit can be used to assist clients in developing a positive self-concept, advocating for their rights, and assuming their rightful place as full members of society.

As we begin exploring the models in this chapter, it is important for the reader to recognize that: (1) Although these models have been selected for relevance and utility in working with clients across disability, other models of practice are also effective and may be the models of choice in working with some clients; (2) due to the structure of this text, in-depth presentations of the models are not possible, and readers should refer to other sources for guidance and information prior to applying the models in a specific context; and (3) although the models are presented separately, in practice the use of these models often overlaps: The case management model may also use elements of the advocacy model, empowerment may be combined with crisis intervention, and so on. Social workers rarely use models in their pure form but instead eclectically, taking what is needed and relevant from each model to best meet the needs of the clients.

As with assessment, it is also essential that social workers address the ethnic and cultural elements in a client's situation and that these be considered in selecting and adopting an appropriate practice model. Advocacy and empowerment models may be culturally dystonic for some clients. The social construct model may not be helpful to a client who views a disability as God's punishment. Case management may be viewed as dependency and therefore may be inappropriate where cultural values espouse self-sufficiency and independence.

The Crisis Intervention Model

Crisis intervention as a model of social work practice developed out of a concern for people who were experiencing severe, acute distress as the result of some event that occurred immediately prior to the distress. It was recognized that, when people are in crisis, they may cope with it in ways that are either adaptive or maladaptive (Hepworth, Rooney, & Larsen, 1997, p. 390). Immediate and intensive intervention is often necessary and effective in ensuring a healthy and functional resolution. For people with newly acquired or newly diagnosed disabilities, the model offers an immediate intervention that can assist clients in coping with the severe stress such abrupt changes in condition can create.

In order to effectively utilize the crisis intervention model, it is important to understand a number of concepts and strategies.

Definition of a Crisis

Gilliland and James (1997, p. 3) define a crisis as: "A perception of an event or situation as an intolerable difficulty that exceeds the person's resources and coping mechanisms. Unless the person obtains relief, the crisis has the potential to cause severe affective, cognitive, and behavioral malfunctioning."

The Precipitating Events and Characteristic Signs of a Crisis State

It is possible to distinguish two kinds of events that are likely to precipitate a crisis state. *Acute situational events,* such as the onset of a serious illness or disability; traumas such as severe automobile accidents; death of a loved one; disasters such as earthquakes, floods, fires, and wars; or being the victim of a violent crime precipitate a crisis state in the individual and often in close family members as well.

Developmental transitions also often precipitate crises: retirement, entering a nursing home, having a baby, marriage or divorce, menopause, a child leaving home, or the onset of adolescence are examples of developmental transitions (Ell, 1995, p. 660). In addition, other events can create a crisis in certain personal and situational circumstances, such as loss of a job, a move, the loss of an intimate relationship or of a close friend or of a home, or an abrupt change in socioeconomic circumstances.

In addition to developmental and situational crises, Gilliland and James (1997, p. 19) suggest a third kind of crisis, which they have called *existential crises.* These "refer to the inner conflicts and anxieties that accompany important human issues of purpose, responsibility, independence, freedom, and commitment." These occur, for example, if we realize that we made some wrong choices in life that cannot be changed, if we feel that we are useless to everyone, even to ourselves, or if we realize we caused great harm to another person, even accidentally, such as by injuring or killing someone in an automobile accident.

Crises must be understood in a cultural context as well. Events that cause crises in some cultures are readily accepted as natural events in others. There is always a cultural meaning attached to a crisis, and any assessment or planning must incorporate elements that are culturally congruent. Crises can be further provoked and conditions worsened when approaches and plans that are not congruent with the client's culture and expectations are attempted.

People in crisis may experience severe emotional upset, anxiety, depression, confusion, or anger; inability to concentrate, to make decisions, to solve problems, or to take action; high levels of vulnerability and memory loss; low levels of defensiveness; disturbance in sleeping and eating patterns; fluctuating sensations of hot and cold; and other physical, cognitive, affective, and relational difficulties (Ell, 1995; Gilliland & James, 1997).

Challenges and Opportunities Are Engendered

People normally function comfortably in a state of homeostasis. The exceptional stress causes by the crisis destabilizes the individual and creates opportunities for extreme reactions and behavior not commonly a part of the individual's patterns. The extremes may present a danger; the possibility of suicide, homicide, or other harmful behavior may be seen as the only way to deal with unbearable stress (Gilliland & James, p. 4), and the behavior of a person in crisis is often unpredictable and erratic. However, because many crises immediately involve professionals such as physicians, nurses, police officers and other justice officials, members of the clergy, social workers, psychologists, funeral directors, and others who are trained to recognize, intervene, and/or refer people in crisis for help, assistance is often quickly available. Recognizing their need for help, people in crisis often reach out for assistance as well.

When people in crisis are not offered assistance and/or do not seek it, one of three patterns generally occur: (1) They may cope with the crisis themselves, gaining new strength and growing from the experience. (2) They may survive the crisis by blocking all painful feelings. The feelings do not disappear but remain under the surface, unaddressed and unresolved, and impede a positive adaptation to the changes engendered by the crisis. (3) They become effectively completely unable to cope and suffer a serious breakdown (Gilliland & James, p. 4).

The stress of the crisis event, and the state of disequilibrium created, offer opportunities for growth and change as well. When a person is vulnerable and when defenses are down, there is the possibility of reflection, insight, growth, and change. Coping with the crisis, developing greater, or new skills, taking chances, making choices—all provide ample opportunities for personal growth and can engender a feeling of confidence and self-respect. As the immediate demands of the crisis diminish, as some of the pain diminishes, clients may become aware of these opportunities.

How can we help people in the crisis of a newly diagnosed disability or an unexpected change in condition to move toward positive resolutions, rather than negative and dysfunctional ones, or indeed to move at all? Crisis states do not persist over long periods of time. It is generally accepted that the maximum period a person can remain in a crisis state is six to eight weeks. After that, a new state of equilibrium—positive and functional, or dysfunctional and harmful—must ensue. Crisis intervention practice models provide helpful guidelines.

The Practice Method

Because crisis intervention generally occurs during the six- to eight-week period following the crisis event, it is considered a brief form of therapy. The goal of crisis intervention is to assist the individual toward a meaningful positive resolution and functional adaptation to the crisis. The effects of the crisis may persist to some degree well beyond the six- to eight-week period; however, the person has regained a sense of control and the ability to use appropriate coping skills in addressing problems.

Gilliland and James have developed a six-step model for crisis intervention that has been widely accepted and utilized by social work practitioners. The model is summarized here and requires ongoing, careful assessment of the client during all phases of the intervention:

Step 1. Define the problem: Listen to what your client is saying carefully, noting both verbal and nonverbal cues. Define the problem from your client's point of view.

Step 2. Ensure the client's safety. Assess your client for physical or psychological risk of harm by exploring both internal states and the external situation. Take any needed precautions to ensure client and others are safe from harm.

Step 3. Provide support. Listen to your client in a caring, empathetic manner. Be available to your client so that you can be depended upon to be a real support person.

Step 4. Examine alternatives. Assist the client to explore options and choices, to develop effective coping mechanisms.

Step 5. Make plans. Assist the client to develop a short-term plan, which includes steps the client can take to effect the plan himself or herself.

Step 6. Obtain commitment. Assist the client to make a commitment to the plan, and to the actions he or she has developed in the plan.

Application to Clients with Disabilities

The crisis intervention model adapts well for addressing the crises of newly diagnosed or acquired disabilities. When there is a need to assist parents to accept their newborn child's developmental disability, an adult to address the major life changes required by a spinal cord injury, or an elderly person in living without the vision he or she had depended upon for eighty years, the crisis intervention model of practice can be utilized appropriately.

Disabling conditions may cause permanent changes in a client's ability to function independently, and social work intervention may be necessary well beyond the crisis period. An important part of the plan developed with the client may be to initiate case management or to refer to independent living or to vocational rehabilitation.

It is also important to remember that the disability itself is not the only potential source of crisis in the life of the client. Disabled clients also marry and divorce, lose beloved family members, get caught in floods, and ask themselves existential questions. It is very important to listen closely and not to assume that the disabling condition is the primary factor in the precipitation of the crisis. Let the client lead in determining the role that the disability plays, if any, in the crisis he or she is experiencing.

The Empowerment Model

As Kemp states (1995, p. 190), "An empowerment approach . . . assumes an engaged worker who helps clients to construct their experience in political as well as personal terms." Social work core values focus strongly on a recognition of human dignity and respect for persons, and social workers have always viewed client self-determination as primary in upholding these values. Self-determination for clients involves placing the client's goals and objectives in a primary position in planning and implementing services. Client-centered practice encourages clients to take an active role in problem definition, assessment, and intervention planning. Workers recognize and build upon client strengths to develop a practice that is grounded in mutual respect.

Disability as Vulnerability

As discussed in the previous chapter, people with disabilities are recognized as a vulnerable population not only because of functional limitations; socially imposed limitations that result from social stigmatization, oppression, exclusion, and prejudice and the individual's internalization of these often create a low sense of self-esteem, powerlessness, and helplessness in clients with disabilities. The empowerment model assists clients to achieve their potential and to promote changes in their environment and in social policy that will promote social justice (Lee, 1996, p. 230).

Society has described the person with disabilities as a "victim" of a "tragedy" with which one must cope. Critiques of this assumption present the concept that (1) disability is not always as disastrous a condition for the individual as nondisabled people think and that (2) it is not the disabling condition itself, but societal reactions to it that create difficulties and victimize the disabled person (Black, 1994, pp. 409–10).

Redefining disability to focus not on what is "wrong" with the individual but rather on what limits his or her ability to function in society moves us away from the medical model and toward a more social work-appropriate model that involves the full range of both individual and environmental assessment that is an essential part of the social work processes (Black, 1994, pp. 396–97).

The strengths assessment is an especially useful tool in working with the empowerment model of practice. By focusing on the client's strengths, the worker can help the client to motivate and to see himself or herself as actor, rather than acted upon. Empowerment practice involves the worker in helping the client to act, rather than in acting on his or her behalf.

Thus, the power we work to help our clients to achieve "is related to the possession and effective use of both psychological and socioeconomic resources," and interventions can include psychological, experiential, and environmental factors (Hartman, pp. 34–35).

The Practice Method

Lee (1996, pp. 231–37) develops eight principles to guide empowerment practice that can be used in working across disability.

1. Utilizing processes and skills that promote coping, adaptation, and/or social change include reflection, thinking, and problem solving. Clients are encouraged to explore not only the problem or need, but also the oppressive and disempowering circumstances that may have prevented its resolution.
2. Increasing motivation through the use of empowering skills and through ensuring that the client's basic needs (food, shelter, clothing, and financial and emotional support) are met. As noted above, working within the client's own problem definition and responding empathetically to the client's sharing of experiences with oppression and difference increase motivation. Using the strengths assessment is helpful as a motivating tool as well.
3. Maintaining psychic comfort and self-esteem to externalize the sources of oppression and reduce self-blame.
4. Enhancing problem solving and promoting self-direction through teaching skills, and the provision of experiential opportunities.
5. Utilizing special worker skills, such as consciousness-raising and education, and practicing in a manner that supports equality, symmetry, and parity between worker and client.
6. Where appropriate, using empowerment skills with groups and communities to promote social change.

7. Assuming a professional stance that includes self-awareness and places the oppression experience as one of the issues to be considered in working with the client. Thus, the oppression experience itself and its effects on the client, family members, and other relationships becomes a part of what is assessed and addressed in the process.
8. Knowing both clinical processes and methods, as suggested above, and political process is essential.

It is essential to recognize that the empowerment approach has developed out of a distinctly Western frame of reference. Encouraging the development of independence, self-actualization, and the primacy of the individual support a value system that is culturally linked. Care should be exercised prior to engaging in this practice model in determining that empowerment is a culturally appropriate model for use with a particular client. This caution should also be used in considering the advocacy practice model described below.

The Advocacy Model

Sometimes the services provided to clients are inadequate or ineffective in meeting needs. Criteria for admission to programs may exclude a client who can benefit from the service. Long waiting lists keep clients in limbo while need for services remain unmet. Environmental barriers may effectively block access to needed resources. Empowerment is the model of choice in these instances, because empowerment enhances self-esteem and provides the client with a sense of control over life circumstances. However, it is not always possible to use this model with all clients.

Hepworth, Rooney, and Larsen (1997, p. 468) define advocacy as a process of working on behalf of clients to: (1) obtain needed services and resources, (2) modify policies, procedures, and practices that negatively impact of clients, and (3) promote new legislation or policies to meet client needs. While this definition crosses practice levels, the focus here will remain with the individual client.

Determining Appropriateness of the Model

The advocacy model meets the needs of clients whose problems cannot be adequately addressed with readily available resources in the community and who are unable to advocate effectively to meet their own needs. Clients with severe disabilities such as profound retardation, psychosis, severe dementia, or Alzheimer's, who are "locked-in" or otherwise unable to communicate needs effectively are unable to advocate for themselves. Social workers using this model assume a proactive role by engaging in advocating for clients with other agencies, community programs, funding sources, and planning agencies.

In working with the advocacy model, it is important to distinguish the clients who are unable to *express* needs from the clients who are unable to do what is necessary to *have needs met*. Expressing needs and exercising choices in meeting them requires at least three abilities: (1) mental competence to understand and reflect and self-assess, (2) ability to consider alternatives and decide on a course of action, and (3) ability to implement the action chosen.

Clients who are frail, who are unable to communicate verbally, or who cannot perform the physical functions required—such as using telephones, visiting government offices, or filling out forms—are often competent, able to express needs, and able to determine courses of action. With such clients, it is essential that the social worker assist in identifying needs and exploring courses of action. With the client's permission, the worker then acts in the client's stead in advocating for benefits and services.

Ethical Issues

Ethical social work practice also dictates that, when clients choose to refuse services or resources that the worker may believe to be helpful, clients' wishes be adhered to and that clients have the right to determine which advocacy actions the worker may engage in on their behalf (Hepworth, Rooney, & Larsen, p. 469). Care must be taken that we do not equate inability to advocate or refusal to advocate with incompetence and thus override the client's wishes in order to pursue what we believe to the client's best interest. Client self-determination in these instances must always guide advocacy efforts.

Clients who are unable to express needs or to reflect upon choices and options because of mental illness or cognitive or developmental disability are unable to provide the worker with either selected goals and courses of action or permission to act on their behalf. In such circumstances it may be necessary for workers to approach family members, guardians, courts, or government agencies in order to discuss potential actions and to obtain permission from a surrogate prior to initiating advocacy on the client's behalf.

The Practice Method

Advocates "argue, debate, bargain, negotiate, and manipulate" (Compton & Galway, 1994, p. 434) the environment in order to obtain the resources and services necessary for client well-being and optimum functioning. Advocacy is often directed toward obtaining benefits and services to which the client is entitled but is not receiving.

As a practice method, advocacy can be used without direct client involvement in the process. Because of this, it is important that workers develop an understanding or a contract with clients that gives them permission to act on the client's behalf (Compton & Galway, pp. 434–35). Where this is not possible, workers should seek the consent of a responsible surrogate.

The Case Management Model

During the last decades of the twentieth century and into the new millennium, case management as a practice model was and is used extensively to address the comprehensive needs of the disabled population, especially in working with clients who are mentally ill or who have developmental disabilities, HIV, or other long-term, ongoing needs (Rose, 1995, p. 335).

The case management model is appropriate when the client's needs emerge from the *disability itself* due to its nature, its severity, and its impact on the client's overall functioning. It is not an appropriate model to use with a client who is disabled but who seeks services in order to address relationship problems, plan educational goals, adopt a child, or receive support due to death of a spouse or partner. In instances where the client is already receiving case management services and seeks assistance with any of these issues, it would be appropriate for the case manager to make a referral and to integrate this need and service into the client's overall plan of care.

Clients who are disabled may require a range of services, including medical care, personal caregiving, transportation, education, vocational rehabilitation, recreation, housing, or nutrition, as well as support. When services are provided piecemeal, they become fragmented, problems and gaps in service are not recognized or addressed, and each service functions independently of the others. Case management oversight addresses fragmentation and provides continuity and coordination in the interest of meeting client needs.

Case management models differ according to client needs and agency or program structures. Client-driven models are strengths-based and generally include advocacy and empowerment goals in planning. Provider-driven models stress the importance of the plan for service and value the client's adherence to the plan; the service providers define needs and evaluate outcomes (Rose & Moore, p. 338).

Case managers identify and engage clients in the process of needs assessment, and develop a plan for meeting the needs with the client. Resources in the community are located to meet the needs, and clients are linked to the services. Case managers typically provide oversight and coordination of services, rather than administering the services directly. However, agencies and programs vary; in some agencies the case manager also provides counseling and support services, crisis intervention, and services to the client's family. In others the role is limited to linkage, coordination, and general oversight of all of the services provided by other resources. Case managers review the plan for meeting client's needs with the client on a regular basis, assessing whether needs are met, or whether other services and resources are needed. Case managers often assume the responsibility for advocating for clients as well.

Determining Appropriateness of Model

Clients with disabilities who need case management services tend to be in these circumstances (Rothman & Sager, 1998, pp. 5–7):

1. They have a severe disability, the nature of which places the client in a position of serious hardship; the circumstances are not amenable to resolution through traditional social work methods of treatment.
2. The disability, and impairments in functioning that accompany it, are presumed to be long term and unresolvable.
3. Client needs are not being met through family, friends, and other people in the client's network, and the social support system available to the client is inadequate for the degree of client need.
4. Clients are unable to meet needs due to poor coping skills, low self-esteem, and lack of information about resources and services.

It is important to recognize that case management clients *do* have many strengths and survival and coping skills that can be encouraged and used to assist them to take an active role in planning and managing services. Consumer-driven models encourage clients' self-determination and value client input in service planning.

Components of Case Management Service

Rothman and Sager (pp. 9–14) identify four major components of social work intervention using the case management model:

Goals:
(a) community living to enable maximum independence
(b) optimal functioning

Intervention Structure:
(a) longitudinal service
(b) interdisciplinary involvement (range of services)
(c) community-based service

Foci of Practice:
(a) supportive, skill development
(b) external/environmental interventions
(c) range is micro to macro

Practice Style:
(a) high level of client participation
(b) readily accessible if problems occur
(c) expresses genuine positive regard for client

Social Worker Functions

Social work in case management settings requires flexibility, creativity, patience, and an extensive and thorough knowledge of both the client and the community's resources to meet the client's needs. When needed resources are absence or inaccessible, case managers may advocate for clients who may be unable to advocate for themselves.

Practice Methods

The model included here (Figure 13.1, p. 216) provides an overview of the case management process. Because of the long-term needs of most case management clients, workers' involvement is often measured in terms of years rather than weeks or sessions. The end point, discharge, may not be possible, and the focus of the worker's interventions becomes one of optimizing the client's situation and minimizing potential harms and losses rather than achieving a permanent resolution.

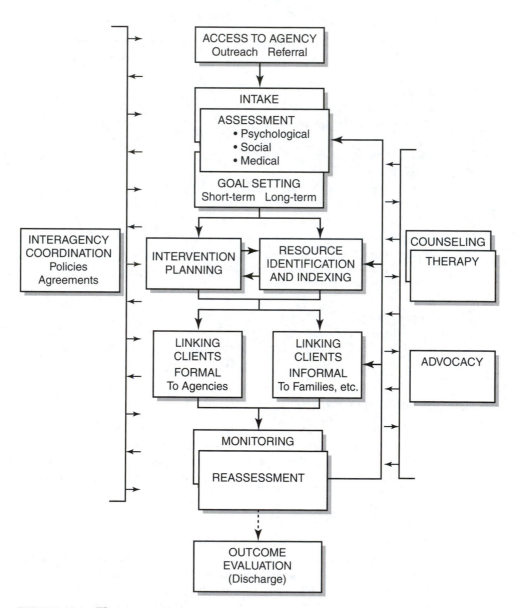

FIGURE 13.1   *The case management process.*

Rothman, J., & Sager, J. (1998). *Case Management: Integrating Individual and Community Practice,* 2nd ed., p. 25, Boston: Allyn and Bacon.

The Social Construct Model, Revisited

The social construct model of disability, as developed and described by Michael Oliver (1991, p. 32), "does not deny the problem of disability, but locates it squarely in society. It is not individual limitations, of whatever kinds, which are the cause of the problem but society's failure to provide appropriate services and adequately ensure the needs of disabled people are fully taken into account in its social organization."

The major emphasis of this model is on the need to reformulate and redesign society such that it is inclusive of all people. This process involves disability advocacy and political action, core elements in professional social work practice. It supports a view of humankind and of society that is inclusive, universal, and affirming. As such, the positions Oliver espouses surely merit implementation, and possible practice models that support this change process will be presented in succeeding chapters.

However, when we consider practice models that address the needs of *individuals,* social construction do not seem to encompass the immediacy of the need or the unique experiences of the person. Yes, it is essential to advocate for change, to assist people to understand that internalized oppression influences self-esteem, relationships and social functioning, perception of choices and options, and indeed every aspect of a client's life. However, to place the disability itself in a central position in the client-worker relationship may undermine and discount the reason the client has come for service. Also, many of the goals of social construct theory, in terms of changing society and involving people in this change, may be fairly long range. The social worker must address the client's immediate needs first.

People with disabilities have noted that there may be a disconnect, or at least a partial disconnect, between the social construct model as a way of understanding disability and the direct experiences of people with disabilities. Social construct does not necessarily encompass the physical experience of impairment and/or pain, nor does it address the real limitations that are intractable and cannot be compensated for through social and environmental change (Oliver, pp. 37–39).

What can be taken from the social construct model and integrated into practice models for working with individuals? Social construct uses many of the tools of two of the models included here, empowerment and advocacy. Linking the theories of social construct with practice models provides both an expanded theoretical base for the models and a practical tool for working with clients across disability while societal changes are occurring.

Exploring the nature of oppression and its meaning for the individual, helping people to see that oppression is societally grounded and individually experienced, and working toward understanding and diminishing the effects of oppression on the lives of people with disabilities are essential both to social construct theory and to these practice models. Helping people to assess and evaluate the role that disability plays or doesn't play in the problem that has brought them to the worker for service helps to clarify and distinguish problems and provides a solid basis for goal-setting and interventions. Assisting people toward an understanding of a commonality in the interests and needs of the disability community empowers clients to move toward social action and group solidarity and view themselves as actors and doers in the process of social change. In this way, clients can "connect the personal to the political" (Oliver, p. 170).

Chapter Summary

This chapter has explored practice models that can provide a useful framework for social work practice with individuals. These models can be used successfully to address the needs and problems of a wide variety of clients and problems and are not restricted to work across disability. While necessary space limitations preclude the inclusion of a greater number of practice models, it is recognized that any practice model can be used to address the needs of a disabled client. It is the client's *problem,* and not the *disability,* that must serve to influence the choice of practice model.

The models included here have been chosen because they provide a methodology for addressing problems frequently encountered when working across disability: crisis, long-term needs, oppression and low self-esteem, and the lack of access to services to enhance life quality are often experiences of clients with disabilities.

The section on social construct is included here in an attempt to relate elements of the social construct position to the practice of social work with individuals whose immediate problems and needs must be considered along with social construct's necessarily long-range goals of societal change. Social construct both supports the empowerment and advocacy practice models and contributes valuable grounding for the utilization of these practice methods. In choosing a practice model, workers must always consider cultural implications and select methods of assessment and interventions that are culturally congruent for individual clients.

Questions for Thought and Discussion

1. Clients with severely disabling conditions often require case management services over long periods of time. How can clients who require such comprehensive and long-range services be helped toward a meaningful role in planning?

2. Crisis intervention services for people who become disabled through trauma are often provided while the person is in intensive care by workers who are specially trained to provide such services. However, clients may be discharged from the ward or from the hospital before the crisis is resolved and control is reestablished. How can crisis intervention services, which are often setting specific, be provided to clients once they leave the setting?

3. The "sick role" can be viewed as an adaptation that is essentially negative and dysfunctional, or as a kind of empowerment—people who are "sick" may demand a great deal of support and assistance from others and may use their condition to exert power over others to get needs met. How can we distinguish between "empowerment," which is appropriate, and such abuses of power?

4. People who are in crisis are often unable to think clearly, utilize coping skills effectively, act, or develop a plan. Additionally, they may be severely depressed. These are all conditions that impact negatively on a person's ability to make self-determined choices and decisions. Should we provide services under the assumption that people in crisis cannot effectively self-determine?

5. Who should decide when a client with a severe disability is in need of long-term case management services? Should the client have the right to refuse such services?

14

Practice Models: Working within the Disability Community

The models for practice with individuals presented in the previous chapter may be applied to problems and practice situations where the central focus of the problem is the disability itself or to any other kind of problem the individual may be experiencing. The assumption was only that the person had a problem that needed to be addressed in the social service context. The models included in the chapter are frequently useful in addressing problems related to disability.

Similarly, the community models may also be used with a variety of communities, problems, and concerns. The models included here are those that may be especially helpful in working with needs related to disability and the disability community.

Weil and Gamble (1995, p. 581) note that community organizations can serve a variety of functions and that there is generally a focus on one or more of the following areas:

1. Improving the quality of life for members of the community
2. Advocacy
3. Social and economic development
4. Service and program planning
5. Service integration
6. Political and social action
7. Social justice

Definition of Terms

Before exploring the models, however, it is important to clarify what and who we are talking about when we talk about models for disability community practice. We shall begin by attempting to define "disability," "community," and "practice" as they will be used here.

Disability

Chapter 7 introduced the reader to a number of groupings that have been used in defining disability in the United States. Major systems include defining disability as activity limitation, as causative condition, as an impairment, and according to medical classifications. The Americans with Disabilities Act (1990) defines disability as having a condition that limits activity and function, having a record of such a condition, and being seen as having the condition.

Individuals with a disability may see themselves as a part of the wider disability "community," or they may identify primarily with others who share their limitation, condition, or impairment. Some people do not identify themselves as disabled and thus do not see themselves as a part of the disability community.

Community

When we think about community, we generally think about a neighborhood or district of a city, a small town, or a rural areas with boundaries. This kind of community is locational; that is, it is defined by its geographic area. In this sense, people with disabilities generally don't form a community. However, other forms of community are directly applicable to people with disabilities.

Many of the communities that exist in society often do not have clear boundaries; also, people are members of many communities simultaneously. A teacher in New York City, for example, might be a part of the African American community, the Methodist community, the educational community, the alumni of City College community, the Harlem community, the community of bikers along the Hudson River, and the opera lovers community. A farmer in Nebraska might be a member of the local farming community, the Congregational community, the dairy farmers community, the Norwegian community, and the single-parent community. A store clerk in Wyoming might be a member of the white water rafting community, the store clerk community, the gay men's community, the Native American community, and the photography community.

It is easy to see how each of these communities addresses a specific characteristic, interest, or quality of the person described. Each person belongs to a number of communities; some of these may be grounded in a specific geographic area but others are determined by interests, shared concerns, vocations, and other characteristics.

Geographical communities are located in a bounded and specific area, and are made up of people who share ties and interests to a specific locale.

Social networks include family and kin, groups of friends, colleagues at work, classmates, and members of an organization. Social networks may provide mutual assistance to members, and/or band together to advocate on behalf of a shared interest of concern (Kemp, 1995, p. 185).

Vocational communities are groups whose connection is centered around a professional identification, interest, skill, or ability. Vocational communities share concerns, help to disseminate new information, and may have special requirements for membership.

Functional communities or communities of interest are composed of a group of people who share an interest or concern. Communities of interest do not need to be located in one geographical area. The Internet, the telephone, and other forms of modern technology have created communities of interest with no face-to-face contact. These communities can provide support and engage in advocacy over long distances (Kemp).

The disability community is multilayered and multifaceted. Within the broad "disability community" are communities of people with specific impairments or medical conditions and people who identify strongly or weakly with the community as a whole. The national disability community is not geographical, but many local geographical communities also exist. The Internet and the proliferation of Internet access has enabled the development of website-based communities related to disability as well.

It is important to recognize that, like other communities, the disability community does not always speak with one voice, act in concert, or agree about priorities in needs or political actions. Therefore, when we think about the application of a model of practice to the community, we must in each instance establish the criteria that will determine community membership.

The disability community of interest does not include only people with disabilities; it also includes family members, friends, others in the person's support network, professionals and caregivers, and other interested people. Some practice models are focused only on the person with the disability; most include anyone who has a "stake" in the problem or concern that is the focus of the model's practice.

Practice Models

Practice with communities involves a number of specific professional skills, such as collaborating, initiating, educating, brokering, linking, political action, and advocacy. The role of the professional may vary according to the kind of model being used and the goals and objectives the specific group develops. However, a general process can be identified that is helpful in conceptualizing the process of community change. The process involves five steps (Weil & Gamble, 1995, p. 581):

1. Identifying the problem and the desired outcome
2. Determining which system will be targeted for change
3. Determining and locating the primary constituency, those most concerned
4. Deciding what will be the scope of concern (area, population)
5. Defining the primary social work roles in an effort that will involve varied numbers of people and situations

All practice models that work for change in communities and in the wider society must have a clear understanding of who is affected by the problem, in what manner, and possible courses of action. Early in the process, a needs assessment must be conducted. Needs assessments can range from informal polling of members to large-scale, sophisticated research designs that are professionally administered and analyzed. The needs assessment model defines some of the essential elements that will be used to define problems and determine courses of action.

One of the oldest and most effective forms of community change is the self-help group. Self-help groups are peer led and provide support, information, and an opportunity for people who share a common problem or concern to draw inspiration and strength from one another. Empowerment groups may evolve from self-help groups, or they may be formed to address issues of concern to members as well as provide opportunities for personal growth and development for members. Social action and social planning groups identify specific problems that are of concern to members and are related to societal and organizational deficits in meeting the needs of the community.

The Community Needs Assessment Model

Communities, even geographical ones, are not static. Rather, they are dynamic and in a constant state of change and evolution. Community assessment provides an understanding of the community structure, its needs, and the changes that affect it both from within and from without. Community assessment can be used in conjunction with other models in community practice. Social action and social change models, empowerment models, and political action models (addressed in the next chapter) can all utilize the information gained from community assessments in order to plan for action and social change.

Assessments can be performed by professionals outside the community or by members. They may be initiated by social change groups, government programs, or special interest groups. In either case, participation and involvement of community members and their representatives in the assessment process provides an educated core of individuals who are knowledgeable about the problems and needs being assessed.

Assessment is a research process. Research methodology is utilized in effecting the assessment, which can be quantitative, qualitative, or both. Assessments often contain several methods, each of which provide a different dimension and ground of understanding.

To be effective, assessments must begin with a definition of who and what is being assessed; in other words, the *population* who are members of the community must be defined. While disability communities are often not geographical, assessments must have boundaries. These can be very large, such as the entire population of a country, or smaller, such as the clients of one agency or people who live in one building The visually impaired "community," for example, may be composed of all visually impaired people in the United States or just those in Sioux City, Iowa, those known to the Lighthouse organization, or those who live or work in the Mission district of San Francisco.

The dimensions and methodologies to be used for assessment must encompass the *need* to be assessed; it is important to determine not only *who* is affected but *how* and possibly *what has been done* in the past to address the problem and *what resources* exist in the community or in the wider society to address the problem. This may require different assessment instruments.

In general, all community assessments should address the following:

1. There should be an understanding of the community, its unique qualities, and its similarities to other communities (Kemp, 1995, p. 194). If we are studying the "community" of people who are visually impaired, we need to understand any special characteristics of the community of people with limited vision, the differences and similarities between visually impaired people and people in other disability communities such as the Deaf community or the spinal cord injury community, and indeed the differences and similarities between the visually impaired community and the community without visual impairments within which the visually impaired community is embedded.

2. A variety of tools should be used to assess different dimensions and qualities of the community and its needs. These methods can include surveys, mailed questionnaires, census data, personal or telephone interviews, observation, and the use of focus or other groups (Kemp, p. 194). The methodologies chosen should always be suitable to the community being assessed; written questionnaires may not be appropriate for assessing the visually impaired community, for example, and automated telephone surveys that require pushing numbers on the dial may not work well to assess needs of people with limited range of motion in their hands. Telephone interviews may also be inappropriate for people who are deaf. Forms that require both privacy and mailing may not be practical for people who have no personal access to mailboxes.

3. Assessors both within and without the community should approach the data-gathering process with an open mind and a willingness to listen and learn (Kemp, pp. 194–95). When members of the community are participating in conducting the assessment, it is particularly important that the social worker encourage self-awareness and stress the importance of maintaining a neutral stance during the needs assessment process.

4. While needs assessments are of necessity needs-focused, it is important to include community strengths and resources in the assessment (Kemp, p. 195).

Because of the dynamic structure of communities and the rapid pace of change in today's world, studies must be timely to been effective. Conditions ten years ago were quite different than they are today, and needs, resources, and populations affected by problems may change rapidly. Current data not only presents an accurate picture but also enables the development of a sensitive and responsive plan for addressing the concern.

The Self-Help Group Model

Individuals with particular problems, experiences, and needs often draw support and assistance from other people who share their problems and concerns. Self-help groups provide ongoing peer support and are effective in addressing needs, providing resources, and teaching coping skills to individuals, The oldest self-help group, Alcoholics Anonymous, was founded in 1935 (Magen, 1995, p. 162). Self-help groups typically are at least nominally sponsored by a national or international organization that has a stake in the problem or concern of the group. The broader organization lends legitimacy and facilitates intergroup communication.

The national or international organizations often provide initial funding, train leadership, define the structure and function, and may provide meeting sites, websites, annual retreats or conferences, or other methods for people to come together around a commonly help interest or concern. However, each self-help group is unique and defines its own goals and purposes within the wider organization. Most self-help groups are open groups: Members can join at any time and are not obligated to any specific number of meetings.

Disability and Self-Help

Because one of the major issues for clients with a disability is often independence, the philosophical framework of self-help is especially useful in conveying strength, self-sufficiency, and personal dignity to members. Self-help groups, as we shall see in Part IV, are an important part of the resource network for people with disabilities and serve a vital function in support, advocacy, and education.

All of the major organizations focused on a specific disabling condition or concern can provide access to self-help groups. The National Multiple Sclerosis Society, the Arthritis Foundation, the Lighthouse, and the Cerebral Palsy Network are all examples of these kinds of organizations. In addition to local networks of support groups that are diffused nationwide, these organizations and others also provide support via telephone and websites for community members who are unable to attend meetings or who prefer these kinds of support. Many organizations at various levels also provide hotlines and helplines for members that are open twenty-four hours a day and staffed by group members.

The Social Worker Role

Social workers serving in professional roles in self-help groups are usually outsiders. They may provide the impetus for group formation, consultation, initial training, and support for group members and help locate and identify potential leaders. During meetings, social workers are available as needed but generally do not assume a leadership role.

Because social workers, too, have needs and problems that may benefit from self-help groups, it is not unusual for professionals to be members of a self-help group as peers. This may create serious role conflicts because most peer-led self-help groups do not have a specific role for peers who are professionals. The social worker/peer member may experience some stress from this conflict; however, this can generally be resolved through discussion and clarification of the individual's role with both leadership and other members.

It is important for members to understand when the social worker is speaking as a professional and when as a peer. It is also important for the social worker to resist requests for personal counseling and advice and to remember that, in the peer role, he or she does not have the legitimization, supervision, and support generally available for workers in a professional setting. In order to benefit personally from the self-help group, the social worker must be comfortable in sharing personal information, concerns, and experiences in a way that is generally not a part of professional behavior.

Self-Help Groups and Social Action

Many self-help groups may take on a social action function in addition to peer support. When people share experiences and concerns, commonalities in experience are often found. Some groups offer support through the process of affirming and validating the members' experiences. Others evolve into empowerment and consciousness-raising groups and eventually become involved in social action. Individual groups generally determine the way in which social action and peer support needs will be balanced. Often, the national or international organization provides the structure for the social action portion of the group's functioning.

The disability community has a strong history of self-help leading toward social action. Part I presented the story of the CILs (Centers for Independent Living), which

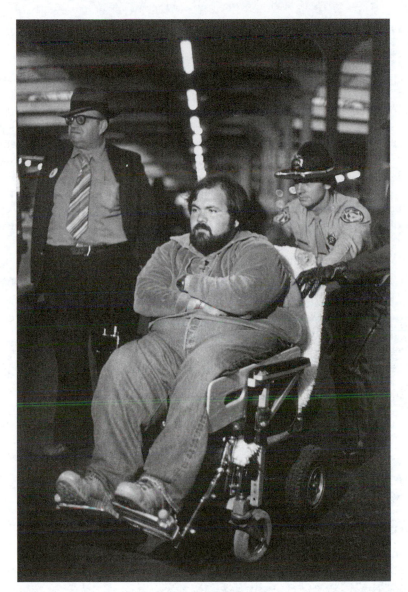

Self-help through social action civil disobedience: Resisting being moved, disability rights activist is pushed from demonstration by a police officer, San Francisco, 1978.

developed out of peer support groups, and ADAPT, a support group that quickly took on social action functions. The disability rights movement like its predecessor movements, has developed out of the efforts of self-help organizations to address member needs and the social, educational, housing, economic, vocational, and recreational disparities between group members and society at large.

The Empowerment Model

The empowerment model for communities is an extension of the empowerment model for individuals and is build upon the same foundations: that human dignity and respect are an essential part of optimal functioning, and that oppression, exclusion, and discrimination undermine self-esteem. On this broader level, empowerment focuses on supporting a feeling of group competence, connectedness, and the group's ability to effect change for the good of all of the members of the group. The skills, abilities, and personal characteristics of each member of the group are used together to promote and achieve the mutually determined goals.

All members of empowerment groups have a stake in the resolution of problems. Thus empowerment group members may be family members, individuals in a support network of a person affected by the problem, or people with a special interest in the member's

The empowerment model in action. A demonstration in support of accessible public transportation, San Francisco, 1978.

concerns. While not all members of the group may initially feel empowered, the positive attitudes and change efforts of some members have a powerful effect on others. When change efforts bring results, each member of the group gains a sense of empowerment. Thus empowerment of some members can become a motivational force to empower others.

Several elements characterize the empowerment model.

Group Member Participation

As noted above, the empowerment model encourages active participation by all group members. Members are considered citizens and consumers, people who are negatively affected by conditions in society that impede their optimum functioning, both in terms of the built and/or natural environment and in terms of social attitudes and behaviors such as oppression and discrimination. As citizens of the wider community, group members are encouraged to explore their mutual concerns and to develop plans for addressing them. Active participation engages members and is individually empowering as well: Group empowerment and individual empowerment support each other (Kemp, pp. 189–90).

Individual participation tends to decrease as the size of the group increases and members feel that the role of their concerns and personal efforts is minimized. When an empowerment group's size becomes so large that effective participation by individual members is decreased, the worker may suggest the formation of subgroups or subcommittees to address particular issues and problems. Members then select the group or committee that best addresses their concerns and allows for the use of their personal skills and abilities.

Empowerment Dialogue

Before an empowerment group can effectively move toward community action, discussions must move individual members from an understanding of their own personal problems and needs to a broader understanding of how the political and societal processes, including oppression and victimization, impacts individuals.

Sharing personal narratives is an effective beginning to this process. As members listen to one another, they hear echoes of their own experience and are able to begin to generalize from personal to group. The group then moves toward generalizing the members' experiences and recognizing common themes. During this stage of the process, the group members develop strong bonds and a group identity that empowers each member.

Because group members and the experiences many share occur in a social context, empowerment dialogue moves toward an exploration of the social and political environment and an examination of the structures within that environment that contribute to the group's experience. When these have been identified, the discussion can turn toward the development of a course of action to modify them and to remedy the conditions affecting members.

Social Worker Role

Work with groups to effect change involves a major shift in the social worker's professional stance. This is not a place for the "nonjudgmental attitude"! Committed workers can inspire and support group members, provide information about resources and strategies, teach interventions skills and methods, and help preserve the group's momentum.

The role of the social worker in the empowerment model is not to direct, manage, or organize. Rather, the worker assists the members of the group to own the process and the results of efforts. To assist in this effort, the worker helps the group to dialogue, reflect, and determine courses of action and goals, to develop strategies, and to build connections among members and with other groups to promote the goals of the group. The worker may also reinforce and teach coping skills, negotiating skills, and advocacy skills to members, and encourage the active participation of all members as able and desired. The leadership of the group remains with the membership and not with the worker, thus supporting the group's feelings of self-direction and self-actualization.

The role of the social worker as collaborator assumes a mutuality of interest and dedication. He or she is an involved participant rather than a distant expert (Kemp, p. 191). In order to fulfil the professional role with authenticity and sincerity, it is important that the worker's personal values and interests be in consonance with the goals of the group. Where there is a serious value difference between worker and group members, the worker may become ineffective and actually impede the group's progress toward goals.

The Social Action/Functional Community Model

Weil and Gamble (1995, p. 583) state, "The central focus and desired outcome in organizing functional communities is action for social justice focused on advocacy or changing policies, behaviors, and attitudes in relation to their chosen issue." Community groups also organize with the specific purpose of advocating for changes in the wider community that impact negatively on a special community. As noted earlier, functional community groups are communities centered around interest, rather than geographic area. Functional communities often organize using social action models to advocate for the community's needs and concerns. The social action model focuses on the attainment of social justice. As such, community members organized into social action groups identify an unmet need related to the interest of the community and organize to effect change so that the need will be met. Social action groups often address the needs oppressed populations.

Workers and group members using this model recognize that there is a scarcity of resources in society for meeting all needs for all people. However, they believe that it is important for this identified unmet need to be addressed and that society's resources should be reallocated to meet this (Sheafor, Horejsi, & Horejsi, 2000, p. 117). Social action implies that the majority cannot always rule, that there are instances in which the needs of the minority groups in the society, such as people with disabilities, must be addressed in order for a socially just society to function.

Functional communities engaging in social action often work to educate the general community regarding their concerns. They may also provide services to members of the community whose needs are not met by existing social and governmental institutions (Weil & Gamble, pp. 584–85). An example may help to illustrate this point. In 2000, a university received a large, unrestricted donation. The governing board of the university determined, through a needs assessment, that the library facilities were inadequate and insufficient to meet the needs of the student body, which had almost tripled since the library was originally designed and built. Although accessibility to all buildings and facilities for disabled students was also defined as a need, the governing board felt that allocating the funds to the library would benefit all students, even disabled ones, while making the campus completely accessible would benefit only a small number. Also, university policy stated that classroom locations would be immediately changed if the assigned location was found to be inaccessible to a student enrolled in the class.

Disabled students were angered by this decision, as were their nondisabled friends. Students complained of being embarrassed and humiliated when classmates were forced to change classrooms to accommodate them. Inaccessibility of certain university offices and officials prevented communication and services when questions or problems arose. Some of the older buildings on the campus did not have accessible toilet facilities and students were forced to go to other locations when the need arose, often a cumbersome and time-consuming procedure. They felt that the basic needs of the few (in this case, the physically disabled student population) must come before providing for additional facilities for the many.

Members of the community approached the staff of the Disabled Student's Program with their problems and complaints. Social workers assisted the students to organize and facilitate a meeting of people interested in this issue and develop a plan for involving more

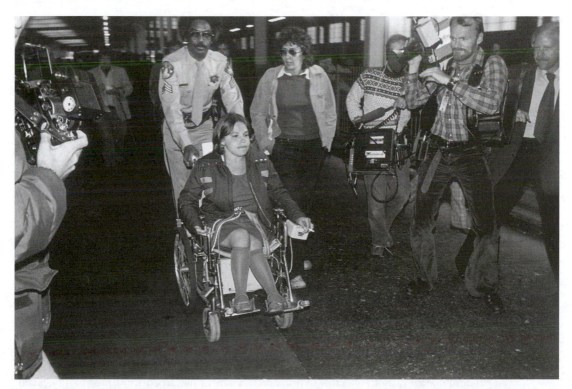

Social action through media publicity: Activist uses media attention to gain a public voice for disability rights, San Francisco, 1978.

people in reversing the decisions of the board. A social action group composed of professionals, disabled students, and other interested students was formed to advocate for a
change in the governing board's decision. The group made posters, distributed flyers, held
informational sessions, and advocated for their cause on the campus radio station. Eventually, they were able to effect a compromise with the governing board that addressed a number of the most urgent needs, and elevators were installed in several buildings to improve
access for students in wheelchairs.

Social Worker Role

In this model (Weil & Gamble, p. 584), the worker serves as:

- Organizer: forming the group and helping to build cohesion and consensus about
  what is to be addressed and how
- Advocate: advocating for the special interest or "cause" of the group, both within the
  group and outside
- Negotiator: assisting the group to work with other special interest groups, elected
  officials, funding sources, and the like to have the need met
- Educator: teaching, rehearsing, and preparing members of the group to approach
  others, give speeches, recruit members, and so on

Group Process and Membership

Social action groups may be tied to a specific need or concern of members of a community.
Resources, both internal and external, are marshaled to address the specific problem identified by the group. There may be a time frame within which the group is working, such as
preparation for a legislative meeting, an election, a community meeting, or other con-
straint. Community social action groups are composed of community members and others
who join together to address specific concerns and to advocate for a population or an issue
(Weil & Gamble, p. 581). Disability social action group membership is generally composed of disabled people personally affected by the problem or concern to be addressed,
other disabled people, family, friends, professionals, and other concerned citizens.

Chapter Summary

Social workers in community practice use models to assist in structuring, defining problems, assessing communities, and assisting community members to plan and implement a
course of action to address the problems. While the worker's role may vary from a very
proactive, organizer stance to a more passive position as consultant and resource, the
process of change in communities functions effectively only if a broad spectrum of community members are involved with the project and committed to its goals.

    A community needs assessment is a necessary part of community practice and must
generally occur early in the change process in order for the process to have validity. Needs
assessments should be timely, involve various methods, be appropriate for the population,
and have support and participation from community members.

Three models of practice that are helpful in working with and within the disability community have been presented. The self-help model involves community members in peer support and service. The worker's role is generally as an outsider. However, there are instances when the social worker is also a peer member of the community. Careful consideration of role conflicts must be given in order to function comfortably and effectively under these conditions.

The community empowerment model builds on empowerment in a group context by fostering connectedness, interrelationships, and joint efforts at change. Social workers in this model serve as facilitators and advisers but enable community leadership to develop and foster the group's development. Empowerment of some members of the group can have a potent effect on others, and serve to motivate them toward full participation and action.

The functional/social action model is built around the concept of communities of interest rather than geographical area and assists community members in organizing to advocate for change related to social justice issues.

Questions for Thought and Discussion

1. Social work professionals who are also members of self-help groups often experience role conflict, as noted above. How would you handle such conflict?

2. In many smaller communities, social workers may find themselves functioning in a professional capacity with a group that includes some personal friends. Do you think this creates an ethical dilemma? How would you resolve it?

3. You have a disability and have been going to a support group for years. You are using the support group primarily for socialization, but you do share personal information. You begin to work with a client with the same disability whom you feel would very much benefit from referral to your support group. Would you refer your client to your support group?

4. What do you see as the essential differences between questions 2 and 3? Do these differences justify different positions? Why or why not?

5. Community needs assessments are often performed for specific reasons with specific goals in mind that could bias the design, the data collection, and the analysis of the assessment. How would you attempt to minimize the effects of such biases?

15

Practice Models: Disability as a Social and Political Concern

The models presented in the previous chapter are effective for community practice. But what happens when the social action needed to effect change must occur at a broader level, such as state legislatures, Congress, or the justice system? Small community groups involved in advocacy may lack the requisite numbers, power, skill, or audience to bring about change effectively at this level. Social and political change often require a wide constituency and the efforts of influential people, legislators, and national organizations. Educational efforts must be aimed at the voting public as well as at individuals within the government bureaucracy. The influence of the media must be enlisted.

In order to effect change at that level, several practice models have been developed for social work professionals. Three of these are included in this chapter. Each has been used effectively in creating the changes in disability legislation that have occurred in the past several decades. Advocacy is an ongoing project at the national level. Lobbyists in Congress advocate for special interest groups, mass demonstrations prompt police department scrutiny, and research informs debates about resource allocations.

The coalition model addresses the need for a wider constituency and a broader power base for social actions aimed at the state or national level. Where one community group may be effectively silenced, the power of many communities cannot be. Coalitions are built upon effective networking, outreach, and the recognition of mutual interests and concerns.

The political action model places the political process at the center of change efforts. This model utilizes various methods for educating elected officials about specific issues and concerns, lobbying for change, and enlisting support among the voting public.

The social movement model, the broadest of the three, addresses the need for change from a long-range perspective and attempts to enlist broad support from both within and outside the disability community by appealing to social justice and fairness. Social movements do not change only laws: They work to effect change in attitudes and behaviors as well and have an enormous impact on society as a whole. The Disability Rights movement is a such a social movement; so is the Civil Rights movement, the Feminist movement, the

Gay Rights movement, La Raza, and the various environmental movements. Each seeks to influence society, and each speaks the language of *rights,* rather than the language of *needs.*

The Coalition-Building Model

Coalitions may involve professional agencies, advocacy organizations, and/or community groups. Human service organizations have been very effective in gaining support and effecting legislative change to assist clients with specific needs. Advocacy organizations that focus on a particular problem or population are often effective in educating the general public and influencing policy and program development. Community groups with problems and needs can claim a constituency of all community members and become a powerful and effective force. Professional social workers in all these groups and organizations play an important role in goal attainment.

When a community of individuals, an agency, or an organization defines a problem or an unmet need and begins the social action process described in the previous chapter, leaders may recognize that the community, agency, or group is too small or the concern to narrow to achieve the goals. In such instances, communities, agencies, and organizations can look outside their own membership for other organizations and communities whose interests parallel or overlap the community's own. Coalitions work to influence organizations and programs external to themselves to support the interests and needs of their members. They are dynamic, generally time-limited, and focused on a particular issue of problem (Weil & Gamble, p. 588).

Building the Coalition

The goal of coalition building in itself is to build an organizational power base large enough to influence programs and policies and to effect the desired change (Weil & Gamble, p. 581). Coalitions usually involve representatives of each organization in discussions regarding individual roles, priorities, and strategies. Goals that are commonly accepted must be set, and this process may create a need for adjustment in the original community's goals to incorporate broader interests.

Once the need for a broader base of influence is recognized, the agency, community, or organization can begin the process of locating and approaching other like-minded organizations, beginning the coalition-building process. Identifying other organizations, agencies, and groups who also have a stake in the issue to be addressed often ensures an interested and positive response.

Effective coalitions frequently include a mixture of community groups, human service agencies, and organizations. In working with problems and issues related to disability, an effective coalition can include major service organizations, human service agencies, and community groups. For example, a coalition addressing classroom size for developmentally disabled students in the public schools might include the Association for Retarded Citizens, local parents' support groups, members of the school board, representatives of the teacher's union, student organizations, and human service agencies providing services. A coalition addressing the problem of low employment in the disability community generally might include members of disability-specific organizations, such as the Cerebral Palsy Association, service providers such as Centers for Independent Living, vocational rehabilitation agencies, and support groups of people with disabilities and family members.

Social Worker Role

Social workers' relationship-building skills are especially important in the coalition-building process. Through knowledge of communities and resources, social workers are able to identify potential coalition organizations. Through professional contacts, social workers are often able to begin the exploratory process and assess the position of the group or organization being approached. Through skills in working with people, social workers can assist with negotiation and mediation. Through knowledge of the community organization, the social worker can act as spokesperson for the organization as needed in the broader coalition arena.

The Change Process

Once the coalition has been formed, set goals, and developed a plan of action, the change process begins. Coalition members meet with elected officials, government representatives, foundations, and other resources that can influence the desired outcome (Weil & Gamble, p. 581). Often, coalitions dissolve when goals are met, because involvement requires a great deal of the participating organizations' time and resources. However, coalitions can also evolve into organization and community networks that mobilize for other causes and concerns that affect members.

The Political Advocacy Model

Political advocacy is effective when it is grounded in sound data and an assessment of community needs. When the assessment is completed, the social worker in the political arena must determine whether the intervention required to address the need or concern involves the administrative, legislative, or judicial functions of government and whether it should occur at the level of policy formulation, implementation, or evaluation. The plan or intervention developed should be suitable to policy level and government function (Haynes & Mickelson, 2000, p. 56).

Political advocacy social workers may choose from a variety of models. Selection should be determined by practical considerations as well as appropriateness to the cause or concern. Haynes and Mickelson (pp. 60–65) have identified six potential models for advocacy appropriate for social work professionals.

The Institutional Model

Public policy must be enacted, implemented and enforced in order to be "public." Thus this model focuses change on the organizational structures that enact, implement, and enforce policy, or on the selection of a level or appropriate place to introduce change.

Example: Public policy measures must be passed both by the Senate and the House of Representatives. As this book goes to press, the Senate is controlled by Democrats, the House by Republicans. Although there are precedents and traditions regarding where a bill begins its travels through Congress, advocates can enlist the support of a sympathetic legislator of a committee and perhaps begin the process with the legislative body most likely to support the measure. This validation can be helpful in getting the bill passed when it reaches the less sympathetic legislative body.

The Process Model

The process of decision making is the focus of this model of advocacy. Workers using this process observe and study the way in which decisions are made, including processes apart from the presentation of data and documentation of need.

Example: In attempting to influence the debate in Congress on the subject of stem-cell research, advocates of the research, including the Alzheimer's Association and the Parkinson's Association, whose members might benefit greatly from the research, were aware that the debate would be intense. Nancy Reagan, wife of ex-president Ronald Reagan (who has Alzheimer's), and the mother of a child with Parkinson's, advocated for passage of the measure allowing the research. Introducing this personal element provided support that was more powerful than the simple presentation of data.

The Group Theory Model

Similar to the coalition model, the group theory model suggests that groups can work together to achieve change goals. However, as noted in that model, tensions and the dynamic process between and among groups often create the need for negotiation. The group theory model focuses on the way in which the different groups function to ensure that their needs are represented. The role of the worker is to facilitate the development of compromise among groups.

Example: In order to ensure passage of the Americans with Disabilities Act, strong coalitions of human service agencies, special-interest and service organizations, community groups, and concerned citizens formed a broad coalition to influence legislators and program developers. The coalition was able to gather such strong public support that, with the successful passage of the ADA, it became the spearhead of the much broader disability rights movement, giving it momentum, media attention, and public interest.

The Elite Theory Model

This model considers that public policy is determined by an elite and reflects the values and interests of that elite. Social workers using this model work to convince the elite group that the desired changes are valuable to them as well.

Example: Access to the polls is often difficult for people with disabilities, and privacy in voting, a value highly prized by citizens, must often be sacrificed. Some polling places are inaccessible; others do not provide ballots for people who are blind or have limited vision, while still others require manual dexterity for the operation of the machines. The Disability Rights movement advocates for accessibility of polling places and for indi-

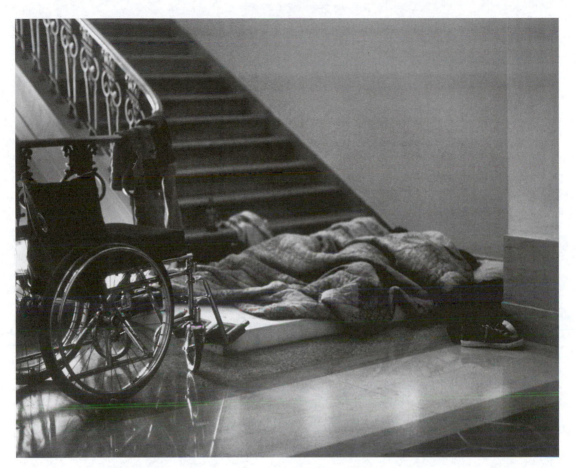

Political advocacy: Several weeks into the takeover of the HEW offices in San Francisco, Governor Jerry Brown sent the demonstrators mattresses. The sit-in lasted 3½ weeks and resulted in the signing of the 504 regulations without segregation of students with disabilities into separate schools as originally proposed by President Carter.

viduals' privacy rights in casting their ballots. States vary in the provisions made for people whose conditions or impairments preclude use of ballots and access to polls.

People with disabilities, as an oppressed group often disenfranchised, tend to identify their interests with other minority groups. Studies of voters and exit polls have demonstrated that a wide majority of minority group members vote for the Democratic Party. Advocates interested in ensuring voting rights for people with disabilities appeal to Democratic members of Congress to press for the enactment of policies that guarantee both access to polls and privacy in the ballot for all citizens. This change would increase the ranks of Democratic voters, and so the power of the Democratic Party in Congress.

The Rational Model

Reason suggests that an appropriate tool for decision making is to consider all the costs and benefits of a particular policy and to adopt the course of action or policy that maximizes good over harm, and that is efficient. Not only those affected directly by the policy but everyone in the society becomes a part of the equation. Social workers using this model attempt to demonstrate that the policy they are advocating for would, in fact, assure this good and benefit not only the group of people advocating for the change but everyone in the society.

Example: Sidewalk cuts benefit people with disabilities who are in wheelchairs or use other alternative forms for personal mobility. They provide access to the public streets, and thus to shops, restaurants, and services. But sidewalk cuts benefit a much broader range of people than these. Among the principal beneficiaries of sidewalk cuts are parents pushing strollers and baby carriages, a vast national interest group. The elderly, people with limited mobility, and small children can all benefit from sidewalk cuts as well.

The Incremental Model

This model is efficient in that it uses existing policies and considers changes in reference to these. Change builds upon existing policy and does not in essence destroy it and then start over from the beginning. Using this system, the worker would find current policy that relates appropriately to the change desired and advocate that the new provision or program be added to the already existing policy.

Example: An example of the incremental model can be seen in considering the 1935 Social Security Act, which covered insurance and public assistance to people who were elderly, blind, and children with disabilities. When the persistent income maintenance problems of people with disabilities was brought to the attention of lawmakers, the Social Security Disability Act of 1956 was eventually passed. This built on the "blind and disabled children," expanded the provisions beyond the "elderly" of the 1935 act, and insured workers under sixty-five who become disabled; widows, widowers, and divorced wives who have disabilities and are between ages fifty and fifty-nine; and the disabled sons and daughters of an insured worker.

Social workers influence public policy in a number of ways. They can provide documentation and testimony of a problem or need. They can be expert witnesses who are called upon to provide information and to express judgment in areas with which they have experience. They can influence legislators by writing letters that present the cause and the action needed and that are grounded in social work knowledge and expertise. And they can lobby in Congress via telephone, letter, or e-mail, or by talking with members and their staffs.

The Social Movement Model

The broadest change model in community practice is the social movement model. Social movements involve both the general public and political systems and parties and seek to effect change in political systems or in public attitudes. Their primary concern is focused around social justice, and the efforts are directed toward addressing issues for a particular group that often are pervasive in the society.

Oppression, discrimination, rights, and institutional and societal bias toward a particular group often form the theoretical grounding for social movements. The disability rights movement is grounded on rights of differently abled people to the goods and services of society and to full participation. Movements often grow out of coalitions and political advocacy; however, they are not limited to one specific issue, not time limited, and organized loosely enough so that groups, organizations, and communities who wish to affiliate can do so with minimal conflict and tension among them.

Although we associate movements with the twentieth century, and often with the United States social and political system, it is important to recognize that movements have occurred throughout history and in many different countries, with different goals and measures of success (Weil & Gamble, p. 589). Globalization is leading us toward an ever-wider potential of causes and populations. The environment and global warming, for example, are issues that surpass national boundaries. As we become more aware of our membership in the global community, we will have more and more social movements involving people all around the world in social movements that can effect social change.

Membership

Because movements are so broadly based, membership is often vast but fluid. Movements tolerate differences within themselves and often have subgroups whose positions and interests vary without significantly compromising the function of the movement as a whole. The Feminist movement, for example, includes people who are interested in equal rights, people who are interested in lesbian issues, people concerned about domestic violence, and people whose focus is reproductive choice. People can become active members of a movement when a specific issue or concern is the focus and become passive or even withdraw completely once the focus or concern has shifted.

Changing Paradigms

Social movements attempt to change the paradigm through which the general population views the population affected by the problem. The Disability Rights movement has been working to change the paradigm for people with disabilities (Weil & Gamble, p. 589). The original thrust of the movement focused on rights such as access to public buildings, theaters, restaurants, education, employment, and public transportation. With the successful passage of laws, leaders and members of the movement realized that, though much had been accomplished, much still needed to be done. With laws removing barriers that had previously impaired full functioning, it was recognized that the achievement of rights and changes in the public image of disability were not synonymous. Rights didn't keep people with disabilities from being pitied, ridiculed, and rendered invisible. To change the paradigm, the disability movement had to make a major shift from within and focus not on disabilities and rights, but on abilities and accomplishments.

Social Movement Process

Social movements evolve around issues and needs that concern members of a population. Haynes and Mickelson (pp. 110–11) have developed a model for a ten-stage process that can assist us in understanding the development of major social movements:

1. Consciousness of a need or problem is recognized and expressed.
2. Consciousness of the need of problem is shared with others who recognize its validity and take ownership of it.
3. This wider group engages in fact finding and in presenting the need or problem to people in a position of leadership.
4. An influx of emotion and a desire for immediate resolution of the problem is experienced by people who are involved, providing energy and momentum.
5. As the problem is presented to more groups and leaders, a number of possible resolutions emerge.
6. Conflicts between the resolutions, and further options and resolutions, will fuel a debate that may last for a period of time.
7. It will be decided that additional information is needed in order to resolve the conflict and determine a course of action. Fact finding can assist in the process, or can stall it indefinitely as more and more information is requested.
8. Open discussion in public forums can last for an extended period of time as groups try to influence the public toward one or the another resolution to the problem.
9. Solutions are tested and, hopefully, a solution is chosen that integrates parts of suggestions from many groups.
10. Some groups who are excluded will withdraw, and a compromise broad enough to have support from most other groups will be adopted.

Social Worker Role

Social workers facilitate and advocate (Weil & Gamble, p. 581) and are a part of the constituency of social movements. Because of their expertise in human functioning and knowledge of the service system, social workers can often take a responsible leadership role in advocating for the goals of the movement. Social workers do not create movements; rather, their work is influenced by the social justice issues that movements espouse (Weil & Gamble, p. 589).

Chapter Summary

This chapter has presented three models for social work practice in social and political advocacy. Social workers can utilize professional skills in the political arena to influence policies and programs that affect client groups. While community models are effective in changing communities, political models of practice are necessary to effect change at the state or national level.

The coalition-building model is effective in widening the base of support to address a specific problem or concern. The agency, group, or community organization that has identified the problem seeks other organizations who share a similar concern and have an interest in addressing the problem. Coalitions are built among organizations such that each organization's efforts are aimed toward resolution of the problem.

Individual organizations send representatives to coalition meetings. The representatives, who are often social workers, must balance the needs and interests of their own organization with the needs and interests of the coalition. Tensions often occur and compromises must be made so that the coalition can advocate as a united voice. Coalitions generally advocate to lawmakers and formulators of public policy; however, foundations, government programs, and institutions may also be approached by coalitions to address commonly felt needs and problems.

The political advocacy model, as its name implies, advocates in the political arena for the needs and concerns of a specified group. Six models of political advocacy were presented: institutional, process, group theory, elite theory, rational, and incremental. Choice of models for political advocacy may be based on the nature of the problem or concern to be addressed, the political level at which the intervention will occur, and practical issues.

Social movements are the broadest forms of political activism and generally involve large numbers of people, groups, and organizations, all of whom share an interest or concern. Social movements generally address rights issues and the needs of minorities and oppressed and marginalized groups in society. The Disability Rights movement addresses issues related to disabled people.

Social movements often begin with addressing a particular unmet need or concern. However, when resolution of the specific issue does not address the fundamental problem, the focus of the movement becomes the development and diffusion of a new paradigm for thinking about the people with whom the movement is concerned. When the Disability Rights movement succeeded in gaining passage of the Americans with Disabilities Act, leaders and members became aware that this bill in and of itself could not resolve the underlying problems of oppression and social difference. The focus has shifted to a reframing of disability with an emphasis on abilities rather than impairments.

Questions for Thought and Discussion

1. Select a disability related organization at the national level. Visit its website and make a list of all of the coalitions, advocacy groups, and special interest groups to which the organization is related. Are you able to clearly identify the reason for each affiliation?

2. Consider the urban problem of accidents to pedestrians that occur within crosswalks at intersections. These kinds of accidents affect many people with disabilities, who may have difficulties in getting across the street in the allotted time or who may be missed by motorists whose eyes are fixed on the light signals. If you wanted to develop a coalition to address this problem, what groups, special interests, or organizations might you approach? What other members of the population might share this concern and be disproportionately affected by crosswalk accidents?

3. Social movements involve a broad societal base, one that reaches far beyond people directly concerned with the issues the movements seek to address. How might the societal base of the disability rights movement be broadened? What issues of concern to the movement also concern large segments of society?

4. One of the members of a peer group for whom you serve as adviser recently fell on an uneven sidewalk. Members of the group want to address this issue. What are some of the steps they might take?

5. The Disability Rights movement has achieved many goals. What do you see as an appropriate agenda for disability rights in the twenty-first century?

Part III Summary

In this essential unit, practice skills for working across disability were presented. The most essential practice skill, without which no interaction can occur, is that of communication, addressed in Chapter 10. People who have a disability may also have difficulties in communication: Blindness or visual impairment may limit the client's ability to receive and interpret nonverbal cues; deafness and hearing impairment limit the client's ability to understand verbal communication; cognitive impairments, developmental disabilities, and mental illness may impact upon a client's ability both to communicate and to understand communication; mobility limitation may impact on nonverbal communication; and the inability to speak necessarily limits verbal communication. It is important to be able to communicate directly with clients, and workers may need both to optimize the client's ability to communicate and to develop alternative methods of communication.

It is important to develop a good relationship with all clients. Often the worker must consider additional factors in establishing the mutual trust necessary for assessment and intervention planning. Clients need to believe in the worker's competence, and both worker and client need to respect the client and have faith in his or her ability to change. When a client has a disability the worker does not share, there may be hesitancy in the development of trust. The worker's empathy and relationship-building skills are important in understanding the client and in assisting him or her to develop a trusting relationship. Workers must also be careful to avoid pity and sympathy, overidentification with the client, or the assumption that they understand the client's experiences because they share a disabling condition.

Any basic soical work assessment tool can be utilized with a disabled client, and it is important not to assume that the disability itself plays the central role in the client's problem unless the client has given specific indications that this is so. Chapter 12 presented several assessment methods that both are commonly used in social work and easily adaptable to include disability where this is relevant to an understanding of the client's situation. Ecological assessment, a strengths assessment based on Cowger's model, psychosocial assessment, a disability-specific assessment methodology, and quality-of-life assessments were presented. The community needs assessment included here enables the worker to assess community as well.

Working across disability occurs at all practice levels. Chapter 13 presented some models for working with individuals that may be especially useful in working with clients with a disability. The crisis intervention model addresses client needs when the disabling condition occurs or when medical or personal crises overwhelm clients. The empowerment model focuses on client strengths and on assisting the client toward a sense of mastery over his or her life, while the advocacy model addresses the needs of clients who are unable to advocate for themselves. The case management model is included to meet the ongoing needs of disabled clients for coordination and management of services.

Chapter 14 presented three models for meeting the needs of the disability community. Self-help groups, the empowerment model for communities, and the social action/functional community model were explored as potential theoretical frameworks for working within the disability community. Advocating for change also occurs at the broadest levels: state and national legislatures, commissions, and programs. The coalition model, the political action model, and the social movement model presented in Chapter 15 present two practice methods for working to effect major political changes in the system as it impacts the lives of people with disabilities.

Devoted to practice skills and models for working across disability, Part III has focused on the provision to specific skills and tools for work at the micro, meso, and macro level. However, it is essential to competent practice that the worker be knowledgeable about resources, services, and support for people with disabilities. Part IV will present various spheres of resource knowledge that are especially applicable to working with people with disabilities. After a discussion of the public and private sector in general, the unit will move on to discuss health care, housing and personal care, income support and employment, the social support and recreation network, and mobility and access.

Part III Unit Assignment

Relationship and communication skills are basic to competent social work practice at all levels. However, when there are barriers to effective communication, the development of an effective helping relationship can easily be compromised. As in all areas of practice, self-awareness and self-monitoring are excellent tools for understanding your personal strengths and weaknesses in communicating across disability.

In Part III, we have considered various skills for effective communication across sensory impairment, speech impairment, developmental disabilities, cognitive impairment, and mental illness. These skills are essential for working with clients at all levels.

In a six- to eight-page paper, explore your personal strengths and weaknesses in communication skills in each of these areas. Are there special conditions that are particularly difficult for you? How could you minimize the negative effects on clients? Are there areas where you feel you would be very effective? Use examples to illustrate your statements where possible.

Example: Speech impairment: I recognize that it is very difficult for me to communicate with people who need to use communications boards. I have a tendency to become impatient and frustrated when communication is very slow. Because of this, I might be tempted to rush clients along by saying what I think they are trying to communicate. I can get very caught up in the creative part of making personal communications boards. A client for whom I was making the board refused to participate or look at me once. I think I was having too good a time and leaving her out of the process. In the future, I think I might _____.

I also know that I am a very poor lip reader. I become embarrassed with my inability to lip read and constantly apologize to clients. I think that this may be related in part to poor vision, so if I have to lip read, it's important for me to have good light on the client's face. I once had a client who could move only her mouth and I found that _____.

On the other hand, I read gestures quite effectively much of the time, and can reflect back to the client what I'm understanding through body language in a supportive and non-threatening way. Once I helped a client _____.

Example: Cognitive impairment: I am very comfortable with people who have cognitive impairments. I don't feel I must "orient" them constantly and can stay wherever they are and have a meaningful conversation. I don't mind reintroducing myself each time. I am aware of subtle changes that indicate "windows of opportunity" and am committed to using these to enhance self-determination. I have had three clients with cognitive impairments that I've been able to help make advance directives and appoint a surrogate decision maker by using "windows of opportunity." One of them _____.

I can work with people whose cognitive disabilities make them anxious and worried, but I especially enjoy people who are at ease and at peace with themselves. I don't do well with people who loudly and repetitively make the same sounds and with whom there is a very minimal possibility for communication. I have a client who just sits and says "ba, ba, ba" loudly all day and I avoid her. I know I don't give her the time and energy I give to other clients—I don't know how to be more effective with this client. Maybe I should _____.

I try not to infantilize, but I am affected by how other people treat people with cognitive disabilities. Sometimes it's just easier to infantilize, especially when clients seem to like it.

Example: Developmental disabilities: I don't like being very authoritative and so it's hard for me to be as directive as is sometimes necessary with clients with developmental disabilities. I also get embarrassed with common words for sexual functions and body areas. I think that, although I can do it, a client might be able to sense my discomfort, and might react to that. Maybe I could try some desensitization strategies _____.

Part IV

The Disability Resource and Support Network

Familiarity with the resource and support network for people with disabilities is an essential part of the social worker's responsibility, and much unnecessary hardship can be prevented through appropriate use of resources. Sandra's experiences with a new friend illustrate the difficulties.

> I've been blind since birth. It's just a part of who I am and I've never been any different. I had always used all the resources available and that made my life a lot easier.
>
> A few years ago, I met someone who had become blind four years ago as a result of diabetic retinopathy. When I met her, she had just started receiving services. She was using a cane and considering a guide dog. But for the first four years of her blindness, she didn't know anything about all the resources that were out there. No one had ever told her. I don't know how her doctor, or the nurses in the hospital, or all the social workers she saw didn't point her toward resources, support groups, and technical devices that make things so much easier for blind people. They just let her flounder. I'm lucky that I knew all those things from the beginning. I think social workers need to be much more informed and never let newly blinded people walk around without telling them about the resources that can help them. I want to be involved in this myself as a medical social worker. (Sandra Arago, personal statement, 4/30/02)

Interest in disability and in meeting the needs of people with disabilities has long been a part of both social planning and private service agency concern. In both the public and the private sector, the programs and services that were developed to meet special needs were often related to the theoretical framework that was dominant.

In considering the complex and inextricably interwoven system of services and organizations that today attempt to address the rights and needs of people with disabilities, it might be useful to review Chapters 2, 3, and 4. Some information from these chapters is included in this introduction to assist you in understanding how the current resource and support network evolved.

In the public sector, people who were disabled and unable to support themselves were included as objects of charity under the Elizabethan Poor Laws, which were adopted by the American colonies. The moral model generally prevailed, and disability was associated with evil and sin. It was the responsibility of the family to nurture and care for disabled people who had families. By the end of the twentieth century, the passage of the Americans with Disabilities Act and the Family Caregivers' Support Act demonstrated a clear shift in theoretical position. The ADA views disability more as a social construct than as a moral failure and places on society the responsibility for ensuring that disabled people have access, rights, and opportunities similar to those of nondisabled people. Therefore, the ADA mandates major changes in the built environment and employment criteria. The Family Caregiver's Support Act underscores that, while families continue to provide a great deal of the ongoing care and support needed by people with disabilities, there is, ultimately, a responsibility on the part of the government to provide for the needs of disabled members of society.

While there was not much change in public sector services for people with disabilities until the twentieth century, there have been massive changes in the past 100 years. The Rehabilitation Act for Veterans returning from World War I marked the first major shift in framework. The Act was expanded in 1920 to include all people with disabilities. It was followed by the inclusion of blind people and disabled children in the Social Security Act of 1935, and government coverage and services were again expanded through the addition of Social Security Disability Insurance in 1956. The Architectural Barriers Act of 1968, mandating access to federal buildings for people with disabilities, was followed by the National Rehabilitation Act in 1973, as well as other acts that addressed civil rights issues, broadened access, and set guidelines for employers. Today, public sector programs address medical needs, housing and housing modification, employment and training, income support, personal care needs, recreational and leisure needs, and many other areas.

Through laws and monitoring, the development of oversight and advocacy agencies, the establishment of programs, research, and the direct provision of benefits and services to people with disabilities, these major trends have been addressed in the public sector:

- Civil rights
- Access and mobility
- Income support
- Rehabilitation and education
- Employment
- Special needs, such as medical care, housing, and personal care
- Research, both general (statistical studies) and particular (regarding cures, prevention, etc.)

The public sector has also defined "disability" and degrees of disability, which establish criteria for program admission.

Private sector involvement can be said to have begun with Samuel Gridley's establishment of the first sheltered workshop for blind workers. Though a number of such workshops were developed, wages and benefits were well below those of other employment. The first advocacy organization, the League for the Physically Handicapped, formed in

1935 in New York and was dedicated to obtaining equal rights for people with disabilities in the public sector—in this case, with the Works Progress Administration. Organizations such as the Society for Crippled Children (now Easter Seals) and the March of Dimes addressed needs for research, education, and vocational rehabilitation. Private organizations opened special schools to meet the needs of blind and deaf children. Private nonprofit agencies addressed needs for housing, personal care, transportation, food, and clothing. In time, these private agencies assumed some of the responsibility for implementing services for people with disabilities which were funded through the public sector.

Private sector resources can be grouped in several ways:

- Organizations dedicated to one kind of disability or condition, such as the American Cancer Society, the National Multiple Sclerosis Society, and the Lighthouse.
- Organizations dedicated to the provisions of one kind of service, such as Lions Club (visual impairment), March of Dimes (research), Canine Companions for Independence (mobility and personal care), and home health care agencies.
- Organizations providing linkages and resource information, such as Physician's Disability Services and Disability Information Resources.
- Organizations providing comprehensive services for disabled people, such as Centers for Independent Living.
- Organizations dedicated to disability and rights advocacy, such as Disability Rights Education and Defense Fund (DREDF).
- Organizations serving a specific locality, population, or region—hospitals and disabled student services in colleges and universities.
- And many others.

The interrelationship between the public and private sectors, the professionals providing services, and the disabled people and family members who are the consumers of services is complex and often unique for each individual. In order to provide the needed services, social workers must be knowledgeable about each client through appropriate communication of needs and assessment techniques and about public and private resources available to meet the client's needs.

Because there is an enormous number of resources, some of which will be useful and some of which will not be appropriate, detailed information about specific resources is not included in this unit except as examples. However, useful Internet sites and web addresses are provided to help you to initiate searches. It is recommended that each social worker develop her or his own system for exploring and keeping a record of resources that might be helpful to her or his clients. A notebook, a telephone file, and computerized listings are three possible systems for keeping resource information, but any system that is comfortable and convenient for the worker will be helpful.

This unit has been organized to provide, first, in Chapters 16 and 17, general overviews of services in the public and private sector separately. Chapters 18 through 22 are organized by need and services and include health care, housing and personal care needs, income support and employment, social support and recreation, and mobility, access, and adaptive technology. It may be helpful to use this framework to organize a personal resource and support network information file.

If there is a specific unmet need or resource required, there are several excellent places to go for assistance, including:

(1) The Internet, which contains an enormous amount of information, linkages, and services
(2) Your agency
(3) The disability resource network in your area
(4) Organizations that serve other client needs
(5) The organizations that serve your client population specifically
(6) A government agency

16

Overview of Network and Services in the Public Sector

Public sector agencies and services are grounded in the right of each person to share in the goods of society, have equal rights, and be accorded dignity and respect. Special programs and services that meet the needs of people with disabilities are generally entitlement services: The criterion for receiving the services is having the disability or impairment included in the service.

Government programs and services are linked to each of the three branches of the federal government and also to state and local governments, creating a dense network of services to address most disability-related problems and needs, such as advocacy and legal issues, employment and income maintenance, housing, medical care, personal care and caregiver services, education and rehabilitation, and other needs related to specific disabilities. The Executive Branch includes the President's Commission and other agencies. The Legislative Branch has passed a series of laws regarding disability rights and maintains various agency websites that include information about compliance, rights, monitoring, and implementation. The Judicial Branch hears cases related to presumed violation of laws related to disability rights; it has begun to build a significant body of case law related to disability. Generally, federal programs are funded at the federal level and are administered and provided at the state level. State programs must meet all of the criteria of the funding agency. States can also provide additional services and resources, as can local governments. Research programs are generally funded and run at the federal level. The federal government also provides information and publications to educate consumers and private citizens about laws, programs, statistics, and research that affect people with disabilities.

Federal Government Resources

Federal agencies provide a multitude of resources regarding statistics, laws, employment, education, and income support. Agencies often overlap and/or provide oversight to other agencies. It is impossible to include all federal resources here; however, an attempt has been made to include a variety of resources as well as suggestions for using the Internet to link to other resources as needed.

Federal programs and resources are often not centered specifically on "disability" but are included in more general and comprehensive programs. A sampling of the kind of information and services related to disability provided by the federal government includes these resources, all obtained from U.S. government-related websites.

Statistics on Disability

One of the functions of the federal government is the maintenance of up-to-date information and statistics on people with disabilities in the United States. A number of government organizations collect and disseminate disability statistics, including:

1. The Census Bureau: Questions about disabilities were included in the 2000 Census. The Census Bureau also maintains a website for disability statistics, which includes information on a state-by-state and city-by-city basis.
   Web address: *www.census.gov/hhes/www/disability.html*
2. The Disability Statistics Center: Funded by NIDRR, the Center collects data about employment and earning, costs of disability, access to health care and long-term care, housing, mortality, and other statistics. Web Address: *www.dsc.ucsf.edu*
3. The National Center on Health Statistics: The NCHS conducted a major study (National Health Interview Survey on Disability) on the use of assistive devices by people with disabilities in 1994, releasing its data in 1998.
   Web address: *www.cdc.gov/nchswww/default.htm*
4. The National Institute on Disability and Rehabilitation Research: NIDRR is the primary source for disability data, both funding statistical research and publishing research findings. Web address: *www.ed.gov/offices/OSERS/NIDRR*
5. The National Organization on Disability: In 1998, the NOD/Harris Poll of Americans with Disabilities found large gaps between adults with disabilities and other adults in regard to employment, education, income, and other measures, with employment showing one of the largest differences. The study showed that employers have less confidence in the ability of people with disabilities to fulfill job requirements. Web address: *nod.org* (*www.dol.gov/odep/public/pubs/ek99.resources.htm*)

U.S. Department of Health and Human Services

HHS is the primary federal government department addressing the needs and problems of people with disabilities. In addition to the Office of the Secretary, there are twelve separate agencies, some of which address specific disability-related concerns.

1. The Office of the Secretary has special offices dedicated to HIV/AIDS policy, veteran's affairs, grants, and civil rights.
2. The Administration on Aging, while not exclusively disability-related, serves the needs of a population with a high concentration of people with disabilities, many of whom have multiple disabilities. As we have seen in Chapter 5, disabilities are dis-

proportionately concentrated among older members of society. Meals on wheels, transportation, and in-home services are among the services provided by AOA, which also addresses the needs of people with disabilities.

3. The Agency for Healthcare Research and Quality supports research and also provides information to assist people in making knowledgeable decisions about health care.

4. The Centers for Disease Control and Prevention monitor diseases, maintain statistics, and support research through twelve centers, including: National Center on Birth Defects and Developmental Disabilities; National Center for Chronic Disease Prevention and Health Promotion; National Center for Environmental Health; National Center for Health Statistics; National Center for HIV, STD, and TB Prevention; National Center for Infectious Diseases; National Center for Injury Prevention and Control; National Immunization Program; and National Institute for Occupational Safety and Health. CDC's mission is "to promote health and quality of life by preventing and controlling disease, injury, and disability." Web address: *www.cdc.gov/aboutcdc.htm*

5. The Centers for Medicare and Medicaid Services provide health care for people with disabilities.

6. The Health Resources and Services Administration oversees the nation's organ transplant system and also serves people with HIV/AIDS through administration of Ryan White funds and CARE Act programs.

7. The National Institutes of Health provide information, research, and informational services through twenty-seven separate institutes and centers. To locate information on a specific condition or disability, use the appropriate institute's information center. Institutes that have information related to disability include National Cancer Institute; National Eye Institute; National Heart, Lung, and Blood Institute; National Human Genome Research Institute; National Institute of Allergy and Infectious Diseases; National Institute of Arthritis and Musculoskeletal and Skin Diseases; National Institute on Deafness and Other Communication Disorders; National Institute of Dental and Craniofacial Research; National Institute of Diabetes and Digestive and Kidney Diseases; National Institute on Drug Abuse; National Institute of Mental Health; and National Institute of Neurological Disorders and Stroke. Web address: *www/nih/gov/icd/*

8. Substance Abuse and Mental Health Services Administration (SAMHSA) focuses on prevention and treatment of substance abuse and mental health programs and needs Web address: *www.hhs.gov/agencies/*

The Department of Labor

The Department of Labor and other federal agencies monitor employment compliance with ADA, post federal job requirements to encourage potential disabled applicants, and provide advice to employers about hiring people with disabilities.

Fact sheets, brochures, reports, and a special "Educational Kit 2001: Win with Ability" are available on a wide variety of subjects related to employment and people with disabilities through the Office of Disability Employment Publications.
Web address: *www.dol.gov/odep/public/media/reports*

The Department of Education

The Department of Education and other federal agencies provide information and resources for education for people with disabilities through the National Adult Literacy and Learning Disability Center, Office of Special Education and Rehabilitation Services, and Disability Rights Education and Defense Fund. Web address: *www.ded.gov/*

Income Maintenance: Social Security Administration Information and Resources

The Social Security Administration was originally a part of Health and Human Services but is now its own independent agency. It provides information online for professionals about disability determinations at *www.SSA.gov/disability/professionals.htm.* Fax requests: (410) 965-0096. Web address: *www.ssa.gov/disability/*

Other Disability Services and Agencies

> National Library Services for the Blind and Physically Handicapped
> Architecture and Transportation Compliance Board
> Veterans Administration Research and Rehabilitation Services
> Rehabilitation Services Administration
> Institute for Independent Living
> Department of Justice Guide to Disability Rights Laws
> Disability Laws and Regulations
> Housing and Urban Development: Fair Housing
> U.S. Access Board (architectural and transportational barriers)

Oversight

National Council on Disability.   The NCD is an independent federal agency whose fifteen members are appointed by the President and confirmed by the Senate. Its function is primarily overview and advising and includes (1) oversight of NIDRR; (2) advising the Commissioner of the Rehabilitation Services Administration, the President, Congress, the Office of Special Education and Rehabilitative Services, and the President's Committee on Employment of People with Disabilities; (3) reviewing all policies, programs, and government activities concerning people with disabilities and standards for Independent Living programs; (4) recommending ways to improve research and services for people with disabilities; (5) submitting an annual report to Congress and President with helpful information that related to disability programs and research.
Web address: *www.Draco.aspensys.com/FCIC/Public/TopicDetail.asp?ti*

Provision of Information to the Public

The federal government disseminates information through publications of the government printing office, websites, and publications of agencies and listings. Some sources of information are provided here but constitute only a very small part of government information resources.

Federal Consumer Information Center: 800-688-9889
ADA-related agencies and sites, such as:

ADA Act Help	ADA Questions and Answers
ADA Disability Rulings	ADA Handbook
ADA Summary	ADA Title II
ADA Technical Assistance Manual	ADA Homepage (Department of
ADA Public Law 106-336	Justice)

Pocket Guide to Federal Help for Individuals with Disabilities
FCC Disabilities Issues Task Force
Disability.gov Internet site for disability resources, including Americans working abroad (Web address: *www.disability.gov/CSS/Default.asp*)

Children and Youth	Housing
Choice and Self-Determination	Income Support
Civil Rights and Protections	Media Resources
College and Adult Education	Recreation and Travel
Disability Statistics	Self-Employment
Emergency Preparedness	Tax Credits and Deductions
Employer's Resources	Technology
Employment	Transportation
Health	

NIDRR (Web address: *www.ed.gov/offices/OSERS/NIDRR/index.html*)
AbleData, NIDRR's information project
Communicating with and about people with disabilities
Clearinghouse on Disability Information
Civil Rights and Disability Rights

State Government Resources

Each state's website also provides information about state resources for persons with disabilities. State governments often utilize an organizational structure similar to that of the federal government: three branches and specialized agencies. In most states, health and human services agencies provide the majority of the programs and resources to meet the needs of people with disabilities; employment, education, rehabilitation, housing, and aging offices may also be helpful in locating resources.

Disability resources from eight states provide a sampling of the kinds of resources states maintain for people with disabilities. State agencies, programs, and resources from these states are presented below and serve to demonstrate some of the variations and similarities in provisions for people with disabilities at the state government level. State listings included are a sample only and are not to be considered as complete and comprehensive for those states. Please see your state listings for further information; all states provide information on services for people with disabilities.

California

California Care Network provides the following services: residential care, medical care, mental health care, alcohol and drug treatment, in-home health and medical services, adult day service centers, home and community services, and veteran's services.

Department of Rehabilitation and Social Services
MediCare and MediCal
Office of AIDS
Hearing Aid Dispensers Bureau
Department of Mental Health
State Council on Developmental Disability
Department of Health and Human Services Disability Programs
Governor's Commission for the Employment of Disabled Persons
ADA Paratransit Office
Office of Deaf Access
Office of Services to the Blind
State Disability Insurance
Disability Business and Technical Assistance Center
California State Library: Braille and Talking Books
Disability Prevention Advisory Committee
Spinal Cord Injury Research Act
CalPERS Programs (disability income)
Attorney General's Office - Legal Rights of Persons with Disabilities
CalVETS
Board of Guide Dogs for the Blind

Illinois

The Disability Assistance Agency's services include: Access Living, CILs, Council for Disability Rights, Fair Housing Assistance, Illinois Internet Disability Resources, Joint Enforcement for Disability Access, Mayor's Office for People with Disabilities (Chicago), Statewide Independent Living Council, and the Disability and Business Technical Assistance Center. Other state agencies that provide services to people with disabilities include:

Guardianship and Advocacy Commission (disability rights)
Veteran's Affairs
Attorney General's Office - Select Committee on Disability Rights
Illinois Council on Developmental Disabilities
Blind and Vision Impaired Health and Social Services
Deaf and Hearing Impaired People Health and Social Services
Disability Coverage Health and Social Services

Kentucky

Kentucky provides a useful online service, Ky Cares, that, on the basis of specific needs and problems, provides referrals and links to appropriate services. For people with disabilities, these include:

Kentucky Relay Service for the Speech and Hearing Impaired
Kentucky Commission on the Deaf and Hard of Hearing
Enabling Technology of Kentuckiana
Cabinet for Workforce Development
Assistive Technologies Loan Corporation
Department for Disability Determination Services
Violations of the ADA in Kentucky (Department of Justice)
Protection and Advocacy
School for Blind
School for Deaf
Vocational Rehabilitation

Massachusetts

The Massachusetts Interagency Disability Coordinating Council coordinates services that include case management, personal care attendants, respite care, protective services, crisis intervention, rehabilitation services, day programs, residential treatment, supported employment, independent living, and transportation. Agencies providing specific services include:

Architectural Access Board
Commission for the Blind
Commission for the Deaf and Hard of Hearing
Rehabilitation Commission
Head Injury Program
HomeCare Assistance
Independent Living Programs
Disability Commission on Employment of People with Disabilities
Mental Health Legal Advisors Committee of the Supreme Court of Massachusetts

Montana

The Disability Services Division provides services to disabled people, including institutional care, residential services, case management, employment counseling and guidance, career training, transportation, adaptive equipment, orientation and mobility services for the blind, rehabilitation for the blind, independent living, medical services, job placement and supported employment. Services also include:

Developmental disabilities program
Vocational rehabilitation

Blind and low vision services
Disability determination services
Olmstead planning document to assist with planning for community-based care

Areas covered by the Public Health Disability Services Division include employ-ment, financial, housing, children's services, legal/advocacy, medical/counseling, and state government, which provides contracting for direct services such as case management, home-based care, counseling, and career training. Toll-Free Disability Assistance 1-877-296-1197 Voice TTD 1-406-444-2590

New Hampshire

The mission of the Governor's Commission on Disability advises the governor, agencies, and the NH Legislature on the needs, rights, and interests of disabled people. The Com-mission oversees the state's compliance with the ADA and oversees both the Architectural Barrier Free Design Committee and the Client Assistance program. The commission's functions include administering a program to distribute telecommunications devices and working with the Independent Living Council.

Architectural Barrier-Free Design Committee
Client Assistance Program for Vocational Rehabilitation Services
Statewide Independent Living Council
Disability Organizations in New Hampshire Directory (government and nonprofit listings)
Veteran's Home
Library Services for Persons with Disabilities
Bureau of Vocational Rehabilitation

Tennessee

Tennessee's Commission on Aging and Disability coordinates services with several other disability-related agencies, including hotlines for traumatic brain injury and osteoporosis. State agencies include:

Tennessee Relay Services (telephone access)
Technology Access
Telecommunications Devices Act
State Library for Blind and Physically Disabled
Opportunities for Artists with Disabilities
Tennessee Developmental Disabilities Council
Property Tax Relief—Disabled Veterans
Property Tax Relief—Disabled Persons
Tennessee Osteoporosis Program
Council on Developmental Disabilities
Department of Veterans Affairs

Texas

Through Health and Family Services, disability services and programs are available including the Deaf Blind/Multiple Disability Program, rehabilitation services, services for the blind and visually impaired, services for the deaf and hearing impaired, transportation assistance, adult day care and interpreter services, and services for people with mental illness and mental retardation. Other agencies and services include:

Commission for the Blind
Commission for the Deaf and Hard of Hearing
Texas Rehabilitation Commission
Mental Health and Mental Retardation
Epilepsy Program
Home and Community Based Services
Intermediate Care Facilities for the Mentally Retarded
Mental Retardation Community-Based Services
Parole Division: Special Caseloads for Terminally Ill, Physically Disabled, and
  Mentally Retarded Offenders
Extended Rehabilitation Services Program
Independent Living Centers
In-Home and Family Support Programs
Hard of Hearing Services
Special Telecommunications Assistance Program
Mental Health Community Based Services

Local Government Resources

Local government service directories can be obtained from both government offices and local government websites. Local agencies tend to provide more direct services, but may also contract for services with other agencies, both governmental and nonprofit. Not all state services are administered directly; many are administered through more localized agencies and are thus are able to be more responsive to local needs and concerns.

Social workers in direct service as well as meso and macro social workers need to be familiar with federal agencies and services as well as with state and local resources. While services and support for individuals are often provided on a local level, new programs and services to better meet the needs of disabled people are often developed at the state or national level and involve broad change efforts using the practice models presented in the previous chapter. Funding for local services is often provided by state and federal agencies and programs.

Chapter Summary

This chapter provides a brief overview programs and services related to disability that are developed and funded through the public sector. A large number of major federal programs address the needs of people with disabilities. The research and statistical data gathered at the federal level provide the information needed to adjust programs and services and to understand the effects of a disabling condition on employment, income, education, and other aspects of life. This research also serves as a ground for the development and/or reconsideration of programs. Major programs address housing, income maintenance, employment, architectural barriers, health, and education are provided and funded through the federal government.

State governments vary in organization and program structure, and some of these variations are evident in our examination of the disability services provided by a sample of eight states. It is interesting to note that most of these states have special commissions and programs to address certain needs, such as the inability to see or to hear. There are also generally programs to address the needs of people with mental retardation or developmental disabilities. However, other services and programs vary by state, and a comparison of the eight shows some differences in priorities and understanding of disability needs.

Local governments are able to be most responsive to special needs and can often adjust state and federal programs to better meet the needs of local communities.

Information on government programs at all levels that address disability is easily accessible on the Internet—several federal government and government-related sites are available. Each state maintains a government site that includes listings of agencies and services, as do many local governments. Information may also be available through the attorney generals' offices, the governor's or mayors' offices, and health and human services offices. Specific public sector services and agencies to meet the needs of clients are easily accessible and often provide a "contact us" listing that can be used to request specific information.

Questions for Thought and Discussion

1. Using one of the federal websites listed in this chapter, explore the services offered and also the links provided to other websites. Is the information included helpful to people with disabilities? To family and friends? To professionals?

2. Based on what you found, do you think that special resource websites for social work and other helping professionals working with people with disabilities would be helpful?

3. Divide your class into three groups: federal, state, and local. Focus on addressing the needs for transportation for people with disabilities and develop programs, funding, policies for who will be served, sources for equipment and personnel, and so on. Consult with each other as needed and explore areas of interdependence.

4. In reviewing the public sector services and programs included in this chapter, do you see any gaps in service? Is there duplication?

5. Imagine that you are a person with a disability in need of housing. You are in a wheelchair and need an accessible kitchen and toilet facilities. Using the Internet, search for information about where you might get help. Search in local resources first; if they do not meet the needs, explore state resources, and finally federal resources. How easy do you think it would be to access these services and actually obtain housing? Were you able to find a specific set of directions or procedures to follow?

17

Overview of Network and Services in the Private Sector

While federal, state, and local government agencies may have a complex and sometimes overlapping system of organizations and functions, it is possible to understand the underlying framework through a basic knowledge of the tripartite government structure and an understanding of departments and agency structures. Unfortunately, these aids do not exist for agencies and organizations in the private sector. Agencies and services often exist independently of one another and have different missions, focuses, populations, and services.

Private-sector agencies provide a major portion of the one-on-one direct services for disabled clients: counseling, vocational training, health care, personal care, transportation, information, support and assessment services, community programs, adult day care, respite care, and caregiver support services are among the many provided to people with disabilities. They also serve an advocacy function, provide information, resources, and referrals, maintain website listings and chat rooms, and provide legal information. While some private-sector entities are for-profit enterprises, the majority of others are charitable, not-for-profit agencies whose mission is to address the needs and better the quality of life of people in their chosen populations. Some agencies are primarily research institutes or disability-related programs attached to universities.

In this chapter, we will explore a number of different kinds of not-for-profit agencies. Some agencies, as we shall see, are disability-specific, such as the Lighthouse for the Blind, the Spina Bifida Association, and the National Alliance for the Mentally Ill. These agencies are generally national; many have local chapters that provide support and services in local communities and regional centers. Some agencies serve all clients with disabilities, such as the National Center for Disability Services or Disability Information Resources; often these are advocacy agencies, such as Disability Rights Advocates or TASH (The Action Starts Here). Some agencies provide specific services in specific geographical areas, such as the Disabilities Board of Charleston County, the Dallas Hearing Foundation, the South-East Deaf and Hard of Hearing Services or the Chester County Down Syndrome Support Group.

Many private-sector agencies provide some or all services under contract to government agencies, and thus receive partial government funding, with the remainder coming from private sources. Others may be funded exclusively by private contributions and grants. Disability-related agencies sponsor special events, such as marathons, walks, balls, sports events, and concerts to help them raise funds for their efforts. In common with other service agencies, those serving clients with disabilities often have a staff that is partially or completely made up of volunteers. National agencies have large volunteer memberships and are able to mobilize groups of people to assist them in their efforts.

Some agencies are composed only, or primarily, of people who are disabled. Others, like ARC and National Alliance for the Mentally Ill, have a strong cadre of family members and friends of people with disabilities. Still others are professional organizations, such as disability legal advocacy agencies whose lawyer members assist people with disabilities to pursue rights in the courts.

To help the reader understand how these various agencies came to be, what their purpose and mission is today, and how their services are provided, the stories of several private, not-for-profit agencies that work with people with disabilities and address disability-specific needs will be presented in this chapter. It is hoped that these stories will provide a basic understanding of the ways in which private-sector agencies function.

Disability-Specific Organizations

Disability-specific organizations are generally national organizations that have local chapters and groups. On a national level, disability-specific organizations are dedicated to education and information, advocacy, and program development. Local chapters subscribe to the mission of the national organization and to its political platforms but function independently in planning activities, providing services, and developing outreach and community programs. National organizations are also often affiliated with international organizations addressing similar problems and concerns, thus forming a part of a global network of organizations focusing on a specific disability. A sampling of disability-specific organizations includes:

> AIDS Foundation
> Alzheimer's Association
> American Cancer Society
> American Diabetic Association
> American Epilepsy Society
> American Heart Association
> American Lung Association
> American Speech, Language, and Hearing Association
> Arthritis Foundation
> Association for the Blind
> Association of Retarded Citizens (ARC)
> Autism Society
> Brain Injury Association

Cystic Fibrosis Foundation
Developmental Disabilities Council
Down Syndrome Association
Learning Disabilities Association
Lighthouse
Lupus Foundation
Multiple Sclerosis Society
Muscular Dystrophy Association
National Alliance for the Mentally Ill
National Head Injury Foundation
National Spinal Cord Injury Association
Spina Bifida Association
Tourette Syndrome Association
United Cerebral Palsy Association

In order to understand both similarities and differences between these kinds of organizations, three are presented here.

The ARC

Mission Statement.   The ARC of the United States works through education, research, and advocacy to improve the quality of life for children and adults with mental retardation and related developmental disabilities and their families. It also works to prevent both the causes and the effects of mental retardation.

History.   "To name the time and place of the beginning of this movement is like trying to isolate the first growth of grass. For truly, this is a grass-roots movement." (Anonymous, *www.thearc.org/history/anonymous.htm*)

Of the groups that became ARC, the Council for the Retarded Child of Cuyahoga, Ohio, was the oldest, founded in 1933 to help area children excluded from the public school system. The Children's Benevolent League, founded in 1936 in Washington, DC, was an organization of parents whose children were primarily in residential care. In 1939, the Welfare League for Retarded Children was founded, composed of parents of children residing in Leavenworth Village in upper New York state. The number of groups increased to 88 by 1950. The largest of these, the Children's Benevolent League, had over 5,000 members.

By 1951, there were over 125 parent groups in the United States. Caring professionals involved with the children and parents encouraged them to found a national organization. The parent groups began to organize, and eventually the National Association of Parents and Friends of Mentally Retarded Children was born. In 1952, the name was changed to National Association for Retarded Children, and its charter was recorded in Tennessee in 1953. The name was later changed to the Association for Retarded Citizens and, still later, the ARC.

At the time of its founding, there were no programs, activities, or support services to help families. ARC's early mission was to help people who were denied day care, education, and work programs, and to educate families and the general public about mental retardation (*www.thearc.org/history/anonymous.htm*).

Current Role and Services.   Today ARC serves the interests of 7.2 million people with mental retardation in the United States and assists them to grow, develop, live in communities, and have access to early intervention, free education, health care, preparation for employment and independent living, leisure and recreation, and family supports.

ARC advocates for research and prevention and for the needs and rights of people with mental retardation at the individual, local, state, and national level. Educational efforts help to provide information to the general public, to legislators and policy makers, program administrators, educators, and others.

Organization.   ARC has a twenty-four-member national board, as well as delegates from each of the approximately 1,000 state and local chapters. There are about 140,000 members: people with mental retardation, family members, friends, professionals, and other interested people. The activities of each chapter are focused on advocacy and on the support of needed services to people with mental retardation and their families. There is a strong component of education and advocacy at every level of the organization (*www.thearc.org*).

The Arthritis Foundation

Mission.   The mission of the Arthritis Foundation is to improve lives through leadership in the prevention, control, and cure of arthritis and related diseases (*www.arthritis.org/ resources/aboutus/history.asp*).

History.   In 1946, a group of scientists and physicians met to begin to address the condition called arthritis. In 1948, there were seven million Americans with arthritis, thirteen chapters, no nationwide presence, no formal treatment guidelines, and only $11,000 was spent on arthritis research in the United States. At that time, there were only seven places where physicians could learn about arthritis and only six treatment and research centers. The organization's first name was the Arthritis and Rheumatism Foundation; it soon grew to thirteen chapters and raised more than $500,000 for research. Three major research discoveries occurred at that time: Rheumatoid arthritis was linked by a blood factor to the immune system, cortisone was developed, and the lupus cell was identified.

During the 1950s and 1960s the foundation expanded its research efforts, began a massive educational program for health-care professionals and the general public, and held a national conference. In 1964, the organization changed its name to the Arthritis Foundation, and the American Rheumatism Association merged with it in 1965 as a section of the foundation. That year, a section of allied health professionals was added to the organization. When funding was cut by the government for arthritis research in 1969, the foundation's efforts engendered donations sufficient to allow research efforts to continue uninterrupted.

The focus of the organization in the 1970s included research, service, education, and fund raising. The year 1972 saw the designation of May as National Arthritis Month. In 1974, the National Arthritis Act was passed, recognizing arthritis as a major health problem in the country.

New medicines and surgical procedures helped to improve the daily lives of people with arthritis.

The American Juvenile Arthritis Foundation was added in 1981, and soon after that the Arthritis Foundation launched its magazine, *Arthritis Today,* dedicated to helping people with arthritis improve their quality of life.

Current Role and Services.   Since 1948, the Arthritis Foundation has raised over $200 million to sponsor arthritis research, supporting the work of more than 1,700 scientists and physicians. The foundation's efforts benefit the more than 43 million Americans with arthritis. The organization also serves people with more than 100 arthritis-related conditions. Annual revenues are more than $113 million, and there are 55 chapters and 150 offices nationwide. Research has markedly improved the lives of people with arthritis, and new medications and surgical procedures continue to do so (*www.arthritis.org/resources/ aboutus/history.asp*).

The Arthritis Foundation projects that, by the year 2020, the number of people with arthritis will be greater than 60 million, affecting life activities such as working, going to school, and raising a family. Ongoing research and community programs are sponsored by the foundation.

One of the foundation's major projects is the annual "Walk or Run" marathon, which is held in different venues both in the United States and abroad. The marathon fulfills several objectives of the foundation (Arthritis Foundation, 2001):

1. Through publicizing the marathon, the Arthritis Foundation disseminates information all over the United States about arthritis and about the research efforts of the foundation.
2. The marathon is the foundation's primary fundraising event. Each marathon participant raises funds for the foundation. In 2001, $4,400 was raised by each person running, walking, or volunteering at the event, which was held in Dublin, Ireland. The Arthritis Foundation provides special training in fundraising and clinics to help participants to remain motivated throughout their fundraising experience.
3. The marathon provides a unique way for people with arthritis to be recognized and supported by friends, colleagues, and members of the community, since participants may run or walk in honor a special person in their lives.
4. Through its "Joints in Motion" training program for both runners and walkers, the foundation assists participants by providing a supportive group environment for training and by enlisting trained coaches to work with participants in all areas of the country. This inclusive approach both broadens support and participation and presents opportunities for people with varying abilities to participate. People with arthritis who are able to participate are especially encouraged.

The foundation provides self-help courses, water- and land-based exercise programs, support groups, home study groups, instructional videos, public forums, educational materials, a magazine, and continuing education for health professionals (*www.arthritis.org*).

Organization.   The Arthritis Foundation is volunteer-driven, and decisions regarding programs, research, budget, and policies are made by volunteer committees. There are 150 chapters and offices nationwide providing services to clients and education to health professionals and the general public. Paid staff provide professional expertise and support volunteer efforts.

The foundation is a part of Arthritis and Rheumatism International, an organization of national associations exchanging knowledge and experiences, supporting research and education and advocacy to promote awareness (*www.arthritis.org/resources/aboutus/ history.asp*).

The National Multiple Sclerosis Society

Mission. "The mission of the National Multiple Sclerosis Society is to end the devastating effects of multiple sclerosis" (Warner, 2000).

History. In 1946, Sylvia Lawry, whose brother had MS, placed an ad in the classified section of the *New York Times* asking to hear about someone who had recovered from MS. All the answers she received, however, were from other people with MS, also seeking help. With a group of friends and advisors—and people who answered her ad—she formed the National Multiple Sclerosis Society to facilitate and provide communication and contact between interested people, between neurologists who were treating MS, and to fund research. These efforts funded research in seventeen countries through grants with funds raised by the society. Dr. Jonas Salk was one of the grant recipients.

In 1950, Lawry and the society convinced Congress to establish a special section of the National Institutes of Health to include MS as a focus, and the Institute on Neurologic Disorders and Stroke.

By 1960, there were 114 chapters of the MS Society throughout the country, each providing services to people with MS and their families. Because of the difficulties inherent in diagnosing MS, the MS Society funded a panel of experts to develop standard guidelines to be used for diagnosis.

The MS Society continued to grow and to provide funding for research and services to people nationwide. In 1967, Lawry broadened the base of research and information by establishing the International Federation of Multiple Sclerosis Societies. Advances in research led to improved treatments and life quality for people with MS.

Current Role and Services. The MS Society provides assistance to over one million people each year through its network of chapters and divisions in every state. The organization serves 250,000 of the estimated 300,00 to 350,000 people with MS in the United States, their caregivers, family members, and children through support groups, information and referral services, video conferences and teleconferences, and educational programs (J. Nelson, Vice President of Field Operations, National MS Society, Denver, private communication, 9/5/01).

There are over a million volunteers who are supported by 2,700 volunteer leaders. Services are free or nominal in cost and include professional counseling, self-help groups, support to keep families with a person with MS together, assistance with medical equipment, provision of information, education, and referrals.

The society supports a library and researchers who can search for information. More than thirty fact sheets and booklets are produced. Because of the complexity and variation of MS, education is especially essential, and booklets provide an excellent avenue for providing information to people with MS, families and caregivers, and the general public. Titles include *Someone You Know Has Multiple Sclerosis: A Guide for Families, Things I Wish Someone Had Told Me, Living with MS, The Win-Win Approach to Reasonable Accommodations: Enhancing Productivity on Your Job, Solving Cognitive Problems, Managing MS Through Rehabilitation, Taming Stress in Multiple Sclerosis,* and *A Guide for Caregivers.*

In 1999, the MS Society raised $134 million in donations, membership dues and contributions, legacies, fundraising, and investments. Half of the 40 percent unrestricted income shared by chapters with the national organization is dedicated to research efforts, and a total of 76 percent of overall expenses is dedicated to research, services to people with MS and their families, and to public and professional education. Fundraising efforts include the MS walk, the MS bike tour, and the annual campaign. The society is the largest private sponsor of MS research in the world.

In 2000, the society invested $25 million to support over 300 MS researchers. Ongoing programs also provide counseling, employment assistance, information about MS, self-help groups, and advocacy for all people with disabilities, and encourage personal empowerment (Warner, 2000).

In 1890, multiple sclerosis was treated with herbs and bed rest, and life expectancy was five years post diagnosis. In 1970, with the advent of steroid treatments, life expectancy post diagnosis reached thirty-two years. Today, the life expectancy of a person with MS is essentially normal (*www.nmss.org*).

Three new injectable drugs have been developed since 1996 that help delay exacerbations in people with exacerbation-remission-cycle MS. They are very costly (about $10,000 for one year per person), and the NMSS has been active in advocacy efforts with HMOs. The Washington, DC, office has also been advocating in Congress for the drugs to be included in Medicare funding. The drugs are effective but have some side effects, and the organization, through its support efforts, works to help people to remain on the drugs in spite of these. Twenty percent of people with MS have the progressive form, and a fourth drug to address the needs of these people has been developed in 2000. The NMSS is also researching the gender differences in MS, since it affects many more women than men. (J. Nelson, Vice President of Field Operations, Denver, CO, 2001, private communication).

Organization. There are several MS Society national offices that serve different functions. The original office, in New York, currently addresses finance, administration, and research-related issues and serves as the center for the national board of directors, a group of volunteers who both govern and provide direction for the organization. The Denver office, founded in 1990, provides support for the chapters, administers fundraising programs, and provides training for the organization. The Washington, DC, office, founded in 1996, focuses on advocacy in Congress and other government bodies. There are about 1,200 paid staff members in the society. There are sixty-seven chapter offices throughout the country, each with a volunteer board of directors and paid staff. Through the chapter president, each board supervises the services and programs in its chapter area (Nelson).

Similarities and Differences

Three national organizations. Three disabilities. Each organization provides similar kinds of services, such as information and education, research funding, advocacy, and support for people with disabilities and families. Each is organized around a national organization with local chapters serving the needs of members. Each emphasizes quality-of-life issues, support, and empowerment. Each is volunteer-run, with paid staff and professionals to provide support and expertise. However, each also remains distinct and reflects the way in which it was formed, the primary interests of its membership, and the specific conditions and problems created by the disability. All three organizations provide advocacy and fund research and educate both the public and the membership about the disability, but the emphasis is a bit different for each. The ARC was formed by families to advocate for the rights of people with mental retardation. The advocacy function continues to be a primary one today. The Arthritis Foundation was founded by a professional group interested in research. One of the major functions today continues to be fundraising for research efforts. The MS Society was originally formed to provide a means of communication for professionals, people with MS, and their families. Education and communication about MS remain a primary focus today.

Cross-Disability Service Organizations

Organizations that serve the disability community as a whole often have a special focus or interest or provide a specific service. The services provided include advocacy, legal assistance specific services needed by wide cross-section of the disability community, political action and monitoring, dissemination of information about disability to the general public and the political community, and linkages to other agencies and services. Some organizations began with a focus on a disability and expanded to include all disability issues. Others are primarily self-advocacy and empowerment organizations composed of people with disabilities and serve as spokespersons for the disability community as a whole. Still others are connected with research organizations or universities, while others are consortiums of organizations. The enormous listing of these organizations include:

> ADAPT (American Disabled for Attendant Services Today)
> American Association of People with Disabilities
> Center on Human Policy (Syracuse University)
> Consortium for Citizens with Disabilities (over 100 disability organizations)
> Disability Information Resources
> Disability Rights Advocates
> Disability Services (University of Minnesota)
> Disabled American Veterans
> Easter Seals
> I-CAN-on-line
> Independent Living Foundation

Make-A-Wish Foundation
National Center for Disability Services
National Family Caregivers Association
Physicians' Disability Services
Society for Disability Studies
TASH (The Action Starts Here)

The stories of the three organizations presented here will assist the reader to understand the ways in which cross-disability organizations develop.

Consortium for Citizens with Disabilities

Mission.   The Consortium for Citizens with Disabilities envisions an American society in which all individuals, aided by an enabling government, have the freedom and opportunity to exercise individual decisions concerning their own lives, welfare, and personal dignity. To achieve this vision, the CCD engages in advocacy for national public policy that: (1) ensures the self-determination, independence, empowerment, integration, and inclusion of children and adults with disabilities in all aspects of society; (2) enhances the civil rights and quality of life of all people with disabilities and their families; and (3) reflects the values of the Americans with Disability Act (*www.c-c-d.org*).

History.   The CCD was formed in 1973 as a coalition of national consumer, advocacy, provider, and professional organizations.

Current Role and Services.   CCD's national offices are in Washington, DC, and the organization continues its efforts to achieve federal legislation and regulations that support rights and good life quality for people with disabilities. Legislative issues addressed by the organization include child care, developmental disabilities, education, employment and training, fiscal policy, futures, health, prevention, rights, social security, TANF/Welfare to work, technology and communication, housing, transportation, and long-term services and supports. Each of these areas is addressed by a specific task force working to improve public policy in these areas. The consortium also produces bulletins and informational packets, announcements of relevant meetings and political action, and other material.

Organization.   The consortium is composed over 100 organizations that have an interest in advocacy and public policy issues for people with disabilities. The organizations include professional organizations, disability-specific organizations, self-help organizations, and others. Annual dues of member organizations, donations, and contributions support the consortium's efforts.

Easter Seals

Mission.   Easter Seals seek to help individuals with disabilities and their families to live better lives.

History.   Edgar Allen, an Ohio businessman, lost his son in a streetcar accident in 1907 at least partially due to the inadequacy of medical resources to provide assistance. Mr. Allen retired from business and began a campaign to build a hospital in his home town of Elyria. He learned that children with disabilities were often hidden away from the rest of society, and in 1919 he founded the National Society for Crippled Children.

To raise funds, the organization launched the Easter Seals campaign in which donors received seals to place on letters and other correspondence in 1934. By 1944, the organization's mission had broadened to assisting adults as well as children. As a symbol of spring, the lily was adopted as the formal logo in 1952. Public support enabled the organization to expand services at grassroots levels. In 1967, the organization changed its name to Easter Seals because its work became so associated with the Easter Seals campaign in the minds of the general public.

Current Role and Services.   Today, Easter Seals is a service organization that assists over one million adults and children, with a national network of 400 service sites. The services of each center are responsive to the needs of the surrounding community, with a family focus and an emphasis on innovation.

Services offered include medical rehabilitation through early intervention, physical therapy, occupational therapy, and speech and hearing therapy, job training and employment, inclusive child care, adult day services, camping, and recreation. Easter Seals also advocates on public policy issues affecting people with disabilities and was a strong force in the successful passage of the ADA. Easter Seals employs 13,000 people and has thousands of volunteers (*www.easter/seals.org/whoweare/story/index.asp*).

Organization.   Easter Seals continues to be a grassroots organization. Ninety-four percent of revenues are spent on direct client services, almost all of these in the communities in which the funds were raised. The Easter Seals national headquarters in Chicago provides support, consultation, and training to the 400 centers dispersed throughout the country. Financial support comes from private insurers, government agencies, fees for service, and public contributions. The Easter Seals campaign continues, raising over $10 million in 1999 (*www.easter-seals.org/faq.asp*).

Canine Companions for Independence

Mission.   Canine Companions for Independence strives to enhance the lives of people with disabilities by providing highly trained assistance dogs and ongoing support to ensure quality relationships.

History.   Canine companions was founded in 1975 in Santa Rosa, California. Bonnie Bergen first got the idea of training dogs as companions for people with disabilities, and a swell of community support was quickly engendered for the project. Charles Schulz (of *Peanuts* fame) and his wife Jean became very involved and donated 12 acres to establish the campus. The first canine companion teams were placed in 1978.

Public interest spurred the development of regional training centers to serve the needs of people with disabilities nationwide. CCI has placed 1,720 dogs from the time of its founding, and 932 dog teams are currently active nationwide. In 1999, 108 teams graduated from the program. The number grew to 114 in 2000, and 64 teams were graduated between January and June of 2001 (*www.caninecompanions.org/facts*).

Current Role and Services.   Mrs. Schulz serves as president of the board of directors today, and the organization continues to grow. There are 325 candidates for team training on the waiting list, and ninety-two active breeder dogs.

CCI breeds its own dogs for the qualities desirable in companion dogs for people with disabilities, qualities such as gentleness, obedience, and positive interactions with people. Volunteers keep females during gestation, and they return to the centers for whelping. Puppies are placed in the homes of 880 puppy-raiser volunteers, who commit themselves to training the dogs both at home and in classes at the centers. When the puppies are ready, the are brought to live "on campus" for advanced training. During the last two weeks, future dog companions come to live on campus as well and partake of intensive training with their dogs. After "graduation" the new dog teams begin their lives together. CCI provides support and follow-up for dog teams in the community through its regional centers.

Canine Companions is the largest service dog training operation in the world. The organization is currently developing standards and guidelines for training that will be adopted by the Assistance Dog Institute, of which it is a member (Johanna Riley, volunteer, Canine Companions for Independence, private conversation, 8/15/01).

Organization.   Canine Companions is a volunteer-supported organization, with over 3,000 volunteers providing a variety of services. Based in Santa Rosa, the national organization coordinates and provides support for the regional centers and satellite offices. Centers are located in Santa Rosa and Oceanside, California; Delaware, Ohio; Farmingdale, New York; and Orlando, Florida, with additional satellite offices in Colorado Springs and Chicago. Volunteers, breeders, and trainers have developed a nationwide network of services and support.

There is no charge to graduates for the dogs; only a $100 team training fee is charged. Funding for the organization is completely through private contributions from businesses, civic groups and service clubs, corporation and foundation grants, and fundraising efforts. The organization does not receive any government funding.

There are four types of canine companion teams: service teams for individuals with disabilities; hearing teams for hard-of-hearing or deaf people; skilled companion teams to enhance communication, range of motion, and social skills for people; and facility teams for professional or educational settings to improve the physical, mental, and emotional health of the individuals served by the facility. Each team is specially trained and supervised. Follow-up services provide ongoing support (*www.caninecompanions.org*).

Location-Based Disability Services

Many communities, cities, and regions provide services for people with disabilities who live in their locality. Services are generally organized in a way that is particularly responsive to the needs and concerns of the local community and thus may be more individualized than the services of many national organizations. Often, location-based services were initiated in order to meet a specific community need and were later expanded to include a broader base of people and services. Location-based communities are accessible: They are a physical presence in the community, and staff and services are more aware of and responsive to factors impacting lives of clients in their daily life. Location-based services may be disability-specific or cross-disability.

While location-based services provide many similar services, there are also differences among agencies that are grounded in the history, the needs and special attributes of the population, and the available funds and facilities. In order to encourage critical assessment of agencies and organizations, three agencies will be presented that all meet the needs of a special population: people who are blind and visually impaired. Readers will note that many services are provided by all three agencies, but also that they differ in important ways. Each organization is also impacted by national issues, policies, and events.

Arizona Center for the Blind and Visually Impaired

Mission.   The mission of the Arizona Center for the Blind and Visually Impaired is to enhance the quality of life for persons who are blind or otherwise visually impaired.

History.   The organization grew from a small group of blind and visually impaired people who were meeting in each others' homes to help each other learn how to become economically independent. Two options were piano tuning and mop and broom making, and the group trained in these two fields. They also discussed ways of addressing problems in everyday living that affected them. With the passage of years, the number of meetings and meeting locations grew, and the group assumed a socialization and support function; skills training was provided to individuals at their request through a "home teacher."

In 1952, the Coordinating Council of the Blind and the local Maricopa Club established a central meeting place for the groups in Phoenix. The Phoenix Blind Center, as it was known, hired its first executive director in 1953. When the building was scheduled for demolition, the local Lions Club began planning for a permanent facility and formed a voluntary affiliation of Lions Clubs to raise the needed funds. The group was named in honor of Melvin Jones, who was a native of Arizona and founder of the Lions Club. Land was donated, funds were raised, and volunteer labor was recruited from both the Lions Clubs and labor unions. The new building was completed in 1964.

By the mid-1960s, center services included rehabilitation instruction services, orientation and mobility instruction, and a special aids service. The client base doubled, but the organization maintained its primary focus on support groups and social and recreational programs. In the 1970s, state and federal funding through the Independent Living and Older Americans Act enabled transportation services.

Budget and funding cuts in the 1980s forced consolidation of programs, and some activities had to be eliminated due to lack of transportation services. The executive director saw a need to make the organization independent of funding and created a business, Arizona's Center for the Blind Paper Recycling, centered in the agency's building and parking lot. The business grew and eventually moved to separate quarters. As the business continued to flourish, the board of directors established paper recycling as a separate, wholly owned, for-profit subsidiary of the organization. Satellite offices were established in Sun City, Mesa, and Scottsdale. The agency's focus continued to be counseling support and social and recreational programs.

With a new director, the center developed as a primary resource for broad-based, fully integrated rehabilitation programs and services for adults. Funding efforts included the United Way, the State Rehabilitation Services Administration, and private foundations. Staffing was expanded and new services provided. The Rehabilitation Skills Center was established in 1995 and included rehabilitation skills training, orientation and mobility instruction, counseling services, information and referral, and social work and community education and outreach. The assistive technology center was created in 1996 at the center to provide cross-disability assistive technology assessment and training at home, in the community, and in the workplace.

Current Role and Services. Under the direction of board president Steve Walker, the organization has expanded its efforts at public awareness about blindness and visual impairment, targeted long-term financial needs, and undertaken a remodeling, consolidation, and expansion effort through a major capital and endowment campaign. Current services include counseling, peer group support, rehabilitation teaching techniques, classes and workshops, assistive technology and technology assessment and training, social work services emphasizing empowerment, orientation and mobility training, and social and recreational activities.

Organization. ACBVI has a multidisciplinary professional staff, volunteers, and an executive director accountable to the board of directors. Funding is received from United Way, state and federal agencies for contract services, endowments, grants, and contributions. The organization serves the state of Arizona, primarily focusing on the Phoenix area (*www.acbvi.org*).

Aurora of Central New York

Mission. The mission is to assist blind and visually impaired and deaf and hearing impaired people living in central New York.

History. Aurora of Central New York was established in 1991 by the merger of the Lighthouse, which was founded in 1917 to assist blind and visually impaired central New Yorkers, and the Central New York Association for the Hearing Impaired. It was felt that the merger of the two organizations would enable the provision of more efficient and effective services to the people of central New York. The agency serves people of all ages.

Current Role and Services. By 1997, the agency was providing counseling services for over 500 people. Orientation and mobility training is provided onsite to over 200 people a year, and about 1400 people were assisted in learning skills for independent daily living such as cooking, cleaning, and clothesmatching as well as money management. Interpreter referral services provide interpreting services, skills assessments, and classes and workshops for interpreters, and over 12,000 hours are provided annually.

Some of the other services provided include supported employment services for people who are deaf or hard of hearing, low vision services to assist people with residual vision to maximize it, senior vision screening for over 800 adults, sign language classes (ASL) for 150 members of the hearing community, youth education for independence through the school system, personal service volunteers, support for a Deaf AA chapter, early intervention services, and fostering public awareness through presentations to community groups and advocacy. An adaptive technology center provides computer and technology-related services.

Organization.   Aurora receives funding from United Way and contracts with government agencies in the provision of services. The Board of Directors formulates policy and provides direction with input from the professional staff.

The agency's professional staff serve thousands of people with vision and hearing limitations, blindness, and deafness in Onondaga, Oswego, Cayuga, northern Cortland and Jefferson counties (*www.members.aol.com/auroracny/*).

Association for the Blind and Visually Impaired

Mission.   The mission of the organization includes assisting visually impaired people to develop skills to become more independent through rehabilitative services; to educate the general public, organizations, professions, visually impaired people, and their families about the nature of visual impairments and the capabilities of visually impaired people; and to promote the prevention of blindness.

History.   Roberta A. Griffith, the founder of the association, became blind due to a childhood illness. She attended Michigan School for the Blind and Ohio School for the Blind, and later was the first blind woman to receive a college degree in an institution not intended to serve blind students, from Western Reserve. She later compiled a the first dictionary for the blind, in six volumes, and dedicated herself to publicizing the needs of blind people. She was one of the original organizers of the American Foundation for the Blind.

With the assistance of eighteen volunteers, Roberta Griffith founded the Grand Rapids Association for the Blind and Sight Conservation, which became the Association for the Blind and Visually Impaired in 1913. The Association established the first integrated sighted and nonsighted classrooms in the nation. It also established the Public Health Institute for training and organizing volunteers to do vision screening in all of the schools in her county, and also the first occupational therapy program to replace the home teacher program for blind students. The association established a preschool program for blind children on the premises of the agency.

In the 1960s, the organization employed the first master's level trained orientation and mobility specialist, and, with funding from the Michigan Commission for the Blind, started a low-vision clinic. It was also responsible for the formation of In Touch Volunteer Braille Transcribers to provide materials for blind people in the community.

A satellite low-vision clinic was opened in Muskegon, and a community outreach program was established to serve minority clients with vision impairments or blindness.

Current Role and Services.   The association currently provides programs to the community through a low-vision clinic, orientation and mobility training, education to prevent blindness and visual impairments, daily living skills instruction, volunteer support for blind and visually impaired community members, an aids and appliance store, leisure time activities, and Braille transcriptions services to enhance the lives of blind people, such as restaurant menus, church hymns, and birthday cards.

Organization.   The association is supported by United Way in all the counties it serves. It also receives funding from the area Agency on Aging, individual donations, the Lions Clubs, memorials and bequests, private foundations, program fees, and special events. The board of directors oversees agency functioning, and professional workers include outreach and minority outreach, rehabilitation, rehabilitation teaching, peer support groups, orientation and mobility specialists It serves a thirteen-county area through two locations (*www.grcmc.org/blindser*).

Comparisons

It is obvious that, while the formation of each of these agencies differed and their history reflects different foci and concerns, there are a number of similarities. All three offer similar services: counseling, rehabilitation training, low-vision services, orientation and mobility training, and assistive devices and technology. All three began to offer specialized services related to the development of new programs to train specialists, and all three were strongly affected by the federal budget, expanding when funds were available for programs, and reorganizing when budget cuts made it necessary. It is clear that these two factors outside each agency's immediate control impacted strongly on service provisions and thus on the agency's ability to meet the needs of the population.

Chapter Summary

Private-sector agencies exist at every level from national to local. Some agencies are disability-specific, while others cross disabilities. Agencies may be funded in a variety of ways through United Fund, government contracts and grants, foundation grants and endowments, fund-raising activities, and contributions. Most agencies use a combination of sources for funding, but private agencies may also be fully privately funded. Agencies generally have a board of directors whose members hire the executive director. Professional staff and volunteers provide services to clients.

Agency services vary according to the mission and goals of each agency, the population being served, and the exigencies of funding. Agencies may provide direct client services, or may advocate for clients through political action and legal services. Most agencies provide a range of services, although some specialize in one kind of activity. All agencies have an education and public awareness function, and recognize that a well-informed public will support their efforts. National agencies also support research efforts.

Clients commonly utilize the services of both public and private agencies to meet needs. This overview has provided the reader with some insight into the way in which both public and private agencies function. In the following chapters, we will explore how both public and private agencies can be utilized to meet specific client needs, such as health and medical care, housing and personal care, education and employment, socialization and recreation, and mobility.

Questions for Thought and Discussion

1. Becoming knowledgeable about the private sector is essential to competent practice. Many communities have directories of services for people with disabilities available. Obtain one of these and explore it. Is it well organized? Is it distributed in ways that reach people with disabilities? Does it offer specific information about services or merely list agency names? How might you improve this important resource?

2. Communities that don't have directories need them. How would you obtain the information needed to develop a directory? With other students in your class, gather information and develop an informal directory of disability services for your area.

3. Select a national organization that serves the needs of people with disabilities. Using their website, brochures, and other information, prepare a report on your organization to share with the class. Exchange reports, and you will become knowledgeable about a number of national organizations! Keep all the reports with this book as a resource for future use.

4. Locate a local organization that serves people with disabilities. Contact the agency and arrange a personal visit to learn about services and programs. Share your information with your classmates.

5. In the last chapter, you imagined yourself a person in a wheelchair in need of housing adapted to enable maximum independence. What resources are available from the private sector to support your needs, and/or to supplement public offerings in terms of housing?

18

Public and Private Intersections in Health Care

> The health care system is an essential infrastructure that can either facilitate functional ability and choice for people with disabilities or make it difficult for people with disabilities to achieve their goals.
>
> (National Council on Disability, 1997–98)

Health-care needs, costs, and availability are central concerns for everyone. Our society recognizes the intimate relationship between life satisfaction and health, and there is a strong emphasis on leading a "healthy lifestyle" and promoting "wellness." Mass-media programming and advertising also encourage us to relate health to beauty. Exercise programs, nutritious diets, regular health checkups, and ample time for leisure and outdoor activities are viewed as promoting health.

Clients with disabilities often find that access to medical care, costs, and application for programs and plans consume an inordinate amount of time and resources. Disability often requires special care needs, high prescription costs, and investment in equipment and supplies. Social workers assist clients by providing case management services to coordinate, advocate for, and obtain needed medical care and ancillary health services.

Comprehensive listings of resources for health-care information and programs are readily available on the Internet. However, in most instances, clients' needs and available health care must be evaluated on an individual basis. Social workers are not the primary providers of health care. However, awareness of programs, legislation, and available resources is essential in assisting clients. Social worker advocacy and expertise is invaluable in helping clients through the complex and intricate healthcare network.

Access to good medical care is often the first issue to be addressed by newly disabled people, immediately followed by the need to arrange for suitable financing. Disability often leads to lower income levels, and many people with disabilities are living at or near poverty levels. Concomitantly, medical expenses are often higher. Private health insurance, Medicare, and Medicaid are the primary sources of funding for medical expenses. The Ticket to Work and Work Incentives Act of 1999 provides extended coverage under Medicare and Medicaid for people with disabilities who become employed.

A major change in federal programs and policies is evolving because of the Olmstead Decision, a 1999 Supreme Court decision supporting the rights of people with disabilities to home and community-based rather than institutional care. Because the Medicaid program has a bias toward nursing home care, new initiatives and programs are being developed to refocus the payment structure in a way that enables people to obtain needed health services in the community. Medicaid waivers are increasingly being utilized by states and communities to fund community based services.

New community-based care initiatives also address the needs of people currently living in nursing homes. Programs to assist people with disabilities to transition out of the nursing home and into the community support the intent of the Olmstead decision and the ADA.

Transportation to needed health-care resources and ancillary services such as nutritional counseling, optometrists, podiatrists, physical therapy, and other health-care needs are also important to maximize the health, independence, and productivity of people with disabilities.

The Department of Health and Human Services funds research projects on various issues in the provision of medical care for people with disabilities. These projects can be accessed at *www.aspe.hhs.gov/daltcp/projects.htm#disability*.

Medical Care

Accessibility

Access to good medical care is essential, but cities and towns in the United States vary in the availability and quality of medical services. This is a national problem, but it impacts disproportionately on people with disabilities, limiting access to new treatments, technologies, and medical resources. Clients who live in rural or economically depressed areas may have to travel long distances to a medical center or health-care facility. Clients who require special regimens such as chemotherapy or dialysis may be faced with decisions about forgoing treatment or moving to an unfamiliar place, without the necessary family and social supports.

For clients who need a limited series of treatments, a possible alternative is to live near the hospital while the treatment is being provided and move back home when it is complete. Though medical follow-up may be limited, the benefits of the social network may outweigh these concerns. Major medical centers provide housing resources and information for people coming from out of town and their family members. Some have housing available through the medical center at nominal cost. Community resources such as the Ronald McDonald House network provide options based on the client's ability to pay and can also provide assistance with food, laundry, and transportation.

Private or Employer-Provided Medical Insurance

People who are employed or whose spouses are employed generally have some medical insurance made available through their employers. Employers vary in the amount of medical insurance they pay for employees: Some will provide partial coverage, some will cover the entire cost of insurance. Policies and benefits also vary, and it is important to check covered services and any limitations on coverage. Many private insurance plans have a cap—a maximum amount that they will pay in benefits. Caps may cover the life of the policy, a single event, or a time period, such as a year. Because people with disabilities often have ongoing medical needs or require costly programs and treatments, they are more likely to reach the insurer's maximum.

Insurance plans also may limit coverage of certain services or may not cover them at all. Mental health coverage and physical therapy are often limited, and costs of eyeglasses, dental care, orthotics, and other services may not be covered at all. If private insurance does not meet the client's ongoing needs, other resources should be explored.

Medicare

The national number for consumer information for Medicare is 1-800-MEDICARE. This help line is staffed by Medicare Customer Representatives. The informative website at *www.medicare.gov* provides general information and also lists Medicare contacts by state. Medicare is available to people who have paid Medicare taxes during their years of employment.

Medicare has two parts. Part A covers hospital care, and Part B covers physician services and other health care, some kinds of equipment, and supplies. Coverage for Part B is optional and is set at $50 per month. The cost of Part B is automatically deducted from Social Security payments if clients choose to add this coverage.

Medicare is tied in to Social Security benefits: If a person is eligible for Social Security or SSDI, that person is also eligible for Medicare Part A at no cost. However, there is a twenty-four-month lag time between the receipt of the first Social Security check and Medicare coverage. This presents difficulties for clients who are eligible for SSDI and do not have private insurance.

Medicaid

In contrast to Medicare, Medicaid is a needs-based program, administered by the Health Care Financing Administrations (HCFA). Medicaid provides medical insurance to 36 million people and is administered by the states. Eligibility is determined by amount of income and amount of resources. See *www.hcfa.gov/Medicaid/ssi0101.htm* for guidelines for SSI recipients.

Medicaid benefits provide coverage for both hospital and physician services, and provide long-term care coverage as well. Long-term care coverage has traditionally been for provided institutional care, but recent court decisions and policy changes are redirecting long-term care toward home and community (*www.hcfa.gov/medicaid/medicaid.htm*).

Managed Care

The majority of health-care coverage in the United States today is provided through managed-care plans. People with private insurance and an increasing percentage of Medicare and Medicaid insured are enrolled in managed-care plans (National Council on Disability, 1997–98). Managed care is privately run and often for-profit.

Under managed-care plans, physician providers and patient recipients may both allow the managed-care company to make determinations of necessity and relevance of treatments, surgeries, office visits, and the like. Patients select a primary-care physician from a list of providers who are members of the plan. In addition to providing primary care, the physician assumes a gatekeeper function in having to refer patients for other services. Plan staff also must approve each physician referral. In many plans, physicians are capitated: that is, they receive a set fee for each plan patient for whom they are responsible. Clearly, it becomes advantageous to provide minimal services, for extensive service provision does not increase the managed-care company's payments to the physician. By controlling costs and access to services, managed care streamlines services and demands efficient and effective use of each health-care dollar. However, managed care providers incurred accusations and lawsuits for not providing needed care, and the Patients Rights Bill (2001) allows plan members to sue companies for damages related to denial of services or care mismanagement.

Because of the greater health-care needs of people with disabilities, managed care has had an enormous impact on the provision of services. People receiving Medicare can choose to join a managed-care plan, and those receiving Medicaid may be required to join a plan in the future. In many states, Medicaid services are provided to all patients through contracts with managed-care companies. Medicaid services may be out for bids to various providers, just as road building and other services are. The provider who is awarded the contract to provide services must undergo an extensive review, licensing and contracting processes, and scrutiny by state officials.

NIDRR is sponsoring several research projects to study the effect of managed care on people with disabilities. Three studies evaluated the impact of managed care on access, utilization, patterns of care, and costs of health care for people with disabilities. One of the studies explores the problems and adverse affects on people with disabilities of managed-care plan membership. Legal issues arise because of greater health-care needs, cost-cutting measures, and nondiscrimination laws (National Rehabilitation Hospital Center for Health and Disability Research, *www.ilru.org/mgdcare/projects.html*).

Several training projects were funded based on study findings. Two of these address the needs of people with disabilities for information about managed-care plans so that they can make an informed decision about health care.

Ticket to Work

In 1999, the Ticket to Work and Work Incentives Improvement Act was passed, providing new options for states to make it possible for people with disabilities to join the workforce without losing their Medicare or Medicaid coverage, so essential in meeting the higher-than-average costs of health care (Health Care Financing Administration Ticket to Work and Work Incentives Act, *www.hcfa.gov/medicaid/twwiia/faq.htm*).

Ticket to Work is an optional program with two parts: One addresses employment and the other medical care. The employment provisions will be addressed in Chapter 19. Title II of the act establishes two new eligibility categories and extends the period of premium-free Medicare Part A coverage for SSDI recipients to eight and a half years. One category, the Basic Coverage Group, extends the Medicaid coverage of people who were receiving SSI. The second category, the Medical Improvement Group, addresses the medical needs of people whose disability has improved so that they no longer meet SSI disability eligibility criteria. States may individually determine whether to charge premiums for these two categories and set the amounts of the premiums.

Home and Community-Based Care

The Olmstead Decision

In July 1999, the Supreme Court decided the case of *Olmstead vs. L.C.*, known as the Olmstead Decision. This decision interprets Title II of the ADA to require that states provide services to people with disabilities in the "most integrated setting" appropriate to each individual. This requires the development of more accessible systems of community-based services for people with disabilities (Olmstead Decision, *www.Medicaid/olmstead/olmslink .htm*). In order to address these changes, HCFA is consulting with each state to develop plans. HCFA will also review all existing Medicaid regulations to see if they are compatible with the Supreme Court ruling.

Medicaid Waivers

Home and Community Based Services waivers (HCBS 1915(c)) offer each state the possibility of planning alternative health care for people with disabilities, in order to support community living rather than nursing home or other residential care facility placement. Waivers may be used to provide services to people who are physically, mentally, or developmentally disabled (Health Care Financing Administration Medicaid Waivers, *www.hcfa .gov/medicaid/hpg4.htm*).

Under this provision, which is a part of the Social Security Act, states may request waivers of certain federal requirements in order to develop Medicaid-financed community-based treatment. The services that may be offered under these waivers include case management, habilitation, respite care, homemaker, home health aide, personal care attendant, adult day health, minor home modifications, nonmedical transportation, and in-home support. There is a requirement that the cost of providing care in the community must be limited to the expected cost of institutional care.

As of 2001, all states except for Arizona have at least one waiver program in effect. There are 240 programs in operation nationwide. More information about home and community services funded by Medicaid may be found in Smith & O'Keefe (2000).

Nursing Home Care

Transition Initiatives Grants

In support of the Olmstead Decision, HCFA has developed a program to provide grants to states to assist in the development of transition programs to move people with disabilities out of nursing homes and into community-based care. In fiscal year 2000, $2,000,000 has been allotted for these grants (*www.hcfa.gov/medicaid/smd53100.htm*).

Ancillary Health-Care Services

Nursing and Nursing Assistant Services

Medically necessary nursing services are available for clients through any public or private insurance plan and may be residential or community based. Home health care and personal care options are available under Medicaid and will be expanded under the Home and Community Based Care initiatives. Community-based services may be provided through contracts with private agencies and resources.

Physical Therapy

Time-limited physical therapy services are offered by insurance plans as well.

Eyeglasses and Eye Exams

Eyeglasses and eye exams may be covered under some insurance policies but are often the responsibility of the individual. For clients with limited resources, the Lions Club offers assistance with both eye exams and glasses.

Lions Clubs International was founded in 1917. This service organization's mission is a commitment to blindness prevention and to service to people who are blind or have low vision. The Lions Club collects and redistributes used eyeglasses, sponsors educational programs, and assists people to get needed assistance to improve their vision. Clients with disabilities whose vision needs are not met through government programs can be assisted through the Lions Club. Services are offered through arrangements with local eyeglass centers and national chains. Contact them through local clubs or through their website at *www.lionsclub.org*.

Dental Care

Medicare and Medicaid do not provide comprehensive dental services. Services generally are limited to extractions and addressing acute problems. Dental societies and associations in many areas provide free or low-cost dental services to clients in need. Dental school clinics offer extensive orthodontia, periodontia, and other dental services. To locate a dental program in your area, contact the local dental society or dental school.

Chapter Summary

The major providers of medical care and health services for people with disabilities are Medicare and Medicaid programs and private insurance. While in the past people with disabilities received medical care primarily through residential facilities, new initiatives grounded in the ADA, Supreme Court rulings, and advocacy have shifted the focus of medical care to the community. The Olmstead Decision, a 1999 Supreme Court ruling, supports community-based care for people with disabilities. In compliance with the ruling, various initiatives on both national and state levels are exploring the development of community-based health services and effective methods for transitioning people with disabilities out of nursing homes and into communities.

Managed care disproportionately affects people with disabilities, who often require extensive and comprehensive medical care over a long period of time. Costs of medical care are often very high for people with disabilities, and managed-care companies that regulate and monitor health-care services may limit access to needed services. Several current court cases are challenging managed-care company decisions.

Questions for Thought and Discussion

1. Managed-care issues disproportionately affect people with disabilities who are dependent on long-term and often expensive health-care services. How would you effectively address the health-care needs of people with disabilities? Do you think that separate programs and health plans should address these unique needs?

2. The higher medical costs of people with disabilities are passed on to all people who are served by an insurance carrier, often raising premiums for everyone. Do you think that this is equitable and fair? What alternatives could be considered, if any?

3. People with disabilities who qualify for Social Security must wait twenty-four months from the date they receive their first check to become eligible for Medicare. If they do not meet Medicaid need guidelines, they must make their own arrangements for health-care coverage at a time when they are facing many disability-connected difficulties and clearly increased health-care needs. What could or should be done to address this gap in essential services?

4. Community-based healthcare for people with severe disabilities is often more expensive than nursing home care. People can require twenty-four-hour nursing supervision, a full-time attendant, provision of oxygen, and other services. Should all people with all conditions and needs for intensive health care be able to live in the community?

5. With classmates, design a community-based health-care service that would serve people with disabilities in compliance with the Olmstead Decision.

19

Public and Private Intersections in Housing and Personal Care Needs

While health needs and concerns are central issues for people with disabilities, where to live, with whom to live, and how to stay independent are major questions that must be addressed as well. Historically, many people with disabilities, especially those with mental illnesses and developmental disabilities, lived in large institutions. With advocacy and the Disability Rights movement, institutional care was seen as undesirable, and community options for living were explored. Today, many of the public institutions that "warehoused" people have been closed.

What housing arrangements can people with disabilities consider? What options are available? To a certain extent, the answers to these questions lie with personal choice, the client's social support network, and available financial resources.

If a person wants to remain in the community, living at home, alone or with family members, is one possible choice. Another is to live independently, and still another to live in a community home or group home where certain expenses and services can be shared. Until the Supreme Court's Olmstead Decision in 1999, policies favored institutional over community living for service reimbursement, but current initiatives will redirect funds toward supporting people in community settings. Nursing homes, retirement homes, life care, and assisted living resources are also possibilities. These are generally private, and are either nonprofit or for-profit. Many accept Medicare and Medicaid.

Several financial issues impact planning. Obtaining housing may be difficult for people with disabilities, who often have lower incomes due to more limited employment opportunities. There are government programs that can assist people to purchase a home or to modify an existing home. Other government programs provide assistance with rental expenses. Medicare does not cover unlimited long-term care expenses, and Medicaid, as a needs-based program, requires that resources be limited before eligibility is attained.

Another issue that impacts housing planning is personal care needs. Where a disability limits the individual's ability to perform ADLs (feeding, dressing, toileting, and transferring) or IADLs (shopping, housecleaning, bill paying etc.), the assistance of another person is required. Many types of residential housing provide for some degree of assistance, and nursing home care can provide complete assistance. For some clients who choose to remain in the community, family members or friends assist with personal care needs. Others require personal care attendant services (PAS) to provide assistance.

In this chapter, we will explore housing and personal care resources. The resources included here are only a small representative sample of resources available to address housing and personal care needs. Both the Department of Housing and Urban Development and the Department of Health and Human Services offer resources and information, as do nonprofit and private organizations. As with all disability-related needs, disability-specific and general cross-disability agencies are among the best resources available.

Community Living

HUD and state governments have agencies dealing specifically with housing for people with disabilities. These can be contacted as resources both for housing and for options in mortgages and rental assistance. However, it is important to encourage your client to express his or her desires in terms of housing arrangements. Most clients will choose to live in the community, either with family members, friends, independently, or in some form of communal living arrangement.

Living with Family

Many people with disabilities live at home with family members. People who are disabled from birth or early childhood grow up with parent(s) and siblings, and, if they remain single, they may choose to continue to live at home with family. If the family relationship is positive and functional, this arrangement provides support and a sense of security. People who become disabled in adulthood may choose to remain with spouses or partners, who often provide personal care and support as well. People who become disabled in later years often choose to live with a child, and, if the child has a positive relationship with the parent, this too is a supportive arrangement.

When disabled people live at home with family members, it is important for the social worker to consider the family as a unit and to be aware of the interactions among members. Family members often need support, respite care, or ongoing assistance in providing care. Chapter 22 will present some resources for assisting family members who are caregivers to live full and meaningful lives while they are providing care for a loved one.

Family housing may need to be modified to accommodate a newly disabled family member. Provisions for housing loans for modifications are presented below. There are also organizations that assist families to modify or rebuild housing to meet special needs. One such organization is Rebuilding Together, a national organization of volunteers (*www.rebuildingtogether.org*).

Independent Living

The Independent Living movement supports disabled people who wish to live independently in the community. Adults who are single often choose to live alone or with friends.

Centers for Independent Living (CILs) exist in many communities across the United States and internationally as well. CILs provide assistance with housing but also offer other services to support and maintain disabled people in the community. CILs in the states of Alaska, Florida, Idaho, Illinois, Maryland, Minnesota, Missouri, New York, Oklahoma, and Texas have joined together to form Statewide Independent Living Councils (SILCs) to share resources and other services.

The first CIL was established in Berkeley, CA, and continues to provide independent living services today. In addition to assistance in locating housing, the Berkeley CIL also provides a range of other services to assist people with disabilities living in the community, including personal assistant services, financial benefits counseling, peer support services, training in independent living skills, deaf and deaf/blind services, the Client Assistant Project, employment services, blind services, and information and referral services to meet a variety of other needs. Berkeley's CIL served over 1,700 people with disabilities in 2001, and 75 percent of the staff have disabilities as well (CIL, n.d.). CILs also maintain websites to assist clients and social workers to locate information about services. These can be accessed through *www.cil.(location).org/services.*

Multifamily Dwellings

Because many people with disabilities have insufficient resources to purchase their own home, many rent units in multifamily dwellings. These may be publicly owned buildings that are specially designated for older people or for both older and disabled people or privately owned units in not-for-profit or for-profit buildings. Section 504 of the Rehabilitation Act of 1973 stipulates that all new construction dwellings of more than four units must provide accessible units for disabled people. However, the number of units mandated is far less than the number required to serve all people (Independent Living Centers, *www.ilsc .org/housing*).

Financial Assistance for Community Living

Fannie Mae Home Mortgages.   The government has developed several programs to assist people with disabilities to live in the community. The National Home Mortgage Association (Fannie Mae)'s "Home Choice" program is an experimental program that assists people with disabilities to own their own homes. Twelve states currently have grants to provide special loans: Alabama, California, District of Columbia, Massachusetts, Michigan, Minnesota, Missouri, New Mexico, New York, Oregon, Washington, and Texas. The grants enable each state to develop its own policies and requirements for home mortgages, which are provided through Fannie Mae lenders. In addition to mortgages for home purchase, second mortgages to retrofit and adapt a home for a disabled person are available. The Housing Finance Agency provides the second mortgage (Parent Advocacy Coalition for Educational Rights, *www.pacer.org*).

To assist professionals working with people with disabilities, Fannie Mae has produced *A Home of Your Own: A Guide for Homeowner Educators,* which includes chapters on the advantages and disadvantages of home ownership, assembling a planning team to assist in the home-buying process, practical advice in shopping for a home, the process of obtaining a mortgage, the settlement process, and some insights into life as a homeowner (*www.fanniemae.com/neighborhoods/home_guide/index.html*).

HUD Section 202 (Elderly, Disabled, Handicapped).   Eligibility for this program is family-income based and generally requires that at least one person be aged sixty-two or older. Some units in multifamily dwellings are also available for people with disabilities who are under sixty-two years of age.

HUD Section 236 (Family, Elderly, Disabled, Handicapped).   This program is also income-based but is available for family with a disabled member who is not elderly.

Below-Market Interest Rate Housing.   This income-based program enables people with disabilities to rent units in private, multidwelling buildings at rates lower than comparable apartments in the area.

Section 8 Housing.   Section 8 provides certificates that enable people to locate housing in the community in a variety of settings, including public housing. Under Section 8, families with a disabled member pay 30 percent of their income for rent only (Department of Housing and Urban Development, *www.hud.gov/local/sdg/sdgmf3.html*).

Communal Living

Independent Communal Living

People with disabilities may choose to live with other people in a communal housing arrangement. Typically, each person has his or her own room but shares a communal living room, dining room, and other public areas of the home. Communal living arrangements provide socialization opportunities as well as peer support; however, it is very important in this, as in all shared living arrangements, to ensure that people respect each other, get along, and abide by whatever rules or policies are adopted by the group.

Independent communal living arrangements are generally peer run. Clients may be referred to communal living by CILs or other disability resources. Communal living has the advantage of offering the possibility of sharing in attendant services, housekeeping assistance, and any other support services needed by members of the group. Houses for communal living may be purchased privately by individuals, or by nonprofit or for-profit organizations. Each member pays a share of the mortgage or of the rent.

Organization-Sponsored Communal Living

Disability-specific and/or cross-disability organizations also purchase and operate communal living homes. Homes that function under the auspices of an organization are generally administered by the organization, which often also provides the personnel and services needed by residents. The communal home is generally one of many services offered by the organization. Others typically include employment services, skills training, education, and counseling.

There is often a "house manager" who supervises residents, attends to problems, mediates disputes, and helps residents to organize and plan activities. Organization-sponsored communal living arrangements are often very effective for people with certain kinds of developmental disabilities, for people with mental illnesses, for substance-abusing clients, and for disabled adolescents.

Financial Assistance for Communal Living

HUD's "Home Choice" program includes loans for "community living," for the purchase of homes for small communities of people. The borrowers can be legal entities, nonprofits, for-profits, limited partnerships, or government agencies (*www.pacer.org*).

Residential Care

Special-Needs Residential Care

People with disabilities who have special needs, such as education, ongoing intensive supervision, a therapeutic setting, or a substance-abuse program may also be housed in larger settings, such as schools or hospitals. These may be public, nonprofit, or for-profit settings and may receive funding in full or in part from public sources. Some special settings are under contract with the government to provide specific services to clients.

Assisted Living

Assisted living facilities differ markedly in appearance. They may be city high-rises or self-contained residential communities. They may be a floor or several floors in a nursing home or in a life-care facility. Assisted living facilities provide residents with assistance and support with activities of daily living (ADLs) and instrumental activities of daily living (IADLs), but generally do not provide intensive medical supervision or nursing care. A nurse is on call, and emergency provisions such as call bells are available in units. Because they do not provide skilled nursing services, assisted living facilities generally are not eligible for public funding through Medicare or Medicaid.

Nursing Homes

Most nursing home residents are seventy-five years of age or older, and many have multiple disabilities. In 1995, nursing home residents who were not elderly (under sixty-five years of age) accounted for only 11 percent of the nursing home population (Strahan, 1997).

Contemporary society recognizes that nursing homes are not appropriate long-term living arrangements for most people with disabilities, and programs and policies are generally moving away from nursing homes and toward community living as the arrangements of choice for people with disabilities. While nursing homes are not the housing arrangements of choice, they do serve the needs of some people who are severely disabled with cognitive disabilities, who are "locked in," or who require continual monitoring of medical equipment and supports.

Choosing a nursing home is a complex task that should involve both the future resident and the family. Important considerations include services offered, proximity to family members, condition of the home, and philosophy of care. In support of self-determination, nursing homes may refuse to admit clients who are brought to the facility against their will and involve residents in planning care, activities, and nursing home rules and policies. Resident councils empower residents to advocate for changes or services and serve as a link between the facility's administration and the residents.

The website *www.members.tripod.com* offers assistance and guidelines for selecting a nursing home. It is always very important to check the facility's performance record by reviewing surveys conducted by government agencies. These nursing home surveys are available on the web at *www.medicare.gov/nursing/home.asp*.

Because there is a strong move away from nursing home care for clients with disabilities, clients are being prepared to return to community living. Transitional support is important in helping clients to readjust positively community living.

Life Care

"Life-care" communities provide a range of services depending upon the needs of clients. While they generally serve older people, most life-care communities do not have a lower age limit for admission. Also, since many people with disabilities are older, life-care facilities provide support and continuity, and a feeling of security about what lies ahead. Independent living provides traditionally equipped apartments or homes where people live independent lives, own cars, and go on vacation. Housekeeping assistance, laundry, and meals are generally provided to clients in independent living units. Assisted living may be provided in traditional housing units, or people may be asked to move to a special area where care can be provided more efficiently. Assisted living provides some medication or medical monitoring and also assistance with personal care and hygiene. Nursing homes that are part of a life-care community provide the same skilled nursing care as freestanding facilities provide and are surveyed and monitored by the same government agencies.

Arrangements for joining a life-care community vary, as the communities vary. There is generally a buy-in where residents purchase their apartment or home. When they leave the home, none, some, or all of the funds are returned to the individual or to family members. The life-care community uses the client's Medicare to pay for medical services, but generally agrees to provide all needed services whether Medicare covers them or not. Personal attendant services often are not included and must be paid for separately. Life-care communities may be administered by nonprofit agencies such as churches or community organizations or by profit-making companies. Because of their cost, life care is generally not an option for people with limited funds.

Financial Assistance for Residential Care

People with disabilities who need skilled nursing care and whose incomes are limited are covered by Medicaid programs. Short-term coverage is also available through Medicare if there is a rehabilitation component to the client's plan. Nursing homes are costly and most people who must pay privately generally run out of funds and become eligible for Medicaid. Private funds may, of course, also be used to pay for nursing home care. Veterans who require skilled care are assisted through the Veterans Administration. The VA also operates its own system of residential facilities and the eligibility standards may be quite different from those of medical assistance.

Life care and assisted living are generally funded by clients through private sources. The cost of these arrangements varies markedly according to location, services offered, facility, and sponsorship. Special-needs residential care is generally funded through public programs, but there are also many private facilities that are paid for individually.

Many private insurance companies are offering long-term-care insurance, and some employers are including long-term-care insurance as one of their benefits. However, there are many problems with this kind of insurance, and consumers may easily be defrauded. Some of the issues clients must consider very carefully include time limits for beginning and ending coverage, ceilings on the total amount of coverage, whether there is a built-in cost-of-living provision, what constitutes a "disability," and exactly what kinds of services will be covered. To assist clients with long-term care insurance issues, a good website is the consumer law page at *www.consumerlawpage.com/article/insurance.shtml.*

Personal Care Attendants

Policy and Legal Issues

Legislation, programs, and policies have tended to support nursing home services rather than community-based services for people with disabilities. This nursing home "bias" is felt most strongly in the area of personal attendant services. As community-based programs are gaining support and the move away from nursing home care continues, issues of concern related to the provision of personal attendant services must be addressed. ADAPT, the organization that began as American Disabled for Access to Public Transport, has changed its name to American Disabled for Attendant Programs Today and is a strong force lobbying for a bill to provide services. ADAPT notes that each state is required to provide facilities for nursing home care, but not for community-based care (*www.adapt.org*).

In support of attendant care, the Medicaid Community Attendant Services and Supports Act (MICASSA) has been brought to the legislature. This act would eliminate nursing home bias in Medicaid policy and establish community-based attendant services.

CD-PAS Programs

The Department of Health and Human Services contracted for a study of consumer-driven personal attendant services in order to determine the best way to implement programs that place responsibility for managing attendant services with users of the services. PAS services are often referred to as home and community-based long-term care services.

Traditionally, health-care professionals and social workers hired and managed personal care attendants for their clients. Empowerment and self-determination values suggested that the consumers of the service should have more control over (1) recruitment, hiring, and training; (2) defining duties and work schedules; (3) supervision; (4) paying; and (5) disciplining and discharging personal care attendants.

Because funds for the service are provided from public sources, several issues of concern arise, such as accountability, compliance, and liability. In order to address these problems, intermediary service organizations, or ISOs, are helpful in providing a balance between government policy and consumer control. Typically, ISOs ensure that legal and policy requirements are met and offer support and assistance to consumers. Some of the functions that must be addressed in hiring a personal attendant that may be provided to clients by an ISO are ensuring compliance with Department of Labor regulations; addressing employee taxes and payroll issues; arranging worker's compensation coverage and disability rules; and verifying citizenship status (Department of Health and Human Services Research, *www.aspe.os.dhhs.gov/daltcp/reports/cdpases.htm*).

Research in this area through HHS includes a study by Doty and Benjamin (1999) of home-supported services for people who are elderly and or disabled that compares the two models: "client-directed" and "professional management." The client-directed model closely parallels the "consumer-driven" model described above. The "professional management" model uses a skilled professional such as a social worker to administer and regulate care provision.

Stavros, a Center for Independent Living in Massachusetts, provides some guidance in understanding personal attendant services. Personal care agencies and state programs determine who is eligible for PAS. Generally, to be eligible, an individual must have a permanent or chronic disability, a need for at least ten hours of services a week, and physician approval. Under consumer-driven systems, the disabled person recruits, interviews, hires, determines the responsibilities of, evaluates, pays, and fires the personal attendant.

Personal care agencies may be independent services providers, or PAS may be one of the services offered by a broader agency, such as a CIL. The agency or service is the intermediary (ISO) between the person with the disability and the attendant. Some programs permit the disabled person to elect to have the intermediary organization assume responsibility for managing the services such as payroll and scheduling or to manage all the functions, including payroll deductions and taxes, individually (*www.stavros.org/pasfaq.html*).

Criteria for Selecting a PAS

To establish criteria for personal attendant services, it is first necessary to define what personal assistant services actually are. We could say that personal assistants provide assistance to people to do the things that they could do on their own if not for the disability. Therefore, the services vary depending upon the nature and severity of the disability and the things the client needs or wants to do. From managing a checkbook to putting on socks, personal attendants are responsive to individual needs. Assistance with ADLs includes meal preparation, dressing, bathing, and toileting. Assistance with IADLs includes shopping, housekeeping, and laundry (*www.stavros.org/pasfaq.html*).

Michelle Caputo (1998) has developed a helpful guide for finding appropriate personal attendants, including sample checklists to assist you and your client to define needs (*www.pn-magazine.com/pn/*). Her suggestions support the consumer-driven model described above and can assist you in preparing your client for the process of locating and hiring a personal care attendant. The first task is for your client to determine exactly what services are needed. It may be helpful to assist your client in clarifying needs and developing a list. (If you are doing the writing, be sure to use your client's own words to describe needed services.)

Because the client is also the employer, it is important to develop an employment contract that includes duties, hours of work and schedule, salary, use of utilities, use of personal items, smoking, alcohol consumption, who pays for social or recreational outings, unacceptable behavior, confidentiality and privacy, and termination notice policy. To locate attendants, Caputo suggests using facilities such as hospitals or colleges rather than ads in newspapers.

When interviewing a potential attendant, clients should obtain basic information (name, address, Social Security number, date of birth, ability to lift/transfer, driver's license, and so on). Ask the interviewee for at least two references. Clients should discuss the job in detail, ask questions, and encourage the interviewee to ask questions. It is preferable that the client not hire someone on the spot; checking references and interviewing several people before making a decision is important. When checking references, suggest that your client ask specific questions about employment, dependability, honesty, and ability to work independently and to take supervision. The client should also ask about personality, reactions to stress, circumstances of termination, and whether the reference would rehire the person.

Attendants can be paid through programs and also through noncash wages such as room and board. Cash as well as noncash wages must be reported. It is important to assist clients to make financial arrangements that meet both client and personal attendant need and legal requirements.

Resources for Locating PAS

Attendant resources may be available through a disability organization or government program. Consulting your local yellow pages under Home Health Agencies will provide a helpful listing as well. Clients may search for and recruit their own personal attendants as well. There are advantages and disadvantages to using a home health agency versus finding your own independent attendant. Agencies can often provide a trained assistant quickly. There is backup if an emergency situation arises, and the agency provides training and directions for your assistant. Financial arrangements are between the client and the agency rather than between the client and the attendant. However, the individual generally gives up direct control over the assistant's activities, which are managed and directed through the agency. The person with the disability tends to be viewed primarily as a patient, rather than as an employer, by the attendant (Tanzman, n.d., p. 2).

Useful information on personal care attendants can be found in De Jong and Wenker, (1983). Helpful internet sites for personal care attendants are:

www.pca-hna.com/ (an online free service)
www.disabilityresources.org/PCA.html (for information and articles)
www.independentliving.org (a personal assistant network)

ADAPTers holding the fence in front of the Bush White House advocating for the signing of the Executive Order implementing the Olmstead Decision.

Homeless Disabled People

Many people who are homeless are also disabled. They may be mentally ill, have HIV, or be chronic substance abusers. A special program administered through HUD addresses the needs of this population through grants provided to public agencies to provide both shelter and support services.

HUD's Shelter+Care (S+C) Program provides these services. Research has found, however, that this group of people with disabilities is often not ready for entry into housing programs. Rather, it is necessary to provide an intensive transitional program of case management and life skills training as well as treatment to prepare people move toward permanent shelter arrangements and support services (Department of Housing and Urban Development, *www.Huduser.org/periodicals/*).

Chapter Summary

Housing is a basic human need. For people with disabilities, who often have special needs and limited incomes, securing adequate and affordable housing can be a complex and difficult task. Knowledge of programs and resources in housing can assist you to work with your client to locate appropriate housing. People with disabilities may live in single-family homes or multiple-unit dwellings. They may own or rent and may live with families, alone, or with others. HUD is the primary government agency providing housing and programs to assist clients with disabilities to pay for housing needs. Programs include housing for families, elderly, disabled and handicapped, below-market interest rate housing, and Section 8 certificates. Fannie Mae also provides assistance with mortgages for people with disabilities who want to buy their own homes or who need to modify or adapt existing housing to meet disability needs.

Communal living arrangements are often useful because they provide a ready source of peer support and the possibility of expense sharing for services such as personal attendants and housekeeping. Communal living arrangements may be peer-run or may be sponsored and/or supervised by an organization. Funding for the purchase of communal housing is also available.

Although there is a strong movement away from nursing home care, some clients' needs cannot readily be provided for in the community setting. Others may prefer to live in residential settings such as assisted living facilities, life care, or facilities supporting special needs.

One of the major issues related to housing arrangements is the need for personal care services. Funding and policy has favored nursing home rather than community-based care for people who need personal attendant services. Currently, there are strong initiatives supporting consumer-driven community-based care, and several states have implemented programs. Research has demonstrated that consumer-driven programs, while providing maximum empowerment and self-determination, may need an intermediary organization to address legal issues, compliance, taxes and payroll, and other concerns.

In order to assist clients to assume control of hiring, supervising, evaluating, and otherwise managing personal care attendants, workers must be aware of the kinds of information and issues that must be addressed.

In the next chapter, we will explore resources related to employment, such as ADA policies, employer responsibilities, job accommodations, and advocacy resources. Vocational rehabilitation services cover a variety of services, including independent living, which supports and maximizes empowerment and self-determination and thus productivity. Unemployment and underemployment of people with disabilities creates the need for income support programs. Social Security and other programs will be described and resources offered.

Questions for Thought and Discussion

1. What qualities would be important for you in choosing a personal care attendant? Of these, are some specific to you and others general?

2. With classmates, develop some guidelines for clients interviewing personal care attendants. What questions should they ask? What qualities should they look for?

3. Family members provide most of the care for people with disabilities. If they were not pro-

viding them, a government agency would most likely be used to obtain care. Do you think that family members should be paid to take care of a disabled relative?

4. What obligations do you think family members have, if any, to care for disabled relatives? Does the degree of relationship make a difference in the obligation?

5. In support of community-based housing, do you think that the government should finance needed modifications for all people with disabilities? For low-income people with disabilities? If so, what modifications should be funded? Kitchens? Bathrooms? Gardens? Closets? Garages? Doorways? Cars? Lifts for steps?

20

Public and Private Intersections in Employment and Income Support

One of the major thrusts of the 1990 Americans with Disabilities Act addresses employment. As we have seen in Chapter 5, people with disabilities have a higher rate of unemployment and partial employment than the general public, and unemployment increases with severity of disability. At the same time, increased medical and health needs related to disability may have a strong impact on disposable income. A greater proportion of people with disabilities are living in poverty, and, again, the more severe the disability the greater the number of people in poverty.

Employment-related issues thus assume an important place in the lives of people with disabilities and may be a reason clients seek help. Increasing job skills, learning new skills that can accommodate disability, preparing for the job search, and working to obtain the necessary accommodations often requires persistence, empowerment, and support. For some people with disabilities, full-time employment or any employment may not be a possibility. For these, other sources of income support must provide the income necessary to maintain the client. These sources include both public and private sector resources.

This chapter will explore several related areas that provide resources for assistance to clients for employment and income support. We will examine the ADA provisions related to employment, how and what accommodations can be made, as well as the Ticket to Work and Work Incentives Act. We will look at preparation for employment, both in terms of social work interventions to prepare and assist clients and in terms of vocational training and/or rehabilitation resources. We will explore resources available through SSDI, SSI, and other disability programs, such as veterans' benefits, and private disability insurance benefits.

Employment

The Americans with Disabilities Act

Title I of the Americans with Disabilities Act addresses employment discrimination, and establishes civil rights for people with disabilities. It applies to private employment;

federal, state, and local government employment; employment agencies; and labor unions. Employers with fifteen or more employees are covered under the act. The Consumer Law Page on the web, which is sponsored by NIDRR, offers links and explanations of specific provisions of the act (*www.consumerlawpage.com/brochurs/disab.htm*). A significant body of case law supports and further defines specific applications of the act.

Job Accommodations

Employer obligations have been challenged and further clarified and defined through both policies and case law. To denote terms or situations where clarification and further definition continues through courts or government agencies, quotation marks have been placed around words or phrases. Each of these may be researched separately if they are applicable to a client situation.

Employers are forbidden to discriminate in the process of hiring, firing, advancement, compensation, and training on the basis of disability. This applies to recruitment, advertising, tenure, layoffs, leaves, and fringe benefits. Both people with a disability and people with a "known association" with a disability are protected. Examples of "known association" include a person with a disabled child, spouse, or parent for whom they are responsible, a person whose partner or family member has HIV/AIDs, or a person who lives with a person who is an alcoholic or who is mentally ill.

The act covers "qualified people," that is, people who, apart from a disabling condition, have the skills, experience, knowledge, and training for the job for which they are seeking employment. Applicants must also be able to perform the "essential functions" of the job with or without accommodations.

Accommodations must be "reasonable," that is, they must not cause "undue hardship" on the employer in terms of expense or difficulty. Extensive renovations, accommodations that may be preferable to the employee but are more disruptive to the facility than other accommodations, or accommodations that impact negatively upon other employees are not required. "Undue hardship" is determined on a case-by-case basis: The nature and size of the business, the availability of resources, and the extent of accommodations required are considered in arriving at determinations (Roessler & Rumrill, 1998, pp. 10–11).

"Reasonable accommodations" may include making the facility accessible, restructuring a job, modifying a work schedule, modifying equipment, providing readers or interpreters, providing a designated parking space, modifying training, examinations, or other programs. If an employee becomes disabled and can no longer perform the "essential functions" of the job for which he or she was hired, "reasonable accommodations" include reassigning that employee to a vacant position whose "essential functions" can be performed by the employee. (*www.consumerlawpage.com/brochuse/disab.htm*).

To understand your client's work environment and barriers that he or she may be encountering, explore all areas of concern. Have your client explain all the things he or she does during the course of a day and think about problems encountered because of the disability. Things to consider might include: Is the workstation very far from other areas where your client must go as a part of job function? Are the water fountain and bathroom in easy reach? Are floors slippery or uneven? Are the hallways the client must use too narrow to maneuver comfortably with a wheelchair? Is the temperature comfortable? Are there fumes, noise levels, or vibrations that impede your client's performance? Is your client lifting heavy objects, filing papers, or using a telephone that he or she cannot hear, or cannot hold?

Some clients will prefer to request accommodations and will advocate and pursue legal recourse if necessary. Some clients may have already made their own arrangements to "accommodate" for disability at work and are comfortable with these. Others may prefer not to tell employers about their disability. When discussing accommodations and working arrangements, it is important to consider and respect the client's wishes. Also, the need for accommodation is not a always a static thing—disabilities change, appear and disappear, or become more severe. What works one month may no longer work the next.

Applicants for a position may not be forced to submit to a medical examination as a part of the pre-employment process, nor to give information about the nature and severity of a disability. Applicants can be asked about ability to perform the "essential functions" of the job for which they are applying. Once the employee is hired, accommodations can only be required when the applicant has made the disability and need for accommodations "known" to the employer (Roessler & Rumrill, 1998).

Particular care should be exercised if your work with a client occurs under the auspices of the organization that employs you both. Employee assistance programs provide counseling and support for clients in the context of the work environment and generally have a goal of supporting the client's effectiveness in the work performed. Ethical issues such as confidentiality, conflicting loyalties and obligations, and advocacy and whistle-blowing present challenges to social workers that may be especially difficult when working with clients with a disability.

Complete information and employer guidance is provided on the World Wide Web. DisAbility resources, disAbility.gov, and other legal sources may be helpful. The Job Accomodation Network (website, *www.janweb.icdi.wvu.edu*) is an excellent source of information, as are the President's Committee on Employment of People with Disabilities (*www.pcepd.gov*), and the Office of Civil Rights, U.S. Department of Education (*www.ed.gov/offices/OCR*).

The Job Accommodation Network is also a personal information network and consulting resource for people with disabilities. Both individuals and businesses can call JAN for advice and consultation. Human Factors Consultants are available to provide suggestions and resources, as well as information on accommodation methods and systems. They can be reached at 1-800-526-7234 by both voice and ttd (Job Accommodation Network, 1999).

Another kind of job accommodation your client might consider is a personal assistant. Personal assistants in the workplace can provide services such as filing and transportation for mobility-impaired people, assistance with decision making for people with cognitive impairments, readers for people with visual impairments, and sign interpreters for people who are deaf. The Department of Labor's article "Personal Assistance Services in the Workplace" provides examples of workplace accommodations using personal assistant accommodations (*www.dol.gov.dol.odep/public/pubs*).

Employee Rights and Advocacy

Applicants and employees should be aware of the ADA provisions and use them as needed and preferred. There are many possible ways to accommodate work sites and responsibilities for people with disabilities: Searching for "reasonable accommodations" involves the employee as well as the employer. It's important for clients to be aware that no accommodations can be expected if the employer is not informed about the disability.

Some conditions that require accommodation are immediately apparent. If a client is in a wheelchair, is deaf and uses a sign language interpreter, is blind, or is unable to communicate verbally, the disability will be obvious and the need for accommodation can be assumed. Some conditions are much less obvious, however, and may only affect work under certain conditions. For example, a person with arthritis may not be able to file or type; a person with muscular weakness may be unable to go up and down stairs without difficulty; a person with hearing limitations may function poorly in a large room with diffuse noise; and a person with chronic fatigue syndrome may have difficulty working eight-hour days. It is important to explore these areas with clients; however, as noted above, it is the client's right to determine whether workplace accommodations will be requested.

If a client has complaints about a job application process or about work accommodations, the EEOC should be contacted. There are fifty EEOC field offices in thirty-three states and the District of Columbia. Complaints may also be filed with the state agency charged with this function: The Fair Employment Practices Agency (FEPA) is an agency of government in every state. The client has 180 days from the date that the alleged violation occurred to file a complaint. The first step is to contact the agency by telephone or in person. Clients will then be given a "charge receipt interview," during which they will be asked some identifying information and about the alleged violation. Medical or other corroboration of disability is helpful in presenting the problem. If your client is unable to call or go for an interview, complaints can be filed by mail. The more complete the information, the better and more quickly the problem will be addressed (Center for Mental Health Services, *www.mentalhealth.org/publications/*). Several excellent websites provide information about employee rights and filing complaints. These can be located by links through *www.eeoc.gov/facts/ADA/*.

Two Supreme Court cases heard in 2002 have had strong implications for disabled workers who are employed. The first, *Toyota Motor Company vs. Williams,* substantially limits the definition of "disability" under the ADA. Ella Williams developed carpal tunnel syndrome as an assembly line worker. She requested a job accommodation and was transferred to another position within the company. After three years in this new position, manual chores were added to her job. She requested to return to her accommodation, but Toyota refused. The parties disagree on what occurred next, but Williams apparently did not go to work and was fired by Toyota. Although a lower court upheld Williams's right to accommodation, Toyota appealed its decision to the Supreme Court.

At issue were the definitions of two key terms in the ADA: "substantially limits" and "a major life activity." The Supreme Court ruled that Williams's limitations from her carpal tunnel syndrome did not meet the ADA definition of disability because she was able to perform major life activities such as brushing her teeth, bathing, and doing some household chores. These disqualified her from claims under the ADA (Disability Rights Education and Defense Fund [DREDF]: *www.dredf.org*).

A second case involved Robert Barnett, a ten-year employee of U.S. Airways, who injured his back loading baggage at San Francisco International Airport. After disability leave, Barnett was transferred to the mailroom, a less physically demanding job. However, in 1992, two employees with more senior status sought this position, and U.S. Airways told Barnett he had to find another assignment, which he was unable to do. He sued U.S. Airways for damages, back pay, and reinstatement.

The Supreme Court ruled that an established seniority system could override a disability claim "generally," saying that seniority was an important employee benefit. The Court's decision further narrows the application of the ADA. Although the Court did recognize that sometimes people with disabilities need special treatment to compete fairly in the job market, disability rights advocates viewed this ruling as a setback with serious implications for disabled workers (Egelko, 2002).

Employer Initiatives

Employment opportunities in the public sector are available at every level. The federal government maintains a website posting employment opportunities through the office of personnel management and information about federal employment (FCIC National Contact Center, *www.draco/aspensys.com/*). The Department of Labor supports one-stop career centers in major cities that provide coordinators to assist in job seeking and employment-related problems of concerns (Department of Labor, *www.dol.org*).

Many local, national, and international companies have developed initiatives for seeking out and hiring people with disabilities. There are also a number of referral sources for employers seeking employees with a disability and employees seeking employment, such as Lift, Inc., and Resource Partnership.

Lift, Inc. (*www.lift-inc.org*) qualifies, trains, and provides employment services to information management and technology professionals seeking employment. It also provides employee-recruitment services for over a hundred major corporations in a number of fields. The insurance company category, for example, includes Aetna, Mutual of New York, and State Farm. The banking and finance category includes a number of local and regional banks as well as Dunn and Bradstreet and Morgan Stanley. Manufacturers include AT&T, Honeywell, Polaroid, and Verizon and consumer goods companies include Abbott Laboratories, Colgate Palmolive, Time, Walgreens, McDonald's, and the Educational Testing Service.

Resource Partnership (*www.resourcepartnership.org*) links people with employers, supports career fairs for people with disabilities, and trains people in interview and job search skills. Job seekers can post resumes on their website. Sponsors include Gilette, Analog Services, John Hancock, IBM, Plexus, tmp.worldwide, and others. Resource Partnership provides services for member and sponsoring organizations that include technical assistance, sensitivity and disability awareness training, diversification with disability planning, and other consulting and advising services.

The Ticket to Work and Work Incentives Improvement Act (1999)

The Ticket to Work program has two parts: One addresses the extension of medical eligibility for people with disabilities who are employed (presented in Chapter 18); the second provides incentives to employment. The program allows states to develop increased supports and services for people with disabilities who work and specifically addresses the needs of people whose disabilities are progressive or who experience periodic setbacks in health that affect their ability to continue to work (*www.hhs.gov/news/press/2000press/*).

The first two states to receive funding to initiate employment programs are Rhode Island and Mississippi, but other states are expected to follow. States must present a plan for a demonstration project and target specific people with specific disabling conditions that meet HHS's criteria, such as HIV/AIDS or multiple sclerosis. Services to be provided include case management, personal assistance, and employment supports.

Education, Training, and Rehabilitation

Rehabilitation Services Administration Programs

Public-sector services and programs for education, training, and rehabilitation are administered through the Department of Education's Rehabilitation Services Administration. The RSA was established as an agency of the federal government to implement the Rehabilitation Act of 1973. The agency is charged with formulating, developing, and implementing programs and policies (*www.ed.gov/offices/OSERS/RSA/rsa.htm*).

Services for disabled people are provided through OSERS, the Office of Special Education and Rehabilitation Services. OSERS offers a broad range of services for people with disabilities through contracts and arrangements with state and local agencies and training programs.

Services and programs for people with disabilities include:

1. State Grants for Vocational Rehabilitation

This is one of the primary programs providing rehabilitation services and training for people with disabilities. To be eligible, clients must have a physical or mental impairment to employment, must be able to benefit from vocational rehabilitation services, and must require vocational rehabilitation services in order to engage in employment. The intent is to provide programs that are "comprehensive" in nature, services that are above and beyond job-training services. These include evaluation, assessment, and provision of assistive technology; job counseling services; and medical and therapeutic services.

The development and use of appropriate social skills are important elements in preparing for and sustaining employment. People with mental illness, mental retardation, and other disabling conditions often need assistance in gaining these skills. Jonikas and colleagues through ULC National Research and Training Center have developed a training manual that includes role plays for socializing with co-workers, friendships and romances at work, requesting a raise, interacting with supervisory personnel, and other work-related scenarios. Their suggestions can be integrated with an overall plan for addressing employment and/or social skills issues with clients.

Counseling and support services for people with disabilities entering the job market may not stop once the job and been secured and employment has begun. Ongoing support, assistance in dealing with situations as they are occurring, and developing new skills are continuing needs. Although vocational training may not be the primary goal of your work with a disabled client who is employed, it is helpful to be able to integrate support for employment into your work. An excellent manual on the subject may be obtained from the UIC National Research and Training Center (Furlong et al., n.d.). Although it was developed specifically for use with clients with psychiatric disabilities, the subjects included will be helpful in working with any client.

2. Client Assistance Programs (CAPs)

Client assistance programs provide assistance and advocacy for clients who are receiving vocational rehabilitation services.

3. Rehabilitation Training

The objective of this program is to provide skilled professionals trained in the rehabilitation fields through the vocational rehabilitation service and independent living. The program supports and provides funding for training programs at institutions. Rehabilitation training includes interpreting and experimental and innovative programs.

4. Protection and Advocacy of Individual Rights

5. The Projects with Industry Program

6. Supported Employment

The Supported Employment program collaborates with public and private nonprofit agencies to hire people with severe disabilities. Cook (1999) demonstrates the use of an employment log to keep track of vocational rehabilitation services provided to persons with psychiatric disabilities who are in supported employment. This accountability tool provides information about the kind of support provided, the time spent, the location of the service, and outcomes related to service provision.

7. Independent Living State Grants

Grants provide funds for the support and development of independent living programs to states, as such programs maximize leadership and empowerment, which leads to independence and productivity.

8. Centers for Independent Living Programs

9. Independent living programs for older people who are blind (*www.ed.gov/offices/OSERS/RSA/PGMS/bvrs.html*)

State Programs

States receive funding through the RSA and develop state and local programs. Some states offer additional services as well. Contact state offices or programs directly.

Veterans' Services

The U.S. Veteran's Administration has two departments that address vocational rehabilitation and training. The Vocational Rehabilitation and Employment Services Division provides for an evaluation of skills, assists veterans to find and maintain employment, and offers vocational counseling and planning, training, education, and ongoing support services. The Independent Living Services Division trains and guides veterans through the independent living process, and provides personal counseling and support services. Clients can apply for VA services online if desired (*www.va.gov*).

Income Support

Some clients may be permanently or temporarily unable to locate employment, may have severe disabling conditions that preclude employment, or may be too old to work. Income support may be necessary to assist clients to meet needs and to remain independent. Income supports are available through Social Security as Social Security disability insurance (SSDI), supplemental security income (SSI), state disability insurance, worker's compensation, and private insurance companies. Under certain conditions, TANF may also provide assistance to disabled clients and their families.

SSA Definition of "Disability" and Applications Procedures

The Social Security Administration determines that a person is disabled if there is: (1) lack of possibility of substantial gainful employment that is (2) due to an incapacity caused by medically determinable physical or mental impairments and that (3) is expected to last at least twelve months or lead to death. "Substantial gainful employment" means the ability to work on a regular basis and earn at least $500 per month.

People who meet these criteria may apply at any Social Security office, by telephone, or by mail for benefits. Each person has the right to an in-person interview. This is recommended because the claims interviewer can review your papers, check for oversights, and offer you helpful advice. An initial determination is made in two to four months' time and will be sent by mail. Clients have sixty days to appeal the decision by requesting reconsideration. The case will be reviewed by a different reviewer. If the claim is denied again, a hearing can be requested before an administrative judge.

Social Security Administration personnel may also be aware of other disability programs for which the client may qualify (Physicians' Disability Services, *www.disability-facts.com/faqs.html*).

Social Security Disability Insurance

SSDI is an insurance program for people who are employed and who become disabled. SSDI is administered through the Social Security Administration and is funded by FICA tax withheld from worker's pay and by employer contributions. SSDI covers both income support via cash benefits and health-care benefits. It covers people who have worked at least five of the ten years preceding the disability. Younger workers can qualify with fewer years of employment. Complete information is contained in the SSA booklet "Social Security Disability Benefits."

SSDI benefits vary depending on past earnings. People receiving SSDI become eligible for Medicare twenty-four months after their first check is received. Because SSDI is an entitlement program, benefits are not affected by unrelated income, such as from investments, or by the income of other people in the household, such as a spouse. SSDI benefits also keep earnings current, so that people receiving SSDI will receive a more substantial Social Security check when they become eligible. When a person becomes eligible for Social Security, SSDI payments terminate. You must be disabled for at least a year in order to qualify for SSDI.

Supplemental Security Income

Supplemental security income provides income support for people who do not meet the employment requirements of SSDI and provides a standard monthly amount to all recipients. SSI recipients qualify for Medicaid immediately. Because SSI is a needs-based program, benefit amounts may be affected by other income and resources, or by the income and resources of people to contribute to the person's support. SSI may even be terminated if there is sufficient income and resources available to the person. The SSA booklet "Supplemental Security Income" provides additional information on services.

State Disability Insurance

Five states—California, Hawaii, New York, New Jersey, and Rhode Island—have disability insurance programs that help people meet short-term disability needs, generally until SSDI benefits are available. Contact the appropriate office in these states for further information.

Worker's Compensation

People whose disabilities are work-related receive compensation through this program. They are available for partial as well as total disability and may pay benefits for up to a year. This is not a long-term resource for people whose disabling conditions are permanent.

Private Insurance

Many people, especially those who are self-employed, purchase private insurance for disability in order to be assured of a continued income. Private insurance policies may have different criteria for eligibility determinations and a different and less rigid definition of disability. Generally, they begin benefits more quickly than SSDI. Some policies and companies reduce their monthly payments when the individual qualifies for SSDI or Social Security, while others do not. Some private insurers also require that people file for SSDI benefits and make reasonable efforts to receive payments.

Temporary Assistance to Needy Families

Historically, it was thought that people with disabilities were exempt from work requirements (*www.hhs.gov/programs/ofa*). However, TANF policies attempt to address the employment issues of people with disabilities rather than placing them in an exempt category.

About 28 percent of TANF caseloads are people with mental health issues, and an additional 40 percent have learning disabilities or low skill levels. TANF programs provide screening and assessment services to determine the needs of each individual and services to assist the person to gain employable skills. TANF collaborates with Vocational Rehabilitation Administration services to meet the needs of clients and to comply with the legal requirements of the Rehabilitation Act of 1973 and of the Americans with Disabilities Act. Where TANF services are limited, vocational rehabilitation (VR) services are not, and collaboration should ensure services that meet the needs of all clients. TANF can purchase VR services for clients as needed.

Where states have limitations in funding for programs, the most disabled clients must be served first. TANF programs themselves are subject to the provisions of the ADA, and must provide "meaningful access" to services for all persons with disabilities.

Chapter Summary

This chapter has provided an overview of the services and resources available for employment and income support for persons with disabilities. Employment rights are addressed in Title I of the ADA and require accommodations for people with disabilities who are seeking employment or who are working. "Reasonable accommodation" is unique to each situation, to the needs of the individual and the resources and circumstances of the employer. People who believe that their rights under the ADA have been violated in terms of employment can file a complaint with the EEOC.

To prepare for employment, people with disabilities may need assessment, training, rehabilitation, education, assistance in job searching and interviewing, and physical or other therapy. The Vocational Rehabilitation Administration maintains federal programs that provide grants to states to serve employment needs of individuals. Programs include rehabilitation training to increase the pool of skilled professionals in the rehabilitation field and support for independent living to foster empowerment and independence. Supported employment provides opportunities for people with severe disabilities to be employed in the public or private nonprofit sectors.

Not all people are able to be gainfully employed. Severity of disability, type of impairment, age, and other factors may limit employment temporarily or permanently. Income supports help individuals meet their needs if unable to work. The primary source of income support is the Social Security Administration, which provides benefits through Social Security Disability Insurance, an entitlement program for people who have worked and paid FICA, and Supplemental Security Insurance, a needs-based program. Some states also provide non-work-related disability insurance to cover time frames and gaps in service provisions. Worker's compensation is available to meet temporary needs (those lasting less than a year). Many people also carry private insurance to support their income should they become disabled. Private insurance companies' definitions of disability may be different than that of the Social Security Administration.

In addition to health care, housing and personal care, and income, people also need opportunities to form and maintain meaningful social relationships, to be involved in activities of interest, and to partake of leisure and recreational activities. Because disability sometimes limits opportunities to meet these needs, assessments should always include both social and recreational dimensions. If client and worker agree that there are unmet needs, exploration of resources will provide some suggestions and ideas for involvement. Chapter 21 will address social networks and recreational needs.

Questions for Thought and Discussion

1. People with similar levels of disability may relate to their disability quite differently and thus have different ideas about their ability to sustain employment. For example, someone who relates to disability as empowerment and is an advocate for disability rights may feel differently about employment than someone with a similar disability who has adopted the sick role. Should both be treated equally in terms of employment and income support?

2. Is there a difference between *enabling* people with disabilities to work and *requiring* them to work? What do you think is the intent of TANF in regard to people with disabilities?

3. With another student, role play teaching job skills, asking for a raise, and relating to co-workers.

4. With another student, practice interviewing a client with a disability who is seeking employment. Ask about the disability, about education, work history, skills, interests, and any other information you think would be useful in assessing your client for employment.

5. Using resources on the web, locate some possible employment resources for your "client." What accommodations will be needed?

21

The Social Support and Recreation Network

While health care, living arrangements, employment, and income support are often central issues to be addressed with clients, it is vital also to remember that our clients live in a society, and that social relationships and meaningful and enjoyable leisure and recreational activities are essential to human being and to life quality. It is important to include these in assessment and in developing interventions for all clients, but especially for clients with a disability.

Clients who have had a disabling condition for a lifetime or for an extended period of time may have resolved issues related to socialization and recreation and may be coming for service for unrelated reasons. Social and recreational issues need not be a focus of client-worker concern unless the client identifies a specific need or issue. However, if the social worker finds that socialization or recreational needs impact upon the client's problem, he or she may want to discuss these with the client as well.

Disability often changes and affects social relationships. Especially when clients become disabled as adults, patterns of social relationships and personal self-concept may be affected. Friends may react in ways that are helpful, but some of their actions may be dysfunctional for the newly disabled individual. New needs for group identification, alternative ways of meeting social needs, and support must be identified and addressed.

As we have seen, family roles and responsibilities may also change with a disability. Family members who are also long-term caregivers have special needs and concerns that often impact upon the client. Self-determination and responsibility, issues of dependence and independence, and physical and emotional strengths and weaknesses impact family members as well as clients. While the effect is greatest among members of the family with whom the client may be living or who assume responsibility for assisting the client, all family members are affected by a disability. Daily routines, schedule adjustment, and vacation and recreational planning are all impacted by a disabling condition.

Appropriate leisure and recreational activities are available and clients, families, and friends should be encouraged to utilize them. Special interests can be maintained, and new ones developed, with the use of adaptive equipment if necessary. Physical activity is healthy and special resources are available for a wide range of disabling conditions. Team sports provide opportunities for socialization and relationship building as well as physical activity.

In this chapter, we shall explore some of the resources and services available to assist clients and families to meet social and recreational needs. We will discuss social support, family caregiver support, and activities and organizations that provide equipment and facilities for recreation.

It is important to remember that communication is essential to social relationship building. Clients whose disability limits communication may first need to address alternative forms of communication and possibly learn to use these effectively. Clients who are not able to communicate or interact with others can have social relationships that are built upon a time, a place, or a shared activity. These, too, are vital parts of social networking. Attending an event with others, sitting next to the same person at meals or activities, or developing an awareness that other people also are with you in a residential facility or are human beings like you are all forms of socialization and social support.

The Social Support Network

The social support network includes family members, peers, friends, social clubs, and organizations. Social relationships help to define us as people. They reflect our interests and choices of activities and relationships. It is vital to understand how your client feels about his or her social support network and not judge your client by idealized standards, formulas, or your own idea of what social support networks *should* be. Every relationship is unique, and everyone is different in terms of what he or she wants or expects from social relationships. What is isolation to one person is quite comfortable to another, and a wide and active network is not desirable to all people. Nonetheless, it is important to assess your client's social needs as he or she perceives them and to work with any areas that are of concern.

Assessment

Several assessment tools presented in Chapter 12 will be useful in helping you and your client to begin to discuss social relationship issues. Classic eco-maps are adaptable and can be built to illustrate social relationships specifically by placing the client at the center and friends, colleagues, clubs, and organizations in the appropriate circles. Alternatively, "social needs" can be placed at the center, and all of the different needs, such as "someone to talk to," "someone to go to the movies with," and so on can be placed in the surrounding circles. It is also possible to place a single social need, such a "friendship" or "someone to talk to" in the center of the circle and to place qualities desired, or qualities important to the client, in the surrounding circles. Building on the assessment, worker and client can discuss any areas of problems or unmet needs, and develop a plan for addressing them.

Building upon Existing Networks

Acquiring a disability often affects a client's social network. Friends who were close may be uncomfortable with the client's changed behavior and abilities and may withdraw, even temporarily. Some people believe conditions are "catching" just by association, even when there is no such possibility. Others may simply be uninformed and not at ease with the changes disability has brought to the client's life. Still others are afraid to talk about the changes and therefore withdraw and avoid the client.

These are some of the mental and emotional barriers that must be considered in exploring the social network; there may by physical barriers as well. An important area to consider is the "visitability" of homes of family members and friends. Accessible housing is, of course, an essential consideration for people with disabilities. But the accessibility of the homes of family members, friends, colleagues, and others is important to maintaining and supporting the social network. For visitability, homes should have entrances with no steps, hallways that are at least 36 inches in diameter, and at least one bath with a 32-inch doorway (Independent Living Service Center, *www.ilsc.org/housing*).

A client with a newly diagnosed disability may withdraw from his or her social network either for a period of time or permanently due to social discomfort, inability to participate in activities and interests, or a desire to avoid painful reminders of the way life used to be. However, the opposite can also occur. People who were quite marginal in the client's network may become caring and interested supporters, and new people can develop relationships as well. New relationships that are built after the onset of a client's disability incorporate the disability and a natural part of the client's identity. A client may find that explaining his or her disability and/or accepting some assistance from others is meaningful and a positive social occurrence.

Workers and clients can explore the client's existing social network in terms of redefining the client's place as needed. However, it is important to maintain continuity for the client in positive social relationships. You may be able to assist the client to share information about the disability with others in his or her social network or talk with a friend about the changes. Clients can include a friend or family member in a session with the worker if worker and client feel this could be beneficial.

If a client belongs to a club or organization or to a casual group that meets around a special activity or interest, encourage the client to explore accommodations or activities that are inclusive. Inaccessible meeting places or times, communications methods, transportation needs, adaptive technology, and special care and attendant needs can all be addressed in order to permit continued participation.

Religious organizations, social action groups, political groups, and other special-interest groups are often good places to seek resources for social network-building. Organizations that have a commitment to inclusiveness or to social justice are often especially welcoming. However, any organization or social group in which the client has an interest or affiliation can offer opportunities for the development of new relationships and the strengthening of old ones.

Peer Support

Peers share a special characteristic that provides the basis for a commonality of experience. Peers can be of a similar age; be of the same gender, marital status, or sexual orientation; be graduates of a particular school or institution; or share a special interest or ability. When we refer to "peer support" in working across disability, we are generally referring to social and emotional support received and offered by people who share a general condition—disability—or a specific kind or degree of disability. In working across disability, peer support groups have been found to be one of the most helpful resources available.

One of the primary sources to contact for peer support is the disability-specific organization that provides special services for your client's needs. Affiliation with such a disability-specific group provides instant support, information, socialization opportunities, and meaningful activities. Peer support groups are open groups that welcome new members at any time, and usually meet at a church, civic organization, library, or other public facility.

Disability-specific programs may offer several peer support activities: a general support group, a "newly diagnosed" support group, one for teenagers or for the elderly, hotlines and telephone support services, newsletters, buddy systems, and other services. The programs are generally sponsored by the national disability-specific organization. To locate a local program that meets your client's needs, first try your local phone book, checking listings for social service organizations or for the specific organization, or contact the area or national organization for local information.

Other kinds of peer support groups may cross disabilities but share another characteristic. There are support groups specific to ethnic groups, people in the military, people who are single parents, and others (Family Village, *www.familyvillage.wisc.edu/center.htm*).

Cross-disability support groups may also be effective in providing meaningful social support for clients. Cross-disability groups may have a professional leader or a professional who serves as a liaison or consultant. Hospitals, churches, hospice organizations, civic organizations, even medical practices and physical therapy practices may sponsor a support group that would be appropriate to your client's needs. Companies that manufacture or market a particular product may also have support groups for people who are using that product.

Caregiver and Family Support

Most people with disabilities in the United States live in the community, either in independent living arrangements or with family members. Elders who are disabled often live with spouses or are cared for by children. Caregivers are an essential part of the client's social support network. In order to enable the client to have a good quality of life, it is important to address and meet the needs of caregivers and family members.

Family members and caregivers need information and resources to better meet client needs. They need to share their experiences and to be able to learn and grow from the experiences of others. They need respite from their caregiving responsibilities at times. Many of the resources for caregivers listed below have been assembled by the National Multiple Sclerosis Society, but other disability-specific organizations also have special support and information for caregivers. There are public resources available through Departments of Human Services in local areas.

Books

Caprossela, C. (1995). *Share the care: How to Organize a Group to Care for Someone Who Is Seriously Ill.* New York: Simon & Schuster.

Carter, R. (1996). *Helping Yourself Help Others.* Random House/Time Books (800-773-3000).

Cole, H. (1991). *Helpmates: Support in Times of Critical Illness.* A personal narrative. Westminster John Knox Press (800-227-2872).

McGonigle, C. (1999). *Surviving Your Spouse's Chronic Illness.* Henry Holt.

Meyer, M., & Derr, P. (1998). *The Comfort of Home: An Illustrated Step-by-Step Guide for Caregivers.* CareTrust Publications (800-565-1533).

Radford, T. (1999). *A Guide for Caregivers.* New York: National Multiple Sclerosis Society.

Strong, M. (1997). *Mainstay for the Well Spouse of the Chronically Ill,* 3rd ed. Little, Brown & Co.

Susik, H. (1995). *Hiring Home Caregivers: The Family Guide to In-Home Eldercare.* Impact Publishers (800-234-4211).

Today's Caregiver Magazine, www.caregiver.com.

Zucherman, C., Duber, N.N., & Collopy, B., eds. (1990). *Home Health Care Options: A Guide for Older Persons and Concerned Families.* Plenum Press (800-242-7737).

Caregiver Support Resources

Remember that your agency will also have information about resources for caregivers in your area and is usually your best source of information due its experience and contacts. However, should you need additional resources, these may help you get started:

1. Caregiver Survival Resources, *www.caregiver911.com*

2. National Family Caregivers Association, 800-896-3650, or *wwwnfcacares.org.* Provides support services to caregivers and advocacy for caregivers' needs. The organization supports self-advocacy for caregivers grounded in the belief that if caregivers take care of themselves and see caregiving as one aspect of their lives, they will be happier, healthier, and provide better care as well. The organization supports a newsletter, a toll-free number and Internet access for advisory services, a prescription discount program, and other services that support caregivers' efforts. It advocates in Congress and in state legislatures for caregivers' needs and serves the needs of over 54 million family caregivers in the United States.

3. The Well Spouse Foundation, 800-838-0879, or *wwwwellspouse@aol.com.* Provides networking and local support groups for caregiver spouses.

4. National Association for Home Care, 202-547-7424, or *www.nahc.org.* Provides referrals to state and local home care agencies and a consumer's guide.

5. National Federation of Interfaith Volunteer Caregivers, 800-350-7438, or *www.nfive@aol.com.* Provides respite support and volunteer services through local congregations.

6. National Respite Locator Service, 800-773-5433, or *www.chtop.com/loctor.htm* Provides information about respite services by location.

7. The Sibling Support Project, *www.seattlechildrens.org/sibsupp/*. Provides support for brothers and sisters of people with special health or developmental needs. Has 350 programs nationwide offering sibling support.

8. Alzheimer's Association National Family Caregivers Support Program, *www.alz.org*. Provides support groups, information and suggestions, newsletter, and a website specifically for this program.

The National Family Caregivers Support Act

This recently passed legislation provides funding for caregiver support to states to be administered through Offices on Aging. The amount of funding each state receives is based on residents of the state over age seventy. Each state develops its own programs, sets its own priorities, and adopts its own guidelines. Caregiver Support Act funds are designated only for family members caring for a person over sixty years of age at present. Contact area agencies on aging for information about programs in your area.

The government has earmarked 10 percent of each state's funding through the National Caregiver Support Act to be used for grandparents or other family members (with or without disabilities) who are providing care for a child (with or without disabilities) under the age of eighteen as a legal guardian or a responsible adult caregiver. The caregiver must be over sixty, the child under eighteen. The program can support grandparents whose disabilities limit child care or create an undue burden and also meet special needs of caregivers for disabled children.

Leisure and Recreation Activities

While social networking and social support needs of people with disabilities and their families are important, providing time and opportunities for leisure activities enhances quality of life as well.

Community Activities

People with disabilities can participate in all community activities, but may also desire contact with disability communities with whom they share a special interest. Clients can be encouraged to participate actively in community events and attend fairs and festivals, political meetings, planning meetings, and other events of personal interest. Disability-specific and cross-disability organizations also sponsor community events and promote disability awareness.

Leisure Activities

Almost any activity or interest can be adapted and pursued by someone with a disability. Explore your clients interests and a broad range of possibilities. Some resources for people with disabilities from Family Village (*www.familyvillage.wisc.edu/recreat.htm*) are included here. See also in Chapter 22 for additional suggestions. Public agencies such as the parks department, the recreation department, and community colleges may also provide consultation with recreational therapists and specialists to assist you and your client in locating the activities your client prefers.

Art, music, theater	Hunting
Camps, recreational, therapeutic, and respite	Internet discussion groups
Cooking	Radio and TV
Cycling	Reading, listening, viewing
Dance	Sailing
Fishing	Sled hockey
Fitness and exercise	Snow skiing
Gardening	Sports resources
Golf	Water sports
Horseback riding	Wheelchair sports

An excellent resource for recreation and leisure time activities is the National Center on Physical Ability and Disability (*www.ncpad.cc.uic.edu/aboutncpad.htm*). NCPAD is funded through a grant from the Centers for Disease Control and Prevention (NIH) to the University of Illinois. NCPAD's website includes pull-down menus for recreation and leisure time activities, exercise and physical fitness, sports and team games, information of specific disabilities and conditions, and resources and accessibility. They may be contacted at 800-900-8086 by both voice and tty, and by e-mail at *ncpad@uic.edu*.

Physical Activities and the Outdoors

Physical activities are important for everyone. They are especially important in maintaining the health and wellness of people with disabilities. It is important for you to explore with your client the kinds of physical activities he or she enjoyed. Some of the leisure activities above have a strong physical component, and the resources offered will assist you and your client to locate activities of choice. This section will offer additional suggestions for physical activities and also for outdoors experiences. *Before beginning a physical activity program, it is important to check with the client's physician and to follow recommendations regarding suggested kinds of activities and frequency.*

Physical Activities, Exercise, and Fitness. Certain physical activities are particularly beneficial for specific disabilities, and disability-specific organizations may be an excellent source of programs. Swimming pools and recreations centers are excellent resources as well. For example, many community pools offer special cardio programs and special arthritis programs. Exercise and fitness programs for people with limited range of motion are available in recreation centers and in senior centers. Specialized yoga, low-impact aerobics, and other programs may be recommended for your client as well. To search for disability-specific physical activity, exercise, and fitness resources, use *www.ncpad.cc.uic.edu*.

Team Sports.   Involvement in team sports provides a double benefit for clients: both physical exercise and social networking. Participation involves commitment, goal setting, and persistence, and is an empowering activity. Many of the major categories of sports have special teams, equipment, and organizations for people with disabilities. The Special Olympics, perhaps one of the most prestigious competitions, offers alpine and cross-country skiing, cycling, roller skating, aquatics (with events that parallel olympic events), equestrian, sailing, badminton, floor hockey, speed skating, basketball, soccer, regular and table tennis, bocce, team handball, bowling, gymnastics, power lifting, and volleyball. The Special Olympics hosts winter and summer games at regular intervals.

If you client enjoys athletics but isn't quite ready for the Olympics, there are other sports teams and organizations to which he or she can belong (National Center on Physical Activity and Disability, *www.ncpad.cc.uic.edu*). A few examples:

Basketball: adapted as wheelchair basketball, bank basketball, or twin basketball, is offered in the Special Olympics but also through the Dwarf Athletic Association and the U.S. Cerebral Palsy Athletic Association.

Football: adapted as Flag Football for the Deaf, wheelchair football is offered by the Universal Wheelchair Football Association and the Deaf Sports Federation.

Hockey: adapted as sled hockey, floor hockey, hockey for the hearing impaired, hockey for power wheelchairs, and ice hockey for the visually impaired is offered by the American Amputee Hockey Association and the Special Olympics.

Softball: adapted as wheelchair softball, beep baseball, and over-the-line softball is offered by USA Deaf Sports Federation, Dwarf Athletic Association, Special Olympics, and the National Wheelchair Softball Association.

The Outdoors.   Outdoor activities restore not only the body but the soul, and many people find that spending time in natural settings such as parks, beaches, forests, and lakes on a regular basis is very beneficial. No matter what the condition or disability, the outdoors is accessible in some way. Recent laws and programs have expanded the accessibility of the outdoors, and accessible trails, beach access, restrooms, and other facilities are available in may areas.

The National Park Service, state park systems, community parks, national forests, and recreation areas are all avenues to explore for outdoor activities. Contact the individual park or beach to obtain up-to-date information on access and resources. Adaptive technology resources suggested in the following chapter will also contain information on transportation and mobility systems that are designed for outdoor access, such as wheelchairs with special "beach wheels" or narrower bases.

An excellent source of information on the web is GORP (*www.gorp.com/gorp/*), a guide to outdoor recreation possibilities for all people. There is a special section for people with disabilities, the disability "community," which lists accessible areas and features special places and events that are accessible for people with disabilities. Recent articles about outdoor access included the Cataract Trails of Marin County, California, with walks through the woods; Hiking in the Oregon Dunes, where there are extensive boardwalks to facilitate mobility; Delaware Water Gap, with calm, flat-water paddling possibilities near New York and Philadelphia; and Everglades National Park, where paved and boardwalk trails include accessible campgrounds and visitor facilities. You can reach them at *www.gorp.com/gorp/eclectic/disabled.htm*.

Chapter Summary

In this chapter, some suggestions and resources for social networking and recreation and sports have been presented. There are many possibilities, and clients and social workers should think creatively about all of the options available. Social networking involves making optimum use of the client's existing social network as well as developing further avenues for meeting social needs. Peer support through a disability-specific organization is often very helpful in providing support and information and also in serving as a source of social contacts. Other kinds of support groups are often helpful.

Caregivers are an essential part of the social network of clients. Caregivers often have complex issues involving conflicted and overlapping obligations and responsibilities. Respite care is needed at times, and support groups help caregivers discuss problems, develop solutions, and advocate for caregiver needs. The National Family Caregivers Association provides an avenue for information, a source of support groups, and advocacy in federal and state legislatures. Disability-specific organizations often also have support groups for family members and caregivers.

The recreation and leisure activities network offers a wide range of activities for all interests, suggests organizations that support these activities and interests, and locates sources of supplies and adaptive equipment. Physical activity and team sports are particularly effective in providing physical exercise and development, opportunities for socialization, and contact with nature and the outdoors.

Chapter 22 will offer some suggestions for helping people to get to the leisure activities, jobs, and friends that are important to them and for providing adaptive equipment that maximizes opportunities for full participation in all life activities and events.

Questions for Thought and Discussion

1. You have a client who is developmentally disabled. Search for resources in your community that would provide social and recreational opportunities for him.

2. You also have a client who is a paraplegic and is in a wheelchair. Prior to becoming disabled, this client had enjoyed running, basketball, and swimming. Search for resources in your community that would meet her needs.

3. The family who is caring for a mentally ill client at home is beginning to show signs of stress and exhaustion. How would you locate help for them, including respite care?

4. You have a client who is "locked in" and bedridden. What kinds of leisure and recreational activities would be available to help him?

5. Explore the GORP website, parks, and recreation centers in your area. What kinds of outdoor activities are available for clients?

22

Mobility, Access, and Adaptive Technology

Clients with disabilities, like all clients, desire a good quality of life that includes functioning in society with dignity, freedom, and independence. This includes the ability to live in comfort in a place of their choice, the ability to control their environment, and the ability to leave home and partake of all of the goods and services offered by the society to its members.

As we learned in Chapter 2, the lives of people with disabilities were restricted in many ways until the major rights movements of the mid-twentieth century. Housing, education, employment, and transportation were often not accessible, and many people led homebound and restricted lives. As laws and statutes began to address the needs of people with disabilities, society began to change. New housing was required to have certain features to make it much more convenient, and old housing was adapted. The concept of Universal Design was introduced, and a whole new way of thinking about the build environment now permeates schools of architecture and design.

Accessibility became a normally accepted fact in public buildings, and sidewalk cuts were placed at street corners. Traffic signals chirped, elevators dinged, and Braille signs appeared. Street-crossing controls were placed at waist height. Parking spaces for those with disabilities were assigned in every shopping mall and on every public street. Public restrooms had accessible toilets and lowered paper towel racks. People came out of their homes and into the streets, restaurants, and movie theaters.

Along with the changes in laws and policies came another revolution that affected people with disabilities: Major advances in technology and increased interest in inventing and creating adaptive technology made eating, dressing, food preparation, house cleaning, moving about, reading, writing, working, using the telephone, communicating, and just about everything else easier.

In this chapter, we will explore access, mobility, and assistive technology. While these subjects, like the previous ones—health care, housing, education and employment, and social and recreational activities—could fill volumes by themselves, a discussion of some of the primary issues and resources related to mobility, accessibility, and adaptive technology will help you to become aware of some of the possibilities available for clients.

It is important to recognize that some home modifications and certain kinds of assistive technology may not be available in whole or in part through public funds. In a 1997 study of payment sources for assistive devices and technologies, LaPlante and colleagues (1997, pp. 17–28) found that only 8 percent of assistive technologies and 33 percent of home modifications were received free of charge by people with disabilities. Where people paid for devices or technologies, 48 percent reported paying for them personally or with family support. More than 75 percent of people with accessibility features in their homes reported paying for them through these resources. Third-party sources paid in whole or in part for 52 percent of assistive devices and 23 percent of home adaptations. However, recent initiatives such as the Fannie Mae program for home ownership and home modification and community-based care have provided additional resources for funding.

Mobility in the Built Environment

The Client's Neighborhood

Once out of the house and into the street, what accommodations can be expected? Cities and towns vary significantly in terms of providing services and accessibility for people with disabilities. However, in any community, it should be possible to designate a special parking space near a client's home, and to have signage urging motorists to be aware of a blind or deaf person in the vicinity. Sidewalk cuts, while not universal, are generally available on at least one side of the street. Traffic lights with sound signals can be requested and installed where needed. Codes generally require that sidewalks be smooth so that wheelchairs can maneuver, and so that people will not trip easily.

Neighborhood theaters offer places for wheelchairs, and restaurants have ramps leading to the front entrance. Supermarkets have wide checkouts, and stores of all kinds often have electric mobility accommodations for customers. Elevators in public buildings have controls at waist level and Braille signage. Offices have an area with lowered counters.

If your client has difficulty in moving about his or her neighborhood, it is helpful to assess this in depth. Walk around your client's neighborhood, with him or her if at all possible. Is the client's home on a steep hill or accessible only by a set of steps? Are the shops in the community older and perhaps more crowded and cramped? Are the sidewalk cuts on the other side of the street? Is the only grocery store with accommodations too far to be accessible? Is the client's home at a noisy, busy intersection that is apt to confuse and disorient him or her?

Each client's needs and neighborhood will differ. It may be helpful to make a drawing of the neighborhood, noting the places your client would like to be able to go. Then, with the client, develop a plan to meet the client's needs. If the problem is on a street or public area, the Public Works Department or other responsible public agency in the client's neighborhood should be contacted. If the problem is in a private area, the responsible person should be reached: the mall management office, the theater manager, or the store manager.

Remembering that the goal is not only accessibility but empowerment, encourage your client to advocate for himself or herself. It may be helpful to give the client the name and phone number of the person or department to contact. Role play, rehearsal, and strategic planning may useful tools. If your client is unable to advocate, ask for permission to advocate for him or her before contacting anyone on your own.

Transportation

People generally leave the immediate area of their homes to go to work, to school, and for health care, socialization, and recreation. This requires transportation, either public or private. Clients who are able to drive but need adaptive equipment can purchase or lease cars with specialized driving controls such as braking and acceleration devices, shifting and clutch controls, steering components, turn signals and light controls, and other driving controls. Specialized vans with lifts and ramps are also available. To locate manufacturers, view descriptions of types of equipment, and the like, see *www.abledata.com/Site_2/ transport_gen.htm.*

Clients may be unable to drive vehicles or may prefer to use public transportation. Mass transit systems accommodate people with disabilities by providing assistance such as buses with lifts, "kneeling buses," lifts and elevators to rail systems, platforms that are level with train floors, and other methods that increase accessibility. However, not all mass transit vehicles may be accessible; accessibility may be limited to certain routes, certain time intervals, or certain stops. To find out about routes and accessibility, contact the mass transit department in your client's area.

Not all clients are able to utilize mass transit systems. Section 223 of the Americans with Disabilities Act states that all public entities that operate fixed-route transportation must also provide paratransit service for people who are unable to use the fixed-route system. One of the major issues in obtaining access to the paratransit system for your client is eligibility. The federal government has established three categories of eligibility:

1. People who are unable to board, ride, and disembark by themselves
2. People who need a wheelchair lift where a fixed route does not provide this
3. People who can't get to a fixed route location due to "environmental or architectural barriers," weather, distance, and the like

For more information on eligibility and other paratransit regulations, see *www.fta.dot.gov/ library/policy/ADA/ada.htm.* Private transportation is also available via accessible taxis and van services.

Air and Long-Distance Travel

The Air Carrier Act mandates accessible air travel for people with disabilities. Regulations stipulate that carriers may not refuse transportation solely on the basis of disability, limit the numbers of disabled people on any flight, deny access to trip information, or refuse transportation because disability may affect appearance or behavior. Should a client experience a problem, an airline complaints resolution official must be immediately available.

Airports generally should provide accessible parking near the terminal, medical aid facilities, restrooms, drinking fountains, ticketing systems, amplified telephones and text telephones, accessible check-in and retrieval of baggage, and assistance in getting on and off the aircraft (Federal Aviation Administration, *www. faa.gov/acr/dat.htm*).

Clients with disabilities no longer need to feel restricted in traveling around the country or around the world. Long-distance transportation by train or bus is accessible and available to every city, state, and country. To make travel pleasant and trouble-free, however, clients need to plan in advance. The Department of Transportation, the Federal Transit Administration, and Project ACTION of Easter Seals has prepared a special traveler's database (*www.projectaction.org/paweb/index.htm*) to provide this information. The database is arranged by state and city and covers public transit operators, accessible van rental companies, accessible taxis, airport transportation, and other useful information. Of course, the information on this website is not limited to distant areas—it's a simple way of finding out about many transportation resources in your own area as well!

Parents with Disabilities

Parents who are disabled and who have young children have special needs far beyond their own medical care. They may or may not have become parents prior to becoming disabled. Parenting is challenging under any circumstances; disabled parents face special challenges and providing support is essential. For them, access to schools, playgrounds, children's special programs, and other concerns can present challenging problems. In addition, parents with disabilities can have special needs in terms of assistive and adaptive equipment to assist them in parenting. Personal care attendants may be required. Project Star, of the Children's Institute, provides resources, parenting tips, education, and support for parents through its website (*www.trfn.clpgh.org/star/index/shtml*). Another helpful resource is Parents with Disabilities OnLine, a national network that provides online support for accessible parenting through their Parent Empowerment Network. Parents with Disabilities OnLine also provides resources, medical information about pregnancy, information about adoption, and adaptive parenting aids (Parents with Disabilities OnLine, *www .disabledparents.net*).

Adaptable Living Space

The Fair Housing Act

The Fair Housing Act of 1968 covers issues relating to disability. It states that landlords cannot forbid necessary modifications or refuse to make reasonable accommodations for people with disabilities, although tenants may be required to return the premises to their original condition before relinquishing them. Landlords who don't allow pets must accommodate pets who serve disabled tenants, and, if requested, must provide reserved parking space near the tenants' apartments. New construction must be accessible, must have light switches and outlets at waist-high level, and must have reinforced walls in bathrooms to allow for the installation of grab bars. HUD monitors compliance with the Fair Housing Act. Complaint forms are available on line at the HUD website and/or the nearest HUD office may be contacted for assistance (Department of Housing and Urban Development, *www.HUD.gov/the/thehous.htm*).

Adapting Existing Living Space

Home modifications can be essential in assisting a client with disabilities to be comfortable and safe in his or her home environment and can assist clients with almost any disabling condition. Through the Center for Universal Design (*www.design.ncsu.edu/cud/ built_env/housing/article_hmod.htm*), Margo Johnson and colleagues. (1999) have developed some suggestions for home modifications helpful in addressing client needs.

1. *Hearing limitations:* People with hearing limitations may not be able to hear routine sounds such as doorbells and telephones and warning sounds such as fire alarms. Modification possibilities include amplifying the sounds, installing visual signals, or installing a TTD (telecommunications device for deafness).

2. *Vision limitations:* People with vision limitations may have difficulty in conditions of low light or glare, may see foggily, or may be unable to see details. These may affect ability to read thermostats, appliance controls, printed material, telephone directories, and other items. Modifications might include increasing the home lighting, especially task lighting focused on specific areas, using blinds or shades to reduce glare, and using nonglare finishes on floors and other objects. Tactile cues such as texture changes are also helpful.

3. *Diminished sense of smell:* People may be unable to detect odors, or distinguish among them. They may not be able to detect those that warn of danger such as fire, gas leaks, and toxins. Detectors with visual and/or auditory cues are helpful.

4. *Altered sense of touch and dexterity:* People may have difficulty sensing heat or cold or textures, and/or be unable to perform fine finger movements such as pinching or gripping. These can cause difficulty with doorknobs, faucets, appliance controls, doors and windows, electrical cords, and other items. It is helpful to use distinctive textures; install levered handles, rocker light switches, and other easy to grasp and operate devices; and, for safety, it is helpful to lower water heater temperatures, install temperature-limiting devices, and use visual markers and stove burner covers.

5. *Decreased strength and range of motion:* People may have difficulty lifting, pushing, pulling, reaching, bending, kneeling, or standing for long periods. Stools and grab bars are helpful, as is placing home controls in an easily accessible place, having pull-out shelves, work surfaces at different heights, easy-glide hardware on drawers, adjustable height closet poles, extra-long hoses on sink spray attachments, and many other modifications.

6. *Decreased mobility and agility:* It is helpful to eliminate or reduce any barriers to mobility inside and outside the home, install ramps and electric garage-door openers, reframe doorways to make them wider, replace or eliminate thresholds, and redesign the spacing and placement of furniture. Bathrooms with roll-in showers, bedrooms with lifts, and ample grab bars are helpful.

7. *Loss of balance or coordination:* These can cause instability when people are standing or walking and there is a risk of falling. It may also be difficult to get into and out of chairs and beds. Helpful modifications include removing scatter rugs, lowering thresholds, lowering beds, and raising chairs.

8.   *Changes in cognition:* People with changes in cognition may not recognize a danger or may wander away. Safe barriers that prevent wandering are helpful, as is limiting access to dangerous objects such as knives, scissors, hot burners, electrical outlets, and medicines.

Some useful resources for home modification and assistance include:

Adaptive Environments, *www.adaptenv.org*
Fair Housing Accessibility Guidelines, *www.hud.gov/fhefag.html*
Fair Lending: A Resource Guide, *www.fairlending.com*
Home Modification Action Network, *www.homemods.org*
National Association of the Remodeling Industries, *www.nari.org*
National Council on Seniors' Housing, *www.nahb.com/builders/seniors.htm*
National Kitchen and Bath Association, *www.nkba.org*

Universal Design

The concept of Universal Design suggests that designing products and environments that can be usable by all people without need for adaptation or specialized design is beneficial for everyone. Universal Design in housing advocates building housing for a lifespan. This includes entrances with no steps, wider doorways, light switches and receptacles at waist-high levels, and bathrooms and kitchens usable by everyone (Center for Universal Design, *www.design.ncsu.edu/cud/*).
Some useful resources for universal design are:

Center for Inclusive Design and Environmental Access, *www.ap.buffalo.edu/*
Center for Universal Design, *www.design.ncsu.edu/cud/*
Philip Stephen Companies, *www.UniversalDesignHomes.com*

Universal Design does not focus specifically on disability. Rather, it attempts to encompass the needs of all people, from children to adults to older people. Light switches and outlets at a universal design height make controls accessible to children, people of short stature, and people who are carrying packages, not only people in wheelchairs. Sidewalk cuts prevent falls for everyone and are handy for children taking small steps, for parents pushing strollers, people pulling shopping carts, and people who use assistance for mobility. Door handles instead of knobs are handy for anyone with wet or slippery hands, are much easier for children to manage, and are very helpful if your hands are full. Park trails that are paved bring the outdoors to all. Multiple sensory stimuli can only increase everyone's awareness; if the traffic light chirps as well as changing color, we have two sensory inputs that reinforce each other to help us to be extra careful.

Assistive Technology

The Department of Education through NIDRR sponsors a special website called AbleData (*www.abledata.com/Site_2/prod_type.htm*), which is a comprehensive database for assistive technology of all kinds. Specialized equipment can be searched by product type, by company, and by brand. Categories of technological equipment include:

Architectural elements such as safety and security mechanisms, and vertical lifts

Communication devices such as signal systems and alternative communication systems

Computers and accessories

Controls, including environmental controls and switches

Educational management and instructional materials

Home management such as food preparation and housekeeping

Orthotics and prosthetics

Personal care such as feeding, carrying, drinking, holding, and toileting equipment

Recreation items such as crafts, sewing, and sports equipment

Seating systems and cushions

Sensory disabilities technology

Therapeutic aids

Transportation such as vehicles and vans

Vocational management such as work stations and office equipment

Walking devices such as canes and crutches

Wheeled mobility such as manual, sport, and powered wheelchairs and scooters

Because communication is essential in working with clients, the reader may want to become familiar with the kinds of communication devices available in order to assist clients to communicate effectively (*www.abledata.com/Site_2/communication_gen.htm*). These include:

- Alternative and augmentative communication systems
    Communicators, such as communication boards and books and encoding and scanning devices
    Oral speech technologies, such as amplifiers, artificial larynxes, clarifiers, and devices to assist stutterers
- Headwands and mouthsticks
- Reading assistance systems
    Auditory output, bookholders, magnifiers, page turners, and tactile and Braille materials
- Signal systems
- Telephones

Special dialing phones and special transmission phones
Signal and transmission accessories
* Typing accessories
* Writing systems
    Braille supplies, tools, training, and writers
    Writing guides, paper, and tools
    Other writing products

You may find that use of one or several of these communication technologies may be very helpful in working with clients. However, some clients may prefer not to use any assistive technologies. While it is important to respect your client's wishes in regard to use of these or any other technologies, adaptive equipment, or home modifications, exploring the reasons for the refusal may assist you in better understanding your client.

Chapter Summary

A good quality of life is important to everyone. Clients with disabilities may find that attaining a good life quality is complicated by lack of access, lack of mobility, or impairments due to the disabling condition. Laws and policies that support access and mobility have made it possible for people to participate in social, recreational, educational, and vocational activities that may have been much more limited fifty years ago. With information and planning, people with disabilities have access not only to their own communities, but to the world.

Access alone, however, is not sufficient to broaden the possibilities for people with disabilities. Modifying and adapting living spaces can enable independence and self-sufficiency. The Universal Design movement suggests a new approach to addressing accessibility and adaptability for people with disabilities. Universal Design presumes that people's needs will change over the lifespan and that the needs of all people can be addressed by designing environments that are readily usable by everyone.

Creative and innovative ideas in adapting technology to meet the needs of people with disabilities has also been a major factor in increasing the possibility of good quality of life. Communications devices enable almost everyone to communicate, and environmental controls and home management aids operated through a variety of technologies enable people to create and maintain a personally comfortable environment. Technology has provided new means of transportation, both personal and public. Vocational adaptive technology has expanded employment and training possibilities, as well as educational opportunities.

As social workers, we can help our clients to maximize their use of all of these changes: to use laws and programs, technology and architectural design, as well as their own abilities and creativity to enable a full and meaningful participation in all that they wish to do with their lives.

Questions for Thought and Discussion

1. Design something useful for the home using Universal Design principles. You can design a furniture item, a room arrangement, a piece of equipment, or the like. Present your design to your classmates.

2. Locate information about paratransit services in your community and find out how to access them.

3. Consider the building your classroom is in. Is it fully accessible? Check the bathrooms, the elevators, the office counters, the layout of furniture in classrooms, the location of handicapped parking, and the ramps.

4. If you have found problem areas, how would you correct the problems? Develop a plan.

5. If you had a client who was very weak and unable to form words intelligibly, what system would you suggest to help her to communicate? Check on the AbleData site under communication for some ideas.

Part IV Summary

One of the distinguishing features of our profession is our ability to research, access, and provide needed resources and services to our clients. We do this by developing a good working knowledge about resources in general and by using specific strategies and resources to help locate services and support systems. There are many services available, both public and private, to meet client needs in relation to disability. It is impossible for us to learn all of them. However, we *can* develop an overall working knowledge that includes where to go to find the special resource or support service our client might need.

This fourth and final part, the Disability Resource and Support Network, has completed the model we have developed for social work practice across disability. Resources in a number of areas that are often helpful in social work practice across disability have been provided, along with links, web addresses, and Internet sites where additional information may be accessed.

Chapters 17 and 18 have presented an overview of the public sector and the private sector. We have seen that the public sector is organized through a hierarchical and interlocking system of government agencies and services that have developed through each of the three branches of government as each sought to address the needs of people with disabilities. The legislative branch has developed programs and allocated funding; the executive branch has implemented and monitored programs; and the judicial branch has ruled on disability rights, accessibility, and other important issues. The private sector appears much less organized and more fluid. Agencies and services have been developed to meet needs on both local and national levels. Organizations may focus on one disability, one need, or one area, or cross disabilities and needs to serve a broad base of people.

In the succeeding chapters, several essential needs were defined and related resources and support networks have been identified. Chapter 19 addressed medical and health needs. Medicare, Medicaid, private insurance, managed care, and Ticket to Work are the principal ways in which people with disabilities meet medical needs. The chapter also addressed housing and personal care and explored resources for home purchase, remodeling and adaptation, rent supports, and community-based housing possibilities, as well as residential care. Personal care attendants often make the difference between sustainable community living options and nursing home care for people with disabilities. The kinds of services personal care attendants provide were explored as well as resources and guidelines for hiring a personal care attendant.

Chapter 20 presented some of the major resources in employment, vocational training, and income support. Employment and accommodation provisions of the ADA were presented, including terms still in the process of being definitively defined, such as "reasonable accommodation." Both public and private sectors were explored for employment opportunities and resources. Skill enhancement, vocational training, and rehabilitation resources were suggested. For clients who are unable to work, income supports and eligibility requirements were presented.

Chapters 21 and 22 considered several other important needs and available resources. First, in Chapter 21, we addressed social and recreational needs, including sports and activity resources specific to particular limitations. In Chapter 22, access and mobility resources included paratransit, regulations for air carriers related to people with disabilities, and travel resources. Adaptive technology can be essential in optimizing life quality for people with disabilities, and resources and kinds of technology available included special technology for enhancing communication, including various alternative forms of communicating and recording.

It is recognized that this resource section is of necessity not inclusive and can only give a sampling of the breadth of services and resources available. However, it is hoped that readers will use suggested resources and internet links to obtain additional information as needed.

Part IV Assignment

Select a disability or condition you are interested in learning about. Read about the disability and the kinds of limitations it creates in functioning. Using the subject areas included in Chapters 18 through 22, locate resources that might be helpful to clients with this particular disabling condition. For example, if the disability you selected was paraplegia, read about what the needs and limitations of paraplegia might be. Develop a comprehensive list of resources to meet these needs structured around:

Health-care and medical needs
Housing and personal care
Employment and income support
Recreation and social networks
Mobility, access, and adaptive technologies

References

AbleData (NIDRR's information project). *www.abledata.com*

Access Unlimited. (1999). Disability Services: Disability Categories. *www.uncwil.edu/stuaff/DISABILTY*

ADAPT. *www.adapt.org*

Albrecht, Gary L. (1992). *The Disability Business: Rehabilitation in America.* Newbury Park, CA: Sage.

Albrecht, Gary L., ed. (1976). *The Sociology of Physical Disability and Rehabilitation.* London: Feffer and Simons (University of Pittsburgh Press).

Allen-Meares P., & Law, B.A. (1993). "Grounding Social Work Practice in Theory: Ecosystems." In J.B. Rauch, ed., *Assessment.* Milwaukee: Families International.

Alzheimer's Association. *www.alz.org*

American Disabled for Attendant Programs Today (ADAPT). *www.adapt.org*

AOL iVillage Better Health Network. (1998). Disability classifications: Definitions commonly used by schools. *www.members.delphi.com/anee*

Appleby, G.A., Colon, E., & Hamilton, J. (2001). *Diversity, Oppression, and Social Functioning: Person-in-Environment Assessment and Intervention.* Boston: Allyn and Bacon.

Arthritis Foundation. *www.arthritis.org/resources/aboutus/history.asp*

Arthritis Foundation, Los Angeles Chapter. (2001). "Need a Reason to Run or Walk the Marathon in Dublin, Ireland?" Los Angeles: Author.

Arizona Center for the Blind and Visually Impaired. *www.acbvi.org/*

Asch, A. "Visual Impairment and Blindness." (1995). In R. Edwards, *The Encyclopedia of Social Work.* Washington, DC: NASW Press.

Aspen, What Did You Soy? (1996). In L. Keith, ed., *Whatever Happened to You?* New York: New Press.

Association for the Blind and Visually Impaired. *www.grcmc.org/blindser/*

Association for Retarded Citizens. *www.thearc.org/history/anonymous.htm*

Auld, W.M. (1927). "The Crippled Child: Why You Should Share the Care." *Cripple's Journal.* Vol. 4 (14).

Aurora of Central New York. *www.members.aol.com/auroracny/*

Barnes, C., Mercer, G., & Shakespeare, T. (1999). *Exploring Disability: A Sociological Introduction.* Cambridge, UK: Polity Press.

Battin, M. Pabst. (1982). *Ethical Issues in Suicide.* Englewood Cliffs, NJ: Prentice Hall.

Berkow, M., editor-in-chief. (1992). *The Merck Manual of Diagnosis and Therapy,* 14th ed. Rahway, NJ: Merck, Sharp, and Dohme Research Laboratories.

Beyond Affliction: The Disability History Project: Inventing the Poster Child. *www.npr.org/programs/disability*

Beyond Affliction: The Disability History Project: The Overdue Revolution. *www.npr.org/programs/ disability*

Beyond Affliction: The Disability History Project: What's Work Got to Do With It? *www.npr.org/ programs/disability*

Bisman, C. (1994). *Social Work Practice: Cases and Principles.* Pacific Grove, CA: Brooks/Cole.

Black, R.B. (1994). "Diversity and Populations at Risk: People with Disabilities." In F. Reamer, *The Foundations of Social Work Knowledge.* New York: Columbia University Press.

Bogdan, R. (1992). "On Construction of Humanness." In P. Ferguson, J., Ferguson, & S. Taylor, eds., *Interpreting Disability: A Qualitative Reader.* New York: Columbia University Teacher's College Press.

Braithwaite, D.O. & Thompson, T.L., eds (2000). *Handbook of Communication and People with Disabilities.* Mahwah, NJ: Lawrence Erlbaum Associates.

Brieland, D. (1995). "Social Work Practice: History and Evolution." In R. Edwards, ed., *Encyclopedia of Social Work,* Washington DC: NASW Press.

Bulhan, H.A. (1985). *Franz Fanon and the Psychology of Oppression.* New York and London: Plenum Press.

Canine Companions for Independence. *www.caninecompanions.org/facts*

Caputo, M. (July 1998). "Quest for the Best." *PN/Paraplegia News Magazine.* Paralyzed Veterans of America.

Caregiver Survival Resources. *www.caregiver911.com*

Carter, R. (1996). *Helping Yourself Help Others.* New York: Random House/Time Books.

Castiglioni, A. (1941). *A History of Medicine.* New York: A. Knopf and Son.

Centers for Disease Control. *www.cdc.gov/aboutcdc.htm*

Centers for Disease Control (2001a). Disability and Health, Healthy People with Disabilities. *www.cdc .gov/ncbddd/dh/*

Centers for Disease Control (2001b). Healthy People with Disabilities, HP2010 Data on Disparities *www.cdc.gov/ncbddd/fact/thpfs2.htm*

Center for Mental Health Services. (n.d.). Filing an ADA Employment Discrimination Charge: Making it Work for You. *www.mentalhealth.org/publications/*

Center for Universal Design. *www.design.ncsu.edu/cud/*

Center for Independent Living. (n.d.). Center for Independent Living Information Packet. Berkeley, CA: Author.

Center for Independent Living, Berkeley, CA. *www.cil.berkeley.org/services.htm*

Charlton, J. (1989) *Nothing about Us without Us.* Berkeley: University of California Press.

Christian Council on People with Disabilities. (2001). Statement of Faith, Principles of Ministry. *www.ccpd.org/statementoffaith.htm*

Cole, H. (1991). *Helpmates: Support in Times of Critical Illness.* Westminster: John Knox Press.

Coleman, Lerita M. (1997). "Stigma: An Enigma Demystified." In Lennard Davis, ed., *The Disability Studies Reader.* New York: Routledge

Compton, B., & Galway, B., (1994). *Social Work Processes.* Pacific Grove, CA: Brooks/Cole.

Consortium for Citizens with Disabilities. *www.c-c-d.org/about.htm*

Consumer Law. *www.consumerlawpage.com/brochurs/disab.htm*

Consumer Law Page (long-term care insurance). *www.consumerlawpage.com/article/insurance.shtml*

Cook, J. (1999). *Instructions for Completing the Supported Employment LogL Logging Format and Case Examples.* Chicago: UIC National Research and Training Center.

Cowger, C.D. (1991). "Assessment of Client Strengths." In D. Saleeby, ed., *The Strengths Perspective in Social Work Practice.* New York: Addison Wesley Longman Publishers.

Darwin, C. (1985). *The Origin of Species by Means of Natural Selection.* Middlesex, England: Penguin Classics.

Davis, L. J. (1997a). "Constructing Normalcy: The Bell Curve, the Novel, and the Disabled Body in the 19th Century." In L.J. Davis, ed., *The Disability Studies Reader.* New York: Routledge.

Davis, L. J. ed., (1997b). *The Disability Studies Reader.* New York: Routledge.

De Jong, G. (1979). Independent Living: From Social Movement to Analytic Paradigm. *Archives of Physical Medicine and Rehabilitation,* 60.

De Jong, P., & Miller, S.D. (1995, November). "How to Interview for Client Strengths." *Social Work,* 40 (6).

De Jong, G., & Wenker, T. (1983). "Attendant Care." In N.M. Crewe & I.K. Zola, *Independent Living for Physically Disabled People.* San Francisco: Jossey-Bass Publishers.

Department of Labor. *www.dol.gov/odep/public/pubs/ek99.resources.htm*

Disability Law Update. *www.disabilitylawupdate.com*

Disability Resources on the Web. *ww.disability.gov/CSS/Default.asp*

Disability Rights Education & Defense Fund (DREDF). *www.DREDF.org*

Disability Social History Project. *www.disabilityhistory.org*

Disability Statistics Research Center (UCSF). (1992). United States National Health Interview Survey. *www.dsc.ucsf.edu*

Doty, P., & Benjamin, A.E. (April 1999). "In-home Supportive Services for the Elderly and Disabled: A Comparison of Client-Directed and Professional Management Models of Service Delivery." HHS and UCLA.

Duffy, K. (1997). Berkeley Shows the Way in Disabled Community. *Berkeley Voice,* Berkeley, CA.

Duffy, Mary. (1996). "Making Choices." In L. Keith, ed., *Whatever Happened to You?* New York: The New Press.

Easter Seals. *www.easter-seals.org*

Edwards, E., Ed. (1995). *Encyclopedia of Social Work,* 19th ed. Washington, DC: NASW Press.

Ell, K. (1995). "Crisis Intervention: Research Needs." In R. Edwards, ed., *Encyclopedia of Social Work.* Washington, DC: NASW Press.

Egelko, B. (2002, April 30). Justices: Seniority Trumps Disability. In SF case Supreme Court limits law's scope. San Francisco: San Francisco *Chronicle,* p. A6.

Equal Employment Opportunities Commission. *www.eeoc.gov/facts/ADA/*

Everson, S. (2001, April). Workshop presented at Adult Protective Services Conference, Palm Springs, CA.

Family Village. *www.familyvillage.wisc.edu/center.htm*

Fannie Mae. *www.fanniemae.com/neighborhoods/home_guide/index.html)*

Federal Aviation Administration. *www.faa.gov/acr/dat.htm*

Ferguson, P., Ferguson, J., & Taylor, S., eds. (1992). *Interpreting Disability: A Qualitative Reader.* New York: Columbia University Teacher's College Press.

Fine, M., & Asch, A. (2000). "Disability Beyond Stigma: Social Interaction, Discrimination, and Activism." In K.E. Rosenblum & T-M. Travis, eds., *The Meaning of Difference.* Boston: McGraw Hill.

French, Sally. (2001). "Can You See the Rainbow? The Roots of Denial." In K.E. Rosenblum & T.-M. Travis, eds., *The Meaning of Difference.* Boston: McGraw Hill.

Funk, R. (1987). "From Caste to Class in the Context of Civil Rights." In A. Gartner & T. Joe, eds., *Images of the Disabled, Disabling Images.* London: Jessica Kingsley.

Furlong, M., Jonikas, J., Cook, J., Hathaway, L., & Goode, S. (n.d.). *Providing Vocational Services: Job Coaching and Ongoing Support for People with Severe Mental Illness.* Chicago: UIC National Research and Training Center.

Gartner, A., & Joe, T. Eds. (1987). *Images of the Disabled, Disabling Images.* New York: Praeger.

Gartner, A., Lipsky, D.K., & Turnbull, A.P. (1991). *Supporting Families with a Child with a Disability.* Baltimore: Paul H. Brooks Publishing Co.

Germain, C.B., & Gitterman, A. (1980). *The Life Model of Social Work Practice.* New York: Columbia University Press.

Gilliland, B., & James, R. (1997). *Crisis Intervention Strategies,* 3rd ed. Pacific Grove, CA: Brooks/Cole.

Goffman, E. (1986). *Stigma: Notes on the Management of Spoiled Identity.* New York: Simon & Schuster.

Goffman, E. (1997). "Selections from *Stigma.*" In L. Davis, ed., *The Disability Studies Reader.* New York: Routledge.

Goode, D., ed. (1994a). *Quality of Life for Persons with Disabilities.* Cambridge, MA: Brookline Books

Goode, D. (1994b). "The National Quality-of-Life for Persons with Disabilities Project: A Quality of Life Agenda for the United States." In D. Goode, ed., *Quality of Life for Persons with Disabilities.* Cambridge, MA: Brookline Books.

Guide to Outdoor Recreation. *www.gorp.com/gorp/*

Hanks, J.R., & Hanks, L.M., Jr. (1948). "The Physically Handicapped in Non-Occidental Societies." *Journal of Social Issues, 4*(4). Ann Arbor, MI.

Hartman, A. (1994). "Social Work Practice." In F. Reamer, ed., *Foundations of Social Work Knowledge.* New York: Columbia University Press

Haynes, K.S., & Mickelson, J.S. (2000). *Affecting Change: Social Workers in the Political Arena,* 4th ed. Boston: Allyn and Bacon.

Health Care Financing Administration Ticket to Work and Work Incentives Act. *www.hefa.gov/medicaid/twwiia/faq.htm*

Health Care Financing Administration Transition Grants. *www.hefa.gov/medicaid/smd53100.htm*

Health Care Financing Administration Medicaid Waivers. *www.hefa.gov/medicaid/hpg4.htm*

Hepworth, D., Rooney, R., & Larsen, J. (1997). *Direct Social Work Practice: Theory and Skills,* Pacific Grove, CA: Brooks/Cole.

Hermann, D.H. (1997). *Mental Health and Disability Law.* St. Paul, MN: West Publishing Company

Hockenberry, J. (1995). *Moving Violations: A Memoir.* New York: Hyperion Press

Howe, Samuel Gridley. (1999–2000). in *Brittanica.com*

Independent Living Centers. *www.ilsc.org/housing*

Iezzoni, L., & Israel, B. (Dec. 2000). "The Reluctant Identity." *Journal of Health Politics, Policy, and Law.* (Durham, NC), 1157–67.

International Paralympic Committee. (2001). Lawn Bowls Classification. *info/lut/ac/uk/research/paad/ipc/lawn-bowling/class*

Job Accommodation Network. *www.janweb.icdi.wvu.edu*

Job Accommodation Network. (1999). Job Accommodation Network brochure. Washington, DC: President's Committee on Employment of Persons with Disabilities.

Johnson, M., Duncan, R., Gabriel, A., & Carter, M. (1999). *Home Modifications and Products for Safety and Ease of Use.* Center for Universal Design. *www.design.ncsu.edu/cud/built_env/housing/article_hmod.htm*

Jonikas, J., Casey, A., & Cook, J. (n.d.). *Sustaining Employment: Social Skills at Work.* Chicago: UIC National Research and Training Center.

Jonsen, R.R., Siegler, M., & Winslade, W.J. (1998). *Clinical Ethics: A Practical Approach for Ethical Decisions in Clinical Medicine,* 4th ed. New York: McGraw Hill.

Kaye, H.S., LaPlante, M.P., Carlson, D., & Wenger, B.L. (1996). *Trends in Disability Rates in the United States, 1970–1994.* Washington, DC: NIDDR.

Kemp, S.P. (1995). "Practice with Communities." In C.H. Meyer, & M.A. Mattaini, eds., *The Foundations of Social Work Practice.* Washington, DC: NASW Press.

Kennedy, M.J., LaPlante, M.P., & Kaye, H.S. (1997). *Need for Assistance in the Activities of Daily Living.* Washington, DC: NIDDR.

Kennedy, M.J. (1988). *From Sheltered Workshops to Supported Employment Syracuse.* New York: Center for Human Policy.

Kleege, N. (1999). *Sight Unseen.* New Haven, CT: Yale University Press.

Kriegel, L. (1969). "Uncle Tom and Tiny Tim: Some Reflections on the Cripple as Negro." *American Scholar,* vol. 38, pp. 412–30.

Kleinfeld, S. (1979). *The Hidden Minority: A Profile of Handicapped Americans.* Boston: Little, Brown & Co.

Kumin, L. (1994). *Communication Skills in Children with Down Syndrome.* Bethesda, MD: Woodbine House.

Lansdown, R., Rumsey, N., et al. (1997). *Visibly Different: Coping with Disfigurement.* Oxford, UK: Butterworth Heinemann.

LaPlante, M.P., & Carlson D. (1992). *Disability Statistics Report: Disability in the United States, Prevalence and Causes.* Washington, DC: NIDDR.

LaPlante, M.P., Hendershot, G.E., & Moss, A.J. (1997). "The Prevalence of Need for Assistive Technology Devices and Home Accessibility Features." *Technology and Disability, 6,* 17–28.

Laucht, M., & McClain, J.W., Jr. (1994). "Quality of Life in the United States: A Multi-Cultural Context." In D. Goode, *Quality of Life for Persons with Disabilities.* Cambridge, MA: Brookline Books.

Lee, J.B. (1996). "The Empowerment Approach to Social Work Practice." In F. Turner, ed., *Social Work Treatment: Interlocking Theoretical Approaches.*

Lenhart, S. (2000). Protecting Workers with Developmental Disabilities. *Applied Occupational and Environmental Hygiene* 15(2), 171–81.

Lift, Inc. *www.lift-inc.org*

Lions Club International. *www.lionsclub.org*

Longmore, P.K., & Goldberger, D. *The League for the Physically Handicapped and the Great Depression: A Case Study in New Disability History.*

Lum, D. (1999). *Culturally Competent Practice: A Framework for Growth and Action.* Pacific Grove, CA: Brooks/Cole.

McDonald, G., & Oxford, M. (1999). The History of Independent Living. *www.acils.com*

McGonigle, C. (1999). *Surviving Your Spouse's Chronic Illness.* New York: Henry Holt and Sons.

McNeal, Jack. (1997). *Americans with Disabilities. www.census.gov/hhes/www/disable/sipp/disab97/asc97.html*

Mackelprang, R., & Salsgiver, R. (1999). *Disability: A Diversity Model Approach in Human Service Practice.* Pacific Grove: Brooks/Cole.

Magen, R.H. (1995). "Practice with Groups." In C.H. Meyer & M.A. Mattaini, eds., *The Foundations of Social Work Practice.* Washington DC: NASW Press.

Mairs, N. (1996). *Waist High in the World.* Boston: Beacon Press

Mancuso, L.L. (1994). *Reasonable Accommodation for Workers with Psychiatric Disabilities.* Boston: Center for Psychiatric Rehabilitation, Boston University.

Medicaid information. *www.hcfa.gov/medicaid/medicaid.htm*

Medicare nursing home surveys. *www.medicare.gov/nursing/home.asp*

Medicare. *www.medicare.gov*

Meyer, C.H. (1995a). "The Ecosystems Perspective: Implications for Practice." In C. Meyer & M.A. Mattaini, *The Foundations of Social Work Practice.* Washington, DC: NASW Press.

Meyer, C.H. (1995b). "Assessment." In E. Edwards, ed., *Encyclopedia of Social Work.* Washington, DC: NASW Press.

Meyer, C.H., & Mattaini, M.A., eds. (1995c). *The Foundations of Social Work Practice.* Washington, DC: NASW Press.

Meyer, M., & Derr, P. (1998). *The Comfort of Home: An Illustrated Step-by-Step Guide for Caregivers.* Care Trust Publications.

Morrow, Howell, N. (1993). "Multidimensional Assessment of the Elderly Client." In J. Rauch, ed., *Assessment: A Sourcebook for Social Work Practice.* Milwaukee, WI: Families International.

Nadel, L., & Rosenthal, D., eds. (1995). *Down Syndrome: Living and Learning in the Community.* New York: Wiley-Liss.

National Association for Home Care. *www.nahc.org*

National Center on Health Statistics. *www.cdc.gov/nchswww/default.htm*

National Center on Physical Activity and Disability. *www.ncpad.cc.uic.edu/*

National Council on Disability. *www.Draco.aspensys.com/FCIC/Public/TopicDetail.asp?ti*

National Council on Disability. (1997–98). *National Disability Policy: A Progress Report.* Washington, DC: Author.

National Family Caregivers Association. *wwwnfcacares.org*

National Federation of Interfaith Volunteer Caregivers. *www.nfivc@aol.com*

National Institutes of Health. *www/nih/gov/icd/*

National Institute on Disability and Rehabilitation Research. (1992). *Disability Statistics Report: Disability in the United States, Prevalence and Causes.*

National Institute on Disability and Rehabilitation Research. *www.ed.gov/offices/OSERS/NIDRR*

National Organization on Disability. *www.nod.org*

National Rehabilitation Hospital Center for Health and Disability Research. *www.ilru.org/mgdcare/projects.html*

National Respite Locator Service. *www.chtop.com/loctor.htm*

Oliver, M. (1991). *Social Work, Disabled People, and Disabling Environments.* London: Jessica Kingsley.

Oliver, M. (1996). *Understanding Disability: From Theory to Practice.* New York: St. Martin's Press

Olmstead Decision. *www.Medicaid/olmstead/olmslink.htm*

Parent, W.S., Hill, M.L., Wehman, P. "From Sheltered to Supported Employment Outcomes: Challenges for Rehabilitation Facilities." *Journal of Rehabilitation, 55*(4), 51.

Parent Advocacy Coalition for Educational Rights. *www.pacer.org*

Parents with Disabilities OnLine. *www.disabledparents.net*

Pelka, F. (1997). *ABC-CLIO Companion to The Disability Rights Movement.* Santa Barbara, CA: ABC-CLIO (Companions to Key Issues in American Life).

Pfeiffer, D. (1993). Overview of the Disability Rights Movement: History, Legislation, and Political Implications *Policy Studies Journal, 21*(4), 724–34.

Phelan, M., & Parkman, S. (1995). "Work with an Interpreter." *British Medical Journal,* 311(7004), 555ff.

Philips, W.R.F., & Rosenberg, J. (Eds.). (1980). *Changing Patterns of Law: The Courts and the Handicapped.* New York: Ayer.

Physicians' Disability Services. *www.disabilityfacts.com/faqs.html*

Piastro, D.B. (1999). "Coping with the Transitions in Our Lives: From 'Afflicted' Identity to Personal Empowerment and Pride." *Reflections, 5*(4), 42–46.

Polio, S. (1996). "Being Sam's Mum." In L. Keith, ed., *Whatever Happened to You?* New York: New Press.

President's Committee on Employment of People with Disabilities. *wwwpcepd.gov*

Project Star. *www.trfn.clpgh.org/star/index/shtml*

Racino, J.A. (1999). *Policy, Program Evaluation and Research in Disability.* New York: Haworth.

Radford, T. (1999) *A Guide for Caregivers.* New York: National Multiple Sclerosis Society.

Rebuilding Together. *www.rebuildingtogether.org*

Resource Partnership. *www.resourcepartnership.org*

Robinson, Emma. (1997). "Psychological Research on Visible Differences in Adults." In R. Lansdown, N. Rumsey, E. Bradbury, T. Carr, & J. Partridge, eds., *Visibly Different: Coping with Disfigurement.* Oxford: Butterworth Heinemann Publishers.

Roessler, R.T., & Rumrill, P. (1998). *The Win-Win Approach to Reasonable Accommodations.* New York: National Multiple Sclerosis Society.

Rolland, J.S. (1988). "A Conceptual Model of Chronic and Life-Threatening Illness and Its Impact on Families." In C.S. Chilman, E.W. Nunnaly, & F.M. Cox, eds., *Chronic Illness and Disability.* Newbury Park, CA: Sage.

Rolland, J.S. (1989). "Chronic Illness and the Family Life Cycle." In B. Carter & M. McGoldrick, eds., *The Changing Family Life Cycle.* Boston: Allyn and Bacon.

Rose, S.M., & Moore, V.L. (1995). "Case Management." In R. Edwards, ed., *Encyclopedia of Social Work.* Washington, DC: NASW Press.

Rosenberg, R.R. (1994). "Capitol People First: Self-Advocacy and Quality-of-Life Issues." In D. Goode, ed., *Quality of Life for Persons with Disabilities.* Cambridge, MA: Brookline Books.

Rothman, J., & Sager, J.S. (1998). *Case Management: Integrating Individual and Community Practice.* Boston: Allyn and Bacon.

Scalise, K. (1998). The Other Activists of the 60's: A New Collection of Original Papers and History Documents Disability. *www.urel.berkeley.edu/berkeleyan/1998/0304/activists.html*

Scotch, Richard K. (2001). *From Good Will to Civil Rights: Transforming Federal Disability Policy,* 2nd ed. Philadelphia: Temple University Press.

Shapiro, J.E. (1994). *No Pity.* New York: Three Rivers Press.

Sheafor, B., Horejsi, C., & Horejsi, G. (2000). *Techniques and Guidelines for Social Work Practice.* Boston: Allyn & Bacon.

Sibling Support Project. *www.seattlechildrens.org/sibsupp*

Smith, G., O'Keefe, J., et al. (2000). *Understanding Medicaid Home and Community Based Service.* Washington, DC: George Washington University Center for Health Policy Research.

Snow, K. "People First Language." *www.modmh.state.mo.us/sikeston/people.htm*

Social Security Administration Information for Professionals. *SSA.gov/disability/professionals.htm*

Stavros. *www.stavros.org/pasfaq.html*

Stone, K.G. (1997). *Awakening to Disability: Nothing About Us Without Us.* Volcano, CA: Volcano Press

Strahan, G. (January 23, 1997). "An Overview of Nursing Homes and Their Current Residents, Data from the 1995 National Nursing Home Survey." *Advance Data Number 280,* National Center for Health Statistics.

Strong, M. (1997), *Mainstay for the Well Spouse of the Chronically Ill,* 3rd ed. New York: Little, Brown & Co.

Sudderth, D., & Kandel, J. (1997). *Adult ADD: The Complete Handbook.* Rocklin, CA: Prima Publishing.

Susik, H. (1995). *Hiring Home Caregivers: The Family Guide to In-Home Eldercare.* Impact Publishers.

Szaz, T. (1970). *The Manufacture of Madness.* New York: Harper and Row.

Tabletennis.org (2001). Functional Classification for Table Tennis. *www.tabletennis.org/ittc/players/classification*

Tanzman, M.R. (n.d.). *Living Independently with Personal Assistance.* Jackson Heights, New York: American Association of Spinal Cord Injury Psychologists·and Social Workers.

Taub, D.E., & Greer, K.R. (2000, November). "Physical Activity as a Normalizing Experience for School-Aged Children with Physical Disabilities: Implications for Legitimation of Social Identity and Enhancement of Social Ties." *Journal of Sports and Social Issues, 24*(4), 395–414.

Thomas, S., & Wolfensberger, W. (1982). "The Important of Social Imagery in Interpreting Societally Devalued People to the Public." *Rehabilitation Literature, 43*(11–12), 356–58.

Thomson, Rosemarie G. (1997). "Feminist Theory, The Body, and the Disabled Figure." In L. Davis, ed., *The Disabilities Studies Reader.* New York: Routledge.

Tripod International. *www.members.tripod.com*

Tropman, J.E. (1995). "Community Needs Assessment." In E. Edwards, ed., *Encyclopedia of Social Work.* Washington, DC: NASW Press.

United States Census Bureau. *www.census.gov/hhes/www.disability.html*

United States Census Bureau, Survey of Income and Program Participation. *www/disable/sipp/disab97/asc97.html*

United States Department of Education. *www.ded.gov/*

United States Department of Education, Office of Special Education and Vocational Rehabilitation Services. *www.ed.gov/offices/OSERS/RSA/rsa.htm*

United States Department of Education Office of Civil Rights. *www.ed.gov/offices/OCR*

United States Department of Health and Human Services. *www.hhs.gov/agencies/*

United States Department of Health and Human Services, Office of Family Assistance. *www.hss.gov/programs/ofa*

United States Department of Health and Human Services, PAS Research. *www.aspe.os.dhhs.gov/daltcp/reports/cdpases.htm*

United States Department of Housing and Urban Development. *www.HUD.gov/the/thehous.htm*

United States Department of Labor. Personal Assistant Services in the Workplace. *www.dol/gov/dol/odep/public/pubs*

United States Department of Transportation. (1993). Paratransit Policy. *www.fta.dot.gov/library/policy/ADA/ada.htm*

FCIC National Contact Center. *www.draco/aspensys.com/*

United States Government Disability Resources. *www.disability.gov*

United States Social Security Administration. *www.ssa.gov/disability/*

United States Veterans Administration. *www.va.gov*

Visier, L. (1998). "Sheltered Employment for Persons with Disabilities." *International Labor Review, 137*(3), 347–65.

Walters, E. (1997). "Problems Faced by Children and Families Living with Visible Differences." In R. Lansdown, N. Rumsey, E. Bradbury, T. Carr, & J. Partridge, eds., *Visibly Different: Coping with Disfigurement.* Oxford: Butterworth-Heinemann Publishers.

Warner, E. (Spring 2000). *Just the Facts: Frequently Asked Questions About MS and the National MS Society.* New York: Communications Department, National MS Society

Weil, M.O., & Gamble, D.N. Community Practice Models. In Edwards, R., (1995) *The Encyclopedia of Social Work.* Washington, DC: NASW Press.

The Well Spouse Foundation. *wwwwellspouse@aol.com*

Wendell, S. (1996). *The Rejected Body: Feminist Philosophical Reflections on Disability.* New York: Routledge.

Wendell, S. (1997). "Toward a Feminist Theory of Disability." In L. Davis, ed., *The Disabilities Studies Reader.* New York: Routledge.

Williams, M. (1997). In R. Lansdown, N. Rumsey, E. Bradbury, T. Carr, & J. Partridge, *Visibly Different: Coping with Disfigurement.* Oxford: Butterworth-Heinemann Publishers.

Wolinsky, D., & Breakstone, A. (1975). "Reporting for the Rehabilitation and Sheltered Workshop." *Journal of Accountancy.* 140(1): 56.

World Institute on Disability. (Spring–Summer 1995). *Semiannual Report.* Vol. II, no. 2.

"The Social Semiotics of Disability." In M. H. Roux & M. Bach, eds., *Disability Is Not Measles.* North York, Ont: Roehrer Institute.

Woolis, R. (1992). *When Someone You Love Has a Mental Illness.* New York: Jeremy P. Tarcher/Putnam.

Woods, M.E., & Robinson, H. (1996). "Psychosocial Theory and Social Work Treatment." In F.J. Turner, ed., *Social Work Treatment: Interlocking Theoretical Approaches,* 4th ed. New York: Free Press.

Zucherman, C., Duber, N.N., & Collopy, B., eds. (1990). *Home Health Care Options: A Guide for Older Persons and Concerned Families.* New York: Plenum Press.

Index